I0831583

Boarding School Voices

Boarding School Voices

Carlisle Indian School Students Speak

ARNOLD KRUPAT

University of Nebraska Press | *Lincoln*

Library of Congress Cataloging-in-Publication Data
Names: Krupat, Arnold, author.
Title: Boarding school voices: Carlisle Indian School students speak / Arnold Krupat.
Other titles: Carlisle Indian School students speak
Description: Lincoln: University of Nebraska Press, 2021. | Includes bibliographical references and index.
Identifiers: LCCN 2021025912
ISBN 9781496228017 (hardback)
ISBN 9781496228901 (epub)
ISBN 9781496228918 (pdf)
Subjects: LCSH: United States Indian School (Carlisle, Pa.) | United States Indian School (Carlisle, Pa.)—Alumni and alumnae—Correspondence. | Indian students—Pennsylvania—Carlisle—Biography. | Off-reservation boarding schools—Pennsylvania—Carlisle. | Boarding school students—United States—Correspondence. | Indians of North America—Cultural assimilation—United States. | BISAC: SOCIAL SCIENCE / Ethnic Studies / American / Native American Studies | LITERARY COLLECTIONS / Indigenous Peoples of the Americas
Classification: LCC E97.6.C2 K78 2021 | DDC 974.8/01—dc23
LC record available at
https://lccn.loc.gov/2021025912

Set in Garamond Premier Pro by Mikala R. Kolander.

What has become of the thousands of Indian voices who spoke the breath of boarding-school life?

K. TSIANINA LOMAWAIMA

We still know relatively little about how Indian school children themselves saw things.

MICHAEL COLEMAN

An incredibly complex Indian world, one full of priests and teachers, schemers and con artists, athletes, artists and singers, people who stayed engaged with Indian politics, education, law, and culture; and people who melted into reservation communities, small towns, and big cities as dentists, clerks, farmers, and mechanics.

PHILIP DELORIA

Contents

Illustrations

Acknowledgments

I'd like to offer brief but sincere thanks to some of the people who helped with this book. Matthew Bokovoy of the University of Nebraska Press was supportive from the first he saw of it and was helpful throughout. The press's Heather Stauffer was consistently generous with aid and good ideas. I am grateful to them both. I am deeply indebted to Jim Gerencser of the Carlisle Indian School Digital Resource Center, who over the long haul helped me navigate the rich digital archive, answered a great many questions, and provided images for many of the illustrations. Tom Schmidt of the Sharlot Hall Museum Library and Archives in Prescott, Arizona, kindly made the Museum's Michael Burns manuscripts available during my visit there. Richard Tritt of the Cumberland County Historical Society provided information and images for illustrations, and Barbara Landis, the society's deeply knowledgeable historian, was prompt in response to any questions I had. I thank them all.

Introduction

Partly inspired by Robert Dale Parker's "Boarding School Poems" section of his *Changing Is Not Vanishing* (2011), and by Jacqueline Emery's *Recovering Native American Writing in the Boarding School Press* (2017), this book is an anthology of mostly unpublished writing by former students of the Carlisle Indian School and a study of that writing. The book's epigraphs, two of which I used earlier for both volumes of my *Changed Forever: American Indian Boarding-School Literature*, are meant to provide the context in which the former students' writing and the critical commentary should be read.

Thus I cite once again the more-than-rhetorical question Tsianina Lomawaima posed in 1994: "What has become of the thousands of Indian voices that spoke the breath of boarding- school life?" and also Michael Coleman's observation a year earlier, that in regard to the boarding schools, "We still know relatively little about how Indian school children themselves saw things." *Boarding School Voices* presents the words of some of those "thousands of Indian voices who spoke the breath of boarding-school life," so that they may tell us something more "about how Indian school children," here meaning those who attended the Carlisle Indian School, "themselves saw things."

Both volumes of *Changed Forever* had a third epigraph, Amelia Katanski's assertion that "Boarding-school narratives have a significant place in the American Indian literary tradition" (2006). I continue to believe that they do. But although the texts published here for the first time or reprinted after obscure publication many years ago (letters, notes, brief newspaper articles, and responses to questionnaires) do indeed benefit from literary readings, they do not—unlike the self-consciously autobiographical texts Katanski and I formerly studied—quite attain "a significant place in the American Indian literary tradition," as that "tradition" continues to develop. For that reason, I have dropped Katanski's words and replaced them with an observation by Philip Deloria that shifts the emphasis from the literariness of these texts—something I will indeed consider—to their representational or pictorial evocativeness. The bulk of this book consists of the words of many former Carlisle School students who are, as Deloria sketched, among the "people who stayed engaged with Indian politics, education, law, and culture," and also those "who melted into reservation communities, small towns, and big cities as dentists, clerks, farmers, and mechanics," as Indian ministers, lawyers and teachers, laundresses and seamstresses. They provide some of the many perspectives of Native people who attended boarding school in the east from 1879 to 1918, allowing us a measure of insight into what they saw and thought and felt.

Some few of their names will be familiar—**Luther Standing Bear**; perhaps **Charles Dagenett** and **Charles Bender**—but I suspect the majority will not.[1] Most readers are unlikely to have encountered **Nellie Londrosh (Nunn)**, **Leonard Tyler**, and the Reverend **Joshua Given**, for example, or **Joel Tyndall, William F. Campbell, Harriet Elder (Stuart)**, and **Julia Powless (Wheelock)**. All of them—and many others—published short pieces in one or another of the Carlisle newspapers while they were students, and then returned questionnaires, and sent letters to the school after they had left. This body of texts has been preserved and digitized by the Carlisle Indian School Digital Resource Center, a rich archive that has not yet been published or studied. It is well past time to hear these former Carlisle Indian students speak.

The Carlisle Indian Industrial School was established in 1879 by Civil War veteran Captain Richard Henry Pratt.[2] It was the first of the federal off-reservation boarding schools and their flagship; it closed in 1918. Summarized in Pratt's often-quoted remark, "Kill the Indian and save the man!"—erase Indian languages, religions, and cultures, and replace them with those of the dominant American society—

Carlisle's ethnocidal program was long taken as the aim of Indian education in America. More recently, it has been trenchantly criticized and condemned as a major engine of colonialism. There is no question that Carlisle *hurt* a great many young Native people, some of whom became sick at the school and died, while others ran away, or survived having endured sufficient trauma to afflict the rest of their lives and, indeed, the lives of generations of their descendants. There is almost no firsthand record of what these people suffered and what they thought about their time at Carlisle; they did not communicate with the school, and their voices are not recoverable in its files. But a fair number of Carlisle students had warm feelings toward the school and, for that matter, toward Pratt himself. This does not mean that they did not suffer loneliness and a sense of dislocation, or that they were not affronted by the denigration of their languages and cultural practices. Nonetheless, as they tell us in their own words, they found much in their schooling to value.

In this regard it should be said that whatever their experience of the school, no student was forced to attend Carlisle; parental permission was required before a child could go.[3] The many accounts of Native children being pulled from their hiding places by police or soldiers and dragged off to boarding school weeping are, for the most part, historically verifiable: but they do not apply to Carlisle. In its earliest days Pratt himself, staff members of the school (Zitkala-Ša, for example), and students (Luther Standing Bear) went out to various reservations recruiting. And while they did not provide Native parents with anything like a full and accurate description of what this thing called "school" would entail, they took no child to Carlisle without his or her parents' consent. In later years it was necessary to apply for admission, and I provide a scan of just one of these applications; there were many. These facts are in no way meant to excuse the damage Carlisle did to many of its students.

The very first group of Carlisle students to attend, Lakotas from Rosebud and Pine Ridge, had been recruited by Pratt himself. Their parents had agreed to their attendance, and the children had acquiesced in their parents' decision—although again, neither the parents nor the prospective students had a clear understanding of what was involved. When, at the last minute, as Luther Standing Bear recalled, his young sister, despite having agreed to go, decided she would not board the boat for the first leg of the trip to Carlisle, she simply remained behind with her father (Standing Bear 1975, 126–27). Nonetheless, once at school, some students did indeed run off, and they did so for a variety of reasons. Runaways—often called "deserters" in the Carlisle files—were young people who found themselves desperately lonely for home; experienced the regimen as oppressive; or thought their agreed-upon stay—usually three or five years—simply too long. But even some who had run away, as we will see, kept in touch with the school in later years.

Pratt's reputation today is about on a par with Custer's; perhaps it is worse. I will not attempt to rehabilitate that reputation, but I will say that there was a complexity to Pratt far greater than that of impetuous Pahuska. Dr. Martin Luther King is reported to have said that the South loves the individual Black man or woman but hates the race, while in the North it is just the opposite. In this respect, Pratt was a southerner when it came to Indians. He liked, respected, and befriended some of the Kiowa, Comanche, and Apache prisoners he oversaw in the 1870s in Florida, and he clearly had a great affection for many of the Indian students he came to know in his twenty-five years at Carlisle. There is abundant evidence that many of them also felt warmly toward him. Pratt's own education had been no greater than that offered at Carlisle—about eighth grade—and while he was shrewd and, for the most part, pragmatically effective, he was not particularly well-read or intellectually adept.

Thus it seems never to have occurred to him that the qualities he consistently found so admirable in Native people—their honesty, seriousness, dignity, and thoughtfulness, for example—must have come in some measure from their cultural formation. It is a bitter irony that the ideology of ethnocide he espoused was not only morally reprehensible but also entirely unnecessary for Pratt's aims, causing pain completely unrelated to the gain intended. That is to say, to socialize Native people as workers and homemakers did not require that they speak only English, wear uniforms, or drill and march, as required at

Carlisle. Making them do so, moreover, was absolutely ineffective in "killing the Indian" in them. I know of only a single former Carlisle student who claimed no longer to be an Indian, as we will see.

Nonetheless, as Brenda Child (2014) has insightfully developed the matter, the boarding schools' ethnocidal practices have become a metaphor for the worst evils of colonialism, a specifiable source for all the ills that beset Native communities today. There is no doubt that the schools caused pain and suffering that often lasted generations; some of their ill effects linger today. But the full story, so far as one can grasp it, is one not only of suffering and pain, loss, defeat, and abjection, but also of what Gerald Vizenor has termed Native *survivance*. It is a story not only of victim-subjects but of ingenious agents, a narrative not only of suffering but of creative syntheses and adaptative actions. Undoubtedly tragic in some ways, in others the story of a great many Carlisle students is an occasionally ironic—or, more often, in a strictly literary sense—a comic tale. Many Native students of the school worked their way through to positive outcomes in their lives, as we can see from their own words.[4]

Most of those students came to accept the concept of privately owned land, and they took land allotments when they could. So, too, did most of them eschew the traditional clothing of their home communities and dress in "citizen's" attire; when possible, they cooked on stoves, not open fires; they washed their clothes with a machine manufactured for that purpose, if one was available. They worked as blacksmiths or carpenters, as their ancestors had not; they farmed or raised livestock despite the many difficulties they encountered, and sometimes they ran a small grocery or dry goods store. Several of them entered the professions. Many spoke their own language at home, but those who chose to keep in touch with the school express pride in their knowledge of English—a knowledge that varied enormously, as will become clear. They were Episcopalians and Catholics, Baptists and Presbyterians, with a few joining the Church of Latter Day Saints. This did not prevent some of them from also participating in the Ghost Dance movement and many more from practicing the peyote religion and in time joining the Native American Church.

Their sense of themselves and their perspective on the world, to extrapolate from what they wrote and said, was, for the most part, *tribal*. They were the oxymoron Pratt could not imagine and never fully comprehended: they were *Carlisle Indians*. They were not, in Luther Standing Bear's phrase, "imitation white men" (1975, 141) or some hybrid creation. Neither unself-consciously "traditional" nor self-consciously "modern," they were a different kind of Indian.

Thus **Grant Left Hand**, having returned home to Indian Territory from Carlisle in 1882, became prominent in the Arapaho Ghost Dance movement in the early 1890s—all the while clerking in a store, as he reported in responding to a 1910 Carlisle questionnaire. Left Hand wrote that he was a member of the Baptist Church, while also reminding the school that he was the son of Left Hand, a principal chief of his Southern Arapaho people—who had also been both an adherent of the Ghost Dance religion and a Baptist. So, too, with another Arapaho, War Bonnet, who was known from his school days forward as **William Shakespeare**. He was opposed to the Ghost Dance but became a prominent southern plains peyotist and member of the Native American Church. While Shakespeare had three wives, he was nonetheless proudly modern, writing to Carlisle in 1917,

> I start to teach my people the way of white people education farming and I was the first one in my people to wear a hat but my people were still had a feathers on their head and few years after I show them how school means.

As for the nonstandard but fascinating language use of William Shakespeare, I offer some observations on it and on that of many other former-student writers, a little later.

In much the same way, while you may recognize the name of George Sword—an Oglala Lakota, an intimate of Crazy Horse, a man who had been in the Custer fight, and who became Captain George Sword of the Indian police and later a tribal judge—it is not likely many will know his son, **Frank Locke**. Sword sent his son to Carlisle, and Locke would live a life very different from his father's. He kept in touch with

Carlisle for some thirty years, always offering thoughtful commentary. These are only three of the interesting men and many women from whom we will hear.

Although I have emphasized the evocativeness of the writings of these former Carlisle students—what they tell us about themselves and their home communities, the perspectives they offer on a wider American world—it would be a mistake merely to pass over those words themselves and the larger narrative structures they form. These Indian people wrote about their lives in some detail, and their stories, like all written narratives, may be read as literary texts inviting attention to their structure and their style. Western narrative—narrative in English—has four plot structures: tragedy, comedy, romance, and what Hayden White calls satire but I prefer to call irony. Readily apparent in fiction or dramatic writing, these plot structures are operative in non-fictional narratives as well—in historical texts, for example, as Hayden White showed many years ago, and in ethnographic and social-scientific texts, as James Clifford and others have shown.[5] Because the writings I present from former Carlisle students are not extended texts—with the exception, to be sure, of Mike Burns's autobiography, considered in chapter 2—I attend only very little to structural matters or implicit plots. I also try, to the extent I can, to identify elements from indigenous, non-Western narrative traditions.

As I've noted in passing, structurally most of the writings by these former Carlisle students taken together are comic texts. To cite Northrop Frye, "Comedy usually moves toward a happy ending, and the normal response of the audience to a happy ending is 'this should be'" (1957, 167). Thus I read the materials by most of the former students on record as telling stories that, all in all, come to a moderately happy ending: she has come through; obstacles may remain, but many have been overcome; he is getting on well for the most part. Ironic narratives present "a drama dominated by the apprehension that man is ultimately a captive of the world rather than its master" (White 1973, 9). Thus protagonists of an ironic narrative can *do* many things but cannot *act* in such a way as to achieve their goals. Some of the materials by these Native protagonist-authors, Mike Burns's in particular, tell stories that are indeed ironic: Carlisle promised me much; I did as I was told and worked hard, but it has not come out well; after all, I have very little.[6]

While I occasionally specify the structural implications of these Native writers' texts, I pay attention mostly to matters of style: syntax, diction, spelling, and punctuation. In doing so, I am rejecting out of hand any summary judgment that these texts are simply "bad English," poorly written. There are a few texts in the Carlisle files for which that might reasonably serve as the last word—not many, but some—and I have chosen not to reproduce them. They are in the digital collection, and any reader who wants to look for them will find them. They demonstrate that an enforced English most certainly did not work for some. But for the writers I do cite, English, however literally foreign and secondary, was a valued resource.

Some few of these writers invert the letters in a word; "indain," for example, several times appears rather than "Indian." This is an error, to be sure; but, when we consider that many Native people did not—and many do not now—pronounce "Indian" as a three-syllable word but, instead, as what would now be written colloquially as "Ind'n" or "NDN" we can understand that the inversion—indeed an error—is interesting as an attempt to render phonetically on the page what the writer had heard. In much the same way, when we find ~~line-outs~~ in some few of the texts, we may read them as indicators of conflict or unsureness on the part of the writer—who nonetheless persisted and managed to say, in one way or another, what he or she wanted to say.

These writers use a number of non-standard spellings, for example, "I am getting along first rat," "I want him to raise my wedges," "I don't eat Indian foots." Punctuation is sometimes unusual, or "incorrect," the use of periods in particular. If one does not simply dismiss these things as "errors," how might they be treated? One option is to treat them as *data,* examples of "American Indian English" (Leap 1993). Or, more attractively in my opinion, as an English dialect that can be called "Red English . . . a pan-Indian phenomenon, with various subdialects" (Mattina 1985, 9).

A linguist, this is to say, might seek to determine the degree to which the "errors" in any given writer's English might be attributed to the individual's ancestral or native language. Does the gender or the age of speakers—the writers, in these examples—inflect their English in the ways it does on the basis of the ancestral language? Is it the case that Athabascan speakers generally render English differently than, say, Siouan or Algonkian speakers? Do the many Lakota writers we will read engage in "preposition deletion" (Leap 1993, 76), while those who work from the base of other languages insert pronouns where standard American English considers them superfluous? Or is it more nearly the case that all these writers, having experienced a "*total unstructured immersion*" (Leap 1993, 158, italics in original) into English at school, generally write a "Carlisle English" that blurs these distinctions, the Carlisle dialect, as it were, of "Red English"? These are interesting questions and I hope the many texts published here may usefully serve linguists competent in these matters.

But these are not questions I take up in this book. Rather, I consider the deviations from standard American English in these texts as not merely linguistically but expressively powerful uses of language, presenting forceful challenges to the reader's imagination. We can readily "correct" the misspellings I've cited and see in our mind's eye "first rate," "wages," "foods," and so on. But why not consider further the possibilities raised by these spellings? Although they are "errors," some of them are nonetheless potentially interesting "errors," suggesting ambiguities or doubled meanings not present in the standard forms. Thus a student who addressed Pratt as "Found" almost surely meant to write "Friend"—but speculation as to the possibilities of "Found" might be worth engaging. So, too, when a young woman writes, "I live in a lack house," she may mean a "log" house, a "large" house, or a house that is lacking in some regard. Or does the word she had actually written suggest other possible meanings? Rather than simply "misspellings"—of course, they are also that—one can consider them interesting elements of diction.

Diction is at issue, for example, when, describing how she is getting along, Cecilia Pickard writes, "I talk white nicely." Or when another young woman, responding to a question asking her to tell anything of further interest in her life, writes, "I am interested in my life." Occasionally meaning is unclear or uncertain (e.g., "lack house," "Found"), but even then, in most cases the energy and determination of the writers to express themselves in English and in writing—in both a language and a medium still new and unfamiliar—is, I think, exciting. I quote as many of them as I do because I believe each piece of writing is in its own way unique and worthy of attention.

We may thus place these Native writers in relation to their older contemporaries, the poets Gerard Manley Hopkins in England, and Walt Whitman and Emily Dickinson in the United States, and their younger Russian contemporary, the theorist Viktor Shklovsky. This is to say, Hopkins, Whitman, and Dickinson, in their verse, and the prose of the novelists soon to be studied by Shklovsky, intentionally and purposefully engage in deformations of language in the interest of what Shklovsky would call the "defamiliarization," or "making-strange" (in English translation, in "Art as Technique," 1917) of everyday life. And deflections from standard usage are today commonplace in literary art.

To be sure, I don't for a moment suggest that the returned Carlisle students whose writings I present were aware of any of those I have named—although it is not impossible that some few were—or that they were consciously or intentionally making language strange in order to defamiliarize the ordinary. But apart from any intentionality, some of their writing has this effect. Thus their "bad English" works on occasion as a kind of "phonetic roughening," another phrase from Shklovsky, that disrupts our automatic or habitual apprehension of meaning in much the same way that poetry can. Again, I am by no means claiming that the writing published here is literary art, or that these Siouan or Keresan or Apachean or Yuman speakers consciously altered written standard English for the esthetic reasons Hopkins, Whitman, or Dickinson did. But the language they produced can nonetheless provoke an imaginative reach for meaning on the part of its readers, doing work akin to literary writing.

Similarly, let me note that two contemporary Native poets also produce some of their effects by defamiliarizing language in differing degrees. I am thinking of the work of Layli Long Soldier (Oglala Lakota) and Tommy Pico (Viejas Band Kumayaay Nation). Here is an excerpt from Long Soldier's work:

til 1890, when a

Wounded Knee. By
left in the continen-
on at the time the
By way of contrast,
were still coming. By
Knee, the population of
a. (Long Soldier 2017, 17)

And Pico:

> What fires your gd engine Rigor, mortis Cold as
> unmoving or unmoved The opposite of music Warm in the
>
> cold universe Molten, forming A rock becoming magma
> becoming lava becoming land Land, the trauma of lava Lava
>
> the lamp of the ancestors and later a cheeky find in the Junk
> shop and rising in our living room Livin groom. (Pico 2018, 6).

These are sophisticated and deeply intentional deformations of language, and the fragments I've cited don't do justice to the longer texts from which they come. But some of the writing of these former boarding school students, however unintentionally, performs work along these lines.

Some of it also performs the work of those whom Antonio Gramsci called "organic intellectuals." Gramsci had a great deal to say about this matter, but for the sake of economy, I cite the summary of his translators, Quintin Hoare and Geoffrey Nowell Smith. Distinct from professional or "traditional intellectuals" in modern, complex societies—clerics, academics, writers, scientists, and, today, pundits—

most of whom, despite claims to disinterestedness, nonetheless speak on behalf of class hegemonies—organic intellectuals, in Gramsci's view, "are distinguished less by their profession, which may be any job characteristic of their class"—and Carlisle students were for the most part trained to be agricultural workers or craftspeople and housekeepers—"than by their function in directing the ideas and aspirations of the class to which they organically belong" (Hoare and Nowell Smith 1971, 3). They write to a public that is "always in excess of its known social basis," as Anthony Webster quotes Michael Warner saying; their writings seek "to create the conditions for a broader social basis" (Webster 2017, 149). But this is not to say that their writings constitute a program or enunciate a common agenda, once more the reason why I quote more rather than fewer of the writers.

Reading the writing of these former boarding school students along these lines should, thus, work to undo some ideological, or indeed mythical, binaries long-standing in the dominant U.S. American culture regarding Native American expression. I am referring to the apparent opposition between the "noble savage," who, from Thomas Jefferson's citation of Chief Logan's "Lament" forward, asserts his elevated condition by producing lofty oratory (in excellent English, of course), and the silent "cigar store" or "wooden" Indian who can articulate no more than a rough "Ugh!" or "How!"[7] Some of these Carlisle Native writers can be eloquent in "good" English, and some of them can be rhetorically powerful and effective, as I argue, in "bad" English. Discussing the Society of American Indians, founded in Columbus, Ohio, on Columbus Day in 1911, Philip Deloria observed: "Not all Indian intellectuals were educated—but . . . at this moment pretty much all educated Indians functioned as intellectuals in one context or another" (Deloria 2013, 32). In what follows we see many of Carlisle's former students who wrote to the school functioning as intellectuals in exactly this way. And the University of Nebraska Press and I have done our very best to present what they had to say exactly as written.

Carlisle did not have its first graduation until 1889, when fourteen young people from various Native nations graduated. In the spring of

1890 Pratt sent a questionnaire to all of Carlisle's "returned students," those who had been at the school and returned home, either after graduating or after running away, becoming too ill to continue, or having the time they had signed up for expire. He asked not only that they fill out the questionnaire but also that they write him a letter describing their current situation: were they married, were they working, had they had any further education, had they obtained employment in the government Indian Service, and so on. We don't know how many questionnaires were in fact sent out, and however many of them were returned, none has been preserved. But 103 of the former students also sent letters to Pratt in 1890, and these have been preserved and scanned. Almost none of them has thus far appeared in print. In chapter 1, I quote from and comment upon 56 of the 103.

The places to which most of these Carlisle students had returned, and the places from which most of their letters came, was *home*, and home—different for each—was the ground on which they stood and from which they spoke, at a particular moment in time. It is with this in mind that I have presented the letters according to a regional organization. The only two of Carlisle's 1889 graduates to respond to Pratt, **William Campbell** and Julia Powless Wheelock, for example, came, respectively, from the White Earth Ojibwe reservation in Minnesota and from the Wisconsin Oneida reservation. No other letters came from Minnesota Ojibwes, but several did from other Wisconsin tribal people, and I cite them before moving to other regions. Conditions in these different places varied, and I provide historical material to contextualize the issues raised in the letters.

Some of these issues appear to be similar regardless of where they are encountered. Thus there are complaints, for example, about the lack of opportunities for work, about title to land, and about the restrictions imposed by government bureaucrats, among other matters, from all over the country. These similarities prompted the first reader to whom the press sent this book in manuscript to suggest that I organize the letters thematically rather than regionally. Initially appealing, such an arrangement upon further consideration seemed likely to introduce more problems than it would solve. For one thing, the letters voicing, say, concern with land titles are only apparently similar. Different parts of Indian country were allotted at different times—some well before the Dawes Allotment Act of 1887, and some well after: and the Pueblos of New Mexico territory were never allotted, for all that the question of who "owned" which lands was—and is—the subject of considerable litigation. To understand these things requires historical information more easily presented in a regional than a thematic structure.

The reader also suggested a thematic grouping of letters by "traditionalists," as distinct from letters by "progressives." But a simple binary of this sort elides a great many interesting complexities. William Shakespeare, whom I have briefly quoted, was proud of his Carlisle education and the fact that he had taken up farming, but as noted, he was also an important southern Arapaho peyotist and lived with three wives. Rather than classify him as either a progressive or a traditionalist, it is far more fruitful to contemplate the various dimensions, even sometimes the productive contradictions, of his complex Indian identity. This is true as well for Grant Left Hand. He had traveled to visit Wovoka and was a staunch proponent of the Ghost Dance. He was also, as I have said, a Baptist who clerked in a store for almost three decades. The writings of Shakespeare, Left Hand, and a great many of the returned students, as the second reader observed, "challenge the restrictive assimilationist-resistance binary that has dominated narratives of the boarding school experience." Just as careful attention to exactly *how* these former-student writers expressed themselves may undo certain "restrictive" binaries, so too does careful attention to *what* they said. Indeed, to provide a "challenge" to all sorts of prevailing reductive binaries, whether of style or content, is a goal of this volume, as a contribution to the critical conversation about the boarding schools.[8]

Certainly the writings of **Mike Burns** (Hoomothya) should be included in such a critical conversation. Burns, a Yavapai, had been enrolled at Carlisle from 1880 to 1884, and chapter 2 begins with his 1890 letter to Pratt. While at Carlisle, and for some years after he left, he published short pieces on various topics in one or another of Carlisle's newspapers—Emery's anthology does not include any of them—and he also sent detailed responses to later questionnaires he received from the school. In 1894 he began a correspondence—it is also uncollected and for the most part unpublished—with his far better known Yavapai contemporary, Dr. Carlos Montezuma, a correspondence the two sustained until Montezuma's death in 1923. From about 1913 to 1929 Burns worked on a lengthy autobiography which appeared only in 2010, long after his death in 1934. *All of My People Were Killed: The Memoir of Mike Burns (Hoomothya), a Captive Indian* is little known, and I quote from and comment on some of it, in particular those passages in which Burns discusses his schooling. I conclude with some comparative observations on the complex Indian identities of two differently educated Yavapai men, Dr. Carlos Montezuma—Wassaja—and Michael Burns—Hoomothya.

Pratt did not send out any further questionnaires in the fourteen years that he remained in charge of the school. But Pratt's successors as superintendent, Major William Mercer (1904–7), Moses Friedman (1908–14), Oscar Lipps (1914–17), and for just a year before the school closed in 1918, John Francis Jr., did send out such questionnaires, in both shorter and longer forms. In chapter 3, I present the responses to some of those later questionnaires, along with other materials sent to the school over the years by students who had and also by some who had not responded to the 1890 questionnaire.

In one of his later communications to the school, **William Paisano**, a former student from Laguna Pueblo, says to give his regards to **Siceni Nori**, also a former student from Laguna, then employed at Carlisle. Chapter 4 takes Nori and his part in the 1914 congressional investigation into the school as its subject but also as providing a frame for the examination of further communications from former students. Nori had served as "orderly" to Pratt, and then, during Moses Friedman's tenure as superintendent, he became the school's chief clerk, handling large sums of money. In an address to Carlisle's 1911 graduating class, Nori named a number of former Carlisle students whom he held up to the graduates as models of "successful" Indians. Most of them—like **James Johnson** and **Caleb Sickles**, teammates of **Jim Thorpe**'s on Carlisle's football team, both of whom became prosperous dentists—are largely unknown to us today, and I consider what they—and many others—had to say before continuing Nori's history.

In these obscure and mostly unpublished writings of former Carlisle students we may hear a range of boarding school voices. The choice of which to include and at what length is, of course, mine, and so I am indeed directing the choir: but you can hear its voices clearly. The book concludes with an appendix that lists every Carlisle student mentioned, a modest attempt to remember the names and tribal affiliations of persons who have long been anonymous. Along with interested readers generally, their descendants in particular will, I hope, be glad to have heard them speak and to see their names.

Boarding School Voices

I

"I talk white nicely"

The 1890 Letters of Returned Students from Carlisle

The Carlisle Indian Industrial School, the first federally funded Indian boarding school, "opened on the 1st of Nov., 1879 with 147 students," as Captain Richard Henry Pratt wrote in his "First Annual Report to the Commissioner of Indian Affairs," published in the Carlisle newspaper, *Eadle Keatah Toh* or the *Morning Star* for November, 1880 (4). The school's first graduation took place ten years later, the graduating class of 1889 being made up of seven young men and seven young women: three Wyandottes, three Wisconsin Oneidas, a Chippewa, a Miami, a Gros Ventre, an Omaha, an Ottawa, a Sac and Fox, a Cheyenne, and a Winnebago.[1]

The following year Commissioner of Indian Affairs Thomas J. Morgan wrote to Pratt suggesting that he contact the recent graduates and other "returned students" to learn what and how they were doing back home or wherever they might be. Morgan asked Pratt to request that "each Carlisle returned student . . . address a letter to [the commissioner] giving information concerning themselves." I take this description of Morgan's letter from a reply to it dated April 10, 1890, by Assistant Commissioner A. J. Standing. Standing thought

> more reliable information would be obtained by sending to those who can be reached, a series of questions to be answered by them, giving the information desired, and at the same time asking them to address a letter to Capt. Pratt embodying the same in substance; enclose both in the same envelope and return to Carlisle; the letters then to be forwarded to you, replies to questions filed at Carlisle.[2]

Morgan approved and instructed Pratt to do as Standing had recommended. We know that Pratt acted promptly, in that replies to the school's communication began arriving by early June 1890.

But as Dickinson College Archivist Jim Gerencser informed me, researchers could "not find those original survey questionnaires among any of the extant Carlisle administrative records . . . so they likely were not preserved" (personal communication, July 11, 2019). This means that we do not know the actual questions posed in 1890, for all that we may infer from the letters on file what some of them may have been. For example, we know from **Joshua Given**'s letter (discussed later) that there were probably sixteen questions. Pratt never sent out another such questionnaire during his time at the school—he left in 1904—but later superintendents did. These have been preserved, and they provide hints as to what the earlier one had asked.

Although some former students probably never received it, and others chose to ignore it—a matter I take up shortly—103 responses to the questionnaire have been digitized and can be found at the Carlisle Indian School Digital Resource Center, under "Documents" carlisleindian.dickinson.edu. The students' letters to the commissioner went first to Carlisle and from there were sent to him in five packets, from June 17, 1890 to July 22, 1890. In that Pratt "appears to have been out of town during the earlier period when the survey was conducted," it was "Standing himself [who] forwarded along the first two batches of letters" (Gerencser, personal communication, July 11, 2019), with Pratt transmitting the remaining three. Some few of the students' letters were published either in full or in part in the various Carlisle newspapers. But most of those printed here are appearing in print for the first time, and apart from ellipses for text omitted, they are completely unedited.

The majority of returned students—indeed, the majority of the 1889 graduates—did not respond to Pratt's questionnaire and request for a letter.[3] Some surely did not receive it, or did not get around to responding—although at least two former runaways, one of them in a Nebraska penitentiary, did receive it and chose to write. But it is entirely reasonable to assume that others who did not respond simply wanted nothing more to do with the school, having found their experience there anything from unpleasant to traumatic. We know a good deal now about what Native boarding school students suffered at the schools: loneliness, contempt, physical punishment, illness, and death, leading to a legacy of substance abuse, impaired relationships, and suicide. If former students who had suffered these things had responded, it is certain that their remarks would be far more negative than what is on record. But although the responses available are from a minority of the students, it is nonetheless a substantial minority. We cannot hear the voices of those many—the majority—who did not speak in writing, but surely it would be unwise not to listen to the words of those who did.

Of the 1890 respondents, most said that once home they had tried to maintain the "civilized" manners Carlisle had taught them, although some reported—proudly or with shame—that they had gone back to the Indian ways they had known before. Many, regardless of the manner in which they were living, expressed disappointment with conditions at their home agency. Some, whom I have called the "organic intellectuals," had given considerable thought to these matters and wrote to Pratt, often at length, expressing anger at the appropriation of their tribal lands by whites or at their current treatment by reservation agents. Almost all nevertheless express fondness for the school and warm feelings for Pratt himself. Several address him as "Dear School Father," something they had been encouraged to do—pure colonial paternalism, on the one hand, yet a recognition of the importance of Native filial relations, on the other.

Many said they were farming, although most of the farmers wrote of lacking adequate tools or materials. Some were employed at their agencies as carpenters or blacksmiths—who also often lacked the equipment they needed—or as interpreters, regardless of the state of their English-language abilities. A few had joined the Indian police or served as army scouts, something of which Pratt did not generally approve. Several had become or were studying to be teachers; one had been ordained a minister; one was applying to law school; two were performing in vaudeville or circus shows—also something Pratt did not approve—and one "played Indian" for a white purveyor of medicines.

There were only a few Carlisle students from the Northwest—from 1880 the Chemawa Indian School in Salem, Oregon, was available to Native people—but otherwise the student body was made up of young Indians from almost every part of the country.[4] From New Mexico Territory, some students who had returned to their Pueblos wrote of being pressured to participate in communal, ceremonial dances that the school had taught them to avoid as pagan error, thus having to negotiate a tension between the old ways and the new. On the southern plains, use of peyote for healing and worship had begun about 1880, giving rise not only to concern among whites but also to divisions among Native communities. (This is not, however, a subject any student from Indian Territory addresses.) Several students speak of having taken allotments, or of the imminent allotment of their reservation lands, although no one makes explicit reference to the Dawes Allotment Act, passed just three years earlier. On the southern plains, the plains, and elsewhere, the teachings of the Paiute prophet Wovoka and the practice of the Ghost Dance were already gaining adherents by June 1890, although more active participation in the dance would not come until the fall.[5] In late June 1890 the massacre of Lakota people at Wounded Knee was only six months away, something Superintendent Pratt, Commissioner Morgan, and the student respondents could not know. Their letters provide a strong sense of what it was like to live on the cusp of history, as it were, before what we now call "history" happened.

As noted, there were 103 letters sent to the school in 1890, and I reprint in whole or in part 56 of these. That is only slightly more than half, but they represent a very substantial selection; readers for the press thought perhaps too many. I ask your indulgence of possible over-inclusiveness: it is in the interest of giving voice to Native boarding school students not previously heard. Why these 56? The choice is of course subjective. But I've tried to cover the range of responses, writing by young men and women addressing questions raised by the school and raising questions the school did not ask. There are largely positive reports of what life back home was like, and more than a few negative reports. I did not include any of the very few letters I found largely unintelligible, although I have quoted a great many that roughen standard English, defamiliarize it, or make it strange in ways that I have found fascinating. In the body of the text or in endnotes, I have occasionally quoted or summarized material in the school's various publications by or about one or another of the writers to provide context for their later commentary. Some of the former students who responded to the 1890 questionnaire continued to stay in touch with Carlisle over the years, while some who did not respond in 1890 did choose to communicate with the school later. I present a substantial number of these later writings in the third chapter and several more in the fourth.

A Note on Transcription

The 1890 letters have been scanned by the Carlisle Indian School Digital Resource Center, so it is possible to see the penmanship of the various writers—their ages range from sixteen to thirty-two—on the website and it is my sense that the penmanship is very good and fairly easy to read in most cases. The letters have also been transcribed, and I have found the transcriptions in most cases to be accurate, although careful comparison with the originals does reveal some errors.

In what follows, [illegible] inserted in the text means the transcriber could not make out what was written—and neither could I. On the few occasions when I thought I could make out what was written, you will find [**whatever I thought it might be**] in bold and in square brackets. A bracketed question mark [?] indicates that I thought I could make out the writing, but I was not certain. What I take to be transcription errors are also [**in bold and in brackets**]. I have inserted three dots of ellipsis to signal that I have omitted something. Where you find three dots, they are mine, but otherwise, I have not added or altered punctuation. Nor have I altered any non-standard spellings, although I have not inserted [*sic*] to assure the reader that there is no typo. While I am unlikely to have avoided errors entirely, what you find on the page is an attempt to reproduce exactly what these Native people wrote.

I have tried to be consistent in spelling the many students' names, but that was not entirely possible. Marcus Poco sounds the same as

Marcus Poko; in the same way, one hears no difference between Randall Delchy and Randal Delchey, John Dixon or Dickson—or for that matter between Julia Powless and Julia Powlas. People raised in a mostly oral culture tend to use different spellings on different occasions because they are equivalent to the ear. Also, someone listed by the school as William C. Bull turns out to be William Crazy Bull—who later in life called himself William C. Girton, just as Charles Wolf (or Wolfe) came to call himself Charles Wolfe Williams. But even in instances like these, it should not be difficult to find any particular student in the text or in the appendix. Because some members of the first graduating class stayed on at the school in one capacity or another, they did not receive the 1890 questionnaire. Of the other graduates, as I have noted, there are responses only from **William F. Campbell**, a White Earth Chippewa, and **Julia Powlas Wheelock**, a Wisconsin Oneida. Campbell sent the longest letter of any of the respondents, and I begin by quoting almost all of it. Although he had entered Carlisle in 1888 at the age of twenty-two with only eighteen months of prior schooling, he nonetheless managed to graduate within a year of his arrival.[6] He writes,

> Dear Sir,
>
> Your circular issued to returned Carlisle students, requesting them to write and inform you of what they were doing their present [**need**] &c., is at hand. I cheerfully comply with your request. Although not a "Carlisle boy" in the full sense of the term, I was greatly benefitted by going there and I shall always look back to my Carlisle experience as the turning point in my life. And if I make a success of life I shall attribute it to the ennobling influences with which I was surrounded during my stay with you.
>
> Before going to Carlisle I attended school only eighteen months, fifteen months before I reached my tenth year, the other three when sixteen. But I [**have**] had a very liberal training [**in the**] school of experience. I have a fair knowledge of practical book-keeping and surveying. I ran a compass on a survey one summer. I began by carrying a shovel and throwing up mounds

around the stakes. I can now subdivide a township and write up my own notes. I have also been a drunkard and a gambler. I did nothing else for four years. In that capacity I have seen humanity in all its lowest and most degraded stages. I lived most of that time in the gambling halls of Dakota and Minnesota, and in other hells, where I have seen carried on, that traffic in humanity, that is far more disgraceful to the American public than were the slave marts of the south. The above was in the mining and lumber districts of northern Wisconsin. I have passed through the ordeal and stand alone to day with my manhood intact, though battered and scarred it is rapidly healing. I have quit my old associates and for the past two years have drunk no intoxicating liquor, and have given my whole attention to improving my mind. The above is entirely personal and is not *just* what you asked me to write, but I would like to prove that an Indian *can* rise—by his own efforts—from the vice and sin of his environments. I have not been idle any since my return from Carlisle. Am now teaching in a contract school[**, a**]lthough not making much money, am improving my education.

I shall make an effort this coming fall to enter the law department of our State University. Although not up to the requirements in education, I have hopes of entering on "conditions." I am going to Minneapolis next week and see what I *can* do.

Now, as to the most important question in your circular—"what is still needed to enable the Indian to succeed in life?"—I would say in reply that better facilities for education is needed, nothing else. Land is only a secondary consideration. I am speaking of the rising generation. Give them an education and they will procure homes for themselves. In order for them to compete successfully with the white man, their schools must come up to the same standard. You could not expect to take a horse that had never been out of his pasture and trot him a winning race with [**Maud S**] or Jay Eye See. Certainly not. He must be well trained. Just so with the Indian. And like the horse, it is better to take him into a broader field than his own narrow pasture. . . to train him. It is my opinion that five hundred dollars distributed among the various Indian Schools of the United States in the shape of prizes, would produce more beneficial results, than five thousand spent in any other way. It would produce competition, something not found in most Indian schools, while it is the very *life* of white schools. Better let it create an ill feeling among the students [**than let**] them continue in the same listless manner that characterizes the majority of Indian Schools at the present time. A few schools should be established where Indians could prepare for college, and let a scholarship, to some good college, be the prize for them to compete for. Competition begins with the white boy the day he enters school.

Johny Smith enters school at scarcely six years old. His sole ambition is to excel. . . . Thus it begins, and ends only with his life. Competition *makes* the white man, and nothing else will *make* the Indian . . . it is plain that competition is the governing force. My objection to Bellamy's ideas of government is, it will destroy competition, then would begin an age of decline.

You have asked me a question. I have answered it according to my own opinions. . . . I will close by asking a favor. (an Indian's great failing) I have a printed copy the proceedings of the Mohonk Conference. I have read it over with a great deal of interest. I noticed where one or two made comparisons between the Indian and negro. I say there is *no* comparison as the champion of our [illegible], I ask you this favor, [**if you**] hear that comparison again. Ask the maker of it this question. Did you ever hear America's most learned and polished orators draw illustrations from the negro, and how many have you heard, that do *not* draw the most beautiful similes from the Indian? The question makes its own argument.

I am Sir your most obedient servant
Wm. F. Campbell (Part 5)[7]

Clearly Campbell is an organic intellectual commenting on matters relating to his class and caste, or as he would have put it, to his "race"—whose oratorical prowess he considers superior to that of another "race." Pratt did not respond to this letter, although between June 1890 and January 1891 he wrote to Campbell no fewer than seven times—without, however, offering any thoughts about the "comparison" Campbell rejects.[8]

Julia Powlas, another of the first Carlisle graduates, addressed her letter not to Pratt but to Indian Commissioner Morgan. (Pratt's cover letter to the students made clear that their responses would be forwarded to Washington.) She writes from the Oneida reservation, the Oneidas being one of three Native nations overseen by the Green Bay Agency in Wisconsin, the other two being the Menominee and Stockbridge. She opens by identifying herself as "Julia Wheelock (Nee Powlas) . . . Age 24 At Carlisle 4 yrs" (Part 5). She is Julia Wheelock because, as she writes, "Few months ago I was married to an educated returned student from Carlisle." Her husband is **Charles Wheelock**, like Powlas a member of a prominent, progressive Wisconsin Oneida family.[9] His student file indicates that he was at the school from 1885 to 1889, exactly the years Julia Powlas attended, and that his grade level upon leaving was "9th (above)"—the highest one could go at Carlisle. But Charles Wheelock was not among the 1889 graduates, nor is a letter from him among the 1890 responses.

Julia Wheelock informs Pratt that she "had quite a little education before I went to Carlisle & could talk the English Language. This I learned in our family." She continues,

> Since my return from Carlisle, I have never been out of work. I did not have much of a vacation when I first returned. But went right to work . . . as clerk for Hon. D.C. Lamb, Special Indian Agent. Clerked for him till I began teaching in September. My school closes on the 30th day of this month. . . .
>
> Few months ago I was married to an educated returned student from Carlisle. He is also teaching school. We are getting on splendid so far. We have built a new frame house & have 30 acres cultivated and 60 acres uncultivated. . . . Our people are all civilized & have

never seen any one wearing an Indian clothes in our country. Most all have good homes. There are two Church Denominations on the reserve-ation. Methodist & Episcopal. (Part 5)

Two years after the passage of the Dawes Act in 1887, Dana C. Lamb had been appointed special agent to carry out the allotment of the Oneida Reservation in Wisconsin. The usual allotment was 160 acres to each head of household and 80 to each unmarried adult. This is not, of course, what Julia Wheelock reports, although the land she and her husband are cultivating was probably part of some allotment—which she likely approves, since she is working as Agent Lamb's clerk. Allotment, however, was opposed by two groups of Oneidas: the conservative or traditionalist Oneidas and also a number of wealthy Oneidas who had on their own secured title to large tracts of land, which might now be threatened by the allotment process.

Powlas's letter has some slight errors, but clearly she is as comfortable with written English as she is with clerking, teaching, farming, and going to church in citizens' clothing. She and her husband would continue to do well, and she kept in communication with Carlisle for more than twenty years (although there is nothing at all to the school from Charles Wheelock). I quote some of what she wrote in later years in the third chapter.

Charles Chickenny, a nineteen-year-old Menominee, whose reservation was part of the Green Bay Agency, like Powlas Wheelock's, offers a response that makes clear the degree to which the workings of the U.S. government in Washington impacted the daily lives of Native people far from the nation's capital. Chickenny expresses fears that the appointment of a new agent will unsettle and disturb the life around him. I quote his letter in full. He addresses Pratt as "Sir":

Very glad to inform you these few lines, to tell you the very trouble I have. I am work for all I am worth to have our present [A]gent Jennings remain + I earnestly + emphatically refuse to receive Mr. C. S. Kelsey as for my agent for they are the one who from time unto time have tried to starve the poor Indians and now I + my father +

grandfather is fighting as hard as we can and *I am* not going to have any one run my tribe like a mule or a dog, if I the said Indian should let Mr. Kelsey do as he please. I guarantee that he will starve my tribe + why should I go back when I am to the foot of the ladder that I have climbed doing the administration of my present agent Mr. Thos. Jennings + further trust in God that my right shall be delivered as I want to have them so that I can lead my tribe in the path of righteous. + I am sure if the Govt want the Indians to be come civilized he is not going to have Mr. Kelsey but them back in the same place where Mr. Jennings found them in wild wood and under the republican starvation. I tell as this that if Mr. Kelsey is agent I + the Tribe will have to out fishing and hunting in order to make our living through the administration of C.S. Kelsey + I am sure this the Govt does not want to heard or see + further to be runned [?] by the Shamans sharks I am going to stand for my right until the day come when I shall leave my home + go to another home your truly

Charles W. Chickenny (Part 1)

I think it is high feeling that caused Chickenny to inscribe himself as Charles *W* here rather than Charles *M* (see just below), but this young man's passionate letter raises a great many issues in need of explanation. Chickenny had entered Carlisle in November 1880, when he was just nine, leaving the school in June 1884. His Carlisle file lists him as Charles Mat Chickeny and his "Home Address" as "Matchickeny (1st Chief)." The name derives from the Menominee, *Ma'tshi-kine'u* or Mahchakeniew, meaning "Bad Eagle"—and it was the young man's grandfather's name (Beck 2005, 54). We also learn from Agent Kelsey—Kelsey did, in fact, replace Jennings—that "Chickeny, aged seventy-three" (234), a leader of the Bear clan, was a judge on the three-member Indian Court (Kelsey, in *Annual Report of the Commissioner of Indian Affairs for 1890*).

Satisfaction and more often dissatisfaction with the Indian agents in charge of the reservations is a common theme in the returned students' letters, and a few words about this may be in order here. Government Indian agents, like Cabinet members, were nominated by the president and confirmed by the Senate. In 1869 President Ulysses Grant's desire to control the rampant corruption of the administration of reservations by what had become purely a patronage system led to his so-called "peace policy," one aspect of which assigned oversight of the reservations to various church groups, who were expected to nominate upright men as agents. But from Rutherford Hayes's election to the presidency in 1876, each newly elected president usually removed all the agents nominated by a previous president of a different party and sometimes even replaced agents installed by a former president of his own party. While federal Indian policy and Congress's willingness or, more usually, unwillingness to appropriate funds for rations, education, and implements on the various reservations played the largest part in how members of any given Native nation fared at a particular point in time, the competence or incompetence of individual agents was still extremely important on a day-to-day basis.

Some of them were thoughtful, honest, intelligent, and sensitive men; others were corrupt, ignorant, and brutal. Nonetheless, as Rani-Hendrik Andersson has noted, all of them were "in a difficult situation; they were expected to carry out the government's programs . . . but at the same time they were forced to face the realities of reservation life." This "dilemma can clearly be seen in their annual reports" (Andersson 2008, 100) to the commissioner of Indian Affairs, from some of which I quote.

Charles Chickenny's letter refers to the fact that under Grover Cleveland, a Democrat, Thomas Jennings had served as the Menominees' agent from 1885 to 1890. Jennings had been in favor of allotting the reservation, but he also had been strongly supportive of the Menominees' logging enterprises, which were threatened by local lumber interests. In 1887, for example, Jennings had overseen the construction of a new tribal sawmill, and this, along with his continued defense of Menominee logging, provoked its opponents to pressure Washington into removing him and installing in his place Charles Kelsey. Kelsey, as David Beck writes, was believed by "most tribal members . . . to be affiliated with the Oshkosh lumber interests . . . scheming to get the tribe's timber" (Beck 2005, 54), and thus his appointment was opposed by tribal leaders—something that is clearly conveyed in Charles Chickenny's letter to Pratt.[10]

Upon his election as president in 1889, the Republican Benjamin Harrison did indeed replace Jennings with Kelsey. But while Kelsey was not as supportive of tribal timber interests as Jennings had been, he was not as hostile to them as Chickenny had feared he would be. In his 1890 annual report Kelsey noted that Menominee logging had earned the tribe nearly two hundred thousand dollars in the past year (235), over five hundred million dollars today (2019)! As a result of their lumber business, by 1905 the Menominees were one of the wealthiest tribes in the United States; they had not, as Charles Chickenny had feared, had to go out "fishing & hunting in order to make [their] living."

Whatever Chickenny's sense of the difficulties his people faced in June 1890, he seems also to have wished to return to Carlisle. I infer that from a letter Pratt wrote to him dated a little over a month later, on July 31, 1890. Pratt informed him that **Dennison Wheelock**, the Wisconsin Oneida bandmaster who had just graduated, would be coming to the Green Bay Agency to recruit students for the school, and Pratt wrote, "I should be very glad to have you here if the Agent approves of you coming" (Pratt letters binder 107; see note 3 for binder detail). But either because Agent Kelsey did not approve the young man's returning east or for some other reason, there is no further record of Chickenny's attendance at Carlisle. Although the *Red Man* for June 1890 did not publish Chickenny's letter, it did say of him that he was "now clerking in a store . . . is not married, [and] goes to Catholic Church" (3). A notation in his student file indicates that in 1910 he was at Keshena, Wisconsin, working as a "laborer," but there is no further communication between him and the school.

From the Winnebago Agency in Nebraska, about six hundred miles west and a little south of Green Bay, Wisconsin, **Susie Young** responded to the 1890 questionnaire. She had entered Carlisle at the age of twelve in 1884 and was enrolled until 1889, when her time expired and she returned home. She begins with some exciting news:

Dear Sir Captain,

I must write, and try to answer the questions as much as I can. I am living with my aunt with papa, for a little while. Well I will tell

> you something, but it isn't necessary to tell before we will But I hope you will keep it to yourself, until the day that we promised Will be very soon. And I will write to you just what day. This is. A white man is going to marry me. Captain do you think it will be very best for me to do it. . . . This man is coming to see papa's land before the 4th, but I will be waiting for you to hear you a word. My parents are willing to let me, because I am big enough.

Pratt does not seem to have answered in a timely manner, but Susie Young did indeed marry the man in question, Louis Cass Kelsey, a white man.[11] The couple would have two children, **Mary** and **Charles Kelsey**, both of whom would attend Carlisle, although their parents' marriage did not last. The reason it did not would be given by Susie Kelsey Mitchell, as she was then, in her response to a Carlisle questionnaire sent in 1912 that I cite in chapter 3.

In her 1890 letter she continues,

> I am well and happy always. The scholars that are from the eastern Schools are doing nothing, especially me, Agent won't give me any work around the Agency. I ask him about twice but no use to bother him. Some of them are graduated from Hampton, doing nothing. The house I am living in nearly worn out but I am trying to kept clean as I can. This house leaks when it rains. So they had been asking the Agent to let them be fixed, but he did not say nothing. The Indians said that he is not trying to help the Indians some ways. This is only house that had not been emptied since it build. So its worn out pretty badly.
>
> I hope the children are all well teachers and officers. Church every Sunday at Indian Presbyterian. Well I must close and sent you love.
>
> I am well and happy. But excuse I had made to much mistake. So [**G**]ood bye to you all.
>
> From your friend,
> Susie E. Young (Part 5)

In his report for the Eleventh Census in 1890, the Omaha and Winnebago Agency agent, Reuben Sears, wrote that he thought the Winnebagos were poor farmers and not industrious. He also expressed his opinion that reservation schools were much better for the Indians than the eastern boarding schools (*Eleventh Census* 378), an opinion that may have been prompted by the fact that, as Susie Young had written, she and a number of Hampton graduates were home "doing nothing."

A very full and moving account of the difficulties of the returned student is **Simon Smith**'s letter to Pratt, also sent from the Winnebago Agency in Nebraska. Smith had enrolled at Carlisle in August 1887, and his student information card records that he was sent home for "Bad Conduct" in July 1889. His age upon enrollment is recorded as twenty, which would make him about twenty-three in 1890, although Smith himself writes, "Age 28." He addresses Pratt as "Dear Friend." Here is his letter in full:

> I received the letter last week I am sorry that I didn't answered right away. I will tell you the reason why I didn't write, I was very busy last week working in the Department barn. a man work in this place he went way to do some work for himself, so I work in his place, I get a dollar day + my board that is all I do the work in this place. I never get any work by month I always work by day since I came back from Carlisle I always working for my self the first summer I came back I didn't do any thing, much, now this summer I plant some corn but not much I have only ten acres because I have no team to work with, this I use in plowing a oxen team, we just use these team only three or four days. now I don't know what I am going to do to cultivated my corn, I have to work for some body, and use his team, some boys get a team this summer they went out to brake some of their land, I like to go out to brake some my land but I cant do it. I got no team to go, work with, I live with my mother all the time since I came back, + I always remember, Carlisle, think about all my friends at the school I am getting along well + happy at present. I hope all my friends at Carlisle are doing well. excuse me for a poor letter, +

using no ink I have no pen, so I use my lead pencil I have not much to say, all the girls from Carlisle are wearing Indian clothes I see them most every day, this is all I have to say to you this time

From your Friend,
Simon Smith (Part 3)

Smith has had trouble getting monthly work, which would pay better than daily work. That he has little access to a team prevents him from breaking more land than the ten acres he has planted with corn. He says he has been living with his mother since his return, but his student file listed his mother as "Dead" at the time of his enrollment at Carlisle in 1887. Smith reports that "all the girls from Carlisle are wearing Indian clothes," but there is only one Nebraska Winnebago woman I could find who was a returned student in 1890, **Nellie Londrosh**, and I believe it is unlikely that Simon Smith would have seen her in "Indian clothes," as I explain later. There are no subsequent communications from Smith to the school on record.

Nellie Londrosh had been at Carlisle from 1883 to 1887 and, now married, she writes to Pratt as Nellie L. Nunn:

Dear Friend:

I have just received your letter with the enclosed questions I have answered them as near as I knew [**how**]. I am 22 years of age, and went to Carlisle in Nov. 1883. . . . I have always talked English and could read before going to Carlisle. I worked at [**General**] housework before I went and while there. I returned home in Feb. 1887 and taught in the Winnebago Industrial school until Dec. 1889. I was married in March 1889 to the Industrial teacher at the school. We attend the Presbyterian Church. I have a little girl five months old. . . . I have got along very well since leaving school and the only trouble I have had was the death of my brother.

I have no land as there was none allotted to me. I wish I could have got land but do not think I can. I have written to the Sec. of the Interior asking for some but have not received any answer yet.

Very truly yours,
Nellie L. Nunn (Part 5)

Nellie Nunn would have two more daughters and send both to Carlisle, although her first child did not attend. She does not seem to have been successful in having land allotted to her, as I note in chapter 3 when considering her later communications with the school.

I have found three responses to the 1890 questionnaire from returned Nez Perce students: **Jesse Paul**, **Charles Wolf**, and **Harriet Mary Elder**, by then **Mrs. James Stuart**, all of whom write to Pratt from the Ponca Agency in Indian Territory. The traditional homelands of these young Niimiipuu were in the Columbia River Basin of the Northwest—parts of Washington, Oregon, Montana, and Idaho—but all three came east to Carlisle from Indian Territory because they had been exiled there by the U.S. government.[12] Chief Joseph of the Nez Perces had surrendered to Generals Miles and Howard in October 1877, bringing an end to the "flight of the Nez Perces."[13] Paul, Wolf, and Elder had all experienced that four-month-long ordeal as very young children, traveling with their people over a distance of some fifteen hundred miles in an attempt to reach Canada. Only in 1885 did the Niimiipuu return from Indian Territory to Fort Lapwai, the Nez Perce Reservation in Idaho Territory, and to the Colville Reservation in Washington Territory.[14]

Jesse Paul, "Nez Perce—at Carlisle 8 years/Age 19 years/Returned Home 1888," writes:

> I can not very well remember just the day and month I left my home, because I did not know then. I was quite small when I left my home (which was at the time Indian Territory), and could not work at any thing. Now about working at school, I was about three years working on farms, and when I returned I went to working at blacksmithing until I left Carlisle for home. . . . I am employed as interpretor for a surveying party which at work in the Nez Perce Reservation.
>
> Well most of the time since I returned I have been in some business. About two years ago I was out again with a surveying company and worked around here several places. The question, what particular trouble have you had? I can not answer very well.

I have not been in ill health for any time. I have no farm at the present, but will have one when the reservation is surveyed.

This is all what I can think and will close.

Yours truly,
Jesse Paul (Part 3)

Paul's Carlisle file indicates that wagon-making was the trade he had learned at Carlisle, but clearly he was a competent blacksmith as well. As I later explain more fully, Alice Fletcher, known predominantly today as an ethnographer, arrived at Fort Lapwai in 1889 as the government agent in charge of allotting the reservation, which she did intermittently until 1892.[15] The surveying party for which Paul is serving as interpreter was likely one that was working with Fletcher. One of the surveyors was Harriet Stuart's husband, James. Jesse Paul writes that once the reservation is surveyed, he expects to have a farm on his allotment.

As a former Carlisle student, Charles Wolf is also doing some interpreting. Describing a rather more complex situation at the agency than Jesse Paul had, he writes to Pratt,

Dear [s]ir:

I received your letter, and so I take pleasure in answering to the Honorable Commissioner of Indian . . . Affairs, which he had made the questions to the former pupils of Carlisle and those that have returned to their homes. Well since leaving dear Carlisle School I have been losing my knowledge, but gained my strength.

When we got home Agent Norris put us to work with Surveyor's party, that only chance we had, earning some money, ever since new Agent came to the reservation or when Agent G. Norris was out. Robin a new Agent from Moscow has never try to gave us any chance where we earn money and strength or gain more knowledge.

Next month the Indians are going to have nomination, . . . and several of Indians nominate me for interpreter. And they are sure I am going to be interpreter for the whole reservation.

> Capt. my dear sir, I was mostly educated at Carlisle and same time I learn to use of English language. This all I have to say and do not know what continued to say.
>
> Yours friend
> Chas. Wolfe (Part 3)

When Wolfe returned to Idaho from Carlisle in 1888, George Norris was the agent at Fort Lapwai, and Wolfe describes having worked with Norris's "Surveyor's party" as a chance to "earn money." "Robin," the ominous-sounding "new Agent from Moscow," is W. D. Robbins, who had come from Moscow, Idaho, and would soon take over from Norris as reservation agent. In chapter 3, we look at Charlie Wolfe's responses to questionnaires sent out by Carlisle more than twenty years later.

Harriet Mary Elder, Mrs. Harriet E. Stuart as she signs herself, writes at greater length and expresses some strong opinions. Mrs. Stuart addresses Pratt as "Dear friend," and writes:

> I have received your letter today. I will try and see whether I can write a letter fit to read. Now it seems to me like a century since I left Carlisle, but at the same time I do not forget that I am a Carlisle student. Now I am twenty-two years of age. I went to Carlisle in the year of 1880 and there remained six years . . . . My ears were filled with, but Indian, my eyes, my brains were shut with ignorance. I breathed with of sound native language untill I went to Carlisle to learn the English language, which I now speak every day since I left Carlisle. While there, I learned how to sew, cut and fit dresses, wash + iron, cook and teach. Now I am housekeeping and have been boarding our principal teacher of this school. . . . In answer to your eleventh question, I have asked the Supt. of this [S]chool to work in the [S]chool, and no answer was granted me. Only that I ought to work for nothing, since the Government has spent so much money on me, ought to work for nothing, whatever comes on hand. I am willing to work, but the Government did not say I should work for nothing to get along. I do not live in a tent, but for present, I am living in a Government

house, since Miss Fletcher came. I do not know how to wear Indian clothes. I dress as a Carlisle student should. I am married to a graduate of Selam Indian School, and who is now assisting in the allotment with Miss Fletcher.

I atten the Presbyterian Church. I have no children, and have got along as well as I could be expected, only I did not expect to help my peopel without unless there was a little trouble before me. But hopes are that may our heavenly father make our way to enable us the returned students to help our poor people from dirt and ignorance. . . . We have 160 acres of land just allotted on which we will have our new house build pretty soon.

> You will fine the letter is written without any help, and
> please remember me to all I know yours truly Friend
> Mrs. Harriet E. Stuart (Part 2)

To understand Harriet Stuart's strong disapproval of what she calls Indian "dirt and ignorance," it is necessary to keep in mind what her early experience—like that of Jesse Paul and Charlie Wolfe—had been. As mentioned, they had experienced as children the rigors of their people's 1877 "flight" and the hardships of their subsequent exile. That had come about because when, after four arduous months of battles and travels, Joseph surrendered to Generals Oliver Howard and Nelson Miles in October 1877, he did so upon Miles's word that the Nez Perces would be assigned familiar lands around Fort Lapwai. Although Miles had given his word honestly, he was overruled by his superior, General William Tecumseh Sherman. This meant that some 431 Nez Perces, mostly women and children, sick and malnourished, were sent south to Fort Leavenworth, Kansas. Then in the summer of 1878 they were moved to the Quapaw reservation in Indian Territory, and the following summer they were moved yet again to the Ponca Agency near presentday Tonkawa, Oklahoma. Wolfe and Stuart would have been about nine years old when they traveled with Joseph, and Jesse Paul about seven. Wolfe would have spent five years in "eekish pah" (Trafzer 1985), the "hot place," Indian Territory, before going to Carlisle, while Harriet Elder and Jesse Paul endured two years there before traveling east to school.

If, looking back, Harriet Stuart recalled "My ears were filled with, but Indian, my eyes, my brains were shut with ignorance," this was because her people's flight and the rigors of their subsequent imprisonment had denied her eyes and brain—and those of Jesse Paul and Charlie Wolfe—a traditional Niimiipuu education. For example, not one of them would have had the chance to seek out their *weyekin* or tutelary spirit power, as both Nez Perce girls and boys had traditionally done. And Stuart is unlikely to have participated in her people's important puberty ceremony for girls. In Indian Territory there would have been no opportunity for the boys to learn to catch and for Stuart to learn to prepare Pacific and Chinook salmon, as their people had traditionally done; nor would they have learned to gather, store, and serve *kouse* or camas bulbs. The Niimiipuu were famed riders and breeders of horses, but there would have been no horse riding or horse breeding for them in Indian Territory. Sadly, it is no surprise that during the people's difficult years of enforced exile, Harriet Stuart experienced "Indian" only as an absence, a lack.

Something like this would have been the experience of Paul and Wolfe, too, although they do not express it as Stuart does. She would rejoin her people in their traditional homelands, going home from Carlisle to the Fort Lapwai Reservation in 1886, where Paul and Wolfe would arrive two years later. By then she had internalized Carlisle's values, as the boys had as well. Nonetheless, as we will see, they never abandoned their identity as Nez Perce Indians—even while also keeping in touch with Carlisle, to varying degrees.

Some further notes on Stuart's detailed letter: the "principal teacher" she is boarding is probably a white man or woman employed by the Fort Lapwai Indian School. Perhaps encouraged by that "principal teacher," she has asked the school's superintendent, Edward McConville, for work. The response she reports having received from him—that "the Government has spent so much money on [her], [that she] ought to work for nothing"—is totally inappropriate. (And in fact, as I note in chapter 3, not typical of him.)

Her husband, James Stuart, was a graduate of the Chemawa Indian School in Salem, Oregon, and if he and his wife spoke English to each other some of the time, both of them had grown up speaking their tribal language and both had retained fluency. Indeed, Fletcher wrote of Stuart that he was a "competent and trusty man who understands both languages" (quoted in Sappington and Carley 1995, n.2, 42). Acknowledging the fact that her allotment work was not welcome to all Nez Perce people—Chief Joseph consistently opposed it—Fletcher observed that Stuart had had "his life threatened for working with her on allotment" (in Sappington and Carley 1995, n.2, 42). Nicole Toncovich has claimed that because Fletcher trusted Stuart, "he was able to accomplish many of his own aims without his employer's notice" (2012, 5). These aims included some that were for his personal benefit—for example, he obtained an especially well-placed allotment for himself—and also some that were for the benefit of his people, as when he

> used his diplomatic acumen and his considerable knowledge of federal policy to establish procedures and programs by which the Nez Perces began to reclaim lands, monies, and cultural patrimonies that allotment had attempted to extinguish. (Toncovich 2012, 5)

Carlisle would hear from Harriet Stuart again in 1911, 1913, and 1915.

In 1867 the government had coerced six southern plains nations to sign the Treaty of Medicine Lodge, confining them to designated reservation lands.[16] These were the Wichitas, the Kiowas, and the Comanches, along with a much smaller population of Plains Apaches, settled around the town of Anadarko, and the Southern Cheyennes and Arapahos settled around the town of Darlington, all in Indian Territory. The buffalo herds on the southern plains were gone by 1881, and in 1884 the federal government outlawed the important religious observation of the Sun Dance. Despite this, Cheyenne and Arapaho Agent Jesse M. Lee,[17] in his 1886 *Report to the Commissioner of Indian Affairs*, wrote that "Many adhere tenaciously to their old customs" (quoted in Berthrong 1956, 139), and expressed his opinion that allotting these Indians' lands would be unwise.

But upon passage of the Dawes Allotment Act in 1887, Lee was replaced by G. D. Williams, "who agreed completely with federal policy" (Berthrong 1956, 139), and proceeded with the land allotment regardless of any opposition. Then, when a change of administration led to Williams's replacement by Charles Ashley, he, like Lee before him, tried to convey to Washington the fact that the Indians were largely against any further allotment. Congress having just passed the Indian Appropriations Act of 1889 authorizing the "opening" of two million acres of "Unassigned Lands" in Indian Territory, the concerns of these agents and the tribal nations they served were ignored. When the returned Carlisle students received Pratt's questionnaire in June 1890, the tribes in Oklahoma Territory were nervously awaiting the arrival of the government's "Cherokee Commission" to arrange for still further allotments and sales of "surplus" lands. The Carlisle questionnaire, this is to say, arrived at a time when both the subsistence and the ceremonial practices of the nations in Indian Territory and the southern plains were under enormous stress.

Peyote had come to the southern plains in the 1880s, and now, near the end of the decade, word came of the vision of the Paiute prophet, Wovoka, and his introduction of the Ghost Dance. Black Coyote, a Southern Arapaho chief, traveled to the Wind River reservation in Wyoming in the early spring of 1890 to learn about these things. A bit later, the Northern Arapaho Sitting Bull—a much younger man than the better-known Sitting Bull of the Lakotas—brought the Ghost Dance doctrine to the southern plains. As also to the north and the west, the spring of 1890 was unusually dry, and those who had planted corn saw their crops fail. At this time several returned students from off-reservation boarding schools, as Donald Berthrong writes, "quickly resumed tribal life, partly because of the conservative pressure of their elders and also from the lack of funds to buy the implements needed for successful agriculture" (1956, 146). The scarcity of tools, wire for fencing, draft animals, and the like is something raised in many of the letters to Pratt.

One student who did not resume tribal life nor become a farmer was the Reverend **Joshua Given**, who wrote to Pratt from the "Kiowa,

Comanche and Wichita Agency/Anadarko, Ind. Terr." Given's Carlisle student record lists his father's name as Satank, or Sitting Bear (c. 1800–71), a renowned Kiowa warrior and medicine person who had been active in raids on neighboring Cheyennes, Sacs, and Foxes, and who, as American settlements expanded, led attacks against them as well. In 1867, however, he had been one of the signers of the Treaty of Medicine Lodge. In 1870 Given's older brother, also named Satank, had been killed by Texans, and the following year the elder Satank was arrested and then killed as he attempted to escape. This is only to note that Joshua Given came to Carlisle not from a family of Native progressives but from one that had engaged in active resistance to the Americans. He was among the first Carlisle students to arrive, in October 1879.

Just after his first year at the school, Given published an account of his early life in the Carlisle *School News* for November 1880. Here is most of it:

> I am a Kiowa Indian 19 years old. My father's name "Satank." I will tell you a little of my life. I was born in Colorado and when very young we went to the Indian Territory about Fort Sill. At that time we lived on Buffalo and in houses made of buffalo skins. The Kiowa men used to kill the buffalo and trade the robes to the white Traders for sugar and coffee. I have killed a good many buffalo.
>
> All this time some of the Indians were bad and used to steal horses and cattle and kill people . . . a great many soldiers went to fight them. . . . I was then a long-haired Indian boy with a blanket. My first white friend was the agency Doctor, Dr. Given he was a good man and took me to live with him, cut my hair and gave me some white man's clothes and then when a school was started I was one of the first scholars and have been at school as much as I could. The Indians are not now like they used to be, the buffalo are all gone and they must look for their living from the ground and from cattle. . . . We want to learn all we can and after a while we go back to our own people and teach them all we can. (1)

Dr. Obadiah G. Given, the agency physician whose surname Joshua Given had taken, would become the Carlisle School doctor, where he and his young namesake remained in touch.

Years later, after a visit home, Joshua Given would publish a long letter in the *Indian Helper* for August 10, 1888, reporting on how former Carlisle students he had known were getting on. He said of **Emily Peatone**, a young Kiowa woman who had entered the school about six months after he did, that she "is the dirtiest returned Carlisle pupil I have met" (1), and that the Comanche student "**Marcus Poco** is no good" (4). Emily Peatone had entered Carlisle in the spring of 1880, at the age of fourteen, and remained for three years. Her student information card indicates that she had married Frank Bosin, but it does not say when. She did not respond to Pratt's 1890 questionnaire, nor are there any further communications between her and the school in her file. But she must at some point have written, for twenty-five years after the Reverend Given had rendered his harsh judgment of her, the Carlisle *Arrow* for May 31, 1912, contained the following note:

> It has been a number of years since Emily Peatone left Carlisle; since then she has married and is now the mother of four children; her husband's name is Bosin. Mrs. Bosin writes of a "good home and a good living on a farm." (3)

We will consider Marcus Poco later.

Given had a much better opinion of **Etadleuh Doanmoe** and his wife Laura. Doanmoe, a Kiowa born about 1855, had fought in the Red River War on the southern plains and in Texas. At the war's end in 1875 he had been sent by the Americans with other captive Kiowas, Comanches, and Southern Cheyennes to be held prisoner at Fort Marion, in Saint Augustine, Florida, where Richard Pratt was in charge. Pratt had enlisted local volunteers to educate some of the prisoners at the Fort, among them Doanmoe, who followed Pratt to Carlisle in 1879, where he continued as a student and also worked as a staff member. While at Fort Marion, Doanmoe had done a series of drawings—"ledger art"—that are now highly regarded.[18] He briefly served as a Presbyterian missionary among his Kiowa people, dying in 1888, just before Given's visit.

Given writes: "The report of so much of Etadleuh's property being destroyed by the Indians is not true. I have seen the house and the wagon, corn-field and other things." He notes that "the Indians are proud of their corn-fields and the success they are making. It was due to Etadleuh's advice." He observes that Etadleuh's wife, "was well," and "remains just as firm in her new life and she should be encouraged" (Carlisle *School News,* November 1880, 4). **Laura Doanmoe**, likewise a Carlisle student, had also been among the first students who entered in October 1879. She was still enrolled at the school in July 1889, although she obviously had been at home in 1888 when Given visited. She did not respond to Pratt's 1890 questionnaire, but she remained in touch with the school, and I review her extensive file in chapter 3.

In Given's 1890 letter to Pratt, he affirmed some of what he had written in his brief autobiography, and continued,

> I could read some before entering the Carlisle School, and of course I could speak little English, as I spent some two or three years in the Kiowa School here at Fort Sill. But in those days, this means nothing—comparing with what has been done at Carlisle Indian School. . . .
>
> At Carlisle School I acted as janitor. Left the Carlisle School in 1884 for good and entered the Lincoln University, Chester County Pennsylvania. I was graduated from the Collegiate Department in 1886, and the following fall, I entered its Theological Department. I spent three years in this department, graduated in April 1889. When graduated I was examined and licensed to preach the Gospel by the Presbytery of Carlisle. Received an appointment, July 20th 1889, from the Board of Home Missions of the Presbyterian Church to be a missionary among the Kiowa Indians. . . . The *Plymouth Church* of which Rev. Mr. Beecher was once the pastor raised the sum of $800 and with this amount they (that is, the Congregation) errected a beautiful frame cottage for my use. While I meet just as many

> difficulties and have as many temptations, like the rest of human beings, I have thus far escaped the putting on of the [**camp**] clothing. In answer to questions 15 and 16, I have to say, that I married an educated white lady, to help me in my work among my people. My wife is a real "yankee" from Connecticut. . . . The Indians . . . even while some of them object to my preaching, are very kind and listen to my humble talk. I have a small farm and have twenty three horses, three mules, thirty head of cattle and seven pigs.
>
> I [**hope**] these answers will prove satisfactory.[19] (Part 5)

He signs himself "with respect, / Your ex-pupil, / Joshua H. Given." Kiowa Reverend Joshua Given would die of consumption in 1893.

Also writing from "Wichita Agency Anadarko I.T." in June 1890 is a young woman who signs herself **Cecilia Pickard**. (Her Carlisle files list her as Celia Pickard.) A Wichita who had entered Carlisle in 1880 when she was only nine years old, she had left in 1884. Her older sister, **Eva Pickard**, whom she mentions, had entered Carlisle a year earlier, in 1879, but had had to leave in 1882 because of ill health, a frequent cause of departures from the school. Cecilia Pickard is a lively, chatty nineteen-year-old whose letter to Pratt filled four handwritten pages with much domestic detail. She begins,

> Dear Sir:
>
> I now seat myself to inform you of how I have been getting along since I left dear Carlisle. I received those printed question's to be answered and all the answer's are very true. I am the best Seamstress here and they say they can not get on without me. I can now make my own dresses as well as any one else. . . . We have a small stockade house it is my brother in law's, we have a small farm too. We have a few peach trees + few apple trees, and we have a garden in the yard it is doing very well, there are onions, beans, tomatoes, cabbages, musk and water melons [**i**]rish + sweet potatoes, pumpkins and different kinds of corn. . . . I had about twelve head of cattle some were lost or killed by the Indians

on the other side of Washita. . . . Eva has two children the oldest is my favorite her name is Elinor Tatum we called her Helen for short + the youngest is May Belle Tatum. [**m**]y mother has got so she wears dresses sometimes on [**s**]unday. All in our family belongs to church except my little brother that is off to school. . . . We sold our farm to one Indian [**w**]oman. We have selected a new place six miles from it. It is a beautiful place . . . and by next summer we will be ready to move to the place. . . . It will make a pretty home if we just had a house to commence with a house here costs so much to get the lumber + then to have it made. I will try and go without getting new Dresses for a while and give the money toward getting the lumber I will give them most of my wages for the house. I could do very well if we just had a house. next summer I will stop working here and go home to stay + keep house for my mother. [**w**]e have no man at our home but my brother in law and he does all the work for we cannot afford to have a man work for us. but I promised my brother in law I would pay a man out of my wages or hire him to help him put up the fence we are going to enclosed ~~us~~ in our land by barb wire fence. and hire a man to break the land where our field will be. I am not married yet. I have had offers but refused them. I do a great deal for my niece's I make them dresses . . . I love them + they love me. Helen thinks that there is no one like her [**a**]untie. both of them have worn dresses ever since babies and will + shall wear dresses and not Indian clothes as long as I have money. . . . I can make anything in sewing but sorry to say I cannot cook much Eva does the cooking but I can do everything else. . . . I can ride a horse as well as any man . . . and a wild horse cannot very easily throw me. I can ride barebacked + straddle + side ways + have run race's lots of time's sunday I was out riding + a runaway horse with a bridle and a rope past me + I race it all around the filed tried to catch it but it went across the creek and I let it go. I must stop now for I must get to work.

She signs herself "From your scholar," and adds: "P.S. excuse me for not writing any better as I do not write much, but I read lots. give my love to Richenda & Nana" (Part 2).[20]

This is a wonderful free-flowing stream of consciousness by a young woman who preceded by a good number of years the expert practitioner Virginia Woolf! And, just as self-consciously literary "streams" would do, her letter leaves it to the reader to fill in details of the matters to which the speaker alludes. Pickard, as noted, writes from the Wichita Agency at Anadarko, Indian Territory. The Wichitas, a Native nation that had never engaged in an attack on whites, had been part of the Kiowa and Comanche Agency based at Fort Sill until 1871, when they were assigned their own agency at Anadarko, on the Washita—another spelling for Wichita—River, just over forty miles north of Fort Sill.[21] Wichita people had long had an agricultural tradition, and were more inclined to take up farming than the Kiowas and Comanches at that time, something to which Cecilia Pickard's letter attests.

She seems to be working as a seamstress "here," where "they say they cannot get on without" her. Although she does not say just where that is or who her employers are, we learn from the Carlisle *Indian Helper* for February 3, 1888, that "a very pleasant letter from the matron of the Wichita School, Anadarko, Ind. Ter.," reported that Cecelia "is at the school there as assistant seamstress, and does her work most thoroughly" (2). When she does go home, that home, as she makes clear, is her brother-in-law's house. Her brother-in-law—a term she may have learned at school, in that most Native people would say, "my sister's husband"—is indeed the husband of her older sister, Eva, and his surname must be Tatum, the surname of her nieces, Elinor Tatum, or Helen, and May Belle Tatum. Otherwise, the family consists of Cecilia, Eva, and their mother, a sister in Philadelphia, and a "little brother that is off to school." There is no mention of their father, and the Carlisle student information cards for both Cecilia and Eva Pickard do not list a father's name, as they did for most students.

With their farm sold to "one Indian woman," it appears that all of the Pickards and Tatums will be living together in the new place—if only they can get the house built. Cecilia Pickard never names her brother-in-law, Mr. Tatum, the father of Helen and May Belle Tatum, but he was a Wichita man named Lawrie Tatum. This emerges from the Carlisle files of his daughters, Helen and May Belle, both of whom entered Carlisle in 1903—but under the names of **Helen Pickard** and Rosabel or **Rose Pickard**. The applications for the girls record that their parents, Eva Pickard and Lawrie Tatum, were dead at the time of their application, neither one of them yet forty years old. But the girls' "father" in some of the Carlisle records appears as Arthur Pickard. This is incorrect because Arthur Pickard is Cecilia's "little brother," who, in 1890, had been "off to school"; he was the Tatum girls' uncle—as is indeed indicated correctly elsewhere in their records.

Eva Pickard's husband Lawrie Tatum would have been named for Lawrie Tatum, a Quaker, who under Grant's "peace policy" became agent of the Kiowa, Comanche and Wichita Agency at Fort Sill in 1869, where he would serve until 1873.[22] Eva Pickard had been born about 1864, and Lawrie Tatum, who would become her husband, was probably born around that time as well. I believe he was the older brother of **John Tatum**, who entered Carlisle at the age of twelve in 1882 and was enrolled until 1887. John Tatum's student information card lists his father—and, if Lawrie was indeed his brother, Lawrie's father as well—as Buffalo Good (sometimes Good Buffalo; occasionally Buffalo Goad), a traditional Wichita band leader involved in several negotiations with the Americans.[23]

John Tatum also responded to Pratt in 1890; here is his brief letter:

> I haven't got much to say in requesting that we should write to you I hope you will be glad to hear from me I am well at present and hope you are the same. All of the Wichita are improving in there work and going on to the ways of the Whites. There is another thing ~~to~~ for me to tell you about. We have a church house. every Sunday we go to church. some of the Wichitas are Christains now and they got a preacher too. I haven't much to say this is all.
>
> Your friend,
> John Tatum (Part 3)

Despite his Carlisle education, and his church going, John Tatum had not entirely abandoned the ways of his people. He was described by the anthropologist Alexander Lesser, for example, as "a Wichita *chief* visiting the Pawnee" (1933, 300, my emphasis) in 1900 to participate in the Pawnee Ghost Dance Hand Game ceremony, the subject of Lesser's study. The 1915 *Census of Wichita and Caddo Indians* gives his wife's name as Chaw wah, a name that suggests she was probably not a former boarding school student.

John's brother, Lawrie Tatum—who in June 1890 was a returned Carlisle student and a married father of two, busy with fencing, breaking farm land, and building a new house for his family and in-laws—was also an adherent of the Ghost Dance. It was just over a year later, in the fall of 1891, that Lawrie Tatum would be part of a delegation visiting the Paiute messiah, Wovoka. James Mooney wrote that "Tatum was a schoolboy and acted as interpreter for the party,"[24] which "came back impressed with reverence for the messiah," and the dance that was to bring about a revitalized world. According to Mooney, Wovoka's Wichita visitors, on their return, "changed the time and method of the dancing, in accordance with his instructions," and "were dancing in this fashion when last visited in the fall of 1893" (Mooney 1973, 160). Is it possible that Lawrie Tatum's mother-in-law, Mrs. Pickard, who, as her daughter had written, "wears dresses sometime on sunday," also participated? And what did his wife, Eva, a former Carlisle student—who did not write to Pratt in 1890 but whose daughters would also attend the school—think about her husband's involvement with the Ghost Dance?

We cannot know what Eva's younger sister Cecilia Pickard thought of the Wichita Ghost Dance because, as we learn from the Carlisle *Indian Helper* for July 10, 1891, she had died in April that year, less than a year after writing to Pratt and several months before her brother-in-law's visit to Wovoka. The *Helper* described her as "one of our dear little girls. She grew into womanhood and had a useful life among her people up to the time of her death" (2). No cause of death is given for this young dressmaker and horsewoman, only twenty years old. We will learn a little more about John Tatum and his nieces Helen and Rose in chapter 3.

Hortie Stevens, "Wichita Age 22 / At Carlisle 4 years / At Home 4 years," also writes from the Anadarko Wichita Agency. He had been at Carlisle from 1882 to 1886, two years of his schooling overlapping the last two of Cecelia Pickard's—he would probably have known her family from home. His English is not standard, but he is free in its use, largely unconstrained by punctuation. His lengthy letter begins,

> I received the letter from you last week ago that the commissioner who he has instructed you to write me and know how I am doing ~~so~~ getting on I am very glad this letter want me to know how I am doing so I try to answer this letter to you so I can tell you what I have doing I am doing working at my farm every day so I think this is the way of civilized people. . . . I consider this is what you want to know so it is my heart get greater But I think you should think that I am throw things away what I learn here I should not do that throw away which is the of White I still on that matter do what is Better for me and become of a man so I am ever try hard to do. . . . I consider the Indians are getting on well But I think my tribe are doing very well that is Wichita Indians doing working they farms very well [**B**]ut the truble have no houses I have no house for my self I live in the tent But I am not wear the Indian Clothes I still, able to wear the English clothes this is the true words I give you in this letter this is all I have to say to you I been Educated here in this school and been worked round here + study thing so I am not throw things away which is I learn here in this part the country.

Housing clearly was a problem for the Wichitas at Anadarko, as Cecelia Pickard had reported, and Stevens notes some of the difficulties farming, as she had as well. Even though he writes that "my crop of corn are very good it is nearly four feet high now," nonetheless,

> it is not very big field so I would like to have more land I break up this little peace of land last fall for myself because it is the Government has not allow to break land for the Ind[**ai**]n now so I am try to make land But the trouble my horses are not use

> to break land so I have not enought field . . . . But I am going to tell you this I have two heads of cattle last year I brought from the Indain in the day tim[. . .] I went hunt that two cattle was lost some body has been draw down to the Washita river and kill there I think it must be wild Indain there. . . . Please Capt R.H. Pratt can you sent Newpaper. (Part 3)

Like the Pickards, Stevens too has lost stock on the Washita to "wild Indain there," to Kiowas or Comanches, perhaps. He is asking for the *Indian Helper*, which seems to have been mailed to most former students.

Stevens is not writing exactly as the school had taught him to write; his grammar, spelling, and punctuation—he uses very little—have many "errors." But he writes with energy—repeating himself for emphasis—and, it seems to me, with more than adequate clarity. Whatever Pratt may have thought of his former student's writing, he did send Stevens the newspaper and received thanks for it from Stevens. We may infer this from a letter in Pratt's papers dated September 22, 1890, in which he says he is pleased to learn that Stevens enjoys receiving the *Helper* (Pratt letters 242).

We have heard from a Kiowa man and a Wichita man and woman from the agency at Anadarko. I turn now to a Comanche from that same agency, twenty-year-old Marcus Poko, who had left the school in November 1884. Poko writes to Pratt:

> Dear Sir:
>
> I received your circular and have answered your questions. You will see by my answers that I have been wearing blanket for sometime but was not my fault. I have a large farm and working hard for the support of my small family. I have cattle, pigs, horses, and mules. On account of having no church near us, I do not attend church. I went to Carlisle in 1880 and remained there for four years. I married a camp Indian but I think I am getting along alright. This is all.
>
> I am your friend,
> Marcus Poko (Part 5)

Poko refers to the questionnaire that had accompanied the request to send Pratt a letter, stating that he has filled it out. No doubt the fact that Marcus Poko had "gone back to the blanket," had married a "camp Indian," and attended no church were the reasons why Joshua Given, after visiting home, sent the negative report about him that ran in the Carlisle *Indian Helper* on August 10, 1888. The pious Mr. Given, once a long-haired boy himself, had written disapprovingly,

> Marcus Poco is no good, in every sense of the phrase. Is married and has one boy—long hair and face painted in yellow and red. The Kiowas told me that Poco loves horseracing too dearly (4)

I don't know whether Poko was aware of this earlier report. But he did not give up on the school, and would respond to its 1910 questionnaire, as we will see.

From the nearby Cheyenne and Arapaho Agency at Darlington came a letter from **William Little Elk**, "Cheyenne. Age about 30 / At Carlisle 3 years. Returned home 1884 / (Was a very good Baker at Carlisle)." He writes,

> I have had never thought of Carlisle since I leave at last I found letter you sent. I hate to write letter, as you want us to tell you about our doings. you see my age. I am man enough and have been school very little. I use be scout inside three years and there I use got $25 a month. and I have just get out scout this year. [**Capt.**] it is very hard there are great many return children that are going back in Indian ways. Why just because there is no work to do. How we going keep up the way that we have learn. if you want us to do right + want us to become like Whites do something for us. sent something that we may wrk at and that will bring us something to keep up. I had have hard time to find something to do.

His command of English is no obstacle to the insightful analysis William Little Elk, a mature and thoughtful organic intellectual, offers of the problems facing the returned student. He writes,

> When School boy comes home and have something in his mind hope to do it. And go to the Agent ask for wrk. And Agent answer I have no wrk for you. And what do you think a boy will do. Will as long as his [**S**]chool clothes else. [**a**]nd as [**soon**] clothes past away he is on Indian ways. this is very poor way Capt. there is no hope us. [**a**]s long as this thing going on this way we will never turn out any other way. Government ough do something for educated children. he ough put all kinds shops on every Agencie. this is all I have to say to you. I am one of your old Carlisle boy

All Pratt himself could do to address these urgent matters was to pass these observations on to the commissioner of Indian Affairs to persuade the government to "do something for educated children."

William Little Elk had married **Minnie Wolf Face**—she is listed in the Carlisle records as Minnie Little Elk—in February 1884, while both were in attendance at the school. She did not respond to the 1890 questionnaire. But she and her husband did communicate with the school later, and I consider in chapter 3 what they wrote.

William's younger sister, **Florence Little Elk**, had entered Carlisle in 1886 and then left a year later because of illness. She writes to Pratt briefly, in effect confirming the situation William had observed of "great many return children":

> Florence Little Elk
> Cheyenne age
> At Carlisle 20
>
> June 20, 1890
>
> Capt. R.H. Pratt
>
> Dear Sir,
>
> I am sorry to say that I am Indian away all the times. I cannot do answered questions and the other girls all go Back in Indian aways (too)
>
> that is all (Part 5)

Twenty years later, upon receiving a questionnaire sent by Superintendent Moses Friedman, Florence Little Elk, although she still could "not do answered questions," nonetheless wished to communicate with the school and found someone to answer them for her, as we will see in chapter 3.

Like William Little Elk, **Leonard Tyler**, another young Cheyenne from the Darlington Agency, had given a great deal of thought to the difficulties of the returned Indian student. Tyler's name was Magpie when he went to Carlisle, where, under circumstances I have not discovered, he was named Leonard Tyler by the aunt of John Tyler, former president of the United States. He writes to Pratt,

> Dear Sir;
>
> You letter is received I shall write [**afew**] important facts requiring in your letter. Since my return I have never made much progress. In fact I did not remain at home but one year. I went back to go school at Haskell Institute, Lawrence, Ks. I remain the three years, but the most difficulties at home is that we have no way of made progress or there is no work here I am always very anxious to go work when I come back but have no means to do so. That is why so many of the return students gone back in Indian ways. There is a subject which I have hold + excepted you assistance is very much need.

He too reports that "there is no work here," and "That is why so many of the return students gone back in Indian ways." Tyler, another organic intellectual, recognizes that "assistance is very much need," and he offers detailed plans to ameliorate the situation. Before considering them, let me note that one of those who had "gone back in Indian ways" was Tyler's wife, also a former Carlisle student, Jennie A. Tyler or **Jennie Black Kettle (Tyler)** who also responded to Pratt.

Both she and her husband wrote on the same day, June 13, 1890. Here is her letter to Pratt in its entirety:

Dear Sir,

It is almost the year since I returned at this Agency. During my return I could not help but going to camp to live with my folks. It is afact that we got no place to going to. This I remain in Camp for two months then I return here in Chey. school to work. If we had place to go to it will be all right. We cannot live in Camps after we had learn the better way. [**nor**] we either agree any more the ways of our people. We desired or need houses, things that are necessary to use.

This is all—yours truly
Jennie A. Tyler (Part 4)

Although she was married to Leonard Tyler in 1890, she nonetheless says that she has been living with her "folks." Cheyenne people had traditionally been matrilocal, so it is likely her husband was also living with them. When she writes, "It is a fact that we got no place to going to," I assume that "we" refers to herself and her husband and to the difficulties they, like many others, faced in obtaining adequate housing.

Painfully aware of such matters, Leonard Tyler offered an elaborate plan to better the lot of the returned students. He writes that he has attempted to "gather 40 return pupils to plant a 'Colony' for ourselves." Such a colony would surely have been modeled on the nearby Seger Colony, founded several years earlier by John Homer Seger (1843–1928). A former Union soldier who had marched with Sherman through Georgia, Seger had been the first white settler among the Cheyennes and Arapahos, arriving in Indian Territory in 1872. In 1886 Cheyenne and Arapaho agent Jesse Lee had invited Seger to lead a group of Arapahos, soon to be joined by a number of Cheyennes, to form a farming colony about sixty miles from the Darlington Agency, and as we will see, several returned Carlisle students were living and working there in 1890. Tyler, however, seems to have wanted a "colony" exclusively made up of returned students—which he could not successfully establish.

He continues,

> Last year I gather 40 return pupils to plant a "Colon[e]y" for ourselves. After talked over + encourage by each young men about the Colony we start to select our farms. After looked over where to made a Colon[e]y we return at Agency and ask the Agent for Assistance, but never pay attention. It was then change of administration.

He refers to the fact that Benjamin Harrison had replaced Grover Cleveland as president in 1889, although this time the "change of administration" did not mean a change of Indian agent, as Harrison retained Charles F. Ashley, who had been appointed by Cleveland. In that Ashley apparently had "never pay attention," Tyler hopes to go over his head. He writes,

> I believe my good friend a separation of return pupils from old Indians is good plan. If the Government wanted enable us once more in our exertion Let the return pupils place in Colony. Let the Government furnished houses furntur team implements + other . . . necessary things. If the Government cannot [**afford**] to furnished these things, then perhaps he can load us money to start with.

Tyler proposes "At least $400.00 each young man to start with for two years," and then goes on to explain in detail how the loans would be repaid. He concludes,

> instead white man getting all money from Indians in breaking their farms. I can but feel this in my heart, that it will be a refuge for the return pupils if you pushed the matter. hoping to see the day when we shall stand on the same ground with our white brothern. Yous truly Leonard Wm Tyler (Part 2)

A. J. Standing, who forwarded this group of letters to commissioner Morgan on June 17, 1890, did push the matter to the extent of calling the commissioner's attention to Tyler's letter as among those of special interest. Tyler's proposed colony was never established, but he continued to be active in tribal affairs, as we will see later.

Ernest Left Hand, a young Arapaho man from Darlington, also wrote in no uncertain terms of the difficulties he, like so many others, faced. He said,

> Found=
>
> The reson why I fall back in Indain way? you don't give me nothing or it don't do me no good. if I have chance to work I would not do any Indian way. I don't care nothing now. I used to go to Agent a ask for work but could not get any work. This is all I have to say. (Part 1)

Left Hand, now twenty years old, had entered Carlisle in October 1883, leaving just a year later because of ill health. He was the son of Niwot or Nawot, known as Left Hand, a principal chief of the Southern Arapaho.[25] Nawot, upon learning that his son was sick and about to be sent home, asked Ernest's older brother, **Grant Left Hand**, who had returned from Carlisle in 1881, to write a brief letter to the school asking that Ernest be allowed stay. The Carlisle *Morning Star* for October–November 1884 published Grant Left Hand's letter as part of a short article headlined, "Chief Left Hand, Cheyenne, Does Not Want his Boy to Come Home" (8).[26] Grant says that his father "wants his boy to stay at Carlisle . . . and learn something," and that "he was very sorry when he hear that his boy come back home. If the boy get well again he will go back to you" (8). Ernest Left Hand did not return to Carlisle, and although his curt note to Pratt in 1890 sounds very much like a last word, he too responded to requests from the school for information in 1910 and 1912.

Grant Left Hand's Carlisle student information card bizarrely gives his name as "U.S. Grant." Left Hand had entered the school in 1879 and left less than two years later, also because of poor health. He did not respond to Pratt's 1890 questionnaire, and one possible reason for that would be his developing interest in the Arapaho Ghost Dance. In August 1891, after the massacre at Wounded Knee, Grant Left Hand joined a party of Arapahos that included **Arnold Woolworth** and **Casper Edson**, both also former Carlisle students, to make the journey to the southwest to visit Wovoka (Mooney 1973, 157). Upon their return, just as the Wichitas had done after Lawrie Tatum's visit to Wovoka, the Arapahos changed their manner of performing the dance (Mooney 1973, 157)—but the dancing continued. James Mooney wrote of Grant Left Hand that "notwithstanding several years of English education, . . . [he] is a firm believer in the doctrine and the dance."[27] He reported as well that Left Hand's wife, Mo'ki, or Little Woman, "is as prominent in the Ghost Dance among the Cheyenne" (1973, 278). Mo'ki was Grant Left Hand's first wife, and I have learned nothing about her. Left Hand later married **Kate Stalker** or **Stocker** , also a Cheyenne, and a Carlisle student from 1886 to 1895. We will hear from her later as well as from Arnold Woolworth and Casper Edson.

The last letter I cite from the Darlington Agency is from **Percy Kable**, a Cheyenne, who had attended Carlisle from 1883 to 1888. His files give no age for him, although the *Twelfth Census of the United States* for June 1900 lists him as having been born in 1871. After spending the summer of 1888 at home, he enrolled in the fall at the Haskell Institute in Lawrence, Kansas. The *Indian Helper* for April 26, 1889, quotes a letter he sent the school from Haskell, in which he wrote:

> I am well and strong. I am still holding on to my trade and using it at this school. I am now instructor in the tailor shop. . . . I have 5 boys and 2 ladies in my shop. Last week we made 21 suits. . . . All the Carlisle boys here are well. I send my best regards to all the teachers and students. (4)

In its September 20, 1889, issue the *Helper* reported that Kable had gone farther east to enter White's Manual Labor Institute, a Quaker school in Wabash, Indiana, expressing concern lest he be the sort of young man given to moving around too much (3).[28] However long he did remain at White's, he was back home in June 1890, by which time he too had experienced the difficulties of trying to farm in Indian Territory.

Here is Kable's brief but cogent account of the government having educated and then largely abandoned its boarding school students:

Dear Sir,

You requiring letter is at hand. I am well at present. It is hard matter require in your letter. I must tell you that we return pupils have no place what we would call a home. no matter how much we may educated after return here we have no means of progress. we need team implements to work with. In fact we got nothing therefore you see if Government desired to see the Indian come civilized he ought start us and be examples of our people. we need to have our houses furnture teams wagons farming implements. We are willing to go on hard work if we had means to doso. this is all

your friend
Percy E. Kable (Part 2)

Inadequate teams to break ground; shortage of wagons and farming implements; no furniture for the houses; and thus "no means of progress"—he describes the dire situation that prevailed elsewhere as well. But hard work did allow Percy Kable to become "examples of our people," as we can see in chapter 3 from his later responses to the school.

Also writing in 1890 were **Henry North**, **Hubbell Big Horse**, **Jah Seger**, and "Jack Bull Deer,"[29] all of whom had come home to Indian Territory to farm at the Seger Colony. Hubbell Big Horse was Cheyenne, and the other three were Arapahos. Their ages and their fluency in English vary considerably, but they are remarkably consistent about several important matters that they may well have discussed among themselves.

Jah Seger is one of the oldest of the returned students, at age thirty-one, and he had surely taken his name from John Seger. He had enrolled at Carlisle in February 1881 and left in 1883, so that he had now been out of school for seven years, a much longer time than he had been in school. His English is sometimes hard to follow—and I have on several occasions differed in my transcription from the Carlisle website's transcriber of his letter—but he has much to say and he is determined to express himself, whatever his difficulties with the language; he sent Pratt no fewer than six handwritten pages. Seger begins,

> Dear [**sri**] Capt. Pratt
>
> as you requestut it I will now writ to you since I left Carlisle I have worked at diferant things the first [**thirteen?**] want after I got Bock I checked in the Traders sto[**r**]e at Darlington I then worked for J.H. Seger on cows Ranch three months then inlisted as a scout one year then [**settld**] at Seger Colony and opend up a farm have surved six months enlistment as scout sice I came hear have bin Polease for one year hear at this Colony and have farmed hender for about six months have kept a small stalk of grosreys which I sell when the Indians come for Rations and make a small profit on them when I come out hear Capt [**Lee**] who was acting Indians [**a**]gent + gave me one 1 cow + have kept [**her**] and have increas and buaght a few head so that now I have 16 heads

"Capt Lee," is Agent Jesse M. Lee, whom we have already met. The transcript has "the first ittristeen want," but I have read what I take to be the adjective as "thirteen," guessing that Seger means "thirteen months"; that is far from certain. One can easily understand that he "*clerked* in the trader's store at Darlington." Seger uses English as he has heard and remembers it—from teachers and staff at Carlisle, from agents and Americans at the Seger Colony—but perhaps never seen in writing during little more than two years at school. Writing, as it were, in the oral tradition, he uses almost no punctuation whatever. (Many other of the writers, as noted, use little internal punctuation.)

He continues,

> I built a house last winter I baught about half the lumber the [**gov**] furnushed the other half I don the Hanling and helped Mr. [**s**]eger and Indians carpenter to do the work in building I have this year 12 acres of wheats most ready to cut about six acres of oats + garden I have his kept bosk a good deal by having to fead Indians friends + relatives though my wife is a camp woman she makes

dreses for my children those in always some camp Indians that redasule as school boys because we try to do like the white man I can take care of myself + family as well as sell a good exampel to the camp Indians if I could have the help oford[**ed**] me.

This is a passionate account of the realities of agency life as Jah Seger lives it. Although "camp Indians" ridicule—"redasule"—the school boys as imitators of the whites, they also expect those school boys to "fead Indians friends + relatives," just as they would have in the old days. And, married to a "camp woman," Seger does exactly that, although he has been kept back a good deal—"have his kept bosk a good deal"—as a result.

He continues insightfully, demonstrating the sort of understanding of the organic intellectual. as I have called it. He now makes clear his awareness that the difficulties he currently faces have much to do with the historical expropriation of Indian lands by the whites and the inadequacy of compensation:

> I want a tital to my Land I nead a better team as I only small horse poneys when I try to farm as I did in Bucks Co. Pa I find I conot do so with a small pare of Pones I nead more cattle to rais stalk from after I get my Land I would like to fuse it so I could use it for the suport of my famely tho[**se**] is a disatesfaction you want to know my education + experien[**s**]e in buisness is behind meney what prson get we or now being braught in close contact with white man what can you do to help as out, bealing among the arapohoe bealing the whiteman k[**e**]ept sayeng we own No Land I share this fealing with the rest as I know from reading Treoteys that theos Indians made with the govermet that they had a large Resonation in Colorado & western Kansas and + beleave if we had our [**just**] dues we would have [**Land**] enough for our own use in farming and stalk raising + enough to spare . . . . why cant we get this amague your self in my plase what would be done
>
> Your Respestfully
> Jah Seger (Part 2)

Others at the Seger Colony had also been "reading Treoteys that theos Indians made with the govermet"; Jah Seger does not write standard English, but his "phonetic roughening" is strikingly vivid. Imagine yourself in his place—"amague your self in my plase"—"what would be done?"

Hubbell Big Horse, a twenty-four-year-old Cheyenne, had left Carlisle in 1882, and like Jah Seger, he had been away from school for a number of years when Pratt's 1890 questionnaire arrived. Big Horse had also served as an army scout and tried to farm, experiencing many of the difficulties Seger had. He writes to Pratt:

> Was glad to get you [illegible] lettler and glad to know that the Hon Commissioner is inturessal in the Carlisle student as doing as well as what they [**need**] to enable them ~~as doing~~ to do better. I have been working a good deal since I came back have Surved one year and six months as Indian Scouts. I did not get a head every while I was a Scouts. Scarsy any ~~I was a Scouts~~ any of the Boys they join the Scouts. I worked on a farm in New Jersey I saw how white men lived way to. I know that is a better way the Indian live now. Had I the chance to do so, I would open up a farm and live on it and make my own Living.

But, as he, too, has found, the means for doing so successfully are lacking:

> to do this I nead a horse a Team a Wagon and Farm Implements I need Sead and Rations of for one year at least I nead wier for fencing to keep my Stock at home so I would not have to spend all my time hunting them. I need about 10 head of cows to start with so that when crops failed I would have something to fall bask own, and live upon until I could rais a crop.

And there is also the matter of land rights:

about all I want a tital to my land so I will know that no white man or Indian can take it from me I wish the Commissioner could give me this start not as a gift but is payner for land that once belonged to my people which the white man is now farming

Very Truly Friend
Hubbell Big Horse (Part 2)

He asks for no gift, but for rightful title, and "payner"—payment—for land that the settlers, with rightful title or not, are working for their own benefit.

Henry North, an Arapaho, has similar things to say. In excellent English, and with abundant punctuation, he writes:

Dear Capt. Pratt,

Your printed letter of recent date was received. And I will try and answer your enquires as well as I can. Us returned students have a good deal to contend with, and I am glad to know that the Honorable Commissioner is interested in us, and we are glad to tell him how we are situated. When we came back, while it is true, we had better education and understood work better than the Indians on the reservation we had no team[s] to begin farming with and no place to make our home while engaged in farming, except with the Indians, and when we lived with them [w]e must live like them, to a great extent. If we worked for wadges the camp Indians begged from us. . . . I married a returned school girl who could keep house, cook, and sow. But she could not prevent her mother + sisters and their families from living with us. . . . I opened up a farm although I had no team. The Agent paid for the breaking of two acres, and furnished oxen for me to break about 5 acres. I chopped the posts and fenced twenty-two acres. The Government furnished the wire, I browed a team and hauled the [**wier**] fifty miles to my farm and completed my fence. I then went to the [**cannons**] and camped twenty miles from my place and cut cedar logs for a house. I borrowed a team to haul them with to my farm.

Chopping the posts to fence twenty-two acres of land is work enough for any man, let alone then hauling wire fifty miles with a borrowed team to string to those posts! North then camped in what I believe are the "canyons" of the Washita, cut cedar logs, and, with another borrowed team, hauled them twenty miles to his farm. The government furnished building supplies, and North and "our Indian carpenter . . . built the house." This is the story of a Native American farmer near the end of the nineteenth century in Indian Territory. Henry North, about twenty-two at the time, had the strength, good health, and will to persevere.

He further says that the agent had given him "a cow & calf" when he was married—to Nancy Lee, also an Arapaho—and he has increased his stock holdings. He has as well "six acres of wheat, and a garden growing," with his "wheat . . . to harvest in a few days." Thus he writes that he has "more laid up, or a better start than many of the Carlisle boys," although if he "had a team wagon and harness," he "could now have a good farm opened up instead of the seven acres." As well as he has done, he writes, "some times I feal like giving up it seems so slow getting along." And, like Jah Seger and Hubbell Big Horse, he has used his education to look into some of the causes of his condition. He tells Pratt,

> Now from what I can learn from reading the treaties these Indians have made with the Government, had we our just dues, we would have land enough to furnish us all a good farm and enough to sell to give us a start in farming and could I get this start, while I am young, the Government would seeon be releaved of furnishing rations for my familes.
>
> I will here state the help, I would like to have to enable me to support my self and family, in a civilized way.

He then proceeds to lay out a five-point program for future improvement, the second of which is unique among the returned students' responses. Like Jah Seger and Hubbell Big Horse, he writes: "1st I want my land given to me with a clear title." Then, perhaps with tongue in cheek, he says, "2nd I would like the old [c]hieves and their dog soldiers + medicine men to be sent to Carlisle for about ten years training."[30] He next asks for "3rd . . . a good span of mules or large American mares to farm with," along with "4th . . . a wagon and necessary farm implements seed and rations for one year." Finally, he would like "5th . . . a little more lumber to build another room on my house, and a few cows to start me in stock raising, ten or twelve cows would do with what I have" (Part 2). I review some of North's further communications with Carlisle in chapter 3.

The last letter to Pratt from the Seger Colony that I cite was transcribed as having been signed by "Jack Bull Deer Indian Police." But there is no student information card, no student file, no photograph, nor any mention in the various Carlisle publications for anyone named Jack Bull Deer. This is because, as can be seen from the scan of the original, the letter was written by **Jock Bull Bear**, an Arapaho who entered Carlisle at the age of nineteen in February 1881 and left because of illness in January of 1884. Bull Bear is in accord with the other Seger Colony respondents. He begins,

> Dear Friend Capt Pratt
>
> Your friendly letter come a few days ago. I am now seating for the porpose of answering. I was glad to be rememberd and also thankfull to know that the Honerable Comisoner is interested enough in us returned students to enquier espesaly after us.

He says that he has been "working at diferant things since I came back. Scouting farming fence building carpertering and now on the police force." Then, like the others, he writes:

> when I came back from Carlisle I had nothing to startt with and if I earned wedges thare was so many Arapahoes friends to assist me to spend it that it was almost unless for me to try to get a head enought to buy a team. Now as Genral Margon has bein kind enough to enquier what is still need to enable me to su[s] eed which I supose means that I support myself and family for

> I would not make much of a success without I done that. I will try and state as near as I can. I need the some chance that a white man would need was he in my sitution that is on a reseration where all are poor, and no one to hire on a land without house barns on fance market or mills exsept the small improvements made by the Indians in four years. While I need a house I can build it myself if I had the lumber, doors and windows nales.
>
> I wants a farme which I can make with my own labor. If I had team, a wagon, [**honass**], and wire to fance with. I have a small farme fenced but not enough to support myself and wife and two childers I need about ten cows to rais my beefs and a few steares to sell to get money to buy clothes and suplyes with should thare be a faluer of crops.

He, too, firmly states,

> I want a ~~tittel~~ title to my land so that I will know that when I plant a tree or build a house on it, it cannot be taken from me I don't ask that all this be furnished me as a gift but that it be taken from the value of land that one time belonging to the Arapahoes in Colorado and western Kansas in the place of which the Goverment has not given us a title to every land though it purtend to do. so when the Cherakee strip was promised us in exchange for our other lands if I can realise something from this when I am young and able to work I can thence hope to be able to provide for my self when I am old. but should I be compeld to live during my [illegible] sorounded with the uncivilized and igronant without some ade to give me a ~~stort~~ start. I am afraid I would not be much better prepared to take care of my family than some of them when I get old.

He signs, "Very Respesfully, / Jock Bull Bear Indian Police," and adds, "answer my letter if you can" (Part 2). Bull Bear's letter was one of the earlier ones forwarded to Commissioner Morgan by A. J. Standing, and Pratt may not have seen it; there is no copy of a letter to Bull Bear in Pratt's June 1890–January 1891 correspondence.

Like Jah Seger, Jock Bull Bear is thinking here of Northern Arapaho lands that had not been secured for the Arapaho nation, its Colorado lands going to the Shoshones and its Kansas land lost as part of the Cherokee Strip. The Cherokee Strip had been established many years earlier, by a provision of the government's 1835 New Echota treaty with a faction of the Cherokee Nation. The treaty provided that the Cherokees, upon removal from Georgia, would be granted a western "Outlet" referred to as the Cherokee Strip in what is now north-central Oklahoma. A survey done as part of the Kansas-Nebraska Act of 1854 placed the northern part of the Strip in southern Kansas—Kansas then moving to contest Cherokee title to that portion of the Strip. After the Civil War the Cherokees leased what lands remained to them in that section of Indian Territory to ranchers for grazing their cattle, something a number of Cheyennes and Arapahos did as well. But in February 1890, President Harrison forbade all grazing on Indian lands, the prohibition to take effect in October that year. Writing in June 1890, Bull Deer is no doubt aware of many of these developments.

Before leaving Indian Territory, I want to look at two letters from the Quapaw Agency in the eastern part of the territory, one from **Charles Dagnett**—as he initially spells it here—a Peoria man, and the other from **Charles Hood**, a Modoc whose traditional homelands were far from Indian Territory. Dagnett was about eighteen years old in June 1890 when he received Carlisle's questionnaire. He had entered the school in 1887, as he notes , and although he gives the date he left (because of ill health) very exactly, "Nov. 28, 1890," that date cannot be correct—because he is writing in June 1890. He means to say he had left the previous November, in 1889. But Dagnett would return to the school, and despite recurring poor health he would graduate in 1891. As we will see in chapter 3, he would go on to a very distinguished government career, serving the Indian Office for some thirty years as supervisor of Indian employment.

Earlier, in July 1888, Dagnett had had a letter he'd sent to the school published in the *Indian Helper*. It appears under the heading, "A Camp

Letter from Charles Dagnette," another spelling of his name. Here is most of it:

> I thought I would write a few lines to you this morning and tell you something about camp. I am sure I like it very much. We came here yesterday and carried everything up from the car me and seven other boys and I went to the mountains to pick huckleberries while some got dinner and some put up tents. We did not get many berries but had a good time. . . . This morning after inspection we had a short service and then writing material was given out. I went to my headquarters—a little tent in the woods—and took a book, and went out to the shade to write, and while I was writing I had a visitor. . . . Arthur Johnson is dining-room boy. Dennison is dining-room boy for Mr. Campbell. (4)

Arthur Johnson, a Wyandotte, had entered Carlisle with Dagnett in 1887 and would graduate in 1893. Dennison is Dennison Wheelock, a Wisconsin Oneida, a cornetist, and soon-to-be Carlisle bandmaster. Mr. William Campbell was the Carlisle disciplinarian, apparently in charge of this outing. The "visitor," I should hasten to say, "was a large copperhead snake about three feet long" (4), which Dagnett dispatched easily.

The "camp" experience he is describing is not one I have found elsewhere in my encounters with Carlisle writing. The excursion Dagnett describes seems to be a rather large-scale encampment (tents have been put up) with at least one dining room, oriented toward study (writing and reading), and also including country pleasures (woods, mountains, huckleberrying, and a potential run-in with a snake). What I want to note especially here is the fluidity and polish of Dagnett's epistolary manner. It has seemed to me that letters from Carlisle students published in the various school newspapers most often appeared with only very light editing; non-conventional punctuation or syntax were often left as the student had used them. In this case, however—I will note others—Dagnett's letter must have been substantially edited, or he had help in writing it. Consider, by way of comparison, his 1890 letter, written two years later.

He addresses it not to Pratt but to the "Hon. Com. of Ind. Affairs, / Washington City, D.C.," to whom, he had understood, it would eventually be sent. Dagnett writes at some length and I quote most of what he had to say:

> In compliance with the request of our good Supt. I submit the explanation of Questions answered, I was fourteen past when I left for Carlisle, arriving there Nov. 15, 1887. I entered the Tailor Shop Dec. 6, 1887. the following May I lift Tailoring + was Orderally. until June 22 when I entered the printing office, + followed that + mail carring, also farming one summer, until I lift Nov. 2[0], 1890. . . . I had went to the Quapaw Mission, some, before going to Carlisle. My father & mother were both educated, + I was brought up to Speak English. I was raised on a farm, + tended to stalk a good deal. We have a large farm, but rent it, + and I have no work only to help tend to stalk.
>
> We live in a large Hewd log house at present, though, we expect to build soon, as the land is allotted.

Dagnett's written English in 1890 is considerably less polished than it had been in his letter of two years earlier. His writing does, however, show him to have adopted the literate habit of providing exact dates (accurate or not), and he specifies printing and tailoring as trades he had learned at Carlisle, along with serving as "orderly," and engaging in work as a mail carrier and student farmer.

"[B]rought up to Speak English," he has previously attended "the Quapaw Mission, some." This is the Quapaw Agency U.S. Indian Industrial School, just north of the town of Wyandotte, and known locally as the Mission. Founded by the Society of Friends, it had opened its doors in 1872 and was supported by the Friends until 1880, when it was taken over by the federal government. Serving Wyandottes, Peorias, Miamis, Quapaws, and students of some other tribes—several young Nez Perces at the Quapaw Agency, as we have seen, and also some Modocs, as we will soon see. Dagnett writes that his family lives in a large house of hewed logs, but they expect to build another as soon "as the land is allotted." The Dawes Act of 1887 mandated allotment on a tribe-by-tribe basis, initially exempting the lands of the Peorias, among many other tribal nations in Indian Territory. For the most part, Peoria allotment, which Dagnett eagerly awaits in June 1890, did not take place until 1893, although even after that date some Peoria land remained unallotted.

Dagnett continues,

> I have had very poor health the last year, + was not in school since Nov. last, + returned for my health. We are living on my step-father's farm. . . . Though I have been among the Indians, I have never wore Indian attire, at all. There is no certain church that holds meetings here, The Quaker + Baptist have a Missionary here, they have a circuit + come here twice a month. considering all things I have got along very well, though the want of good society + *real* civilization, to-gather with bad health, was + is my principal obstacle. I have not had my land allotted yet, but will soon,
>
> Closing, I am + remain,
>
> Yours most Raspt.
> Charles Dagenett (Part 3)

Dagenett's health would improve sufficiently for him to return to school and, as noted, to graduate in 1891. He would then continue at nearby Dickinson Prep School and go on to a distinguished career, as we will see later.

Also writing from the Quapaw Agency was Charles Hood, a Modoc, whose people's traditional lands, like those of the Nez Perces also held there, were far from Indian Territory, the Modocs' lands being in northeastern California and southwestern Oregon. Although their Carlisle files do not record it, these young Native men and women were intimate participants in what the West calls history. They were caught up at an early age in events of great importance to their peoples and to an American history of domestic colonialism: the Modoc War of

1872–73, the Custer fight of June 1876, and the Nez Perces' "flight" of 1877.[31] Charles Hood would have been no more than five or six years old in those years, and he does not speak of any memories he had of that experience. But the surrender of his people to the army in the fall of 1873 is the reason why this young Modoc man is writing to Captain Pratt from the Quapaw Agency in Indian Territory.

Hood begins by identifying himself as "Chas. Hood, Quapaw / Age abt 23 / At Carlisle 3 years," but he is not a Quapaw. He tells Pratt,

> I am very glad to let you know that I am getting along very well in every way that I know how. As soon as I returned home, I commenced working right away on our farm: [t]hat is part of fathers and my brothers. Now, I am farming for myself. I have about [t]wenty acres of corn and eight acres of oats. It was the same summer that F.C. Armstrong, U.S. Indian Inspector met me. I told him I was a returned Carlisle student. The resigned U.S. Indian agent J.V. Summers reported to him (Armstrong) that I was not afraid of work. On his own account F.C. Armstrong made me a request to Indian Department that I should have a team of horses, harness, farming implements, wagon, livestock, lumber to build a house and necessary tools.

Hood's English is obviously very good, and that may be because he had had more than five years of schooling before entering Carlisle.[32] Nonetheless, the school put him in the fourth grade on his arrival, and recorded him as having reached only the fifth grade on his departure three years later. But his writing is far more mature than that.

Hood writes to Pratt of having returned "home" to the Quapaw Agency. Given that he had spent twelve years of his life there—since 1873 when the Modocs were sent east—and only his first five unsettled years in the Northwest, it is no surprise that he calls the agency "home." Much later, however, in 1909 when the Modocs were given the opportunity to return to the west, he was one of a minority of the people to do so.[33]

John Van Meter Summers had been Quapaw Indian Agent since 1885 and was at the agency when Frank Crawford Armstrong, U.S. Indian inspector, arrived on an official visit in the summer of 1888, when Hood returned from Carlisle.[34] What Armstrong requested for him is, as we have seen, exactly what so many returned student farmers said they needed. Nonetheless, that request does not seem to have been accommodated. Hood continues, "F.C. Armstrong was here last fall"—that would be the fall of 1889—"and I asked him what the Indian Department has done for me." Hood writes,

> He said he would again see when he would return to Washington. Hon. Com. Morgan requested me to refer this to him after the 1st of July 1890 I have one mare that Maj. Moore the agent gave me. I am still looking for the articles promised me by the Department. I am getting along well in every way. I am well and out in the field every day. (Part 4)

Did the Indian Department eventually furnish Charles Hood "the articles promised [him]?" I think it probably did not, for in his August *Report to the Commissioner of Indian Affairs*, Major Moore would write, "I have estimated for 20 young brood mares and 50 heifers for this tribe, and hope to be allowed to put this stock into their hands at once, as they are greatly in need of them" (84). The agent, thus, is making the same request that had earlier been made by Inspector Crawford, both of these employees of the Indian Office cognizant of conditions on the ground and the needs to be addressed. Was this second request more successful than the first in getting Charles Hood some of what he needed? I cannot say.

The only other Modoc student to attend Carlisle prior to 1890 was **Lucinda Clinton.** Three years younger than Charles Hood, she had arrived at the school from the Quapaw Agency with him, on September 16, 1885, and left for "home" with him on July 6, 1888. She did not respond to the 1890 questionnaire, but she and Charles Hood would marry and be together in Klamath, Oregon, in 1917, as described further in chapter 3.

I turn here to the Southwest to consider, first, letters from students who had returned to the San Carlos Agency in Arizona Territory. I then look at letters from the Pueblos of New Mexico Territory.

Brian Early Bird, an Apache, had been at Carlisle for a little more than five years, from 1884 to 1889, and his written English is far from standard. Here is his letter in full:

> Dear Sir Capt. R.H. [**rott**],
>
> that you[**r**] want to know Something about me, and [**I**] want to tell your what I have ding here. this countriy and let Sumners were come back. here, I do not work anything. agency and I came our here working Saw mill for $15.00 Dollars a month, and he say to me Cap John Bunth mon. and I will say to [**your**] [**afew**] this a letter and I fell sick for 3 month and this tim get well. and talk [**careinofra**] myself and I dind lik to wear Indian clothe[**r**] I always trying to all my best here at San Carlos and that this all I Say to your good by. (Part 4)

He signs himself, "your friend/Brian E. Bird," reducing part of his name to a middle initial.

Established in 1872, the San Carlos Agency brought together several Apache bands along with Yavapai people, who as we will see in chapter 2 were often referred to as Tonto Apaches—as Early Bird was—or Mojave Apaches. "Bunth," the agent to whom Early Bird is referring, is Captain John L. Bullis. Bullis had been captain of the 118th United States Colored Troops, made up of freedmen and runaway slaves during the Civil War, and he had later fought in Indian wars. All the returned San Carlos students speak well of him. Brian Early Bird says he had been working for Bullis at the agency saw mill for $15 a month (approximately $414 a month in 2019 dollars), and, if he "do not work anything" just now, his former employment may have been terminated because of his lengthy illness. And things did not go well for him after this, as we learn from his later communications with the school.

Constant Bread, also listed as a Tonto Apache, had entered Carlisle in February 1884, departing in July 1888. He had earlier written to the school from San Carlos in the spring of 1889, and some of his letter was published in the May issue of the *Indian Helper*:

> I was very glad to read in the INDIAN HELPER of sixty school boys leaving for the east and not coming back to a wild country like I have got out here. It is a miserable pace [*sic*] here.
>
> Jose that came home with me is working for the post trader at this place. Capt. Bullis got him his place. He did not want to see him and me go to Indian camp. He gave us a nice room.
>
> Capt. Bullis will not allow the boys that have been from here to come back and wear Indian clothes and paint their faces.
>
> When they don't behave themselves Captain tells them that he needs their assistance down on the field very much. There is a great deal of work to be done at place.
>
> The Captain has all hands out at work plowing, and he goes out himself with all the gang . . . and he never leaves the field until everyone else does. (2)

Bread may have sent cash or stamps (see below) for a subscription to the *Indian Helper*, or he may not: but clearly it was sent to him, as it was to most former Carlisle students. Whoever the "sixty boys" he had read about were, he is glad they are not returning to a "wild country" like San Carlos.

"Jose that came home with" him is **Jose Nadilgodey**, and not only did the two go home together in July 1888—both because of ill health—but they had also arrived at the school together in February 1884. Although Nadilgodey had been trained as a harness maker, Bread reports that he is working for the San Carlos trader. The young men—Nagilgodey would have been about twenty-one and Bread about nineteen in 1889—have "a nice room," and Bread is helping with farming at the agency.

In his 1890 letter Bread tells Pratt, "I am well and happy all the times and ever Since I came back from two years ago," but he notes that he doesn't "work for Captain Bullis any more since last Jan 1st I Stoping work there at agency." This does not seem to be a problem, for, he writes, "now I belonged to the Indian Scouts, and I am first sergeant, and also I do [**I**]nterpreter for Indian here, I have very busy works each day around the agency." Immediately following this positive assessment, however, he says: "one things I would like to tell you, about killing peoples every year and [**t**]he Indians they dont behave [**t**]hemselves and they try to kill Some one all the times."[35] Serious as "killing peoples every year" might be, Bread does not elaborate, but goes on,

> Captain Bullis he ha[**s**] very largeds Indian school at San Carlos, about 80 children in school [**t**]his years and some girls too. Dear Captain I thank you for what I have learn at you school at Carlisle and so much better for me, do interpreter and work beside Some thing[**s**] of the times ever since I came back from school. So I have nothing more to tell you anything about here at San Carlos agency So goodbye to you, from your school boy.
>
> Very Truly your friends,
> Constant Bread
> 1rst Sergeant
> Indian Scout (Part 4)

There is no further communication on file from him to the school later than this June 1890 letter.

Also writing to Pratt is "**Rendell Delchey**, Apache," who signs himself "Interpreter, / Randall Delchy," and who appears in the Carlisle records as "Randal Delchey (Cork Screw)." He writes at some length, and although like Constant Bread he is an agency interpreter, like Bread's, his written English is not standard. He begins,

> Dear Sir Capt. R.H. Pratt,
>
> I have reciver you letter in few days ago and since to me that very much interested for you send use every boys at San Carlos. but only I will say that I am [**doing**] right well will Capt. Bullis

> Becauser I try all my best as I can do just as well as any other people have in this country.

Although he says he is doing well, he reports that

> some of the boys are doing are not because we at work Capt. Bullis now we can not go any please will Madoc Wind and myself will we every way we go and think you want know about you school boys what there doing. Some of the school boys are doing nothing at Indian camp this summer . . . the rest of boys are doing right well will there work but I am sorry [t]o say some of the boy ar not. Nothing to do but play I suppose . . . but these boys are at work, yet at San Carlos Madoc Wind + Constant Bread + Obed Rabbit + Reuben Whiteman and Roland Fish at San Carlos and Remember the boys in this letter. From you school boy
>
> Interpreter
> Randall Delchy
> at San Carlos Agency (Part 4)

Delchy is reporting that the agent, Captain Bullis, will not allow him and his schoolmate, **Madoc Wind**, to leave the agency, a problem more than a few returned students encountered.[36] He says that while some returned schoolboys are not working, he, Madoc Wind, Constant Bread (from whom we have just heard), **Obed Rabbit**, **Reuben Whiteman**, and **Roland Fish** do have work.

Pratt may well have remembered "the boys in this letter," and in some measure so may we. Madoc Wind, Obed Rabbit, Reuben Whiteman, and Roland Fish, along with Brian Early Bird, Constant Bread, Randall Delchy, and thirty-five other young Apaches had all taken the long journey from San Carlos, Arizona Territory, to Pennsylvania, to enroll at Carlisle on February 2, 1884.[37] There were only four young women in that party. One of them, **Mabel Kelcusaway** (or Kelcusay), succumbed to the cold and damp of Pennsylvania and died at the school on Christmas day, 1884, at the age of about fifteen. Another, **Eva Dezey**, about sixteen years old, died just a year later, in February

1885. Six of the boys also died, and five were sent home sick before their enrollment period (five years) expired; four ran away.

Ida Whiteface and **Amelia Elseday**, the other two girls who had entered the school in February 1884, did not return home until July 1890 and September 1890 respectively, so they would not have been sent the June questionnaire. Fifteen of the boys stayed longer than the end of term in 1890, so they too did not receive the questionnaire. With seventeen of the San Carlos Apache young men and women not yet home, and eight of the original forty-three students having died, that leaves eighteen students—including the four who had run away—who might have received the questionnaire. But only three of them wrote back, and it is not possible to say whether these three are representative of what the other Apache returned students thought.[38]

To return to Randall Delchy and those he has mentioned: Reuben Whiteman ran away from the school in May 1889, apparently unwilling to remain until later in the year when he might have gone home with Rabbit, Fish, Wind, and Delchy himself. (Constant Bread had left more than a year earlier due to poor health.) In January 1890 the *Indian Helper* had reported that Fish, Rabbit, and Early Bird had gotten married. Rabbit and Fish, the paper also said, were working at the agency sawmill, and as we have learned from him, Early Bird would do so as well. Bread at the time was a shoemaker, a trade he had learned at Carlisle, and he also served as interpreter, as did Wind and Delchy.

Several students from the Pueblos of New Mexico Territory had enrolled at Carlisle as early as 1880.[39] Among them was a young man from Zuni named **Frank Cushing**, who died within a year and was buried in the school cemetery.[40] Others entered a bit later, in 1884 and 1885, a number of young women among them. I have counted seventy students from seven of the nineteen Pueblos who had been to Carlisle and returned home in time to receive the 1890 questionnaire. Of those seventy—again, my figures are as exact as I can make them but still approximate—only thirteen responded, three of them women. As mentioned, that the majority did not respond may be because they regretted their experience at the school, rejected the lessons to which they had submitted, and wished to have nothing more to do with Carlisle. It's also possible that some returned students never received the questionnaire; were too busy to bother; or did not feel their English was up to the task. Nonetheless, like some others, a few Pueblo students who did not respond in 1890 chose to write to the school later. Here are some of the letters of those returned students from the Pueblos who did respond to Pratt in 1890.

Juan Antonio Chamon (also Chamo or Chama) wrote from Jemez Pueblo. Although his student information card recorded his age as eighteen when he entered the school in 1884, in his 1890 communication six years later, he writes that he is thirty. His file says that when he left in 1889 he was at third grade level, but his written English seems more advanced. Chamon writes,

> Since leaving Carlisle most of the time I have been working on a farm. Would like to work at my trade- which is that of black smith, and could no doubt succeed, if I had sufficient tools to enable me to do so. About 11 months since, I married, and have a babe one month old. my wife however, is not educated. There being but poor facilities for education on this Pueblo. I have tried to keep up my studies and be industrious since my return, to the best of my ability. Dear Mr. Pratt, should be in your power, I hope you will see that I have implements that will enable me to get along more satisfactorially to myself.
>
> Thanking you very much, for the kind interest you take in my behalf.
>
> I am very respectfully yours
> Juan Antonio Chamon
> Jemez Pueblo (Part 4)

Just as most Indian farmers lacked adequate equipment and implements, the lack of implements similarly prevents this Indian blacksmith from pursuing the trade he learned at Carlisle as he would like to do. But Chamon did eventually manage to earn a living as a blacksmith, as we learn from his responses to later questionnaires from the school.

Lorenzo Martinez, from Taos Pueblo, wrote to Pratt,

> In answer to the questions I answered all, and is correct. To give you further informations of my doings at home, I will say, that ever since I came home, I have been very busy and so will continue in making the use of my education gained at Carlisle.
>
> I have been working in the printing office of Mr. Lorin W. Brown . . . and now as he sold out his printing outfits I struck out to find a place in the office and been working in the office of "El Monitor," published in Spanish at Taos. But at present I feel obliged to leave on account of the dullness. the Company of this paper haven't got enough money they can't afford to pay high wages. On Monday of next coming week, I am going to start out for "El Durango," Colo. So you see I am trying to better my education.

He then writes, "I have a good deal of trouble with my people of this village. But you may bet, I win my cases every time." He does not say what kind of "trouble" he has, although the likelihood is that it involves attitudes toward the schools—many people continued to oppose them—and toward the ceremonial dances performed at Taos Pueblo—in which Carlisle students from the Pueblos had been strongly admonished to avoid participating. Other returned Pueblo students also report "trouble" of this kind.

Martinez proudly adds, "When Dr. Dorchester was out here Inspecting the Indian [S]chools I reported to him which I believe he has taking in" (Part 3). He is referring to Dr. David Dorchester, superintendent of Indian schools, who had recently visited all but one of the New Mexico Pueblos.[41] In his *Report to the Commissioner of Indian Affairs*, dated August 16, 1892, Dorchester concluded of Taos Pueblo: "The parents have no desire to see their children educated" (14), likely an aspect of Martinez's "trouble." We will learn more about Martinez from his further communications with the school.

From Acoma Pueblo comes a letter to Pratt dated June 18, 1890, from "**James H. Miller**, Pueblo Acoma Age 22," who notes that he was "At Carlisle 5 ½ years." Pratt also received a very different letter dated June 26, 1890, from a young man the transcriber records as "J. H. Miller, Pueblo / Age 18 / At Carlisle 6 years / Pueblo of Acoma." The signature appears twice on the letter, and I believe **F. H. Miller** is more nearly accurate. The student information card for James H. Miller says he entered Carlisle in February 1881 at the age of thirteen and left in June 1886, so he would indeed have been at Carlisle for five and a half years and would have been twenty-two years old in 1890. But there is no student information card for an F. H. Miller (or a J. H. Miller) that might clarify matters.

Certainly James H. Miller and F. H. Miller might be the same person. It would seem unlikely that two young men from Acoma with names that similar were at Carlisle at the same time—although, to complicate matters, there was also a **James Y. Miller** from Acoma (unrelated to James H.) who attended Carlisle, from 1884 to 1892 (so he would not have been sent the questionnaire). As for the two other Millers, we will see that their two letters are very different—although to my (untrained) eye the handwriting, while not identical, is similar.

James H. Miller's letter to Pratt is dated June 18, 1890. He writes:

> I received your question letter last [s]unday week ago which the Honorable Commissioner of Indian Affairs wants it. I was quite enjoyed to read + I will try answered all the questions if I can, and you may know that I am still needed more education of the American civization. I hope this will fined you in a good comfortable life still I am living yet, never had any sickness to me ever since return from school. my wife she is very kind we have always live with joyfully she is a good housekeeper just exactly as good as an educated girl she always does whatever I promised to do it.
>
> But the trouble with her she does not understand the English as like we do. But any how she is sitting by me here now with ~~samilly~~ smilling face wishing to see captain's face.
>
> Well I have [**larg**] of farmmer and stocks + Ranch to keep Our stocks west of McCa[r]ty I think it is good enough for me to[**do**]

> these and every things going an right well every day. The corn + wheat growing very fine
>
> Yours sincerely friend
> Jas. H. Miller,
> Of Acoma Indian (Part 3)

Miller does not mention the sort of division at Acoma that Lorenzo Martinez noted at Taos, but it did exist and apparently got him into difficulties with the traditional authorities, a matter he must have later reported to his old superintendent. I know this from a letter Pratt wrote to Miller on December 4, 1890, in which he expressed regret at his former student's treatment at the hands of the conservatives of his Pueblo, and assured Miller that the "punishment you have received at the hands of the Governor and the officials will react on them in time" (Pratt letters 444). If Miller had indeed been punished because of his refusal to participate in traditional, ceremonial dances, this would have been of considerable interest to Pratt at the time because he was then actively involved in supporting the publication of Marianne Burgess's novel, *Stiya, a Carlisle Girl at Home*, which dealt with exactly this matter, as I will explain.

F. H. Miller's letter to Pratt is dated just over a week later, June 26, 1890, and not only is it different in tone and manner from James Miller's, but it also makes no reference to a wife. The original has some writing at the top of the page, at right angles to the body of the letter—that is where the two signatures are—and the transcriber has put that at the end, reasonably assuming that Miller put it where he did because he had run out of space to complete his thought and did not wish to use another sheet of paper. I follow that practice as well. Miller begins,

> In regards of [**M**]y attention for I have written [**at**] to you since three months because I have not been at home for a time [+] have always attention some little business. So since I cannot write to you I will ask[**e**] you my kindest to please excuse me you know how much I miss my school.

I have always thought of ever since I lift Carlisle school now for u [?] three months ago. All my path[**e**]s for others + sisters are quite well no sickness but have [illegible] comfortable in daily my cattle, horses, burro, and sheep all well them and myself. I am just home from the field at last the message was received it gave me great satisfaction towards it, with, my great expectation is rather dull during I was surely get [**u**] letter before July but then hold on my great [illegible] for a good while, until this minute Certainly excuse me probably I cannot be on hand to ans an sooner.

Miller expresses warm feelings for Carlisle, and he is effusive in explaining why he could not "be on hand to ans an sooner." Eighteen years old and only home for three months, he is extraordinarily active, whether it is "always attention some little business," or in caring for what would seem to be a variety of livestock. He goes on to describe his active engagement in crop raising as well:

I am getting along right well about my work I have plant corn, wheats, oats, and potatoes. It is with great pleasure to tell you that I used the [**Or**]dorless [**P**]hosphate on every piece of garden ground, and was astonished I see its wonderful effect in making that plants to grow It is really the best fertilizing phosphate that I have ever used, crops are doing right well indeed. I am engaged myself doing the farm work I farm all by myself and see what I can do the, I am always song- around my field so the crops will be pleased with it. Some ago the old Indian come out my field and aske me how I plant potatoes and said what I go to do with them.

Note the wonderful conjunction here of tradition and modernity in the field, where we have Miller spreading the odorless phosphate he had learned to use from Carlisle's agricultural program, and also singing songs that his Acoma people had sung for generations "so the crops will be pleased with it." Rather than ridiculing the school boy, "the old Indian" who, I imagine, had noted the abundant yield, "came out to [Miller's] field" to ask how he plants potatoes (not a traditionally grown crop), and—perhaps because there were so many—what he was going to do with them. It is here that Miller ran out of room and went back to write across the top of his first page, "I told I am going to eate them he say are they good to eat I [**ans**] him [**n**]o sir they do not good to eate" (Part 5). Is Miller teasing the "old Indian," saying he is going to eat them—but no, they aren't good to eat? I can't say. Is he trying to prevent the older man from asking for some potatoes for himself? This young man's name and handwriting are very much like those of James H. Miller, but the two express themselves very differently.

Henry J. Kendall from Isleta Pueblo wrote to Pratt from Albuquerque.[42] The young man had come to Carlisle in 1881 at the age of twelve and had left in February 1890 because of illness. The Carlisle *Morning Star* for October–November 1884 reported that Kendall had shared first prize with "**Hattie Porcupine**, Sioux" in a contest to summarize an "interesting talk to our pupils . . . by Rev. Dr. Spinning of Cleveland, O." (8).[43] "Henry Kendall's Account" of that talk is given at some length.[44]

In his time at Carlisle, Kendall seems to have learned a certain epistolary ease of manner, although about midway through his letter, he expresses some serious concerns:

> Your circular, came to hands, but as I have been on a "*spree*" after wood for several days, I failed to comply to your request. But since my return here, I have found that in order to convince the old + the younger people, was necessary to put my wits and muscles. ([**o**]f the former I posses none, of the latter, I am gaining steadily.) to work. I came to many of the men that needed hands. Several days were wasted in hunting work. But when these very men saw that I meant, what I said, they aided me to find work + when I found it I work to prove myself worthy of the kindness shown me + gained friends, that are valuable to me now. Do not take this for a boast, but in many instances, I have heard prominent men say that "an Indian unconscious of Kindness."

The charge that Indians are "unconscious of" or unappreciative of any kindness shown them may have been especially galling to Kendall because of the particular "prominent" man who seems to have expressed that opinion. He writes, "For a certain clergy, I will not mention you know him well, said that he has in this many years he has failed to find an Indian that is *true*." It is very likely that the "certain clergy" referred to may well be the man from whom Henry Jiron Kendall got his name, the Reverend Henry Kendall. He continues,

> There are many Carlisle boys at that village, + they have proven themselves true and trustworthy to others. So there must be another kind of "true Indians" that the Reverend wants. All of us return children need as much, if not more of Indian support, than American. That is if the parents + a few relatives favor the childs views, + proposed changes, there is little if any danger of that child being forced back to the old ways. The majority of the ones that have gone back are either orphans or children of parents that are not independent thinkers.

Like Lorenzo Martinez, Kendall reports in closing that "In my behalf the village is evenly divided" (Part 3); this is to say between those in favor of the schools and those opposed. But for all the assurance of the twenty-one-year-old's generalization, the matter is more complex than he suggests. Whoever the "independent thinkers" at Isleta may have been, it is not likely that the "majority of the ones that have gone back" were orphans.

A bit later that summer Kendall must have written to Pratt asking that Pratt recommend him as a clerk to the government Indian agent. I infer this from a copy of a letter from Pratt to Kendall telling him that if the agent wished to consider him for the position of clerk, he would be glad to offer him a strong recommendation, but that he thought it inappropriate for him propose anyone for the position to the agent (Pratt letters 189–90). Six months later, on December 4, 1890, Pratt responded to another letter he'd received from Kendall, in which the young man must have reported further trouble with his "divided" community. Pratt wrote, "I am glad that you are there to stand up for us" (Pratt letters 446).

That letter would also have included a request from Kendall to Pratt for advice about where he might best continue his education, for the Carlisle superintendent wrote to him suggesting he consider attending Amherst College and offering to help with his Amherst admission. Kendall, however, opted for Rutgers University in New Jersey. His file indicates that he would have been in the class of 1893 but left without graduating. He died at home, at Isleta Pueblo, about 1894.

John Dixon (or Dickson) from Cochiti Pueblo had gone to Carlisle in 1882 when he was already a man of twenty-five, returning home in 1886. He is the oldest of the 1890 respondents. His letter also testifies to the "divided" Pueblo. After leaving Carlisle, Dixon had taken work with a surveying party "for the Rio Grande Irrigation & C. Co." He writes,

> Not very long ago I came back from that party. At the present time I am at home. Last two weeks **Cyrus Dixon** and I worked over to Pena Blanca, for a mexican put up a building. Cyrus has got married last two months ago. I am sorry to let you know that the two girls whom were to Carlisle, and also some of the boys, have gone back to the same way of living and doing superstitious things. Most of the time when I am at home, have trouble with the old Indians, which they call themselves (Los Principales) They have tried many times to force me to do some superstitious dances; but I have not give up your advices. I am very afraid that Cyrus Dixon will do the same because he has married an uneducated Indian girl. (Part 3)

Just as we have encountered two—or three—Millers from Acoma, so we find there are two Dixons at Cochiti, John and Cyrus, and, we will learn, the two have worked together before. Regarding the Principales, Joe Sando explains, "The office of pueblo governor, an institution introduced by the Spaniards, was incorporated into the Pueblos' own governmental institutions" (Sando 1992, 14) after the departure of the Spaniards. The elected governor heads what Sando calls the "Secular Government" of each Pueblo, which is subordinate to the traditional "Cacique Society" (15). "The titular head of the traditional pueblo is the cacique . . . the theocratic leader" (13), and he holds office for life. The Principales to whom Dixon refers would be the elected governors of the Pueblo, enforcing the determinations of the cacique.

The Pueblo's dances are communal and seasonal ceremonies, performed to assure rainfall and the general wellbeing of the community. Just as the Sun Dance on the plains and southern plains had been deplored by missionaries and outlawed by the government, so too were the Pueblos' dances under American attack. As already noted, they would be the particular evil at the heart of Mariana Burgess's novel *Stiya, or a Carlisle Girl at Home*, serialized in Carlisle's *Indian Helper*, beginning with the first installment in the September 20, 1889, issue and published in book form in 1891.[45]

John Dixon had earlier worked as a carpenter in Albuquerque with Cyrus Dixon. We learn this from a letter he had written to Mr. Campbell, a Carlisle disciplinarian, that was printed in the *Indian Helper* for March 18, 1887. John Dixon describes himself, Cyrus, and "John M. Chaves, (another Carlisle boy)" participating in the celebration of George Washington's birthday at the Albuquerque Indian School (1). The three Carlisle boys were working at the government school, "doing the carpenters work, and take charge of the boys." He says, "It seems the school is getting on pretty well. How are the Carlisle scholars getting on?" and he closes, "I remain your sincere friend" (1).

Another letter from John Dixon appeared in the *Helper* for February 24, 1888, not quite a year after the previous one quoted. He is still at the Albuquerque School with Cyrus Dixon, but on this occasion there is no mention of **John Menaul Chaves**. The two Dixons are "still working in the shop. . . . Cyrus and I work all day, we don't go to school at all" (4). But this is not the main focus of his communication. In what would be a very detailed account, Dixon began,

> Since I am at this school, I have been up and down almost in every Pueblo village. The Superintendent of this school takes me as an interpreter to the Pueblo Indian villages, trying to get all the children we can get for the United States Albuquerque Indian School, but sorry to say in some villages we haven't succeeded . . . most of the children in some villages are willing to come to school, but the parents . . . are not willing, especially the mothers. Last month the Superintendent and I have been up to my place twice—to Cochiti Pueblo, about fifty miles north of Albuquerque—and by hard work and by the governor's effort, the first time we got five boys and at the second time four boys. Also, just before Christmas the late governor of the same village brought two boys and a girl. (4)

Toward the end of his letter Dixon informs the reader that "Cyrus' father is the governor at our place, from him we got good many children" (4).

From Dixon's account, it would appear that Cyrus's father, Serafine Quintana—(Cyrus Dixon's "Indian" name in the Carlisle records is Santiago Quintana)—Governor of Cochiti Pueblo in 1888, was progressive in outlook, at least in regard to education, in that he allowed Cochiti children to go to the Albuquerque Indian School, and "just before Christmas" even "brought two boys and a girl" to the government school himself. But if Serafine Quintana was still an elected governor in 1890—something I have not been able to determine—he would have been one of the "Principales" who had attempted to "force" John Dixon "to do some superstitious dances." This would mean that in his capacity as governor the elder Quintana had supported the schools, on the one hand, while insisting, on the other hand, that even those who had been to the schools must participate in the important Pueblo ceremonial dances. We have several times seen that the meanings of progressive and conservative or traditional can be complex, and this would seem to be the case here.

The matter of ceremonial dances prompts Dixon further to seek Pratt's "advice and opinion," going on in his 1890 letter to ask:

> Would not be right for me to apply, to be admitted to the citizenship? I would like to do this, for the reason is that the old Indians or rather Los Principales of each village say, no matter if we young Indian boys + girls were educated, if we are not citizens, we are obliged to do their Indian superstitious dancing. And I don't like to do them nasty things. Please answer, P.O. Pena Blanca. (Part 3)

Pena Blanca is the nearest post office to Cochiti Pueblo, about six miles to the south.

There is no copy of a reply from Pratt to John Dixon in his outgoing letters from June 1890 to January 1891, and while I am certain Pratt would have exhorted Dixon to avoid the "Indian superstitious dance," I cannot guess what his advice would have been regarding Dixon's desire to seek American citizenship, something that for Pueblo people at the time had nothing to do with land allotment. The Pueblos were never allotted, and further, as the *Eleventh Census of the United States* for 1890 clearly stated, "The Pueblo Indians, who live in 19 pueblos or towns, *are citizens of the United States*" (397, my emphasis). Although Dixon did not know it, he was already a citizen—or perhaps citizenship, despite federal law, was withheld from Pueblo peoples in New Mexico Territory in 1890.

There is no community division mentioned in **Maria Analla's** letter from Laguna Pueblo. Analla had attended Carlisle from 1884 to 1889, and in June 1890 she was twenty-one years old and married to Robert G. Marmon of Ohio, who had come to Laguna as a surveyor after the Civil War.[46] Analla addresses Pratt:

> Dear friend,
>
> Since I have left Carlisle I having written you any letter. So I am very glad to write you this lovely morning. I will try to answer

> all the questions I can. I know you would like to know how we Carlisle children all getting along. I think we are all got along well, for my part I think I am doing well. I have very comfortable home. I have most everything I need. I have a very good sewing machine, cost $27.

She writes that she does a great deal of sewing, along with "fancy work," and she is "now busily engaged crocheting a bed spread" that she may send to the State Fair. Her letter concludes,

> Christine Showtematry is dead. She dead 1st of June. We have a very good farm, and great many horses, great many sheep and many cattles. And we have good home. I am very well & happy.
>
> Very Truly
> Maria Analla (Part 2)[47]

Maria Analla Marmon would communicate with the school in later years, and I consider some of that later.

Laura M. S. Reid, another Laguna woman, wrote not from the Pueblo but from Albuquerque, where she was working and perhaps also attending the Albuquerque Indian School. She tells Pratt,

> I was very glad to get your letter but I am at working now I had been at school but all the Children gone home and I am going to go home next month for I am going to try to teach Sunday school. Well and I am trying to learn all I can and I want to come back to Carlisle again so I hope some boys + girls are coming home this summer. Well I hope I will see you again and talk to you and now I hope some of you will come and visit us now.

She has been to Carlisle and she wants "to come back to Carlisle again"—she will repeat the desire—but there are no records for Laura Reid's time at the school at any time. A brief note in the *Indian Helper* for September 16, 1887, announced that she would be coming to the school soon (3), while the issue for August 2, 1889, reported that she had already left. It noted as well that "Laura Reid at Laguna, New Mexico wants to come back to school with her brothers" (3). (There are no Carlisle school records for Laguna boys named Reid.) Those mentions would suggest that she had attended for some two years at most. She continues,

> I am trying to do well and trying to be happy here but I am very home sick but I hope to get use it. I am going to see my papa + mama and all the rest. Well I hope you are all well here, I do not believe that Mary Paisano is dead + Harry Marmon too I hope there are in heaven.

A great many Laguna people named Paisano attended Carlisle. **Mary Paisano** had been at Carlisle from 1884 to 1889; she died at the age of sixteen in April 1890. **Harry Marmon**, listed as a "fullblood" in the Carlisle records, was the stepson of Walter G. Marmon, Robert Marmon's brother. Harry had entered, left, and re-entered the school beginning in 1881, and he died at the age of seventeen early in 1890.

Laura Reid is homesick for Laguna—to which she will soon return for a visit—and also for Carlisle. She says,

> I will write a nice letter to you when I get home because I have not time so I will tell you a little about any thing at home [t]he I had little pony for myself and all each got one and now. how is Dear old Carlisle getting I like to see it very much. I wish I could go back to Dear old school and stay with her there and now I think so many children want to come and I do hope you Remember me yet Dear school how is all my maids at school are they all well I hope they had good time and so I will go home and have nice time to help my mama and I hope I will see Dear school again Well good by I will ~~R~~ writ again when I get home and tell you more about at home from you old school friend

I don't believe Laura Reid ever did go back to Carlisle again.

The 1890 responses also include a moving letter from **Mattie Reid**, Laura Reid's older sister. She had been at Carlisle from 1881 until 1885, and she addressed her letter to Pratt from "Cubero N.M.," not far from her home at Laguna. She will make clear why it is that she is there, and I quote her letter in full:

> My dear School Father R.H. Pratt,
>
> As I sat down to answer the question[.] what you have wanted it breaks my heart to remember the School and of pupils. I have answered all they have asked I am getting along first straight I am working ever since I come from School. [s]till working. I have worked for my people all I can[.] and yet they are not satisfied. for theirsake I have done. very worng. dear me, no one to forgive me for having a Child[.] but if I learned my child about God and every things about Bible sure God will help me along as long as I live in this wicked world. Now I am staying about six miles from my home, working for Mrs. DeArmond, a [s]panish lady. I get 8 dollars a month from her. Capt. I *will* never go back in Indian ways no matter if any Indians want to give me a house. No sir I d[i]**spices** the Indian ways. My Brothers all dress in white man ways also my sisters. I have been thinking about the School. I cant heardly write the letter to you because my tear comes to run. For all thing I wish I was in School of Carlisle. take my son along with me. Remember me to all who knows me. pray for me not to do wrong again. I closed the answer and the letter with mine tears.
>
> Good-bye, A Dios
> from Mattie Reid (Part 5)

As described in chapter 3, Mattie Reid's son James would enter Carlisle in 1906; his age at the time was listed as nineteen, so that he would have been born in 1887, when his mother would have been about seventeen. Like her sister Laura, Mattie Reid also expresses a desire to return to Carlisle, along with strong affirmation of its disapproval of "the Indian ways." She would marry a Laguna Pueblo man named

Martin Luther, with whom she would have a son. I look at her further communications with the school later.

Among the Paisanos from Laguna who had been to Carlisle was **Frank Paisano**, in attendance from 1884 to 1889. He responded to the 1890 questionnaire, noting that he was "Age 15, at Carlisle 5 yrs." He tells Pratt that he is continuing his education and is deeply involved in religious activities. He writes from Albuquerque:

> I have received your circular, and filled it out the best I could. I was very glad to learn of your interest in us, And I am delighted to have the opportunity of still going to school I am now attending Albuquerque Indian Mission School under the care of Rev. Robert Coltman. . . . We attend Classroom every day and change work in the other department every tow weeks. We have churche service every Sab., morning. And Sab. school every Sab., afternoon. Also two Missionary Meetings every month Home and Foreign. We are looking forward with much pleasure to our vacation which commences on the 18th of July then we will go to our homes and in two months we hope to return to [**our**] school. Since I left Carlisle I keep up what I had learned there and I always will remember my old school with pleasure. As I told you I have been going to school since October and never wear Indian clothes neither do I dance. . . . In the Fall I will come back to school and try to get a good education and hope some day I may be able to teacher my own people. With best regards
>
> Your Sincerely
> Frank Paisano
> Pueblo Tribe Laguna, N.M. (Part 4)[48]

The devout young scholar assures Pratt that he "never" wears Indian clothes, nor does he participate in the ceremonial dances of his people. It is interesting to note in this regard that Frank's father, Jose Paisano, was one of the Pueblo's Principales or governors, and we can only wonder whether, having sent his sons—I consider Frank's brother, **Willie Paisano**, just below—to off-reservation boarding school, he also supported their avoidance of the ceremonial dances upon their return.

Regardless of Frank Paisano's refusal to dance or to wear Indian clothes, he too would be elected governor of Laguna Pueblo in 1911, as we see in chapter 3. The meaning of "traditionalist" and "progressive," we see once more, was complex among the New Mexico Pueblos, although it was not simple anywhere in Indian Country.

Frank Paisano's older brother William—he is listed as Willie Paisano in the Carlisle records—"Age 24 / At Carlisle 2 years, from 1884–6," directs his letter to the "Hon. Commissioner of Ind. Affairs." He says:

> The letter from Capt. R.H. Pratt, the Supt. of Carlisle Indian Training School was received telling that you like to hear from us how we are getting along with our works at home.
>
> In reply that I got back from Carlisle School in June 27 1886, soon in after that I was placed on my father's business as farming + stock raising. he have over 40 agres of farming land and over a hundreds of cattle, 2,000 heads of a flock of sheep, 15 mules, and 12 donkeis, and 50 mares and horses. I also bought a set of carpenter's tools this trade I had learned at Carlisle . . . . so that I am doing that work whenever it necessary around the house, but that was no time for me to keep on my trade, as my father thinks it would be best for me, however let me do of my trade whenever it necessary to us. In after one or two years of my stay then I got a wife to the girl that she had been in Carlisle 6 or 7 years her name was Mary Perry.

His father's stock holdings are substantial, and Willie Paisano, unlike many other returned students, has the means to purchase tools for himself. That he is doing well and had married a Carlisle girl does not, however, undo the tensions between old and new at Laguna. For example, Willie Paisano writes of his wife, saying,

> in after 2 years of her stay at our house then she felt to dress up like the rest of the family. I refused her question, but then whole family were in her help, so they overcome of me she is now dressed in Pueblo dress. somehow she is behind of my learning her stay was long than mine which was one year, and ten months.

> My age was 24 years. I used to go to school in Albuquerque N. Mex. Before I went to Carlisle at the time I was 18 years old. Now if there are I missed that you like to know, I shall be glad to receive your question, as I am just in willing to answer[**e**].

Before closing, he reports, "also I had been elected as Sec'y + Treas. for this Pueblo. I will keep on my duty until next year" (Part 4). Many things are at issue here.

Both Frank and William Paisano might have had less positive feelings toward the school than they express in their letters because, as Laura Reid mentioned, their sister **Mary Paisano**, who had entered with them in 1884, died at the school, at the age of sixteen, just over a month before her brothers received the June 1890 questionnaire. Their fourteen-year-old sister, **Minnie Paisano**, who had entered more recently (1889), would be sent home sick at the end of the summer, and they would have been aware of her difficulties.

Mary Perry, William's wife, had indeed been a Carlisle student, and one who, as he wrote, was at the school longer than he was, attending from 1880 to 1884, then reentering and remaining until 1886. Pueblo peoples had traditionally been matrilocal, so that "our house," the couple's own home, would have been near her family's dwelling, and although they had allowed her to attend Carlisle, the family still wears "Pueblo dress." The young husband writes that although he "refused her question," because the "whole family were in her help, so they overcome of me," and "she is now dressed in Pueblo dress." Dressed in Pueblo clothes, would she and her family—her father's name is given as *She we* and he, too, is listed as a Principale—have participated in the Pueblo's ceremonial dances, in spite of the fact that they had sent her to school? Would her "whole family" also have persuaded William, unlike his brother Frank, to participate? Although Mary Perry Paisano did not respond to Pratt's 1890 request for information, she did communicate with the school years later, as we will see. Having been to school in Albuquerque and the East, and "refusing" his wife's wish to wear "Pueblo dress," Willie Paisano was nonetheless elected

"Sec'y + Treas." of Laguna Pueblo, becoming one of the Principales, like his father-in-law.

The June 1890 Carlisle questionnaire came to South Dakota at a very interesting time. The Lakotas, having heard about the Ghost Dance from the Araphos, sent a delegation of their own south to visit the Paiute prophet, Wovoka, and learn of it directly from him. As the great chronicler of the Ghost Dance James Mooney wrote, "Good Thunder, Flat Iron, Yellow Breast, and Broken Arm from Pine Ridge; Short Bull . . . from Rosebud, and Kicking Bear from Cheyenne River agency," along with several others traveled to find Wovoka (Mooney 1973, 64) in November 1889. They returned in March 1890 with positive reports, but as Rani-Hendrik Andersson has written, there were "no large gatherings of ghost dancers on any of the Lakota reservations as early as June 1890" (2008, 42), when the Carlisle questionnaire arrived. That would change by the fall.

There were a great many responses to the questionnaire from Pine Ridge, but only three from Rosebud—and one of those was from a Pine Ridge Oglala, **Frank Locke**, who had come to Rosebud Agency the year before to take work as a blacksmith. Another of the Rosebud respondents was **Luther Standing Bear**, who would become well known as a performer, film actor, and writer. The third was from **Plenty Living Bear**. Shortly after the massacre at Wounded Knee, he would become better known to history under the name Plenty Horses. I begin with them before turning to Pine Ridge.

Frank Locke describes himself as "Sioux, Age 24 / At Carlisle 7 years," from 1882 to 1889. His student information card records that his Indian name in English was "Lock of Hair," neither this nor the name Locke providing a clue to the fact that he was the son of George Sword, a Sun Dance participant, a medicine person, a warrior who had been at the Little Bighorn, an intimate of Crazy Horse, an Indian policeman and judge, and an ethnographic consultant. As Sword explained to Dr. James R. Walker, Pine Ridge Agency physician, "My name is George Sword. My name was given to me when I quit the ways of the Indians and adopted those of the whites" (quoted in Red Shirt 2016, 63). He said, "I took the name, of *Mila Wakan*, which means a mysterious knife. This I did when I saw the swords [of] the officers of the army. I thought that the sword was an emblem of power and authority, so I chose this name. . . . I do not know who gave me the name of George" (Red Shirt 64). Sword had joined the Episcopal Church, and in 1879 Pine Ridge Agent Dr. Valentine McGillycuddy appointed him captain of the Indian police[49]—one of Locke's Carlisle files lists his father as "Capt. Geo. Sword"—and he later became a tribal judge. Sword served as a consultant to Dr. Walker, who was also an amateur ethnographer, writing for him many personal narratives in Lakota and also texts illuminating aspects of his people's rituals and traditions.[50]

His son, Frank Locke, did not often appear in any of the Carlisle publications, but he did have a brief piece in the *Indian Helper* for March 16, 1888, that I think worth reproducing in full:

> **Books as Ponies**
>
> I am enjoying the fair weather here and the good time, but often thought of the old places, where we have had lots of fun in training and lassoing young ponies and how we were often unhorsed, and how we used to set traps to catch foxes and wolves and how we would go to fish and search bird nests and how we used to come home with big hearts, having plenty of game and how we made old folks happy, how I used to try to have my ponies run faster than yours, and how we tried to have fat ponies; but I have now adopted the school books as my ponies, and so if I desire to have my books run fast, I study them harder and there is no doubt that you can't beat me in that race.

In early 1888 Frank Locke would have been twenty-two, twenty-three, or twenty-five years old; his Carlisle records differ. In any case, when he arrived at Carlisle in 1882, he was a young man who had already had a mostly traditional Lakota education. Although I think his brief piece may have been more heavily edited than many other student contributions—like Charles Dagenett's, it is more polished than the letter he sent two years later—it nonetheless has some of the feel of oral composition, as Locke tells his story in a single sentence with almost no punctuation.

In 1890, he addresses Pratt as "My Dear Friend" and begins,

> Your request of which you were so instructed to obtain information of every Carlisle pupil, came to me last week. It has been forwarded from Pine Ridge post office and this is what delay my immediate writ[t]ing. Wishing my report will reach you, before other go in to the hand of the honorable Commissioner of the Indian Affairs.

He then goes on to address a matter that had not been raised in the questionnaire but which obviously concerned him:

> We are very much fear that our friends in East will hear the report of the out break of the Rosebud, which will be a story. There was a little confusion among Indians and Indian police men over a lock up man who ran away from the lock up. The Rosebud is just quiet as before that confusion occured but we afraid that newsman will make too big a picture of that might excite our friends.

He signs himself "You[s] friend / F.L. Locke," adding, "Please write to me soon and inform me of what important to know" (Part 5).

As he explains, the "out break" involved "a lock up man who ran away from the lock up," quite literally the breaking-out of a single individual. But Locke's fear that a "newsman will make too big a picture . . . that might excite our friends," is shrewdly prescient. This is to say that reporters from both the local and national papers would soon play a part in "exciting" outsiders about the Ghost Dance; and the events at Wounded Knee would specifically be referred to as an "outbreak."[51] Locke was correct in assuring Pratt that the "confusion" had not generally disturbed the "quiet" at Rosebud. In fact, J. George Wright, the agent at Rosebud, in his 1890 report dated August 26, 1890, makes no mention whatsoever of any outbreak or confusion, while singling out the Indian police at Rosebud for praise (Wright, in *Annual Report of the Commissioner of Indian Affairs* 1890, 62).

Locke married **Hope Blueteeth**, also a Carlisle student, who had enrolled with the first group of Lakotas from Pine Ridge and Rosebud on October 6, 1879; she left the school with him in July 1889 but did not respond to the 1890 questionnaire. The student files for Blueteeth and her husband contain materials that allow us to follow them later in time, as I do in chapter 3.

Writing from Rosebud on June 6, 1890, Luther Standing Bear addresses Pratt as "Dear Friend," and begins,

> I take pleasure in writing and answering the questions you have sent. I am now twenty-six years old. I went to School at Carlisle in 1879, and remained there six years. . . . I could not read before I went to school. I learned to talk English at Carlisle. . . . While I was at Carlisle, I worked in the tin[-]shop. I am now working at the Agency school as assistant. . . . I live in a small frame house, and it is my own. I do not wear Indian clothes. I married an educated girl, she was educated at Hope School, Spring field, South Dakota. I attend the Episcopal Church. We have two children. I have got along very well since I left school. The particular trouble I have had was about a girl. I have no farm, but have a little garden and raise enough potatoes for my family. I have four mares, and three cows, but I have no pigs. Now I think I have answered all the questions you asked.

He signs,

> I am sincerely your friend.
> Luther Standing Bear
>
> P.S. I have been working eversince I came back from school. (Part 1)

Then, on a separate slip of paper, he adds, "I did not drink no liquor, no smoke, and never swear, eversince I came back from school," inscribing himself this time as "L.S. Bear," a practice we have seen before.

Standing Bear had married Nellie de Cory, whose father, Peter de Cory, was a prosperous white man. The school she had attended, the Hope Indian School for Girls (later the St. Mary's School for Indian Girls), was an Episcopal school established in 1879 by the prominent Episcopal bishop in the Dakotas, W. H. Hare. I have found no information concerning the "particular trouble" Standing Bear had "about a girl" at this early time in his life.

On his departure from Carlisle, Standing Bear had obtained a recommendation from Pratt, which "led to immediate employment as an assistant teacher" (Ellis 1985, 147) at the agency school, a position that required him, like other Native teachers, to wear "citizen's" clothes. Later in his life, however, Standing Bear would change his mind a good deal about the matter of Indian dress. In his autobiographical *Land of the Spotted Eagle*, he would write, "According to the white man, the Indian, choosing to return to his tribal manners and dress, 'goes back to the blanket'" (1978, 190), a derogatory phrase. Standing Bear insists to the contrary, that "'[G]oing back to the blanket', is the factor that has saved [the Indian] from, or at least stayed, his final destruction" (190). Some of his further communications with Carlisle appear in chapter 3.

Plenty Living Bear was several years younger than Standing Bear, but the two probably knew each other at school as they would likely have known each other at home. Having left Carlisle in 1889, he addresses Pratt as "My Dear Sir" and writes,

> I am getting along [F]irst rat. We have nothing to work at now because our Agent would not g[a]ve us anything to work at it. he just gave a white people to do things to work at Agency. [S]o [S]ome of the school boys has nothing to do it and they didn't have any wagon o[r] some other things too. The Agent say he promise us a buggy from Carlisle Barracks so we would like to know when it is time to gave them now. I could not do any work this time because my left hand has being cutting of with a rope.
>
> From yours
> Plenty Living Bear (Part 3)

The agent referred to is J. George Wright, mentioned earlier. He had come to Rosebud in September 1889, and like agents elsewhere he may not have had much work for hire—or he may indeed have given what work was available to whites. Wright's report within the *Report of the Commissioner of Indian Affairs* of August 1890 stated that "All Indians employed at the Agency are required to be legally married" (62), a requirement that does not seem to have been in effect at all the agencies. In any case Plenty Living Bear was probably not married yet, which may or may not explain why he had not gotten work. That Wright had spoken of a wagon or buggy to be shipped from Carlisle by train, a very long distance, is certainly possible—or Plenty Living Bear may have misunderstood him.

I do not know the degree to which Plenty Living Bear was interested in or involved with the Ghost Dance at the time he wrote to Pratt, although the promise of a return to traditional life would have been attractive to him as it was to many others, among them, as noted, several former Carlisle students. I return to Plenty Living Bear after examining some of the letters from students who had returned from school to the Pine Ridge Agency.

The letters from returned Lakota students at Pine Ridge indicate that those who had obtained teaching positions, like Standing Bear at Rosebud, or gotten work at the agency, were doing fairly well, although here too the number of positions available was limited. Several returned students managed to farm, but even when they had sufficient land, there was the usual shortage of implements or materials. And the spring of 1890 had been drier than usual in an area where droughts were common. A few young men write of joining the Indian police, and one performed in a traveling show that took him as far as San Francisco.

Wallace Charging Shield, "Age 20, at Carlisle 4 years, at Home 3 years," also addresses Pratt as "Dear School father." Here is his letter in full:

> I want to say a few words, to let you know that I am still working at the Pine Ridge. Col H.D. Gallegher has giveng me a position

in Oglalla Boarding School under Wm. Malugen, who is the Supt. of this school. Mr. [**Clearnece**] Three Stars used to have this position [**B**]ut he is resigned it, so I am now a principal of the boys at the school, and I like my work very much. the teachers are all help me so I am enjoying very much. (Part 3)

Agent Hugh G. Gallagher had been appointed by President Grover Cleveland in 1886, and Benjamin Harrison, elected president in 1889, kept him on. The *Annual Report of the Department of the Interior for 1890* lists Emory E. Van Buskirk as superintendent of the Oglala Boarding School, with J. H. Malugen as principal teacher.

Clarence Three Stars, mentioned by Charging Shield as having had a supervisory position at the Pine Ridge Boarding School, had been among the first Lakota students to enter Carlisle in October 1879. After two outing assignments on Pennsylvania farms, he had gone on another with Luther Standing Bear to the John Wanamaker Department Store in Philadelphia in the summer of 1884, leaving it—and the school—at the end of that summer. Although there is no letter on file from him in answer to the 1890 questionnaire, he had already written to the school at some length in 1887, sent in a brief report of a visit he had made to Rosebud in 1888, and then addressed another long letter to the school in 1889. All these appeared in the *Indian Helper*.

Under the headline, "Letter from a Young Indian Man Who Spent Five Years at Carlisle," the 1887 article explains that its author is the "New Assistant Teacher at the Pine Ridge Agency Boarding School." It is dated January 14, 1887, and I quote most of it. A young man of twenty-four, Three Stars writes:

Mr. Man-on-the-Band-Stand, Dear Sir:

Herewith enclosed 10 cents worth of stamps for your good little paper for one year. Perhaps you want to know some thing about the Boarding School at this agency. There are some 189 pupils, they learn just as fast as at Carlisle, but they don't talk English to each other unless some one make them talk.

Of course there are some half-breeds here who talk as well as any Carlisle boy, but they are too bashful, besides they are getting in the habit of talking Indian. I am getting in the habit of talking Indian, too, but I shall never let Mr. Ignorance pull me down .... Some of the large boys who have been here long Enough to understand the English language are now employed at the agency, learning trades, so you see that the Pine Ridge Boarding School is doing some thing for the Indians. A man named——was in charge of the school last spring, was inexperienced among the Indians. He used to make the girls pull weeds in the field with the boys, causing much excitement among the Indians. Of course it is a good thing for the girls to learn to be farmers but they are much better at the house work. He had a great deal of trouble with the Indians, but he is not here now, and the school is getting on much better than last spring.

Respectfully,
C.T. Stars (4)

The signature, of course, is one of the odder habits some of the students had picked up, as we have seen on several occasions. Three Stars addressed his letter to "Mr. Man-on-the-Band-Stand," and many pieces in the various Carlisle newspapers appeared under the byline of the Man-on-the-Bandstand, a kind of all-seeing figure of surveillance, today assumed to be not Richard Pratt but rather Mariana Burgess. There are some pieces in the papers, however, where Burgess is in dialogue with the Man-on-the-Bandstand, and while she may have written both parts, it is also possible that at least in these instances the Man is someone else.[52] We will also find Clarence Three Stars a bit later addressing the Man-on-the-Bandstand as "Grand-pa."

In its issue of July 20, 1888, the *Helper* published parts of a letter Three Stars had sent from Rosebud, where, the paper said, he was staying at the home of Luther Standing Bear. Quoting directly and also paraphrasing, the *Helper* has Three Stars reporting that "Luther holds the same position in the school he has had for some time" (2). He also provides some encouraging information about several of the returned male former students, and speaks well of **Martha Bordeaux**, who had been at Carlisle from 1882 to 1887 (she did not respond to Pratt in 1890 nor communicate with the school later). But, says the *Helper*—and this sounds to me like Mariana Burgess—"Clarence has heard of the doings of some of the girls which he is ashamed to report." It then quotes him as wishing these girls "to conduct themselves well when they are tempted," for we "all know that it is very hard for us to do right all the time among our people who are not Christians—both Indians and whites on the reservation" (2).

Another letter from Three Stars appeared the following year in the *Indian Helper* for May 3, 1889. The headline introducing it this time characterizes it as "A Newsy Letter from the Pine Ridge Agency," Three Stars's home. He once again writes to the Man-on-the-Bandstand, this time addressing him as "Dear Grandpa," and he goes on at some length, raising a number of issues about Indian education. I quote most of what he had to say:

> It is a long time since I have written to you and I feel like say a few words in your paper if you will permit me in regard to these children here in the boarding school. Some of their ways and doings are similar to your children at Carlisle.
>
> They break so many dishes, some of them are greedy at the table especially among the new girls and boys. . . . I think they don't go forward with their studies and work without being disturbed, as their parents are here after their rations once a month, some of them every two weeks, then they have to talk Indian with their parents one day.
>
> I was at one of the trader's stores, there were many Indians. In fact, it was crowded when an old woman came up to me suddenly, took hold my coat-collar asking me through whose authority I nearly starved her boy to death.
>
> She talked very loud so that every eye was turned upon us.
>
> It was nearly true, her boy ran away from the school, he was brought back and was fed with bread and water for a certain number of days as a punishment.

I then turned around and told her kindly that I have no power to bring severe punishments upon the boys, I also told her that I was not a chief of the school (Supt.) then she was satisfied. . . .

Another thing occurred while we were trying to secure some children for this school. Mr. Wendell Keith, the Industrial teacher of the Boarding-school here, and I went to Wounded Knee Creek, fifteen miles from the Agency to bring some children if we could get them with the consent of their parents.

While going through a camp named Orphan's Camp, an old man came upon us. . . . He said, "You young men who return from the Eastern schools are not helping your people. Instead of helping your people you help the white man to take our children from us."

I turned upon him and told him that one of the greatest helps I can do for him is to get his children in the school to be educated. . . .

One thing more, one day I was in the sewing room making a pair of pants with the assistance of the girls. They thought it very funny to see a man sewing. . . .

Of course they never saw a tailor before.

Some of these girls are really good workers. I hope they will go East some day to see the outside world.

Your Grandson,
C.T. STARS (1–2)

Three Stars provides vivid illustrations of the divergent opinions at Pine Ridge regarding the white man's schools, something we have seen elsewhere as well. The Pine Ridge School was a boarding school, but it was on the reservation, and as Three Stars notes, the children saw their families once or twice a month, something that he, very much in accord with Pratt, finds an impediment to their acquiring English.[53] He finesses the question as to whether a bread-and-water diet is appropriate punishment for a young man who has run away, saying that he is not the one who imposed—or could impose—that punishment: but it is a reasonable question the woman raises nonetheless.

Reporting on a recruiting trip to Wounded Knee—Three Stars could not know it would later be the site of the massacre of Lakota people by the U.S. Seventh Cavalry—he accurately notes that parental consent is required before children can be taken to the boarding school. He and his colleague will not be removing any child contrary to their parents' wishes. And he describes the old Indian man who does not approve the recruiting activities of Indian students returned from the East. As for the girls who had never seen a man sewing, it is true that Lakota men did not sew—but Hopi men did—and "tailor" Three Stars records the amusement of the Lakota girls. We learn more about Clarence Three Stars in chapter 3.

Edgar Fire Thunder had also been in Carlisle's first class, entering at the age of seventeen with Clarence Three Stars and Luther Standing Bear in early October 1879, then leaving in October 1884. He writes to Pratt,

> Dear Sir:
>
> I will tell you how I am getting along. I am getting along very nicely. I am still work at Agency. I want to say one thing about my wedge. The Agent promise me when I first came to work. But since he left here my wedge not up four years.
>
> I was go back to school again but Dr. McGillicuddy told me not to go and he said if I stay and work at Agency for five years. He will pay me fifty Dollars per month. I work six years now but I don't reach yet. So I wish the commissioner of Indian affairs would rise my wedge. If required about my conduct I would Respectfully refer you to Mr. T.J. Reedy Blacksmith at Pine Ridge under whose supervision I have been working for the last four years.
>
> Now that is all I will say.
>
> Your respectfully
> Edgar F. Thunder (Part 1)

Fire Thunder, like Wallace Charging Shield, is working for Agent Gallagher, and he is a blacksmith under the supervision of Mr. Reedy. If he has worked for six years, he would have begun soon after his return home in 1884. The agent who had advised him not to go back to school, promising him higher wages after four years' work, was not Gallagher, but rather Dr. Valentine McGillycuddy, in charge at Pine Ridge from 1879 to 1886. When Gallagher replaced him, he seems to have kept Fire Thunder on but without raising his wages. We will hear more of Edgar Fire Thunder.

One thing **Charles Bird**, in attendance at Carlisle from 1882 to 1886, seems to have learned with a vengeance is literacy's capacity for exact enumeration. He writes,

> Dear sir:-
>
> I received a paper and questions that you wished to be answered. I will tell you "full and strictly truthful" As I am getting on very well. Well, I went to Carlisle 30th days of Nov. 1882. I was that time 16 years of age, I remain there as far as 22nd days of June 1886. So I have been at school 3 years, 6 months and 22 days.

He lists some of what he studied, recalling, "Before I went to Carlisle I learn to say 'A man' 'A dog' that is all I could said but when there I could talk English fairly well." It was only four days after his return home, he writes, that

> the Agent gave me a job as office-boy for three months and then after all rest of months for two years working at Agency Saw-Mills, but I was discharge years of 1888. The reason was sickness to made me discharge. Now I stayed with my father to live a log house. From years 1888 to 1890 so as this month[,] So I came back from [**the**] school to among this Indians next 26th days of this Month will be four years to live among this Indians. My progressing was a little farm about 12 acres of land to work at, and when I got that done then I take care about over one hundred head of cattle.

He then breaks that number down, distinguishing, it would seem, between the stock belonging to his father, to his uncle, and to him. He also specifies the exact number of horses he and his father own and records the fact that "I have 3 pigs only." He concludes, "My age is 24 years old, single man I attend to Episcopal church. I never wear an Indian clothes since I left Carlisle." Then, along the side of the page, Bird wrote: "Never my hairs let it grow an inch" (Part 2), a fact he surely thought would please Superintendent Pratt.

Marshall Hand entered Carlisle in 1886, and a year later was sent on an outing assignment to a farm in Bucks County, Pennsylvania, where he remained until the fall of 1888. He may have attended public school during that time, as many students enrolled at Carlisle on extended outings did—or, because he would at that time have been in his mid-twenties, it's entirely possible that he did not. In 1888, he "Ran away," but the 1890 questionnaire found him at the Pine Ridge Agency and he responded:

> I read that the Honorable Commissioner of Indian Affairs wants to know something about Carlisle Indian students as I am getting along first rate in every way during just as well as anyone Working to make my own living I am trying to write answers to the questions all I could.

He notes that he had attended boarding school at the agency and had learned some English before going to Carlisle, and

> when I was at Carlisle I was sent out on a farm to work and also I was a shoe maker. But now I am working in the Agency. I earn 15 dollars a month. I like to earn money But can not earn much. I am working every day. I am living in L house of our own. I don't wear Indian clothes and I don't think I will because I never wear Indian clothes every since I know how to take care myself. some boys came back here and wear Indian clothes I am married now I marry an Educated person. I attend in Holy cross church we had a little boy four years old. I am getting along very well since I came back. we have a little farm our not very big. But working to mak something for ourself. . . .
>
> yours friend,
> Marshall Hand (Part 3)

I don't know what he meant by "L house"; possibly he meant to write "Log" house, as several others had. Nor have I discovered the identity of the "Educated person" Marshall Hand had married.

Marshall Hand's younger sister, **Emma Hand**, also responded to the questionnaire. She wrote:

> Dear Friend,
>
> The Honorable Commissioner of Indian Affairs wants to know something about us Indian once we Carlisle Students I getting along first rate in every way. just as well as one can. during well. working to maken my own living I am trying to write answers to the questions all I could. and says the letter will be read by the commissione[s]. I was sent to Carlisle School in Nove 1882. I stayed there four year and 7 month. . . . I could read little Before I went to Carlisle Because I go to day school here at White Birds near the Agency But could not talk any English when I went to Carlisle there I learn to talk English.

She has much more to say, but I interrupt her for a moment here to note that I think it likely Emma and her brother Marshall discussed the letters each would send to Pratt. Emma, for example, opens in much the way Marshall had, writing, "Emma Hand Sioux 20 yrs / at Carlisle 4 years," although she adds: "at home 4 years." Using "Department of the Interior / Indian School Service" stationery, both date their letters "June __"—but give no date, and neither fills in the year the stationery provides, leaving it "189_." Both open with reference to the Indian Commissioner and both say they "are getting along first rate in every way"; both report they are "during" as well as anyone or as one can; and they note the date they were sent to Carlisle.

While Marshall had attended the reservation boarding school, Emma says she had attended the White Bird Day School. That Marshall, at a boarding school and thus at home less, could speak some English before attending Carlisle, and Emma, going home each day from school could not, would seem to provide support for Pratt's belief in the pedagogical value of keeping students away from home as much as possible—although many day school students learned English very well.

Emma continues,

> I could not work before going to Carlisle But going to school every day. and when I was at Carlisle I was sent on farm to work. But now I am working for my self to make something I don't earn no money Because it is hard to earn money. I am working every day. I living in lack house not very nice my own house.

Marshall had said he was "living in L house," and Emma says she is living "in lack house": does this mean each lived in the same sort of house? Had they discussed in Lakota how they might describe their houses in English, Marshall offering an "L" and Emma venturing "lack?"

Like Marshall, Emma continues,

> I don't wear no Indian clothes and I never will wear Indian clothes Like some Carlisle Indian student came here and dress them self in Indian clothes I am married now have my own house I marry Educated person. I attend in Holy cross church Apostolice I had a little boy one years now. I am getting alright since come back school. I had a little farm myself not very Big. But working to have some horses, cattle, mules and pig I wish to have some of this things. This is all I will close my writing.
>
> Emma Hands Means
> Carlisle (Part 3)

Like her brother, she writes that she had married an "Educated person." This was Charles Means, who, like Marshall Hand's wife, had not been educated at Carlisle; at least there is no record of him.[54] The marriage did not last, as I describe further in chapter 3.

I turn now to the report sent to Pratt from Pine Ridge by **Newton Big Road**. He had entered the school in 1882, then left, was readmitted, and left again because of illness in 1886. He writes,

In answer to your letter of recent date I will say that I am now 32 years old. And went to Carlisle in 1882 I was in school 4 years. . . . And I learned to talk English at Carlisle. . . . Now I am farming I earn no money for there is no work for me to do for anyone. I live in my own log house. I wear citizen's clothes. Am married have one child dead. My wife does not talk English I attend Episcopal Church. I have got along very well since I left school.

The principle trouble I have is that I have very few tools to work with. The government does not furnish us with enough stiring plows + mowing machines And besides this is not good farming country.

Last year while at the Agency where the Sioux Commission was here my crops were destroyed by the cattle. We ought to have reapers to cut our wheat + oats. So far we have no reapers at all. I have 20 acres plowed Have 6 horses + 8 cows. I would like to farm more if I could get the tools + more wire to fence with.

Yours truly
Newton B. Road (Part 3)

When Big Road entered Carlisle in 1882, his age was listed as eighteen. That would, of course, be an error if, as he says, he is thirty-two in 1890. Like so many other returned students, he is trying to farm, and like them as well, he finds this difficult in that where he lives "is not good farming country," nor does he have the plows, mowing machines, and reapers he needs. There were actually two "Sioux Commissions" at Pine Ridge in 1889, both with the aim of persuading the Lakotas to sell some of their lands. The first, headed by none other than Carlisle Superintendent Richard Pratt was unsuccessful; the second, led by General George Crook, was somewhat more successful. During one of those visits Big Road's crops were destroyed because he did not have "more wire to fence with" to keep wandering cattle out. Newton Big Road died in 1895.

Difficult conditions and further assaults on the Native land base, were the concerns of **William Crow**, a Northern Cheyenne man of about twenty-eight, settled with many of his people at Pine Ridge.

He had entered Carlisle in 1885 and left because of illness in 1888. He writes, however, that he was "At Carlisle 1 year," and this sort of discrepancy usually means extended time away from the school on an outing assignment. Crow's information card, however, lists no outings for him, which is unusual. He is recorded as having reached the second grade by the time he left, and he clearly is not at ease with written English. Nonetheless, like many others, he has much he wishes to tell Pratt, and he wrote at some length, grappling, in English, not only with his personal well-being but with concerns the Cheyennes at Pine Ridge must have discussed among themselves. Crow's letter to Pratt demonstrates considerable awareness that it will be sent to the commissioner of Indian Affairs. He says,

> Dear Sir,
>
> What ~~prest~~ Commissioner says we never forgot it. This land is give to Cheyenne in White River I never go way from white river I stay in white river all time. I will stay in my land and they pay for my people Every thing I say yes and I got a house now, so I don't go away tall. and I'll make a corn, and I have every thing. Every people in white river don't have a farm or cow. ~~I don't want tongue river~~ I don't like tongue river my people want stay here in white river. about 100 Indian Because commissioner send the white river. the Indian I want you send [**him?**] small way on also I have sign to writts to pay for the Indians about three Stars what say here I have remember. what is good place now[**.**] all I want you tell me.
>
> How long is to go Tongue River the Cheyennes let me know it. some Cheyenne Have no work and some go work Because Has no things if to do work about Carlisle. School learn Indian Children if come home [**H**]as no any things.
>
> If that you say for me I care from friend Red Eagle, Chief Chey
> *and Little Wolf, Chief*

I will once more mark with admiration the energy of this communication, although some of William Crow's meaning needs sorting out.

He names Red Eagle as chief among the Cheyenne, but I have found nothing about a Cheyenne Red Eagle. Little Wolf, however, was a renowned Northern Cheyenne chief, who, after leading an escape of his people from exile in Indian Territory in 1878, settled with them in Montana. A Northern Cheyenne band leader whom Crow does not name here—he refers to him later in his letter—is his own father, Little Chief. I believe Little Chief to be his father because one of Crow's Carlisle file cards list his "home address" as "Little Chief," and an address of this kind usually references the student's father's name.

In 1877 Little Chief had been exiled with Little Wolf to the Cheyenne and Arapaho Agency in Indian Territory, the "hot place," not far from the Nez Perces, against whom they had often fought. But Little Chief did not join Little Wolf in the 1878 escape, and in 1881 his band was allowed to return to Pine Ridge, settling near the White River, which runs through the northern boundary of the reservation. William Crow, born about 1862, would have experienced with his father Northern Cheyenne warfare, defeat, exile, and, since 1881, a fairly stable existence in South Dakota Territory among the Lakotas on White River. Regarding Crow's dislike of Tongue River, note that the Northern Cheyenne Indian Reservation established in southeastern Montana Territory in 1884 is bounded by the Tongue River on the east and by the Crow reservation on the west—and Crows and Cheyennes were traditional enemies. Having heard that the Cheyennes might leave Pine Ridge—White River—and go to Tongue River—where Little Wolf's people had gone—William Crow is not pleased.

One might think the "three Stars" he references is Clarence Three Stars, prominent at Pine Ridge, but this is not the case. Crow's concern is the question of "what is good place," and he mentions "writts" he had signed "to pay for the Indians." I believe these reference the second of the two Sioux Land Commissions of 1889 headed by General George Crook. Crook, who had refused to undertake the enterprise initially, had later agreed. He had been known by the Lakotas as "Three Stars" for the stars he wore on each shoulder and on his hat. While most of the fullbloods opposed the Commissions' proposals for the sale of their land, Standing Bear Sr., Luther's father, George Sword, Frank Locke's father, and American Horse, Maggie Stands Looking's father, were all in favor. Was William Crow's father, Little Chief, a supporter as well? I think he was, for, his son continues:

> Little Chief has sign to writt to go Tongue River. . . . agent not give any things if to do with work. Also I will take that what here say for commissioner one time I work for him for Land But no pay me. and next time I teacher school all good now. everybody like Carlisle it is good school. what is good place. I wish you tell me about new paper and Carlisle to know something. I will try hard to do work. But I have no anything. if wagon pigs just I have Horses and House and farm.
>
> Wm. Crow, Chey. (Part 4)

These last sentences, as the transcriber noted, were written "upside down on the top of [the last] page."

Despite his son's antipathy to the Tongue River area, Little Chief had indeed signed "to writt to go to Tongue River," and he would move his people to the Northern Cheyenne Reservation just a year later, in 1891. Perhaps this was because, as Crow wrote, "some Cheyenne Have no work," "Has no things to do," "has no any things" at White River, Pine Ridge. William Crow tells Pratt that he has taught school, maybe with Clarence Three Stars at the Pine Ridge boarding school, or perhaps at one of the day schools, and he has also done some agency work, for which he was apparently not paid. He has horses, a house, and farm, but his overall assessment is bleak: "I have no anything." Carlisle would not hear from him again.

Moses Culbertson, twenty-five years old, writes, "Eversince I came home from Carlisle I have never met any misfortune nor any thing that will interfere whatever I have been doing," and that "On acct. of my behavior that the Agent here had given me several work since." That work did not last, however, and, currently, Culbertson says, "I am now in the police force & have been still with the Police-force."[55] The rest of his letter—I quote it in full—offers once more the thoughtful, organic analysis sent by several other returned students, making clear the difficulties they faced at home on the reservations. Culbertson explains,

> As a general thing that when the students of Carlisle comes back to their homes, they afterwards turned back to their old ways, habits &c., + finally become good for nothing. The reason why that this thing is happening so is that on account of **scar[s]e** of employment for the graduates of Carlisle.
>
> And also on account of this, some of the old students of Carlisle became members of some of the white show or circus. In doing this they wanted to earn something for their own living. I thought that according to the treaties of the past, that as soon as an Indian is capable of filling a position with good qualifications *he is* certainly *entitled to it*. After this when a student leaves Carlisle, he ought to learn with the understanding that he gets a position at his Agency. With the best wishes from your friend,
>
> Moses Culbertson (Part 1)

That there were not enough positions for the returned students at their agencies we have seen and will see again, as we have also seen that the wages paid to those who did obtain positions were inadequate. The "treaties of the past," as other returned students also referenced them, were supposed to guarantee Indian land boundaries and sometimes annuity payments. They did not promise positions at the Indian agencies for those "with good qualifications" because, for one thing, many of those agencies did not exist at the time the treaties were made. The Pine Ridge Agency itself, for example, was actually no more than fifteen months old on the exact day Culbertson wrote, June 2, 1890.[56]

Culbertson went to Carlisle in 1885, and it is possible that he had been told by recruiters for the school that an agency position was guaranteed by attendance. But we have seen again and again that problems arose for returned students "on account of scarce of employment for the graduates of Carlisle."

Faced with the difficult conditions at their agencies, some former Carlisle students, as Culbertson wrote, "become members of some of the white show or circus" in order "to earn something for their own living." In offering this observation, he may well have had a particular student in mind. Writing ten days later, **John Rooks**, "age 21 years. At Carlisle *7 years*" (emphasis in original), sent a letter to Pratt that begins,

> Captain Pratt,
>
> My Dear friend,
>
> I am going to write a few lines to you this evening to let you know that I am well and also tell you that I seen something last week I mean Claton Brave I saw him ~~and~~ he wear Indian clothing on and rest of are doing well. (Part 3)

As for himself, Rooks writes that he works "on farm at home," and had recently "married an educate woman she from *Genoa Neb.* she talk English and write and she knows how to take care of house."[57] He would later go on to serve in the Indian police at Pine Ridge, and perhaps he is already doing some policing by informing Pratt that he had seen **Clayton Brave** wearing Indian clothes. Clayton Brave had indeed been at Pine Ridge around this time, and as Rooks does not know or say, he was someone who would do just what Moses Culbertson reported and become a member "of some of the white show or circus."

Nor was this anything Brave wished to hide.[58] Less than a week after Rooks had seen him, Brave also wrote to Pratt. Here is his letter in its entirety:

> Clayton Brave, Pine Ridge Sioux
> age 25, at Carlisle 4 ½ yrs
> at Home 3
> Pine Ridge Agency SD
>
> June 18, 1890
>
> R.H. Pratt, Dear Sir,

> I was exceedingly glad to obtain you kind and welcome letter a long time. [a]s I am waiting and had little time I will try to write to you and you as a communication was received by me in good health always and I would like to let you know that I have had been working the show business into Theater in San Francisco also my Acts is first thing I do in feats on the slack wire walking, again fancy rifle shooting and I got through the hoops too. And I get $25 a week & $100 a month. So I can't answer some questions hope excuse my written and I have be travel always never stay one place either. That is all I have to say.
>
> Most Respectfully
> Clayton Brave (Part 3)

Brave is correct in writing SD (not Dakota Territory) because South Dakota had become a state some seven months earlier, on November 2, 1889. His letter strikes me as intended to be the communication of one man of the world to another. Brave is not only unashamed but quite proud of his performance in the "white show or circus," in the great metropolis of San Francisco. I doubt he would walk the streets of San Francisco "with Indian clothing on," as John Rooks had seen him do at home at Pine Ridge, although he may sometimes have performed in Indian costume. And as a performer, Brave is definitely earning a great deal more than he could have earned at home, for had he been paid at that rate for ten months a year he would have earned exactly what Pratt was earning, $1,000 a year, roughly $27, 000 today (2019). Clayton Brave would be at Pine Ridge at the time of the massacre at Wounded Knee, and would (mistakenly) be reported killed, as we will see.

Lucy Day gives her age as twenty-two, noting that she had been at Carlisle for three years, having arrived in October 1879 with the school's very first group of students and leaving in June 1882. Day's student record indicates that she had later returned to the school briefly, reentering in January 1889 but then having to leave in March because of "ill health." She writes at some length, occasionally using the first-person plural, "we." This may mean she was married, but my guess is that she is referring to her parents or relatives. She affirms her loyalty to Carlisle and the lessons it taught and proudly notes, "I talk white nicely." She begins,

> My dear sir Capt. Pratt,
>
> I was very glad to get your letter last week. I am sorry because I did not answers your letter. I was not came in agent so often. thats way I didn't get your letter. . . . I lives in house. I do want to get Indian lives ways. I never forget what I learn in Carlisle. I always talk English when I see white mans so my person was very glad for me that I talk white nicely. I keep my house nicelys can be. . . . we live just like white mans farm + we plenty everything that we have to eat the foots I always remember what I study in Carlisle. We go to church Mr. Cook. every time. he is nice man. Carlisle girls went to church every evening. so I hope we never forget to what we studies to Carlisle. I heard that Rose Bud girls + boys they wears Indian clothes.

Then, she turns abruptly, writing,

> I want tell you some thing that we going to have another agent this summer. so this agent going home in fourth of July. I guess he did not take good care of the people. the people all don't want this agent keep in here. they pretty nere kill.

She says nothing further about this, concluding,

> I always remember off you all. Please Capt. I wish you tell her. Miss Phillip write to me very soon if she is remember me. You must tell thems Miss Phillip + Miss Iriven. I sent my loves +to never forget them. . . . Good by write soon.

She signs, "From Lucy Day," then adds,

> When I was sorry I always said I wish in Carlisle to day I say that way every time. When I remember school girls + boys tell Maggie Old Eagle write to me. (Part 5)

Lucy Day's "person," who is glad she can "talk white nicely," is probably the Rev. Charles Cook, for whose family Day was then working. Miss Phillips and Miss Irvine were teachers at the school, and **Maggie Old Eagle**, several years younger than Lucy Day, had entered Carlisle when Day reentered January 1889. Agent Gallagher did not leave the agency in July; he would be replaced in October, and I do not know just what the trouble was for which "the people all don't want this agent keep in here. they pretty nere kill." Lucy Day died in January 1898.

Another of the very first Lakota girls to attend Carlisle writes to Pratt giving her name as Maggie Belt and also as **Maggie Guy Belt**. She had come to the School as Maggie Stands Looking, the fifteen-year-old daughter of American Horse, one of the first of the Lakota chiefs to send his children to the school. She had left Carlisle in 1884.

There were two Sioux leaders named American Horse—the name is said to mean "He has a white man's horse"—and Maggie Stands Looking's father was the younger, born about 1840. Several of his children—**Ben**, **Joseph**, **Lucy**, **Alice**, and **Sophia American Horse**—would later attend Carlisle. A young man named **Robert American Horse** came to Carlisle with Maggie, and his Carlisle information card lists American Horse as his father. If that were true, he would, of course, be Maggie's brother. But she herself, in a letter we will consider, calls him her cousin. Maggie Stands Looking did have a brother at Carlisle, however, a young man of seventeen named **Guy Bear Don't Scare**, who had come to the school with his sister and their cousin Robert in 1879. Pratt's memoir, *Battlefield and Classroom*, makes mention of both Maggie Stands Looking and Robert American Horse, but I have found no further information about Guy Bear Don't Scare, other than that he probably died in 1888.[59]

The Carlisle *School News* for January 1881, published a letter from Maggie Stands Looking to her father, American Horse, explaining that she had "told this letter to an interpreter and a teacher wrote it down" (4). This is to say that in the slightly more than two years she had been at the school, Maggie's ability to write English had not advanced sufficiently for her to write a letter on her own. Addressing, "MY DEAR FATHER AMERICAN HORSE," she tells him that she is glad to learn of one of her brothers' marriage, and says, "My cousins, and brothers, and I are all very well at this Carlisle school." As I have said, the only cousin at the school with her at the time was Robert American Horse, and the only brother—other siblings and half-siblings came later—was Guy Bear Don't Scare. She expresses concern for her elderly grandfather and asks her "brother Two Dogs to write to [her] again." Two Dogs may or may not been the brother back home who has just been married, but in any case, he is apparently able to write or to have letters written for him. She acknowledges not having been a prompt respondent to letters she has received earlier, but that "is because I can not write. As soon as I get so that I can write myself, I will write as often as I can" (4).

She continues, "Tell Brave Bull that Dora (Her Pipe) has been a little sick, but is most well now." Brave Bull's daughter, **Dora (Her Pipe)**, had come to school with Maggie Stands Looking, and although she had apparently recovered from illness in late January 1881, she would take sick again and die in April that year, to be buried in the Carlisle cemetery. Maggie writes of having heard from "my cousin Robert" that American Horse now has

> a house to live in, and lots of pigs and cows and such things, and I was very glad. You've got a white man's house to live in now and I am anxious to learn all that I can, so that I can come home by and by and live with you.

She reports more students recently having arrived at the school, a number of girls among them, observing, "There are a great many of us here now, and Capt. Pratt is very kind to all of us. . . . Give my love to all of my friends" (4).

A brief letter from her while she was away on an outing assignment also appeared in the *School News* for July 1881, and at this point in time it would appear that she could indeed write for herself. She reports that she liked washing dishes, learning English, and praying to God (4). The Carlisle *Indian Helper* for February 12, 1886, two years after she'd left Carlisle, announced her wedding—but it did not give the name of the man she had married. His name was Guy Belt, and he had not been a Carlisle student, nor is it likely that he had gone to school at all—although his wife, Maggie Guy Belt, as she calls herself, would tell Pratt that he was avid to learn. She begins her 1890 letter:

> I have received the questions that you send me, and I have been Thinking what I am going to [s]ay. Well I am getting along very well and happy and good house keeper. I am always happy with my husband and I want to tell you These. My husband is learn more than any of the School boys. So I am not forgot what I am learned. My husband and I study the lessons some times so my old man is talking some English and also my baby is learning how to talk in English too. and I also teach him to read some too.
>
> My baby is about three years old now. I have just one yet. Well Capt. Pratt you have told us that we must tell the truth to answer those questions. So I will try and tell the truth. Some times I get into trouble but I am always trying hard and keep going on do all the best I Can. as I am always ask God to help me to do all the right ways.

She has picked up the American slang expression "my old man" to refer to her husband, and she has adopted the role of teacher of English to him and to her three-year-old boy, who is perhaps a bit young to be learning to read. But Maggie Guy Belt had had some experience as a teacher, as we may learn from Pratt, who noted in his autobiography: "After her three years at Carlisle away from camp life, with no knowledge of English to begin with, Maggie returned to her people and was . . . made teacher and head of a reservation day school" (Pratt 1964, 275). He observes as well that her husband—Pratt does not give his name—was "the chief of the Indian police" (275), and that among his duties was the task of seeing "that the pupils were prompt and regular in attendance" (276).[60] I can only wonder what "trouble" Maggie Guy Belt got into "some times." She continues,

> I am sure I never never wear Indian clothes since I come back from the school. My husband has 8 acres of land and he is a good work of all the Indians so our Boss Framer is know very well about us. I wanted to tell you one thing well poor James Fox is died two year ago, so no one can not answer his questions. I am not work any where but I am always try to take good care of my own house. Capt. I hope you will not think that some one else write and answer this letters for me. [n]o sir I am sure I have answer all my questions and write this letter too and write with my own hand as some of them could not write. so the school teacher here that write and answer the questions for them. I will be ashamed if some one else write the letter for me. Don't you?
>
> Yours truly
> Maggie Guy Belt (Part 3)

If Maggie had been "a teacher" and even "head of a reservation day school" (Pratt 1964, 275), she does "not work any where" now. But she and her husband, she says, are such good workers that the Boss Farmer—the chief agency farmer, who was probably a white man but possibly an Indian in charge of a great range of crop-raising tasks—has taken note. Their eight acres—the Pine Ridge reservation had not yet been allotted—is not very much land. **James Fox**—his Indian name was Ta ko la, which does indeed mean small, gray fox—had entered Carlisle in September 1885, already eighteen years old, and left because of illness in June 1886. His Carlisle file lists the date of his death as 1887, and Maggie Guy Belt informs Pratt of his death as the reason why there will be no letter from him. She then goes on to assert that she has answered the questions and written to Pratt on her own, offering the observation that some of the returned students are actually getting "the school teacher" to "write and answer the questions for them," something she would "be ashamed" to do—"Don't you?"

I conclude this sampling of letters from returned Pine Ridge students with one from a young man the questionnaire had found away from home, although unlike Clayton Brave, not by choice. **Dana Long Wolf**, "4 years at Carlisle, Age 25 yrs.," writes from "Lancaster Nebr.," where he is incarcerated at the Nebraska State Penitentiary. His situation, thus, differs considerably from that of the other returned students, and I quote his letter to Pratt in its entirety. First, however, there are many interesting things worth noting about this young man. He was the son of the Oglala leader Long Wolf (c. 1833–92), a warrior and medicine person. Long Wolf may have been at the Custer fight in 1876 (Gallop 2001, 197), and if he was, and if his family was in the Lakota camp circle, then his son Dana, about eleven years old at the time, would have been an eye-witness to the battle.

The June 11, 1886, issue of the *Indian Helper* had a brief article reporting a visit Long Wolf had paid to Carlisle. The piece opens, "Long Wolf, Dana's and Hattie's father, visited the school on Tuesday and Wednesday" (2). Dana had come to Carlisle in 1882, and as he would write to Pratt, he had remained "4 years at Carlisle," until June 26, 1886, when he ran away from the school little more than two weeks after his father's visit. **Hattie Long Wolf**, Dana's younger sister—we learn more of her later—had come to Carlisle earlier, on October 6, 1879, with the very first group of Lakota children from Pine Ridge and Rosebud. She left in 1882, so she was not at the school when her father visited. She would, however, return in 1887, with her younger sister, **Hannah Long Wolf**.

The *Helper*'s piece is for the most part an example of Carlisle self-congratulation; I believe it is the work of Mariana Burgess at her most unpleasant. For example, in describing a visit Long Wolf paid to the printing shop—of which Burgess was in charge—the article observes that "we felt sorry . . . that he could not speak or read a word of English." Then, after mocking the fact that Long Wolf wore an Indian blanket,[61] the writer praises the fact that "the Sioux boys who were anxious to hear from their homes, did not speak Indian to their friend, although they had permission to, but talked to him through an interpreter" (2).[62]

Alan Gallop writes that Long Wolf joined Buffalo Bill's Wild West in 1886 (2001, 197). If that is correct, he may have come to visit his children at Carlisle just after performing with the show in Philadelphia on Sunday, June 6, 1886.[63] Would his son Dana's desertion from the school have had anything to do with Long Wolf's employment by Cody and the show's proximity at the time to Carlisle? Almost exactly a year after his visit to Carlisle, Long Wolf was probably among the Wild West performers who played before Queen Victoria in London on June 16, 1887, in celebration of her Golden Jubilee. We know he was present the next time Cody's show played London—another command performance—in 1892, for that was when he contracted pneumonia and died. Long Wolf was buried in a fashionable cemetery in West Brompton, in a plot that Cody had purchased.[64]

Dana Long Wolf writes,

> Dear Friend R.H. Pratt
>
> I am very glad to get you are welcome letter. Was very much please to hear from you. That you have not forget me yet and now my friend I will answer you letter [**S**]oon as possible + let you know about that I have being state prison about [**S**]even months ago. Since I being convict at N.S.P. my Sentence was [**R**]eceive for Seven years at hard labor at Penitentiory. So I can not say any thing about my home because I am being convict already any how but I think I will try to make up my mind write you a letter Today and now I never was a Donkey once yet when I was here but I have tried to make a man of my self like civilization Since I know I'm not half worthy of any body else in the whole convicts. but I've tried my best as I can because the Bible is the Word of God. We should value it very highly. What a blessing it is that we are permitted Read it How great affliction to be deprived of this Privilege. [**t**]he following narrative illustration of this truth is exceedingly touching and I am here is I feels my self to be a Sinner.
>
> I Desires to learn the way of Salvation. And now Dear friend, Do you know that I am Indian boy from Pine Ridge Agency. S. D. I could not answer [**S**]ome of you questions because I was

not at P.R.A.S.D. R. H. Pratt Sir I am very glad to the kind and affectionate interest you have ever ex-pressed in my sister Hattie or Lizzie leads me to feel assured that in and Perhaps you will think it strange[.] that I should write upon such a subject as I intend to [A]nd perhaps also after telling you that I hope I am a follower of the Lamb. You will wonder that I have not said anything to you befor I will tell you my friend why I have not. It is because my own wicked heart would not permit[t]me to but I am Determined I feared no no more but with my whole soul and I want you to write to me again. tell me How is getting on at Carlisle my sister [a] Hattie L. Wolf, L.L.W. Emma B. Bonet[t]. as I wish you tell her Hattie that I want her write to me any time she wants. I am getting along very well at penitenti[o]ry. from you truly friend I am here for nothing

Dana Long Wolf,
but my name is Thomas Skunk Head 1651
Lancaster Nebr.
write Soon (Part 3)

This is an extraordinarily thoughtful, rich, and complex communication!

Having entered Carlisle in 1882 at the age of seventeen, Dana Long Wolf, as I have said, ran away from the school in June 1886, some two weeks after a visit from his father. He says nothing of what he had been doing between that time and the time of his conviction seven months earlier, nor does he say for what crime he was convicted.[65] He is being held in the Nebraska State Penitentiary, opened in 1869, and the only penitentiary in Nebraska. Stating that he "never was a Donkey," Long Wolf says that he was not stupid or obstinate or foolish, and in view of that he is still desirous of making "a man of [him]self like civilization." This turns him toward a passionate statement of faith in the Bible, as he confesses himself "a Sinner" who "Desires to learn the way of Salvation." He will return to his religious feelings shortly, but here, abruptly and poignantly, he writes: "And now Dear friend, Do you know that I am Indian Boy from Pine Ridge Agency. S.D.," apologizing that the Indian Boy "could not answer some of you questions because I was not at P.R.A.S.D"—Pine Ridge Agency, South Dakota—and then thanking Pratt for "the kind and affectionate interest you have ever expressed in my sister Hattie or Lizzie," both of whom he will refer to again as "Hattie L. Wolf" and "L.L.W.," Lizzie Long Wolf.

Dana Long Wolf's younger sister Hattie had an interesting career at Carlisle. As noted, she had entered with the school's very first class in October 1879 at the age of twelve—or perhaps ten or eleven: different records give different ages for her. She stayed until June 1882, and then reentered in 1887. She had—probably a year or so earlier—married a man named Hall Pretty Weasel and given birth to a daughter they named Lucy. (See below.) But she was at Carlisle in 1890, the time her brother is writing; she would remain at the school and graduate in 1892.

Lizzie Long Wolf did not attend Carlisle—although her brother asks Pratt for news of both Hattie and Lizzie. I believe she was a bit younger than Hattie and was born about 1870. Gallop writes that she was with her mother and father when they joined the Buffalo Bill Wild West in 1886, and taking a different path than her brother and two sisters at Carlisle, she traveled to England with the family in 1887–88 and again in 1892. She was with her father when he died in London (Gallop 2001, 198).

Another of the few faulty transcriptions I have found is the transcriber's rendering **Emma B. Bonnet** (sometimes spelled with a double "t" in Carlisle records, as Long Wolf spelled it) as "Emma B. Boneth." This was Emma Bull Bonnet, Long Wolf having used an initial in place of an important part of her name as others had learned to do—Luther S. Bear, Wallace C. Shield, Clarence T. Stars, Dana L. Wolf. Bull Bonnet was an Oglala, also from Pine Ridge, who entered Carlisle at the age of about fifteen in August 1887, the year that Hattie Long Wolf returned to the school with her sister Hannah Long Wolf—who, curiously, is not named by her brother, Dana. Bull Bonnet was also still at the school in 1890, not leaving until 1894.

Long Wolf returns to his religious concerns, saying, "Perhaps you will think it strange that I should write upon such a subject as I intend to and perhaps also after telling you that I hope I am a follower of the Lamb." There were Episcopal missions at the Pine Ridge Agency, and the Holy Rosary Catholic Mission had opened a school there in 1888. But Dana Long Wolf's Carlisle record states that he had not attended school before he came to Pennsylvania, and there is nothing in his Carlisle files to indicate his religious affiliation. He tells Pratt that he had "not said anything" to him before "because [his] own wicked heart would not permit" it. But, he writes, "I am Determined I feared no no more but with my whole soul and I want you to write to me again," and he wants Pratt to encourage his sister—or sisters—to write as well. The simple statement, "I am getting along very well at penitentiory" leaves a great deal to the imagination—as does the manner in which he closes: "from you truly friend I am here for nothing." He signs, "Dana Long Wolf, but my name is Thomas Skunk Head 1651." I suspect "1651" is his convict's number—but is he known at the prison as Thomas Skunk Head? His real name had to have been on file, otherwise the questionnaire Pratt sent would not have reached him. He would communicate with the school again many years later, as would his sister Hattie, and Emma Bull Bonnet as well.

2

"I have always liked to write"

Selected Writings of Mike Burns (Hoomothya)

One of the respondents to Superintendent Pratt in 1890 was **Mike Burns** (1865?–1934), enrolled at Carlisle from 1880 to 1884. He wrote at some length from the San Carlos Agency, Arizona Territory, on June 4, 1890:

> Dear Sir:
>
> I have at hand the letter and the questions which to be answer-ed by the ones formerly at Carlisle Pa. as a student of that Indian School. I have always liked to write and say something about my personal welfare and also behalf of my race as a 'Red Man' and so that the Honorable Commissioner of Indian Affairs can seen how far up in the line of education and civilization of the Indian are at present. In 1880 I first intered at Carlisle Barracks, at being 16 years old and now being at 25 years old. . . . Before intering Carlisle School I used to attend, Post Schools in the Army.
>
> I was raised by the officers in the 5th U.S. Cavalry and I could understand the English Language before attended Carlisle School I lived with an Officer in the Army + worked for him. When I was at Carlisle I found that every student a boy or girl has to learn some trade, so I was a carpenter. At this agency I am now employed as an issue Clerk for Capt. J. L. Bullis as our Acting Agent. . . . I have found no trouble in attaining work at anywhere. I am living in a Dobe house finely furnished and belong to the Agency buildings. Since I have adopted the civilized habit I have never changed to Indian. As I have been to Atlantic to Pacific

Ocean, ~~And as~~ far north as to Montana and as far south as to Texas. So I came to conclusion to settle down. So I got me an Indian wife. In among the Apaches. You can not get one who can read or know something about house-keeping but have to get one and teach them. I was regularly member of the Presbyterian Church. But since I came back here, I have never heard a sermon for five years now. I am sorry to state that I have been ~~to~~ married but a little over a year, and have no children.

Since leaving Carlisle School I have attended several other schools Public and have been doing well in on farms or carpentering and no cause for leaving school only short of financial. I can not mentioned a thing the troubles I had at school as a pupil. I have about 20 acre farm, below the Agency about 2 ½ miles. Of course I have a small property, as five horses, and three cattle.

This closes the questions I beleave.

Very respectfully yours,
Mike Burns Mojave Indian. Would be pleased to received an answer Sir (Part 1)

But Pratt was away when the first responses came in, and this, too, was a letter he may not have seen. His surviving correspondence from June 1890 to January 1891 contains no copy of a letter from him to Burns.

Young Mike Burns reports an unusual history: "raised by the officers in the 5th U.S. Cavalry." What of his parents? What of his people? Although the Carlisle files usually listed the names of each student's parents, and whether they were living or dead, this information is not given for Burns. He signed himself a "Mojave Indian," but the school listed him as an Apache—and he says he has an Apache wife. What was Burns's tribal affiliation, in fact, and what was his wife's? He is the only respondent to the 1890 questionnaire to note travels so extensive as to have taken him from the Atlantic to the Pacific, from Montana to Texas, and one may wonder how those had come about. Burns reckons that he "remained but one and one half years" at Carlisle, but his student file records him as enrolled between 1880 and 1884. And what of the other schools he had attended? There are other matters Burns raises about which one would like to know more.

As he said near the beginning of his letter, Mike Burns did indeed like to write. Between 1880 and 1884, the years he was officially enrolled at Carlisle, he had no fewer than nine pieces of varying length appear in one of the school's several publications. Three more of his contributions appeared between 1886 and 1890, after he had left Carlisle, while the last of his writings to be published by the school, a long letter he sent more than twenty years later, was printed in the 1912 *Carlisle Arrow*. Two more of his letters to the school—another one dated 1912, and one sent in 1915—like his 1890 response, have never been published.

Mike Burns's writing first appeared in the Carlisle *School News* for February 1881. A short piece introduced as "By a boy who has read through his Geography" (4), it informs the reader that having read through his geography book, the boy-author has "learned more marvelous things and about different countries, and different things that I have never dreamed about before," among them the fact that "there are cities and countries greater than in our America. As the city of London, Paris and Calcutta." But there is no need for concern, he writes, because if there should be war with these great foreign places, although "we cannot do anything on the water . . . let them come on land and [w]e can take two to one, or four to one on land. That is all for my story." The author signs himself "Michael Burns / An Apache boy" (4). There is not much to say about this first appearance; perhaps its most interesting feature is the fact that it is followed in the paper by an account of a visit to Baltimore by another Carlisle student at the time, a young man about Mike Burns's age, named Luther Standing Bear.[1]

Burns is next represented in the *School News* for April 1881, under the headline, "What Michael Burns, an Apache Boy, Thinks on the Indian Question." Burns observes that Indians

> have been treated bad by the white man for the last 10 or 15 years, decreasing our numbers. But that kind of treatment for my nation

will soon stop. As for the starting of Carlisle Barracks, and Hampton and Forest Grove it is the very thing our people needed.

Along with Carlisle and Hampton, he is noting the Forest Grove School in Oregon, the second federally funded Indian school, opened in 1880. It would move to the Salem area in 1885 and become known as the Chemawa School, still in operation today. Burns has found his theme, for, he goes on,

> Good many Indians are saying to their children here at this school that they wish them to learn the white man's ways. . . . But how does the white man know which way is the best to do. Was he born that way? No! Education gives him the light of knowledge. Education is the greatest thing human beings need, and to learn God's words. That they may have spiritual wisdom to go by, here and gain in the great, forever eternal life. (1)

This is the view of sixteen-year-old Michael Burns on the "Indian Question" in the spring of 1881.

Burns next appears in the *School News* for June 1881, with a short autobiographical essay called "An Apache Boy Writes Something About Himself." Brief though it is, it is a more developed composition than the ones he had published earlier, and I reserve examination of it for later, continuing here with his slighter efforts.

In August 1881 Burns is once more in the *School News* with "An Apache Boy Tells What He Thinks About Work." He begins by reporting that he has heard some "say the children of Indians at Carlisle Institution are put to work too hard, more than the youth ought to do." He appreciates the concern but observes, "I think the work we are put to do is just to make us more use and will be great and important to us, make ourselves something in the future to come." He then offers the personal testimony that having caught a severe cold in June, he determined nonetheless to work as hard as he could. "I went to my trade of carpentering. I worked for about two weeks, began to feel better," and "now the middle of August I have never felt happier before as I feel now" (1–2).

In October Burns is once more in the *News* with a brief piece, again largely unedited, titled "Anniversary," in which he celebrates the second anniversary of the opening of the Carlisle School:

> Last evening October 6th, the Indian Training School was two years old for the Indian education. And the school gave an entertainment of the amusement and exercises by the boys and girls who have been here since the opening of school and just came from their camps not know anything of civilization. (1)

He expresses dissatisfaction with some of those students' address to the assembly, and wishes "to say a word or so" about it:

> Some spoke as they were earnest of learning and do what they are told and also saying what they will do when they go away from here. But I am really alarm to say that they do not try as they should by Saying they are trying hard and will try hard to learn. Only one or two spoke last evening did it well, as my thoughts was, there were Ruben Sioux and Joe Taylor. They tried to speak more distinct they could not of course. But those two have been trying to learn in all thing they are to do. The rest who spoke I have never heard use English language out their mouth only when they had to say a word or so. But another thing they can hardly hinder themselves they are two many together of same tongue.[2] (1)

Burns has wandered from celebrating Carlisle's second anniversary to confronting a subject the school did not usually address, a measure of inter-tribal tension.

Burns remarks that although Carlisle has an English-only policy, the many Lakota students in attendance—"two many," as he writes—regularly speak to each other in their own language. In fact, he says, he had never before even heard some of them use English. Burns has a certain sense of superiority to these students in that, unlike them, he did not just come from the "camps"—the reservation—and already knew something "of civilization." But there is also surely some envy that there are so many Lakotas at the school who can speak their own language among themselves, regardless of the rules, while there are few or no students with whom he might speak his language. This may be all the more unfortunate in that in his eight years with the army, Burns would also have had very few opportunities to speak it, and he had almost lost the ability by the time he came to Carlisle.

Burns's next appearance in the *School News* comes in November 1881, with an essay called, "The Amount it Takes to Kill One Indian Would Establish Many Schools Like Carlisle and Hampton." In it, he argues that since "it costs nearly a million dollars in trying to kill an Indian and it only costs $150 a year to educate an Indian," surely education is the wiser course for the government to pursue. He writes of the Indians, "I think we can hardly blame them for trying to have their revenge as they remember the broken promises and slaughtering their poor children destroying them, such treatment would harden any nation" (1). Although he has in earlier pieces included himself among any Indians referred to, here he speaks of the Indians as "them" and "they," and uses "we" when speaking of those non-Indians who ought to withhold blame. But when he disparages "the ignorant race of Indians," who must "depend on the promise of our superior friends at Washington to help us," he shifts pronoun use to include himself among the Indians—and thus perhaps implies that not all of them are "ignorant" after all. He is not "afraid to say many things have been done unjust to the red men," and assures the reader that "Some time, or another we will come for that yet," his use of "we" again placing him among those Indians who in time will receive justice, when "The glory of Heaven will open for the red man to show his face to the Great Father." He signs himself "Michael Burns, Apache" (1).

The first *School News* issue for 1882 contained a number of brief comments by students on various topics mostly having to do with daily events at the school. **Jah Seger**, whose response to the 1890 questionnaire I considered in the previous chapter, affirmed at this time, "We are here at this school to learn a better way," for "at the Indian camp we all wicked." Seger understands that "Some white people they wicked also just same Indians," offering the bleak, concluding observation, "I think after while, no more Indian people" (3). **Lewis Brown** notes that he liked "to write English words, and . . . to try every day"; "Raymond, Sioux" expressed pleasure at his outing work on a farm "because I want to be strong man when I go home;" while "Ed. Myres, Pawnee," noted a snowfall that "is gone. It went to his own home." (3).[3] Burns's brief contribution is introduced as something "Michael Burns wrote in his diary." Whether or not this is an actual diary entry, it very briefly records that Burns had heard an "old man" in a store blurting out the words, "I'd rather see that man hung than to see him go to an asylum," in response to which Burns says only, "I presume he meant Guiteau." He is referencing the recent assassination of President James Garfield.[4]

Then in May 1882 Burns is represented by a frontpage piece in the *School News* titled "Communicated," a title I cannot logically tie to the essay that follows. It begins with reflections on American slavery and then moves to what are by now predictable observations and exhortations by Burns. He again praises Carlisle for the opportunity it offers Indian students: "we too may praise and feel thankful that we have the privilege as we have now at this school. Though we are not like the colored people. We have many opportunities to learn and to be as men and woman." There are also the familiar religious observations:

> The time is fleeting and once passed we can never have it back again. God has given us certain times to do what we want and we should not neglect his orders. While we have this opportunity let us be at our work. We are moving step by step onward to a civilized life. The first thing we have to learn is the English language. That it is a hard language to learn, there is nothing like trying at a thing.

He then illustrates his maxim with a description of his own attempt to learn "to walk up a ladder without holding at any part at all!" Though this might appear to be a rather less important skill than mastery of English, Burns reports that he nonetheless finally achieved it. "In all," the pious young man concludes, "we must never forget that God has promised to help those who help themselves, and we must ask him for help for he is almighty and full of wisdom" (1).

The last of Burns's writings to appear while he was still officially enrolled at Carlisle is a letter he had sent describing a lengthy outing assignment in "Lore City, Guernsey County, O[hio]." It appeared in the Carlisle *Morning Star* for September 1883, and I present it in full later and consider it in relation to the more developed account of the Lore City outing in his autobiography—the piece would mark a turning point in his life.

I return here to the autobiographical essay Burns had published in the Carlisle *School News* for June 1881, "An Apache Boy Writes Something of Himself." This is the first time he provides hints as to his background, although as in his 1890 letter to Pratt, he leaves a great deal unexplained. He begins,

> About the year 1871 or 1872 I was out in the wild country, with my native friends. And now I have looked back from the time I was taken prisoner, until the present time. I cannot imagine how I came safely through instead of death. But I found now that the happiest things ever happened. I was taken from the wilderness to the whites. (4)

In late 1872 Burns was indeed "taken prisoner," as he would specify in his 1890 letter, by "officers of the 5th Cavalry" who "raised" him.[5] The phrase "from the wilderness to the whites" suggests a progressive narrative of the sort implied by the titles of later autobiographical texts like *Tahan, Out of Savagery into Civilization* (1915) by Joseph Griffis (Chief Tahan) or Charles Eastman's *From the Deep Woods to Civilization* (1916).

At the time he is writing, 1881, the life story of Mike Burns, Carlisle student and precocious author, would indeed appear to be developing as a progressive tale of a Native man's journey to God and civilization. But the phrase "taken prisoner" suggests that there is quite another story that Burns is not yet able to articulate, an inverted captivity narrative, as I call it, and one he shared with the far-better known Dr. Carlos

Montezuma, with whom he also shared a tribal affiliation.[6] Burns would not begin to tell it fully for another twenty years.

Burns's *School News* text goes on to provide a boiler-plate account of the deficiencies of Indian ways in comparison to the superior civilization of the whites, things he had surely heard many times from the army officers as well as from Pratt himself—and, indeed, had attested to in his youthful journalism. As with his other early writings, he includes an extensive catalogue of Indian faults, like being "too fond of hunting, fishing, horse-racing and gambling," as if the first two were not subsistence activities but pastimes. He is also critical of Native people as fighters, although he qualifies this judgment by noting that "the Indians have been giving hard tussle for *our* hunting grounds"—resisting the invasion and depredations of white settlers—although "*we* are so few of *us* now in trying some way to do some thing for *our*selves" (4, my emphasis). To develop this theme further, he turns to "the Modocs in 1873." Although they were few, perhaps no more than sixty of them, he writes, they "held out until they were compelled to give in" (4).

In 1864, as a response to aggressive white settlement, the government placed the Modocs of northern California on the Klamath reservation in southern Oregon, an arrangement satisfactory to neither Native nation. In 1870 Kintpuash, a Modoc leader known to the whites as Captain Jack, led his people off the reservation, and in 1872 government troops were ordered out to force the Modocs back. At a meeting between the Modocs and General Edward Canby in April 1873 Kintpuash shot and killed Canby; Reverend Eleazar Thomas, who had been in attendance, was also shot. Kintpuash was captured in the summer of that year and hanged in October.[7]

As Burns describes it, the defeat of the small band of Modocs was not so much the consequence of the superior numbers and weaponry of the American soldiers but instead came about because

> God saw and watch the movement of the war and he just know how is going to be ended. If we had been good being and be faithful to his promise. We would not have had the suffering and hard time as

> have had serving in wilderness and darkness, afraid of the light that descends from the glory of heaven. (4)

The seventeen-year-old Mike Burns represents this history as he has learned it from the army, the church, and the schools he has attended; from the perspective, that is to say, of Christian Manifest Destiny. He does include himself—"We"—among those who experienced "the suffering and hard time" occasioned by this particular Indian defeat at the hands of the American army, but of course Burns is not a Modoc. "We did not know," he concludes, himself apparently among those who did not know, "what the day would be before us what had passed nor know how old we were only some of our old friends remembers by so many moons" (4). This would seem to be an attempt at the conventional rhetorical formula, "We did not know our day had passed," a familiar nineteenth-century trope assigned to the "vanishing race," along with its corollary, that soon only the elders would recall those former times.

Why would Michael Burns, who refers to himself as either an Apache or a Mojave, turn to the Modocs and their battles with white soldiers from late 1872 until their defeat in about May 1873? I suggest that Burns writes of "the suffering and hard time" of the Modocs as a way to speak of his own and his people's suffering and hard times in exactly those same years, displacing onto the Modocs the personal and communal tragedy he had himself experienced. Almost thirty years later Mike Burns would represent that history directly and from a Native perspective, writing, near the beginning of his autobiography:[8]

> All of my people were killed in a cave by the soldiers and by Indian scouts [enlisted by] the government. This was in 1872. There lived in [this] cave on the north side of the Salt River . . . 225 souls, men, women and poor innocent children [who]were slaughtered like cattle. (Burns 2010, 26)[9]

These words did not appear in print until 2010, long after Michael Burns's death.

We learn from the autobiography that Mike Burns's name was Hoomothya, or Wet Nose, and that he was a Kwevkepaya born about 1865. The Kwevkepaya, as Timothy Braatz explains, were one of "four Upland-Yuman speaking peoples—Tolkepayas, Yavapes, Wipukepas, Kwevkepayas—who have become known, collectively and misleadingly, as Yavapais" (2003, n.p.). "To U.S. citizens who entered Arizona in the nineteenth century, . . . all mountain bands, even the Yuman speakers, were 'Apaches' of some sort. . . . Kwevkapayas were usually 'Tonto Apaches' or simply 'Apaches,'" while other Yavapais were considered "Mojave Apaches" (Braatz 2010, iv).[10] It is no wonder that Carlisle recorded Burns as an Apache, or that Burns, as we will see further, refers to himself as Mojave, Apache, and Yavapai—although, curiously, not "Tonto."

On December 22, 1872, Hoomothya had been captured by American troops of the 5th Cavalry. Less than a week later, on the 28th of the month, he would be present as those troops, along with Apache, Pima, and Maricopa scouts, killed his father, his grandfather, and his siblings; his mother had been shot by soldiers some three years earlier.[11] The Salt River Cave massacre was merely one incident in what have been "called the 'Yavapai Wars,'" as Timothy Braatz writes, although his sense is that they are more accurately described as "one-sided, murderous onslaughts, carried out by well-armed and organized soldiers against scattered bands of malnourished and poorly armed families" (2003, 137), under the overall command of General George Crook.

Crook's work, as Daniel Herman bluntly puts it, "was killing Indians" (2012, 7), and Herman concurs with Braatz in believing that to call the campaign against the Yavapais "a 'war' is misleading. It was little more than a prolonged massacre" (74), and it took place in just the years that American troops were harassing the Modocs, 1872–73. The "worst of the atrocities in these years was the Skeleton Cave (or Salt River Cave) massacre in late 1872" (Braatz 2010, vi), named for the place where Hoomothya's family and other Yavapai families were camped, and where they would be slaughtered.

Although Hoomothya, as I have said, had not been with the Modocs in northeastern California, he was at Salt River Cave in Arizona on

December 28, 1872, and what happened there was probably still too fresh in his mind and too painful to reference directly in 1881. Captive of the soldiers and a witness to the massacre, Burns would later write in his autobiography that at the time, he thought, "No more hope; no more kinfolk in the world. What shall I do? Give myself up . . . to be killed there with my family [or] . . . forget those awful deeds against my people and take up a new and manly courage, and resolve to become a different man and hope for betterment in the future?" (2010, 29) This, at least, is how Mike Burns later articulated the dilemma he had faced as a boy of perhaps seven years of age. "The slaughter of my people," Burns would write, "ended at about four o'clock that afternoon. There is no history of a civilized race [that] murdered [others] as the American soldiers did to my people in the year 1872. They slaughtered men, women, and children without mercy, as if they were not [of the] human race. I am the only one living to tell what happened to my people" (29).[12]

He lived to tell what happened to his people because he had indeed been "adopted" by the soldiers, in particular by Captain James Burns, leader of the expedition against Salt River Cave. He was the officer who gave Mike Burns his surname and who was the "Officer in the Army," as Burns wrote to Pratt in 1890, with whom he "lived" for a time.[13] Although he could not then have formed the resolve, as Burns later put it, "to become a different man and hope for betterment in the future" (29), it should be noted that Hoomothya was not entirely without "kinfolk in the world." His parents, grandfather, and siblings had indeed been killed, by far the majority of his relations. But as he later explained, although he was in the custody of the American troops, some Indians "tried to persuade me to run away from the camp, and that they would take me so far away that the soldiers would never know where . . . to hunt for me" (42). Although he "had no near relatives" with whom he might live, he did learn that those Indians' intent was to take him to "a lonely cousin of mine," someone who "was crying so hard for me to leave the soldiers' camp." The boy remains reluctant to go to that cousin, but when he is told "that the soldiers were going to sell me off to some Pimas," or that they themselves "were going to kill me," he does leave the camp.

Hoomothya slept in a tent with Captain Burns, and Mike Burns gives a vivid description of how, "at about midnight, the whole camp was so quiet, and I noticed Captain Burns was so sound asleep" (42), that he managed to escape and make his way to a Yavapai encampment where he found his cousin, "the one who begged me to leave the camp of the soldiers to come to his place" (43). His cousin takes him "to the chief who was another cousin of mine, too" (43). Despite their relationship, the chief fears the soldiers' retribution if he were to take in one of their captives. He tells Hoomothya that he

> thought [it] best to go back to the soldiers' camp and to stay with them for as long as I could, for there was no use for me to come back to the Indians again, because there were no relations [of mine] left with whom I could live. . . . The rest said the same, and most all cried. (43)

Burns writes that he "cried, too, and went away," at this advice of a relation, the chief, his cousin. He returns to the soldiers' camp, carefully makes his way past Captain Burns, who is "snoring . . . hard" (43), and manages to pass the rest of the night with his absence undiscovered. This scene clearly marks the moment when he will leave his home country and his people to travel with the army. He will go on to fight Plains Indians—he is even somewhat boastful about the fact that as a twelve-year-old he had fought against the Sioux and perhaps even killed some of them when his cavalry troop was posted to the Plains and engaged them after the Custer fight in 1876. And he will go on to attend school with the officers' children, enroll at Carlisle, and write early pieces that are models of the assimilationist ideal, as we have seen. Burns presents just as clearly the moment when he decides to go home, after which time his writing begins to change.

Mike Burns's formal education began in 1879, when he was still with the 5th Cavalry, now under General Wesley Merritt at Fort Laramie in the eastern part of Wyoming Territory. One of the officers suggested that he "go to day school at this post with the officers' and soldiers' children." So, as he would write in his autobiography, he "went to school," and proved so avid to learn that "after four months I was ahead of all the rest of the class" (183). But the "next year, summer 1880"—just before he would go to Carlisle—he "did not go to school but . . . was asked to ride the mail route, . . . a distance of about one hundred miles" (183). It would be General Merritt, with the concurrence of his superior, General Crook, who obtained a place for him at Carlisle. Having looked at some of his writing while there, I turn now to what Burns wrote about the school and his education later, in his autobiography. In *All of My People Were Killed* the single chapter "Carlisle Indian School and Pursuit of an Education" takes up only nine pages.

Burns wrote that he traveled east to Carlisle in the fall of 1880, stopping on the way in Omaha and visiting with General and Mrs. Crook. As with Captain Burns's part in the massacre that killed his family, it is not clear whether Mike Burns was aware that it was Crook who had specifically ordered this. He continues on his journey, expecting to "telegraph to the superintendent at Carlisle Indian School so there would be a team to meet" him when he arrived in Harrisburg, Pennsylvania. "So," he writes, "I got safe to Carlisle Indian School in about the latter part of September 1880 where Captain R. H. Pratt . . . was the superintendent" (187). He was enrolled on October 26 of that year and "found there were only 175 pupils of all kinds of Indian tribes." "I was the one from the farthest west as a Yavapai Indian of Arizona," on this occasion not calling himself either Apache or Mojave. "But I was not sent from the reservation" (187), as almost all the other Carlisle students at the time—mostly Lakotas, as he had reported—had been. Burns writes,

> I had already been graded to third grade. There were hardly any in the whole school [who] were in that grade, so I had to study by my-self. It was very slow at that time, as I had to go to school in the forenoon and work around the other half of the day. (187)

His fellow students did the same, regardless of their grade. He continues,

> On Saturdays all the boys would be out policing the whole grounds. On Sundays we went to church and Sunday school in the morning.

> In the afternoon we all went to hear the preaching of Dr. Lippincott of Carlisle. He . . . preached the gospel touching almost anybody's heart. Since that time I have never heard a man give such a nice talk about God's teaching through the Son, Jesus Christ. (187)

Burns's own invocations in his school publications of God's will at work in Indian-white relations may well have been influenced by Lippincott's preaching.

"On other days, when we boys had spare time," he continues,

> I showed the rest how to play baseball. I had learned while I was with the soldiers at Forts Brown, D.A. Russell, and Laramie, Wyoming. I had a hard time making the boys understand, but by the next year there we got up sides and played games. (187)[14]

Thus, Mike Burns, a Yavapai from Arizona Territory, recounts how he brought the game of baseball to the Carlisle Indian School![15] The school first fielded a team in June 1886, and its initial game against "outside parties," announced in the Carlisle *Indian Helper* for June 25, 1886, was unfortunate. Playing against nearby Dickinson College, the Carlisle team suffered a 33–16 loss (3).

In the autobiography Burns writes that his first "outing" assignment took place during "the summer of 1881," when he "was sent to New York state to a farm close to [the] Hudson River" (187). En route to the farm, Burns paid a visit to nearby West Point, where General Wesley Merritt, whom he had known for some time, was in command. There he is treated royally and invited by General Merritt to become a West Point cadet himself. He declines, and—perhaps somewhat ruefully—imagines how well he would have done had he accepted Merritt's offer. He continues to the Hudson valley farm and he writes that when winter came he "was told to stay and go to the country school." He is being well paid, and the local school is only two miles away, so although the farm work is substantial, he does not regret further absence from Carlisle. He "stayed on . . . until next spring, 1882" (190), when he decides the time has come to return.

Back at Carlisle Burns finds another 125 pupils in attendance, a substantial increase in the student body. He mentions various activities only briefly—mealtimes, for example, but not classes—before generalizing about what he sees as a disparity between Carlisle's reputation and the education it actually provides:

> Carlisle Indian Training School has turned out its scholars and has placed many young men and women in . . . responsible positions as any white men and women whereby the officers of that school can well be proud to say they have done their work well. [However,] I cannot say I had got my thorough normal education at Carlisle Indian School on account of the fact that I did not stay long enough at that school. . . . I found out that [with] a half-day study at the schoolroom and the other half day just doing odd jobs . . . one could not progress very fast. (191–92)

To progress more rapidly in his education, he says, "I made up my mind to go to some other place where I could go to school all day and study my lessons all day and would work on Saturday for wages or board" (192). Pratt has no objection to this and obtains a place for Burns at a farm in Lore City, Ohio.

As mentioned, Burns had a letter sent to Carlisle from Lore City, Guernsey County, Ohio, dated September 24, 1883, published in that month's *Morning Star*. It is much more mature in narrative manner than some of his other writings of the time, and it is full of detail. Here it is in its entirety:

> I will give you an account of my journey from Carlisle to Lore City, Ohio, in the vicinity of which I am now making my home. You will readily recall my departure from school on the 12th of June last, in company with five others, four girls, two Kiowa, two Cheyenne, and one boy, Comanche. We had a pleasant trip together as far as Pittsburgh where we separated with regret. The other five proceeding to their homes in the west, Indian Territory.

While I went by a different route to Wheeling, West Va., and thence by the B.O.RR. to Lore City. Mr. A.W. Johnson the young farmer, with whom I am making my home, and his excellent wife, gave me a kind reception and from that day, now four months since, have treated me with the utmost kindness, doing all in their power to help me along. Although I am a member of a race between which and the white race, there has always been hostility and strife, and although I came into this community an entire stranger, yet no one has shown toward me or our people, the least spirit of enmity or prejudice. On the other hand all have shown me kindness and in many ways given me much encouragement. I have been a regular attendant at the church services and the Sabbath School at Lore City Pres. Church, and have been greatly benefitted thereby. On the Fourth of July I made an address, to a large audience, which was listened to with deep interest, and highly spoken of by a number of persons. I have also addressed the Sabbath School, thanking them for their interest in me, and making in that way an appeal in behalf of our race which is melting away as fast as ice does before the sun. I am glad to be able to tell you that my surroundings here are so pleasant and favorable and I hope that all the Indian boys and girls are as well situated. I often think of you all and would like to see you. I still feel that I am one of you; and it will always be a source of pleasure to me, to hear of the success of our school I remain yrs truly,

Michael Burns, Apache (4)

Burns is very conscious of himself as an Indian among the rural whites; it would be several years more before he stopped believing that his "race" would "melt . . . away as fast as ice does before the sun." He states his attachment to Carlisle and hopes for "the success of *our* school" (my emphasis). If this has not been edited, or was only lightly edited, it represents Burns's written English as about the best it ever would be. Years later, in the autobiography, Burns again recalled this Lore City outing experience:

> I stayed with these good people nearly two years. I went to school two winters and received a fair education including good, sensible English. . . . In two winters attending country school I learned more than if I had gone five years to Carlisle. (193)

In September 1884 Burns wrote to Pratt saying he thought his time at Carlisle should be up, and that rather than returning to the school from Ohio, he wanted to go home. Pratt responded, saying that he was free to do as he pleased. The time Burns had spent in New York state, and now in Ohio, explains why, although Carlisle listed him as a student from 1880 to 1884, he could accurately state in his 1890 response that he had been at the school—physically present—"but one and one half year."

When Burns informs Alvah Johnson, the farmer with whom he had been living, of his intention to return home, the man asks him to stay on. To encourage him to do so, Johnson offers Burns twenty acres of land, with a house and barn. He also makes clear to Burns that either of "two nice-looking girls whom you have been associated with and going together to meetings and fairs . . . would offer their whole soul to you as a husband" if he remained (193). This is a very substantial proposal, one that, had he accepted it, would have altered the course of Burns's life quite as much as an acceptance of General Merritt's proposal of a West Point commission. But, Burns says, "I had made up a strong mind that no matter what was said to persuade me to stay I was going westward . . . to my old home," and thus, he writes, "I foolishly said no" (193). "Foolishly" perhaps, in that he was not prospering in Arizona at the time he wrote these words, but as he represents it, almost inevitably. This is to say that at some deep level this young man—raised by cavalry officers, schooled (in part) at Carlisle, a committed Christian comfortable on an American farm—seems to have felt that there really was no choice but to go home.

Looking back on his decision, Burns later wrote,

> I was going westward where [I] belonged. In that way I might reach my home—Arizona. That land of my mother's was more dear to

> me than to have the whole farm of Alvah Johnson and all the girls he had near his home. I wanted to come out West and finally reach my home where my mother and father used to live—the land of Arizona. (193–94)

The young man starts west in August 1884, and although it will be some time before he gets to Arizona Territory, he does finally reach his home, never to leave it again.

Burns's train westward has a day's layover in Kansas, and he decides to use the time to visit "A good young friend . . . while I was at the Carlisle School, Elwood Doran, an Iowa Indian who lived on the Sac and Fox Agency in Nebraska" (197).[16] Once he meets up with his schoolmate and friend, Burns's plans change. Learning that a building at the agency needs to be repaired and the pay is good, he puts off his trip home and spends a month working with his friend, just as they "used to work together in the carpenter shop and the painting shop at the Carlisle Indian School" (198). Told of a Presbyterian school called Highland University in nearby Kansas, Burns, who had not mentioned any interest in continuing his education, decides to enroll.

Unlike the country public schools he had attended, and unlike federally funded Carlisle, Highland University charges for tuition, board, and books. The cost is substantial, but Burns has earned enough to pay, and, he recalls, he was pleased to be "attending a highly respected [school like] . . . a Christian young man" (198). He does well, although by March 1885—almost eight months since he had started for home—he can no longer afford the tuition, and must leave Highland University. He does so, however, with a letter of recommendation and a teaching certificate provided him by the president of the university.

A certified Indian school teacher would certainly have been welcome in Arizona Territory, but Mike Burns is not quite ready to continue his journey west. He has heard about an "Indian [school] a few miles out from the town of Lawrence, Kansas, which is called Haskell U.S. Indian School," and he "went out to make a few days' visit to Haskell School" (201). The Haskell Indian Institute—now Haskell Indian Nations University—had opened only the year before, in 1884. When

Burns arrives, the superintendent invites him to enroll as a student, but he wants to be taken on as a teacher.[17] He displays his teaching certificate, but the superintendent "said no he could not enroll any Indian as a teacher when he first entered the school." Burns makes a case for himself that the man is willing to explore, but then decides that it is not worth the trouble (201). I suspect that when he had rejected farmer Johnson's offer to marry and settle down in Ohio, he had not been fully conscious of just how definitive a decision he had made, so that his enrollment at the Presbyterian Highland University, and then his attempt to secure employment at Haskell, were, in effect, a manner of testing himself to see whether his resolve to return home was really as strong as he later said it was. Although his route is less than direct, he does indeed go home.

Burns's history is such is that he has soldier friends almost everywhere, and Carlisle Indian School friends in many places. Through these contacts, he will now work his way back to Arizona. Visiting nearby Fort Leavenworth, he is apprised of scouting work available with the army three days west at Fort Reno. From there he is to proceed to Fort Elliott, in Texas. To get there, he needs a horse—which he obtains with the help of "a schoolmate of mine, named Tom Roberts, a Cheyenne boy" (203).[18] Burns then obtains a letter from General Crook to General Miles ordering his transfer "out to Arizona to join the parties of scouts going after the Chiricahuas" (206), Geronimo's Apache band. This allows him to visit San Carlos, where he arrives "on about the 5th day of December 1885" (247).

He had not seen his people for thirteen years. Most do not recognize him, but, he writes, "one among them came right to me and called me by my Indian name. . . . He was a cousin of mine . . ." whose name "was Quak-ni-due-yah (Summer Deer)." He notes that this young man had gone "to Carlisle and returned to San Carlos as James Roberts" (247).[19] Burns completes his service in the Geronimo campaign, receives "an honorable discharge . . . in 1886" (281), and settles at the San Carlos Agency. Then, he writes, many older people, "women and old men came to see me. As soon as they came in sight they all recognized me as soon as they saw me [and] cried. They had long given me up as either having been killed or died many years ago" (249). Hoomothya has come home.

But Carlisle is by no means forgotten. In June 1886, for example, soon after coming home, Burns sent a brief letter to the school addressed "to one of his tribe" that was published in *Eadle Keatah* (the *Morning Star*). In it he picks up where he had left off some years before, encouraging the unnamed young Indian student to remain in school and announcing his own intention—never carried out—"to attend school at Tucson, A.T. as soon as [he] can pay [his] expenses" (8). Burns next wrote a letter to Pratt that the Carlisle *Indian Helper* published under the heading, "A Carlisle Boy in Arizona," on May 4, 1888. In it he wrote that he had "been a scout at the San Carlos Agency for nearly two years and have had no time to write to any of my friends in the East, and have read no newspapers. You can see," he observes "that it is very hard for a school boy to keep from falling back to ignorance" (4), something other returned students averred. "As for myself," he continues,

> I can fight my own way which I always have done.
>
> I left San Carlos Agency on the 15th with nineteen others, ten Prisoners, seven witnesses and three of us guards, for Tucson, where the prisoners are to be tried for murder.
>
> I am here as interpreter for the Mojave prisoner and the two Mojave witnesses. . . .
>
> When I was on the way here I met your first Lt. Davis, Commanding L troops at Fort Grant. He was much interested in me for I told him I was a scholar under your superintendence at Carlisle. (4)

"Lt. Davis" is Lieutenant Britton Davis; it is not clear why, in writing of him to Pratt, Burns calls him "*your* first Lt. Davis" (my emphasis) unless he means simply to reference Davis as a fellow soldier, like Pratt. Davis was an officer generally trusted by the Indians, and he had played a part in the campaigns against Geronimo in which Burns served as scout.

But Burns could not have met Britton Davis "Commanding L troops at Fort Grant" in 1888. Opened as a cavalry post in Arizona Territory in 1872, Fort Grant would play an important part in the government's engagements with Geronimo and the Chiricahuas. For a time Lieutenant Davis had indeed had a command, but he had resigned his army commission in 1886 and would not have been commanding "L troops at Fort Grant" in the spring of 1888, or even a year earlier, when this letter suggests Mike Burns had met him. I mention this only because it may, in a modest way, testify to the fact that Burns's sense of historical chronology was tending to vary somewhat from that of the mainstream culture. This is a matter I take up at some length in relation to an extended narrative he presents in his autobiography.

The next communication from Burns to the school comes two years later, when he addressed a letter to the *Helper* that appeared with the title, "Right from the Apache Field / By one of our old Pupils." Published in the issue of April 18, 1890, just two months before his response to Pratt's returned-student questionnaire, this letter marks a turn from Burns's earlier writing to and for the school. For he now informs the *Helper* that the Indians are not at all "melting away," and that its eastern readers would do well to attend to their diversity and the difficulty of their situations. No simple affirmation of the school's ethos, Burns's letter offers a complex report from the field by a Native participant-observer.

He begins amiably enough, writing, "I do enjoy the reading of the little INDIAN HELPER," which he had been receiving in the mail. The paper "comes and tells me the news and doings of my old friends and schoolmates at Carlisle," he continues. "It does not seem to me long ago since I left Carlisle Indian School"; indeed, it is "seven years since I used to prance on the green parade of the old Barracks," not something he had written of previously After these nostalgic reminiscences, he turns to weightier matters, taking up important events occurring far from Carlisle, Pennsylvania. He writes, "I have learned much interesting news through the HELPER about Indians throughout the United States. But I have seen nothing about the Apaches on the White Mountain Reservation" (4). White Mountain, to the northeast of San Carlos, is the reservation of which the San Carlos Agency is a part. Burns tells his readers of the "five San Carlos Apaches [who] killed a freighter named Herbert" there about a month earlier, about the beginning of March. He does not tell them that in response to the killing, ten men from Troop K of the 10th Cavalry, a troop of "Buffalo Soldiers" from Fort Grant, had been sent after the killers, leading to what has been called the Cherry Creek Campaign.

This was news that citizens of Arizona Territory would have followed, and Burns sought to bring it to the attention of the Carlisle paper's eastern audience. The campaign may have been of particular interest to Burns because the soldiers engaged in it came upon and killed some of the Apaches in a cave on the Salt River, near Cherry Creek—a cave on the same river where Burns's own family had been slaughtered. He reports that later, on March 10, 1890, "about eighty of the San Carlos Apaches" were sent "away to Fort Union, N.M.," eventually to be moved to Mount Vernon Barracks in Alabama, where Geronimo's people had been held for a time.

Burns's concern here is to inform his eastern readers that "there are many different families of the Apaches living on the White Mountain reservation"—certainly true of the San Carlos Agency as well—and that the Mojaves and Yumas are "Apaches" who speak a different language from Geronimo's Apaches or related groups, and who do not engage in the sorts of hostile actions charged to them. Burns writes that "the Mojave and Yuma Indians had no trouble since they came to this Agency from Fort Verde Reservation," alluding to the fact that his Yavapai people had been removed from Camp Verde and settled at San Carlos in February 1875.[20] He continued,

> and it is the reason that the Mojave and Yuma Indians wanted to return to Verde Reserve because the Tontos, and San Carlos Apaches have had many troubles and blame it on the Mojaves and Yumas.
>
> The news goes out saying the Apaches are doing so and so, but the Mojaves and Yumas never have killed or stolen horses from the white men.

I have seen in the Tucson *Weekly Star* about the expected outbreak of the Mojaves and Yumas sometime this year, but it is not true. Some one must have written false reports from here.

School boys from Carlisle most of them have been enlisted as scouts but George Nyrnah is still interpreter and doing well. There are reports that Fort McDowell of Arizona has been set aside for an Indian School, and I think it is well selected for the spot, for the Indian children to be educated.

I have been working on the farm since I returned to this Agency. Hoping you are all well and with much respect to all of my old schoolmates I am,

Michael Burns, Mojave Indian[21]

Engaging with and reporting on the affairs of his people is a turn for Burns, one that he develops in another brief piece he published in the *Indian Helper* for January 16, 1891. This would not, at first glance, appear to be the case in that the headline is "**Michael Burns thinks the Apaches Need a Missionary**," with Burns describing a Christmas celebrated at the San Carlos Boarding School attended by the families of some of its Apache students, who have no understanding of the meaning of Christmas. Consistent with an older manner, Burns writes, "I should think it is time for the Christian people to come out here and try to teach the Apaches something about Christ." But then, very much as in the piece just cited, he turns to say:

> The Apaches have a record of a wild people, but they are not as bad as the white people making up statements throughout the country. Of course it is the same with us as with every class of white people, there are some bad ones who commit wrongs and get punished for them, but many of the Apaches living on the White Mountain Reservation are a just, kind, and innocent people. (2)

I think his interest in speaking up for "many of the Apaches," among whom he would certainly include his Yavapai people, may well be the result of his decision "to settle down" and to marry, as he had written to Pratt in his 1890 letter. In fact, the woman he had married just two years earlier was not an Apache but "a Tolkapaya woman" (Langellier 2010, 274).[22] She was a western Yavapai named "Che-ha-ta, or Hata for short, meaning 'Laughter,' known among whites as Hattie" (275).[23] If Burns had taught her some of what he knew "about house-keeping," as he told Pratt in 1890, she had surely taught him to become fluent once more in the language he had rarely spoken since he was a boy, while her father, "a leader of the Apache Yuma, or Tolkapaya (Western) division of the Yavapai tribe" (Sullivan 2010, xxxiii), served "as a major source of information on events that had occurred before his birth, or while he was living with the soldiers or in the east" (Langellier 2010, 274). It was also around this time, the late 1880s, that Yavapai people were pressing the government to leave San Carlos and to return to their traditional homelands. Burns was "deeply involved in these events" (274), and in 1894 in his second letter to Carlos Montezuma, he would urge the Chicago doctor to come home, too.

Carlos Montezuma was also a Kwevkepaya, whose name was Wassaja, "Beckoning" or "Summoning." He was born about 1867 and captured by Akimel O'odham (Pima) people, traditional enemies of the Yavapai, in October 1871, just over a year before Hoomothya was taken by American troops. His story, too, is an inverted captivity narrative in that his captors sold him to Carlo Gentile, an Italian photographer and gold prospector, leading to an education exclusively among whites, although under very different circumstances than those of Burns.[24] Montezuma graduated from Northwestern University's Chicago Medical College in 1889, and then served for a time as a doctor in the Indian service in Dakota Territory, service he found difficult. He returned east to become school physician at Carlisle from 1893 to 1896, having years earlier begun a correspondence with Captain Richard Pratt, with whom he kept in touch all his life. Upon leaving Carlisle, Montezuma returned to Chicago and established a medical practice.

Burns had learned that Montezuma was the physician for the Carlisle School and wrote to him on April 16, 1894. The two would correspond for almost thirty years, until Montezuma's death in 1923, a correspondence that has not been collected, edited, or published. In his first letter to Montezuma Mike Burns says,

> I have seen your picture and on the back you have written about your capture by the Pima Indians. I have made inquiry about you and have succeeded in getting a little light of your relations. Would you know that the place named a high table land mountains on the range of the Pinal mountains was called by the Mojaves Mot-noo-jaih-mah-jo [?]. The camp was raid by the Pimas in the night during a very good moon light night.

He then reports that Montezuma's mother and father had

> come to San Carlos and stayed here afew years. But your father died and your mother learned that you and two others were at Fort Verde where the northern Mojaves camp in at the post.

He gives Montezuma's father's and grandfather's Indian names, and reports that the grandfather had died at the Salt River Cave. He continues,

> As I did not finished about your mother. ~~We~~ she started to go to Fort Verde but was overtaken by the Apache scouts and was killed.
>
> But we do not know anything about your sisters only your old uncle is the only one now living, an old chief . . . your father was my uncle. and we were boys and played together. My Indian name is Hoo-mo-thigh-a. . . . You was taken by the Pima Indians and about one year afterward I was captured by the U.S. soldiers . . . and were taken to east and attended schools at other places and have also attended the school at where you now at. Well sir, I would liked if you could answer me and hope that you will know me as your play-mate-as your jee-kave-vi—or cousin.
>
> Will hope to hear from you soon. . . . Ask some of the old teachers about me, as Miss Elly.[25]

Burns's written English is not quite as good here as it had been in years past (or perhaps it had then been edited more than I have supposed). This may be because, having been married for about six years, he had not been speaking English at home—although having been employed for the past four years by Agent Bullis, he would have been speaking and perhaps writing English some of the time. Montezuma responded on April 24—his reply is not among his papers at the Newberry Library, but Burns's letter gives that date as his response—and Burns wrote to him again on May 3, 1894.

Having initially addressed him as "Dr. Carlos Montezuma," Burns now writes, "My dear Cousin." He says,

> Your letter dated April 24th was just rec'd, and you may know how much I was pleased to get your letter. and have told many about you. and that afew remaining relatives joined together and shed tears. Many here know you well, and your name is Wise-ejah and your mother's name was Thil-a-gee-ah as I had stated in the first letter, that your mother heard about you and others were near Ft. Verde and she has gone away from here but Indian Scouts were sent out from here and over took her near Tonto Basin and killed her. But your sister I just lately heard is now living at Globe married to a Mexican and has many children and I going up there and she see her and will call her by the Indian name E-char-naw-ga-wow-spuckja it means scattering hair.

Having himself reacquired his native language from his wife and her family, Burns thinks Montezuma might be interested doing so as well. Along with providing several Indian names, he says, "I will mention some of our language as you are belonging to Mojave Indians. Maw-mee-du-ute jaw-lav-ve. It means that you have many relatives still living here," he says, despite having earlier told Montezuma that "your old uncle is the only one now living." And he explicitly invites Montezuma to come home, writing, "And would be glad if you could come and be a Doctor here." Before passing along other local news that might be interesting to the midwestern doctor, Burns writes,

> Some Carlos Indian woman that claims you are son but she is an other woman whose children captured along way from the place you was taken and she speaks an other language Your younger sister's name was Hoo-lac-vah. We heard nothing about her yet.

He reports that "there is going to be plenty juicy cactus fruit this year which our people goes many miles for them. We used to go to Wee-ka-ja sow-ah. That large mountain north of Florence." He closes, "This is all. and hope that you will write me a long letter again," signing, "I am your lonely cousin / Michael Burns."[26] Lonely though his cousin was, Montezuma did not go home to Arizona for almost thirty years more, nor would he ever serve as a doctor among his people. But he would eventually meet Burns, and the two would be in touch until the end of his life.

Burns may be correct in believing that he and Montezuma were relatives, but it is impossible to determine whether the two had in fact "played together" before the latter's abduction by Pimas in 1871. This is not a subject Burns addressed further in his letters. Early in his autobiography, however, Burns writes at some length of a train trip east that he had taken as a boy, with Montezuma also on the train for the first half of the voyage. Burns's narrative is interesting for, among other things, the ways in which it conflates the literate conventions he had learned from Carlisle—and from his experience in the U.S. Army and as a government employee—and the conventions of a traditional Yavapai oral storyteller.

Early in his autobiography, Burns wrote:

> There came to Camp Date Creek a one-armed man. I learned afterward that he was General Howard, and [he] said he was sent out among the Indians by the Great Father in Washington [the president of the United States] to have some [meetings] with chiefs. [He] wanted to talk of peace. (70)

General O. O. Howard had lost his arm in battle during the Civil War in 1862. In charge of the Freedmen's Bureau after the war, he went on to found Howard University in 1867 and to serve as its president until 1873. During those years he was also an Indian fighter who would soon be involved in the Modoc War and, later, the "Flight of the Nez Perces." Burns gives no dates here, although at the end of his trip, as I note, he provides a single date, and an important one.

Howard had come to Date Creek in May 1872 to gather a group of southwestern Indians to travel to Washington and meet with President Grant.[27] The object, as Howard wrote in his own autobiography, was "first, to cement the ties of good will, and, second to show [the Indians] the hopelessness of resisting a government as powerful as our own" (Howard [1907] 2019, 163). Howard would arrive in Washington with—probably—ten southwestern Indians in June 1872. Burns says, "There was a man there named Mr. Gentile, . . . and he had a boy who could speak Apache Mojave who was captured by the Pima Indians." "This Indian's name was Wissay-jah (Motioning to Come)," he writes, and "This man Gentile made an arrangement with General Howard to take us along" (72).

In the manner of oral narrative, Burns, writing, does not make clear who is meant by "us"; it might mean just himself and Montezuma, or it might include two other Yavapai men he has mentioned. Nor is it clear why General Howard would be interested in an "arrangement" with Gentile and his ward—who are not, as we soon learn, going on to Washington in any case. After days of wagon travel, the party arrives "on the opposite side of Albuquerque, New Mexico," where they find the Rio Grande to have risen so much that "flatboats" are necessary to get across (73). In two more days they reach Santa Fe, and then, Burns wrote, "It took four days and four nights"—narrative pattern numbers, but perhaps accurate[28]—on a stage to get to a city he believes to be Denver, where the entire party waits no fewer than fifteen days until "at last there came a train, and we were told to get on and get seated." After going "north and then east for two nights and three days," Burns writes, "Someone sang out 'Chicago!' At that place Mr. Gentile shook hands with us and [he] and the boy, a native and relative of ours, got off" (73). Absolutely no interaction with Wassaja during the train travel is reported.

"At last," Burns writes, "we were told we were in Washington. We were there about two weeks before President Grant was ready to see us" (73).[29] He then represents the meeting with the president, offering an eye-witness description of the man himself. Burns reports that when he first saw Grant, the president "was seated"; when he rises, Burns observes, "He was a short, thick-built man, [with] a short beard" (73). Grant urges his visitors to work for peace once they have returned to the Southwest and gives them a paper and a picture of himself to testify to the fact that he has named them all "chiefs." Burns continues, "So he handed us a written letter and a medal with his own likeness, and told us to show it to all the people who doubted our story" (74). Burns has narrated here in the first-person plural; he is one of "us"; he has been present and seen the things of which he speaks.

He then briefly shifts to the third person as he describes the president giving "*them* notes to go [so that *they*] could draw some money," going on to describe how "they" go on a steamer to New York and Philadelphia, see "many ships and steamers," and come finally to "a large city . . . that must have been New Orleans" (74, my emphasis). But despite the momentary shift in pronoun, it turns out that Burns was nonetheless one of "them." He next writes, "After *we* saw most of the great ships and steamers [*we*] were taken back to Washington" (74, my emphasis). There they have a last meeting with the president before setting out for home.

The return is an epic journey. First, the party travels by train, with a stop in Chicago as before, and then they travel for another "four nights and five days"—pattern numbers but also likely accurate ones—"to reach San Francisco." When Burns next has himself "on the steamer to the Gulf of California," and then onboard "a smaller steamer up to Yuma following . . . the Colorado River" (74), a contemporary reader may well think he is narrating a mythic voyage rather than actual travel from Washington to Arizona Territory. But the abundant notes to the autobiography make clear that Burns's description of such a trip "coincides with many contemporary accounts" (358 n. 27). This is to say that "not until 1878 did Arizona have its first railroad," and "travel by ship along the California coast and transfer to smaller steamboats for the trip up the Colorado River . . . remained common . . . until after the arrival of the railroad" (358 n. 27). It would seem that Burns's account is probably accurate.

But Michael Burns did not take a train trip with General Howard, Wassaja, and Carlo Gentile, to Chicago and then go on to Washington to meet the "short, thick-built" president with a "short beard." To be sure, Grant was about five feet, seven inches, and in 1872 at the age of fifty, might accurately have been called "thick-built," with, for the time, a "short beard." That Burns was fairly accurate about the president's appearance and got right so many details of the trip from Washington DC to Arizona and back suggests that he may have heard of it from the two Yavapai men who had actually taken it. He calls them "Paw-go-tay [A Big Man], who afterwards was given the name Jose Coffa . . . and another young man, his cousin, who was named Tee-god-a-waw [Hanging on a Limb], and who afterward was called Washington Charlie" (70).[30] Burns concludes, "We had been gone about seven months. It must have been the *early part of November 1870* [when we left], and when we returned it was the beginning of summer" (75, my emphasis); that would be the summer of 1871. These are the only dates he specifies, and they make clear that he could not have been on the trip he had described in great detail.

Burns cannot possibly have been on a train with Wassaja and Carlo Gentile in "the early part of November 1870," returning in early summer 1871, because at that time both Yavapai boys were still with their families. Wassaja was not captured by Pimas until the fall of 1871, while American troops did not capture Hoomothya until late December 1872. But Howard's trip to Washington had indeed taken place six months earlier, in June 1872. Why would Burns disqualify his account as factual and accurate for the historical reader by providing the dates he does? I think it is surely because Burns had learned at school and in the army and in government service that the dominant culture regularly preserved exact dates in writing, and he was writing for an American audience. But by the time he came to write, he had probably become immersed in oral story-telling conventions, and so presented the events with which he was concerned as an oral myth-narrative (in writing).

He tells the story of an earlier time as though he had actually been present, in the manner of the oral tradition.

To be sure, the narrator of a traditional oral story readily acknowledges that he was not, in fact, actually present by means of the formulaic repetition of phrases like, "so they say," or "as we have heard." But this does not disqualify the oral narrator from offering an eye-witness account, nor does it make the events recounted any less "true." The convention pertaining is that these things happened whenever they did, a long time ago—maybe as far back as November 1871. But in the present, I, the narrator, recount the events of which we have been told as though they are occurring here, now, before us; and I tell the story as though I had been there myself, so that you too can be there as you listen.

Of course, when it came to the history most important to Mike Burns—an account of what had happened to himself, his family, and his people—he understood completely that its authority would derive from the actual facts of his personal participation and observation. As he wrote to Montezuma,

> I am going to tell the white people that they have heard only one side stories about how bad the Apaches were to the whites, but the Apaches were forced to do so and they tried to protect themselves, their families, their homes and their land, and who would not do the same thing?[31]

And so he tells the story of the Salt River Cave massacre from his own eye-witness testimony, and this testimony, fully open to documentation, comes from the perspective of one who had himself suffered "how bad" the Americans were to the Indians. The autobiography, as edited and published, provides Mike Burns's full account of his capture by the troops, the slaughter of his family, his time with the army, education at Carlisle, and his return home to a life of hard labor as he reintegrates himself with the Yavapai people and works with them—sometimes in concert with his distinguished friend, Dr. Carlos Montezuma—to improve their living conditions.

In 1912 Mike Burns wrote to Carlisle Superintendent Moses Friedman on February 25, and again on May 31; then on July 27 he completed the questionnaire the school had just sent to returned students. The letters testify to his present condition—hard work at low pay—but they also review some of his very eventful life in the past. These communications to Carlisle suggest that he had either begun work on what would become his autobiography or was actively planning it.[32]

Burns's February 25, 1912, letter to Friedman appeared in the *Carlisle Arrow* for June 7, 1912, in a section of the paper called "Notes of Returned Students," under the headline, "From Bumble Bee Arizona, comes the following letter written by Michael Burns." I quote it in full:

> It is going on 32 years since I entered your institution (being a lonely Apache Indian from Fort Laramie, Wyo.) in the summer of 1880, by the request of General Wesley Merritt who was then a Colonel of the 5th U.S. Cavalry. The school had only 365 pupils. I remained there two years, then asked Captain Pratt to let me go out on a farm where I could go to public school and earn money. He sent me to Ohio. I stayed with a good family for nearly 2 ½ years. Then I made my way to Kansas, found work on some farms and went to a university for one year. In 1885, I joined the soldiers again and made my way back to this country, my motherland. I was a scout while Geronimo was on the warpath. I was employed as issue clerk in the Service for four years until the civil service reform went into effect. I have not had work under the Government since 1894. I would like to have the paper printed at the school. I am growing old and weak and cannot write as I used to write. (7)

It is the *Carlisle Arrow* that Burns wishes to have sent to him, and he was assured of its receipt by Friedman's prompt reply. On March 5, 1912, the superintendent wrote to say, "I shall be very glad to add your name to our Arrow list and will send you under separate cover, some of our publications which might be of interest to you."[33]

Burns's letter offers an outline of his life from 1880, when he came to Carlisle, until 1894, and his last employment in the government

Indian Service. He had lived a life of hard work, and now, at about forty-seven years old—average life expectancy for American men in 1912 was fifty-one and a half, although that of Native men may well have been less—perhaps he did indeed feel himself to be "growing old and weak." And if he was in fact unable to "write as [he] used to write," that would threaten the substantial task he had set himself, to tell the Indian side of what happened to his people.

This may well have been on his mind when he wrote again to Superintendent Friedman on May 31, 1912, further detailing his hard work and the low pay he received for it. Describing his own difficulties—these were not unique to him—Burns wrote,

> I have been so busy working daily at the very hardest labor cutting mesquite trees and cut the branches at 4 feet length for cord wood and some sticks at 7 ft. long . . . and it is for fenceposts. All of the trouble for $2.00 per cord wood. . . . and I do all I can get as it is a contract job. and I have about 8 to 10 other Indians to help me: and it cost much to live too.

We learn from Mike Burns that in 1912 in Arizona, "The flour is always at $5.00 per 100 lbs, sugar at 12 ½ cts. per lb.," and that an Indian laborer usually earns between $1.50 and $2.00 "a day. and no more: and have to board themselves out of thier wages. Worst still," he explains,

> all the Indians who are able to do anything they have to work in order to live. For the Government had stop given the Indians ration and clothing for the last fifteen years now. But it would not look so bad on the whole Indians if the Government would gave to some reliable person money enough to buy some food and clothing at certain time of the year: for help along the older Indians.

At this point Burns had come to the bottom of the sheet of paper he was using, and since there is no signature—something he always included—I suspect there was at least another page to his letter, which did not get preserved in his Carlisle file.

A few months later Burns responded to the 1912 questionnaire. He had probably received others since 1890 when he had written to Pratt—Friedman had sent out questionnaires in 1909, 1910, and 1911 as well—but if so, he did not return them. He had already written about himself to the school, but he seems to have welcomed this new opportunity nonetheless. Following are the nine questions the returned students were asked in 1912 along with Burns's responses to them in full.[34]

1. *Are you married and if so to whom?*

   Yes, to full blood Indian of the Apache-Mohave.

2. *What is your present address?*

   Bumble Bee, Arizona.

3. *Did you attend or graduate from any other schools after leaving Carlisle?*

   Yes. To public School at Lore City, Ohio about 2 years and attend University at Highland, Kansas. only received a certificate to become teacher.

4. *What is your present occupation?*

   Just only common labor such as to work on roads, clearing brush land for farmers and grub roots per acre.

5. *Tell something of your present home.*

   I have no fixed home, only stay at places where I have work to do.

6. *What property in the way of land, stock, buildings, or money do you have?*

   I have no property, no land, no stock, no any money. Only I have to work daily in order to earn a living for myself and family by hard labor.

7. *Have you been in the Indian Service? Army? In what position? How long in each?*

I have been Indian scout for the army many times and became an Issue Clerk for 4 years at San Carlos Agency under Capt. J.L. Bullis of the 24th Infantry from 1890–4.

8. *What other positions have you held since leaving Carlisle?*

   I have had no position under the government service since I have been released from that of being issue clerk at San Carlos Agency.

9. *Tell me anything else of interest connected with your life.*

   I have had much hard times since I have returned back to Arizona. and I was the first educated Apache Indian in Arizona in that time of 1885. When I reached San Carlos Agency there was no school and no man was employed to teach the Indian children. So the officer was acting agent who was Captain Pierce, the 11th Inf. He employed me to help a carpenter to repair the old building was there so that some Indian children could be gathered for school. I was paid at $2.50 per day as asst carpenter. When we had done the building in good shape there were about 75 long haired children from all sizes were gathered and I was still kept there to help the teachers to make the children mind them. and my pay was going on as usual at $2.50 per. and I thought I was doing well and by after awhile my pay and the position in the service will be greater but after awhile my name was lost and never was respected as being a helper to educate the wild Apache. But in 1887 I was again enlisted scout and after serve two terms I was taken in the Indian service again as issue clerk under Captn J. L. Bullis for 4 years. I have done my duties as well as first class clerk. There was no fault of my duty but some Indian Inspector made some reports about Indians were not qualified to hold a Government offices. Just to get some of their friends in view for that position I was holding. So I was turned out of my job in 1894 and have never got back in Government service since then. So if you can help me to get to some position in this country I will be ever so appreciate you. and I am

> completely worn out from working so hard as though having no education and I am laughed at by many.
>
> I am very respectfully
> Michael

His pay was $2.50 a day because he was employed by the agency as a carpenter; that is, he was not simply picking up what work he might find on a day-to-day basis, which would have been paid at a lower rate, as he had written earlier. Having said not long before that he was feeling old and weak, so too does Burns now announce himself "completely worn out from working so hard." If he was indeed "laughed at by many," that might have been the bitter result of his community's sense that the education he had obtained and of which he was proud had not served him well.

If we were to take this late communication to the school as the conclusion of the story Burns had for many years been telling of his life, it would indeed mark that story as bitterly ironic. Michael Burns, the protagonist of this narrative, has obeyed officers of the American army and fought on behalf of the United States; he has attended the flagship government boarding school; he has returned home and worked hard, only to find himself "worn out" and "laughed at by many." But Burns's story did not end here; there would be more positive additions to it, for all that he did not succeed in publishing his autobiography in his lifetime nor achieve a more economically secure condition.

He returned a brief postcard form to the school on January 8, 1913, writing that his "Occupation" was "grubbing stumps by contract," and in his "Remarks" noting, "I wish you all at the Carlisle people a happy New Year and do all in your power for betterment in future." An undated letter from Burns to Friedman is also in the file. It is written on "Department of Justice / Office of United States Marshal" letterhead from a Phoenix Court. I suspect Burns had once again been engaged as an interpreter for Yavapai prisoners bound for trial in Phoenix, and that this brief letter references the form he had completed and returned. He writes,

My Dear Sir:

I had received a card from you some afew months ago for inquiry to how I have been living since leaving Carlisle in 1882. I had answered all that was needed and returned it you. The little paper arrow comes very regular but I could not see anything about my home or mentioned a thing about me. So please answer me as soon as you can as I had asked the supt will help me through the Department to secure me a place at my present home now at Fort McDowell: back to my old people and I have found that they need much help there from the Gov.

So long sir:

I am yours truly,
Mike Burns

Burns is well aware that the Carlisle *Arrow*, which he is receiving regularly, often published letters from former students or excerpted answers they had provided to questionnaires they had completed. He has now left San Carlos and settled on the Fort McDowell Yavapai reservation officially opened in 1903 and comprising only a small portion of what had been traditional Yavapai lands. He once more asks for help obtaining an Indian Service position, something he would do again in a letter he sent to Superintendent Friedman on February 8, 1913, from Yavapai County, Arizona:

My dear Sir:

I have asked my representative of this new State the Hon. Carl Hayden to speak for me to have a place open at Camp McDowell to become a farmer or an issue clerk at that Agency. So an application blank was sent to me by him to fill out and return to him and I mentioned your name for reference: and I hope earnestly you will use all your influence as much as you can understand me. As I am about the only educated Indian living out west and had no chances to improve what I have learned while I was at School: nor could I help my people in no way: as I am now working at the hardest kinds of labor, which it requires no education. I have just merely made a living: for myself and my large family and lived up an honorable life:

Since I have been here among the Apaches: For the last 28 years—

I am yours Very respectfully
Michael Burns[35]

Arizona had become a state almost exactly a year before Burns wrote, and Friedman responded that while he could not recommend him on the basis of personal acquaintance—they had never met—he would consult the available records and do all he could for him. But Burns did not obtain a position as an agency farmer nor, as before, as an issue clerk.

The last letter from Burns to the school in his file is dated December 29, 1915. Burns probably knew that Moses Friedman had been dismissed the year before, although he may not have known that Oscar Lipps was now superintendent, since he addresses his letter "To the Supt. / Indian School Carlisle, Pa." Burns's letter comes from McDowell, Arizona, the Yavapai reservation. It too has never been published, and I cite most of it:

Dear Sir,

I have never written a letter back to old Carlisle Barracks since I have been away: that was in 1882 and it is going on 34 years. That school must have been changed to a wonderful institution and I may not know the place now. Being there only a few old buildings quarters for the soldiers and quarters for the officers and I cannot forget that old Guard house because I was locked in it with another boy for fighting him. It was at the entrance of that gate: going out to Carlisle a town by that name.

Of course Burns had written several letters back to Carlisle since leaving. That he had been locked up for fighting is not anything he had noted in his earlier writing, nor did he include any such incident in his autobiography. He continues,

> By the way I would liked to know how could it be arranged by the Supt and the Government to get transportation for 4 or 5 boys and one person to take them to Carlisle School from here to there and back as an escort.

He explains that he would like a nephew of his "and 3 or 4 cousins" who had been to the Phoenix Indian School to go to Carlisle where they would better "learn some useful professions." He develops some thoughts on that matter, and concludes,

> As I was a student once at Carlisle: and I would like to see some of my young kin folk to have a chance to enter that School: and to make arrangements for me to take them over: Sir,

signing himself "Michael Burns / (Apache)."

He received an answer—the copy on file is not signed, although I assume it was Lipps who wrote—on January 11, 1916, noting, "The old guard house you mention is yet standing and was in use until very recently."[36] The letter explains that no travel money could be provided any longer to anyone escorting prospective students to the school, and it outlines the procedure to follow in order for students to transfer from the Phoenix School to Carlisle. There is no further communication from Mike Burns to Carlisle, and I do not believe he ever saw the school again.

I close by returning to Hoomothya's cousin Wassaja, or Dr. Carlos Montezuma, and reference an essay by Maurice Crandall that presents what he calls "A Yavapai Perspective on Carlos Montezuma's Search for Identity." Crandall begins by noting that "As a people, *we* Yavapais regard Carlos Montezuma as a favorite son" (2014, 1, my emphasis).[37] Acknowledging the many aspects of Montezuma's life and work that have caused some to consider him a progressive assimilationist, Crandall constructs an alternative narrative, the moral of which is, "You can always come home" (23). What "Wassaja means to *us,*" he writes, "is "that *we* can always come home" (23, my emphasis). This is an unfortunately reductive reading of a complex life, eliding any number of factors in order to achieve a simple narrative of return.

For example, Crandall alludes only vaguely to the fact that although Montezuma worked diligently to maintain the Yavapais' Fort McDowell reservation, he had nonetheless spent his whole life trying to get the federal government to abolish Indian reservations altogether. Although their strong wills and large egos militated against the successful marriage of Montezuma and Zitkala-Ša around the turn of the twentieth century—they had been engaged for a time—a major point of contention between them was her determination to work for Indian people on Indian reservations and his determination—in large part influenced by his two years' service on western reservations—to work for Indian people while living away from the reservations. In 1913 Montezuma married Marie Keller, a Romanian-American more than twenty years his junior, and the two lived in Chicago, where he maintained his medical practice until near the end of his life.

As Crandall shows, Montezuma did attempt to learn more about his family and he also kept in touch with cousins—one named Charles Dickens—on the reservation. He also worked with Mike Burns to get the remains of those slaughtered at the Salt River Cave properly buried and memorialized. But Crandall entirely ignores the fact that as late as 1920—Montezuma died in 1923—this Yavapai "favorite son" attempted to enroll as a San Carlos Apache rather than remain a Yavapai. (The attempt was unsuccessful.) Crandall writes that Montezuma "had been living among [his Yavapai people], *even if not physically*, for many decades" (22, my emphasis), but surely one may have doubts. Montezuma had been violently torn from his "home" when he was no more than four or five years old, in 1871. But he simply was not ready to "come home," "physically" to live among his people in Arizona until near the end of 1922, when he was mortally ill. His story is perhaps all the more impressive for the many strands woven through it.

Michael Burns is not regarded by the Yavapais as "a favorite son"; his grave, not far from Montezuma's, is far more modest, and no prominent cultural site bears his name. But after years with the army, and school in the East, he did come home in 1886—as he would urge Montezuma to do in 1894—and he remained among his people until the end of his life. Nonetheless, for almost thirty years he continued to keep in touch with Carlisle. To speak accurately of Burns and Montezuma, it is necessary to recognize the ways in which their lives were marked by what W. E. B. Du Bois called "double consciousness."

If one is a Black American, Du Bois wrote, "One ever feels his two-ness—an American, a Negro; two souls, two thoughts, two unreconciled strivings in one dark body, whose dogged strength alone keeps it from being torn asunder' (Du Bois 1989, 3). For Native people Du Boisian double consciousness would be articulated by, for example, Charles Alexander Eastman in the last paragraph of his autobiography, *From the Deep Woods to Civilization* ([1916] 1977). That paragraph begins with the words, "I am an Indian" (195), and it ends—as does the book—with the words, "Nevertheless, so long as I live, I am an American" (195).[38] Like Eastman, neither Montezuma nor Burns "lived in two worlds," but they did find themselves living with the double consciousness of being deeply Indian and also—by circumstance and historical experience—being, in whatever changing degree, American. This is expressed in Mike Burns's writing from his days at Carlisle to the end of his life.

1. Superintendent Richard Pratt (*center*) with members of the Carlisle staff, a group of students, and—probably—a few staff children. Courtesy of the Beinecke Rare Book and Manuscript Collection, Yale University, New Haven, Connecticut.

2. The first class to graduate the Carlisle Indian Industrial School in 1889. *Back row, left to right*: Frank Dorian, Joel Tyndall, William F. Campbell, Edwin Schanandore, Thomas Wistar, Joseph B. Harris. Middle row, left to right: Kish Hawkins, Eva Johnson, Esther Miller, Lillie Cornelius, Julia Powlas. Front row, seated, left to right: Clara Faber, Kate Grindrod, Cecilia Londrosh. Photograph by John Choate. Courtesy Cumberland County Historical Society.

3. Dennison Wheelock, cornetist and bandmaster of the Carlisle Indian School Band, 1890. Photograph by John Choate. Courtesy Cumberland County Historical Society.

4. Etadleuh Doanmoe, about 1888. Photograph by John Choate. The printed caption reads: "Etadleuh Doanmoe, Kiowa. Taken prisoner in 1875 and sent to Ft. Marion, Fla.; was released in 1878; spent one year at Hampton Institute, VA.; entered Carlisle 1879. In 1882 married Tone-adle-mah, an educated girl of his own tribe, and reentered to the Indian Territory. Served as Helper in the School and Interpreter. In 1888 was appointed by the Presbyterian Board as a missionary among the Kiowas, but died soon after, having lived an exemplary life and exerted a good influence among his associates." Courtesy Carlisle Indian School Digital Resource Center.

5. Joshua and Julia Given, about 1886. Photograph by John Choate. Courtesy Dickinson College Archives and Special Collections.

6. Grant Left Hand and his father, Left Hand. Courtesy Cumberland County Historical Society.

7. John Dixon (*left*) and Cyrus Dixon. Courtesy Cumberland County Historical Society.

8. Michael Burns while at Carlisle, about 1882. Studio portrait by John Choate. Courtesy Cumberland County Historical Society.

DR. MONTEZUMA, APACHE INDIAN—Resident Physician at School '95-'97.
Trained Nurses at Hospital.

740

APPLICATION FOR ENROLLMENT IN A NONRESERVATION SCHOOL.

Full name of child Wallace W. Tyndall, Indian name is ... Name of father Joel W. Tyndall, Name of mother, ... Tribe Omaha Reservation, Omaha Degree of Indian blood of child, three-fourth Is either parent white, if so, which? Mother-¼ white Are either or both allotted? both On what reservation? Omaha Age of child, 18 What reservation school attended? Fort Yuma School How long? about 2 years If ever enrolled in a nonreservation school, name of school, Chamberlain, S. D. When? year 1901–1903 How long? about 2 years If ever dismissed from a school, where, —— ; when, —— and for what reason? ——

(Signed.) Joel W. Tyndall,

NOTE—The above blank to be signed by the child, if old enough to understand its import; if not, by the parent, guardian or other person cognizant of the facts.

CONSENT BLANK.

I, Joel W. Tyndall, parent, guardian or next of kin of the above-named child, Wallace W. Tyndall, do hereby consent to transfer of enrollment for a period of five (5) years in the Indian school at Carlisle, Pa. Dated at Fort Yuma School, Cal on the 22nd day of April, 1905.

(Signed.) Joel W. Tyndall.
(Parent, Guardian or next of kin.)

PHYSICIAN'S CERTIFICATE.

I hereby certify that I have personally examined the above-named Wallace W Tyndall, and have found him physically sound, and recommend the transfer so far as his health conditions are concerned. Dated Yuma Calif. on the 22nd day of April, 1905

(Signed) J. A. Kitchenside
School Physician

AGENT'S OR SUPERINTENDENT'S INDORSEMENT.

Fort Yuma School, Apr 22, 1905

The statements concerning the above-named Wallace W Tyndall are believed by me to be correct, and I hereby recommend the transfer.

(Signed.) John S. Spear,
~~U. S. Indian Agent~~ or Superintendent

NOTE—Age limits, twelve to twenty years, preferably fourteen to eighteen. Students must be at least one-fourth Indian, preferably full Indian.

9. (*opposite*) Dr. Carlos Montezuma and nurses at Carlisle. The caption reads: "Dr. Montezuma, Apache Indian—Resident Physician at School 1895–97. Trained Nurses at Hospital." Photograph by John Choate. Courtesy Dickinson College Archives and Special Collections.

10. (*above*) Wallace Tyndall's application for nonreservation boarding school admission. Courtesy Carlisle Indian School Digital Resource Center.

11. Richard Davis and family. Note reads: "Richard Davis (Cheyenne) Richenda-Mary Nannie Davis (Pawnee)," about 1891. Photograph by John Choate. Courtesy Dickinson College Archives and Special Collections.

12. Mattie Reid Luther, her husband, Martin Luther (*left*), her older son, James R. Luther, and her younger son, whose name is not given. Photographer unknown. Courtesy Carlisle Indian School Digital Resource Center.

Post-Office.

WILLIAM PAISANO, Post-master.

Casa-Blanca, New Mexico, Jan , 1913

Mr. M. Friedman. Supt.
Carlisle Indian Training School.
My Dear Friend!
I am such in a
big hurry in writing to you this
I am been elected Governor
this year again. and also I have
been appointed delegate to
Washington D.C. on busine[illegible].
Trust Deed proposition. and
we have to start tomorrow on
1st of Feb. and from Santa Fe. N.M.
we all have on 2d inst. two
delegate each Pueblo. Indian[illegible]
in New Mexico. and if possible
for you to do us your help a[illegible]
to allow Sicini Nari. to come

13. William Paisano letter to Superintendent Moses Friedman, January 31, 1913. Courtesy Carlisle Indian School Digital Resource Center.

U. S. Post-Office.

WILLIAM PAISANO, Post-master.

WILLIAM PAISANO,

DEALER IN

General Merchandise

FEED AND PROVISIONS,

CATTLE BOUGHT AND SOLD

COUNTY OF VALENCIA.

1473 Casa-Blanca, New Mexico, Jan 31—, 1917

to Washington. that is, when we get there then we can call by phone. that is if he can come at his own expence to do something for the sake his own land, and people. this is only sending ahead so you can have a talk over with him. I will bring two Carlisle man or students as my interpreters Ulysses G. Paisano, and Yamie Leeds, all Laguna people in the meeting are expect Mr. Nari him to help less or much that is if he can, and if you can spare him a day or two either I will be glad. I am your Sincerly Friend. Wm Paisano.

14. (*above*) Three Carlisle Indian soldiers. The caption reads: "#1 Little Hawk, #2 Jannies, #3, Wm. C. Bull." The note below reads: "Frank Jannies, Sioux, Entered Carlisle 1883; remained the full term of five years; was employed as a carpenter at Rosebud Agency S. Dak.; enlisted in the Army Dec. 1891; became 1st Sgt. Co. I 16th Infry., and served as school teacher at the Post. William C. Bull and Samuel Little Hawk, Also members of the same tribe, served their full term at Carlisle and enlisted in the Army July, 1892." Courtesy Carlisle Indian School Digital Resource Center.

15. (*opposite*) James E. Johnson (Stockbridge) in football uniform, about 1903. Photographer unknown. Courtesy Carlisle Indian School Digital Resource Center.

16. Thomas Metoxen, his wife, Elizabeth Sickles, and their four children, about 1909. Photographer unknown. Courtesy Carlisle Indian School Digital Resource Center.

17. Fred Sickles, about 1909. Postcard photograph. Courtesy Carlisle Indian School Digital Resource Center.

CHARLES E. DAGENETT (*Peoria*)
Vice President on Membership.

Mr. Dagenett, who is the U. S. Supervisor of Indian Employment, has been one of the most energetic wokers since the beginning of the Society. In many a financial crisis he has been the business head.

18. Charles Dagenett, about 1911. Society of American Indians, photographer unknown. The caption reads: "Charles Dagenett (Peoria), Vice President on Membership." The printed note reads: "Mr. Dagenett, who is the U.S. Supervisor of Indian Employment, has been one of the most energetic workers since the beginning of the Society. In many a financial crisis he has been the business head." Courtesy Carlisle Indian School Digital Resource Center.

19. Charles Bender, pitching for the Philadelphia Athletics, about 1910. Photographer unknown. Courtesy Carlisle Indian School Digital Resource Center.

20. Superintendent Moses Friedman shaking hands with Jim Thorpe, around 1912, as coach Glenn Warner, Olympic marathon runner Lewis Tewanima, and others look on. Photographer unknown. Courtesy Carlisle Indian School Digital Resource Center.

3

"I am interested in my life"

Further Words from Former Students of Carlisle

Like Mike Burns, many other former students who responded to the 1890 questionnaire answered Carlisle's requests for information in later years; several who had not written in 1890 did write back later. Pratt does not appear to have sent out another questionnaire between 1890 and his departure in 1904, but in 1907 his successor, Major William A. Mercer, sent a very brief questionnaire to graduates of the school. Moses Friedman, superintendent from 1908 to 1914, was much more active in contacting returned students, sending them nine to twelve question forms in 1909, 1910, 1911, two in 1912, and then again in 1913 and 1914, before he was dismissed. There are also communications on file to Oscar Lipps, superintendent in 1914–17, and a few to John Francis Jr., superintendent during Carlisle's last year of operation. In addition, there is a body of letters and news clippings sent to the school by former students over the years.

It needs to be said once more that those who kept in touch with Carlisle are far fewer than those who did not, and their silence may indeed testify to memories of the school that were anything but positive. This must be kept in mind as we read from the record that is available. But that record is substantial, documenting the thoughts and feelings of a very considerable number of young and no longer young Indian people about their time at school and their subsequent lives. These former Carlisle students, to cite Philip Deloria once more, were members of "an incredibly complex Indian world" (2013, 39), and their words can help render that world vivid and real, often providing a detailed and nuanced sense of how it felt to live what would later be called "history." Their descendants and many other readers, I hope, will find their words of interest.

All but three of the communications on file are handwritten, and none has been transcribed before; presented here are my transcriptions with no additions, corrections, or other editorial amendments; ellipses, once more, are mine, indicating omitted material. Like the 1890 responses, the originals of materials in this chapter are available for any reader to consult on the Carlisle Indian School Digital Resource Center website, under "Student Records."

While **Julia Powless Wheelock**, a Wisconsin Oneida, and **William Francis Campbell**, a White Earth Chippewa, were the only members of the class of 1889 to respond to Pratt's questionnaire of the following year, other graduates of that first class would correspond with the school in later years—as would Wheelock and Campbell. I begin with these two and go on to some of the 1889 graduates who had not responded to Pratt in 1890.

William Campbell, as noted, had something of a private correspondence with Pratt. But his only further communication with the school was his response to the brief questionnaire Superintendent Mercer sent to Carlisle graduates in 1907. Dated January 21, 1907, Campbell's reply states that he is married, that his address is Mahnomen, Minnesota, and that he is a lawyer and "County Attorney of Mahnomen County, Minn." In answer to a question asking whether he has "lived in the East any part of the time since [his] graduation," he informs Mercer, "Three years in Washington as Attorney for Chippewa Indians." These are his last words to Carlisle; in large handwriting across the upper righthand corner of his response is the word "Dead." I have not found the year of his death.

Julia Powless Wheelock wrote to the school several times, so that it is possible to get a sense of her life for almost thirty years after her graduation. She too responded to the brief 1907 questionnaire, writing that she was "married to Charles Wheelock" and that her "present address is Wind River, Wyo.," far from her Wisconsin home. At Wind River she is "laundress at the Wind River school, Shoshone Agency."

Responding to a question asking whether she has been in the Indian Service, she says, "Right after my graduation I became a day school teacher at Oneida Wis for two years. Then as asst cook at Osage Indian School Okla one year and laundress at this Wind River School for three years." She says she has not lived or worked in the East. A bit later, in March 1907, she wrote to Major Mercer, either in response to a letter he had sent her or simply wishing to expand on what she had said on the brief questionnaire. Here is her letter in full:

> Dear Friend,
>
> Since you would like to hear something about the graduates as well as the returned students, I will try and tell all I know. William Shakespeare was one of the old students at Carlisle. He is doing well, he is a government farmer. Dresses in citizens clothes. His children are attending this school. Jimmy McAdams is also another student from Carlisle. He is also doing well. He was a school gardner for a time and was a good employee. There are no graduates in this locality from Carlisle. I met Charlie Driscal today, and spoke well of Carlisle. There are few of the boys at this school would like to go to Carlisle this year. I like the work in the Indian Service pretty well. My husband is asst engineer and Band leader. The band are doing fine this year. I have two girls that I intend to send them to Carlisle as soon as they are old enough. I am anxious to see them have better education than I have. I am always thankful for what Carlisle has done for me.
>
> My girls are 10 and 12 years old respectively. They are both bright and quick to learn. They have studied music. But since we been here the is no one that they can take lessons from. I would like so much to have them take a special course in the music if they go to Carlisle.
>
> Yours Respectfully
> Julia P. Wheelock

One of the pleasures of reading these files comes not only from learning more of people already known in some measure but from encountering others who had not thus far come to attention. Former Carlisle students, like the alumni of a great many schools, often kept in touch with one another, sharing and passing along news. Thus we hear of **William Shakespeare**, a Northern Arapaho whose Indian name in English was War Bonnet, who had entered Carlisle at the age of sixteen in 1881 and left because of poor health in 1883.

He had sent a very brief response to the 1890 questionnaire saying that he was "getting along very well," with a "good house," that he was "working at Mission"—the Shoshone Agency—and that he was "also Indian Police." At the time, he wrote, he was "not able to sith on chair long and with for I am sick for two weeks now" (Part 5). Years earlier, in 1883, when he had returned home from school very ill, Shakespeare's father, Scarface, concerned for his son, had sent him south to Indian Territory to learn about the curing powers of peyote. Shakespeare returned much improved in health, and "The Northern Arapahoes give William Shakespeare credit for bringing the cult [*sic*] to Wind River, Wyoming about 1895" (Trenholm 1986, 296–97). It is not surprising that Shakespeare did not mention his experience of peyote's healing powers to Pratt, who would not have approved.

Virginia Trenholm explains that "Shakespeare taught the ritual to John Goggles, who later went to Indian Territory, where he studied under Cleaver Warden. . . . Thus evolved what is known as the Arapaho Way at Wind River" (297). As it happens the practiced peyotist **Cleaver Warden** had also been a Carlisle student, enrolled at the school from 1880 to 1887. Jesse Rowlodge, an Arapaho in his eighties interviewed by Julia Jordan in 1967, remembered Warden as one of those "that organized this Native American Church" (Jordan 1967, 13) among his people. As for John Goggles, he had not attended Carlisle, but he did send his son Christopher to the school, and we may note that **Christopher Goggles**, enrolled at Carlisle early in June 1904, ran away the very next month.

But this did not prevent him from keeping in touch in later years. He responded to the 1909 questionnaire, and wrote again in 1910 to say that he was well, and avoiding tobacco and whiskey. In March 1912 Goggles wrote to Superintendent Moses Friedman at some length, mentioning in passing that his mother's sister was married to Cleaver Warden. Late in his letter Goggles, the one-time runaway, addresses Friedman warmly as "Moses," the only Carlisle student I have found on record to do so.[1]

Although Julia Wheelock had found Shakespeare wearing "citizens clothes" in March 1907, as mentioned in the introduction he "had three co-wives" (Fowler 1978, 230). He does not seem to have experienced his English name as odd or discomfiting, bestowing it upon his son by his youngest wife. Bill Shakespeare, a student at the Wind River School at the time Wheelock is writing, became "a Hollywood actor and a world traveler, and in later years . . . an informant for anthropologists studying Arapaho language and culture" (Fowler 1978, 227). He did not, however, follow in his father's footsteps and attend Carlisle.

Here are some further communications from William Shakespeare to consider before going on to the others mentioned by Powless in 1907. Shakespeare would respond to a questionnaire he received from Superintendent Friedman in 1910 to say that he and his wife—he lists only one, "Cut [?] Nose Arapahoe tribe"—lived in "Arapahoe Wyoming," on the Wind River Reservation; that he "controlled several allotments"; and that he had "some land leased to a white man for farming." As for Indian Service employment, he wrote that he had been "police, farmer, herder and in all about twenty years." He had also by then served as a consultant to the anthropologist Truman Michelson. In 1917 Shakespeare sent a lengthy letter to John Francis Jr., superintendent during Carlisle's last year of operation. It is dated April 29, 1917, and it also comes from Arapahoe, Wyoming. Its address and first line have been cut off in the scan of the original:

> I am still alive out here in Wyoming where I am located and doing very well on my farm only now I am kind of over or run down by hard works. Its a long time since I left there the year was 1872 and the Supt was General R. H. Pratt and the more I thank him for what he has taught me I only were at second reader and that help me well I can talk with a business man alright the reason I left the school so soon is I were in very ill health

> Now I will tell you about my pass present years since I left the school.... Indians when so foolish on account that what they call Ghost dance I been giving big feast and I thought I was a big chief then + when I broke nobody give me a feast then when I first came back that is returning home I start to teach my people the way of white people education farming and I was the first one in my people to wear a hat but my people were still had a feathers on their head and few years after I show them how school means I have been wishing to visited the Carlisle once more but I am getting old now.... I have seven children five are married + two are attending school yet their are growing very well I support them by my own hand + raise them in doing agriculture from my own land too I have liveing at my allotment few years after I returned home and still I am located here as my father found this place for me to run 4 years ago when I was a boy he use to tell me that I should go to school finely the day came when I was sent to Carlisle I was the first one to go to school off my people my father just died on 1910 he was 104 years old.... At this part of Wyoming where I am located the Ground has his White Blanket yet well I must now come to close with kind and + best wishes to dear old Carlisle its make think of it when I receive the Carlisle arrow + always enjoying reading them giving my best wish to all
>
> I Remain
> Mr Wm Shakespeare

Like some other former students, Shakespeare tends to avoid punctuation, giving a more oral feel to his writing. He notes that he has been receiving the Carlisle *Arrow*, and has been pleased to have it, and apparently there was still snow on the ground in Wyoming in late April of 1917. Less than a week later Superintendent Francis responded to Shakespeare's letter to say he wished to have it printed in the *Arrow*. I imagine that would have pleased the writer, but because the United States had entered World War I only a few weeks earlier, and the *Arrow* had begun to fill up with war news—many young men who had been and currently were at Carlisle had joined the army, and a number of

Carlisle women joined the nursing corps—Shakespeare's letter does not seem to have appeared. It is a fine piece of writing and I am pleased to publish it here.

Shakespeare's long-lived father, Scarface, an Arapaho chief, had been among the people's leaders who sought to avoid conflict with the white invaders, and he chose to send his son to Carlisle, the first Arapaho leader to do so. Shakespeare misremembers the date he left the school more than twenty-five years earlier; it was 1882, not 1872, and unsurprisingly, he does not mention the role of peyote ceremonialism in improving his health. He does refer to what he considers the foolishness of the Ghost Dance, an opinion shared by a much later Arapaho student at the school, the artist **Carl Sweezy**.

As for the others Powless Wheelock mentioned, **Jimmie McAdams**, a Shoshoni, had entered Carlisle with Shakespeare in 1881. He seems to have left after three years, but then reentered, and he remained enrolled until 1893. He responded to a very brief questionnaire from the school in 1913, indicating that he was still at Wind River and, like Shakespeare, farming. **Charlie Driscal**, as Wheelock gives it, also a Shoshoni, has more different spellings for his name in the Carlisle records than any other student I have encountered, and that is saying something. He appears as Charlie Driskell, Driscall, Driscoll, and Driskill. He was sixteen years old in 1907 and, according to his student records, still enrolled at the school when Julia Wheelock ran into him at Wind River. He had by then been at Carlisle for three years. Although Wheelock says she had spoken well of the school to him, he would nonetheless run away—or, more precisely, he "Did not return from leave"—the following year, 1908. But like several other Carlisle students who had taken it upon themselves to leave the school, he did not entirely abandon it. Driscoll would respond to a brief 1911 questionnaire sent by Carlisle to say that he was at Fort Washakie, on the Wind River Reservation, living in a tent with a group of other men, and digging irrigation ditches. Twenty years old at the time, he wrote that he was not married, and he had "120 or 160 acres of allotted lands," although he was apparently not working them.

Sometime before November 1907, Julia Wheelock's husband of more than seventeen years, **Charles Wheelock**, died. We learn this from a letter in her file from the Carlisle School to the Indian Bureau dated November 1907, noting that she had applied for a teaching position at the school shortly after the death of her husband. At that point there had been no opening for her, but the letter indicates a place has now become available, and the school hoped she might indeed come to teach at Carlisle and enroll her two daughters as students. The letter informs the Bureau that she had formerly been a teacher at an Oneida day school and that her "personal record shows that she has passed the teacher exam."

But when Assistant Commissioner Henry Greene searched Bureau records under the names Powlas and Wheelock—I assume he also searched Powless—he could find nothing to indicate that she had ever taken the teacher exam. This means she had been hired by the Oneida day school strictly on the basis of her having graduated from Carlisle, by no means an unusual practice. Commissioner Greene did find that she had "failed in the assistant teacher examination in 1904," but, he wrote, if she would take the exam again and be successful, the position at Carlisle could be hers. No correspondence from Wheelock about this matter appears in her file, and because by this time she had worked as a cook and a laundress for many more years than she had earlier taught, Julia Powless Wheelock probably did not once more sit for the teaching exam.

On March 23, 1908, she wrote to Carlisle Supervisor Charles H. Dickson responding to his invitation to attend the school's forthcoming commencement ceremonies, an invitation the school extended to many of its former students. Her letter has a large handwritten X that appears to be a crossing-out through its first page, and there are markings on its second page that appear to join several paragraphs into one. Those markings are surely not by Powless herself, and I assume they were made at the school with the intention of preparing her letter for publication in one of the Carlisle newspapers, words of encouragement, as she says, to the new graduates. I have not found it in any of Carlisle's publications, but here it is in its entirety:

Dear friend,

I wish to thank you for your kind invitation to your commencement exercises. I heartily regret being so situated that I cannot go as I can not be spared from my work here. But these few encouraging words to the class of 1908 will no doubt be as good as if I was there personally. It seems impossible that it is 19 years since I left Carlisle. It seems but a few days when I look back to my school days there. I have always been very thankful for what Carlisle has done for me and it has helped me out wonderfully in every thing that I have undertaken to do. I have been in the Indian Service part of the time and part of the time in my own home since I left school. I sincerely hope that the young students that are going out into the world to fight their own battles futures will be bright and crowned with success. We find in our paths sunny days as well as dark days. But always keep up our courage and overcome difficulties by being truthful and honest.

Wishing you God speed,

I remain yours sincerely,
Julia Powless Wheelock

Carlisle heard from her again the following year in response to the 1909 questionnaire, when Wheelock listed her address as Morris, Minnesota, and in response to the question asking whether she is married, she wrote, "I am a widow for nearly two years," her husband having died in 1907, as noted. She says she has "never attended any other school but Carlisle," works presently as a laundress, and has "a good home. My home is on the farm with a nice barn and a frame house with four rooms in it." As for money in the bank, she writes that she has a "Considerable sum." Question nine asks about Indian Service work, and she says, "I have been in the Indian Service most of the time since I left Carlisle. I was a teacher in a day school for three years then I resigned. Few years later I was appointed as laundress which I have held since." The tenth question asks about other positions, and Wheelock replies, "In 1904 my husband was given a transfer as asst engineer and band leader at Pawhuska Okla and I was given the position as cook which I held for a year."

Question eleven asks whether she had "done anything for the betterment of [her] people," to which she replies,

> I think I have done much good for my people in every way and in speaking of educating the Indians. I think it pays to educate the Indians just as much as the white people. I know a great many returned Carlisle students that are doing well. They have good comfortable homes and are good citizens and I know some that are in the Indian Service that are really doing better work and better employees then their pale faced brothers and sisters. I am thankful for what—

she uses the space for the twelfth question, "Tell me anything of interest connected with your life," to continue—

> —Carlisle has done for me and I hope that the Carlisle School will continue to help us for many years to come for the Indians. There are a great many young Indians that are very anxious to go to Carlisle and I have always given the very highest praise for Carlisle. One can always tell the difference between the educated Indians and the uneducated. The uneducated do not know the value of money or property and are cheated from the white people in their land &c. While the educated ones transact business as good as any white person. A great many Indians would not be what they are today if it had not been for Carlisle or some other big school.
>
> Very Respectfully
> Julia Powless Wheelock

In 1910 Wheelock returned to Keshena, Wisconsin, where she had obtained an appointment as an Indian Service assistant matron; and in 1913 she married Nelson Metoxen (1869–1963), also a member of a prominent, progressive Oneida family. They had met while she was laundress at Morris, Minnesota, where Metoxen had an appointment teaching blacksmithing and wheelwrighting; they may have known each other before.

Nelson Metoxen had attended the Hampton Institute in Virginia, which he had entered in 1889 at the advanced age of thirty. The records indicate that he ran away from his first outing assignment in the summer of 1890, but then returned to the school the following year, remaining until 1893, when he left because of poor health. The Hampton newspaper *Southern Workman* for May 1892 notes a program the month before that included "a quartette by Wheelock, Hubbard, Nelson Metoxen, and Israel Hill" (73). This refers to another musical Wheelock, Lehigh Wheelock, who played brass. I have not discovered what Nelson Metoxen's instrument was, but clearly he too was musically talented, as Julia Wheelock's first husband, Charles, had been. One may read her story as a narrative in the comic mode: she has engaged with life's difficulties and, in all, she has come through well.

Edwin Schanandore, an Oneida from Green Bay, Wisconsin, Julia Powless's home, and also an 1889 graduate, stayed on at the school until 1892, and so he did not receive the 1890 questionnaire to returned students. He responded to the brief 1907 questionnaire to graduates to say that he was divorced—I have not discovered whom or when he married—and had been "Baker and Band Master at Cherokee, N.C. for two years and from there I was transferred to Carson City Nevada as Disciplinarian and Bandmaster." He presently writes from New Mexico, where he holds a position at the Albuquerque Indian School. In March 1907 Schanandore wrote to Superintendent Mercer to report on three Carlisle graduates employed with him at Albuquerque—**Charles Dagenett**, **Nancy Seneca**, and **Annie Kunie** (Kowuni), Mrs. Joseph Abner—to say that all are doing well. He speaks of two other former students he has seen, **Yamie Leeds** and **Bennie Thomas**, and he says they are also doing well. While in New Mexico Schanandore married Carlota Gutierrez, and the couple had three children.

Schanandore had said of Dagenett that "he is an outing agent here for the Indians in this part of the country. His wife is teaching here." Dagenett, a Peoria from the Quapaw Agency in Indian Territory, had been a respondent to Pratt's 1890 questionnaire, having returned home in November 1889 because of ill health. But he had later returned to the school and graduated with the class of 1891. His wife, **Esther Miller**, was a Miami and she had been a member of Carlisle's first graduating class in 1889. She had not responded to Pratt's 1890 questionnaire, and her student file includes no further communications from her to the school. Her husband's file, however, contains no fewer than sixty-nine pages. In charge of outing for the Pueblos in 1907, when Schanandore wrote, Dagenett would become U.S. supervisor of Indian employment in 1914, and we hear more about his work in that capacity in the next chapter.

He would also be among the founding members of the Society of American Indians (SAI) in Columbus, Ohio, in 1911. The Luce Press Clipping Bureau of New York and Boston, to which Dagenett subscribed, provided him with copies of newspaper articles in which he was mentioned—many of these are in his Carlisle file—and these included photos of him with such luminaries as Charles Eastman and Carlos Montezuma. In May 1914 he seems to have become president of the Carlisle Alumni Association, an organization occasionally mentioned by various former students but about which little is known.

Dagenett had also responded to Major Mercer's 1907 questionnaire to graduates, noting that he was indeed in Albuquerque, serving as supervisor of Indian employment. He elaborated in response to the lengthier 1909 questionnaire, writing that after graduating from Carlisle he had attended nearby Dickinson College and then Eastman College in Poughkeepsie, New York. He said he owned two homes, one in New Mexico and one in Oklahoma, and listed chickens, hogs, farm implements, and machinery as among his possessions. As for his Indian Service record, he wrote that he had entered the service in 1894 and served as "Teacher, disciplinarian, Issue Clerk, Day School Teacher, Head Clerk"; his present position was "Supervisor Indian Employment." Asked whether he had "done anything for the betterment of [his] people," he wrote succinctly—and surely with pride—"See reports Commissioner of Indian Affairs 1906, 1907 + 1908."

Esther Miller Dagenett's student file has the notation that she was living in Rocky Ford, Colorado, in 1914, the year Dagenett went to Washington; the couple had probably divorced by that time. In 1916

Dagenett married Cornelia Skidmore. Although Charles Dagenett is mentioned frequently in discussions of the SAI and the so-called "Red Progressives" of the first quarter of the twentieth century, I have found no biography of him. Dagenett died in 1941.

Nancy Seneca was indeed a Seneca from New York. She had graduated from Carlisle in 1897, staying on at the school as a nurse, a profession she would continue to follow. She too responded to the brief 1907 questionnaire to graduates and, later, to forms from the school in 1909, 1910, and 1914. After Carlisle she attended and graduated from the Medico-Chirurgical Hospital nursing program in Philadelphia in 1900. She seems never to have married, and like other Carlisle students who joined the Indian Service, she moved around a good deal. In 1907, she had reported, consistent with Edwin Schanandore's communication, that she was a nurse at the Albuquerque Indian School. Her 1909 questionnaire says she had moved to Chilocco, and the 1910 questionnaire found her in Rapid City, South Dakota. Overall, Seneca seems to have been a woman of few words: she left blank question eleven on the 1909 form, asking if she had "done anything for the betterment of [her] people," and also question twelve, asking for anything "else of interest connected with [her] life." Nor did she answer the latter question on her 1910 response. In 1914 Nancy Seneca was in Pawnee, Oklahoma, still working as a nurse.

Annie Kowuni, a Pueblo woman, had also graduated in 1897, and she too responded to Major Mercer's 1907 questionnaire. She writes that she was married to Joseph R. Abner and was employed as a laundress and a seamstress at the Albuquerque school; she had formerly been an assistant clerk at Carlisle and an assistant matron at the Santa Fe, New Mexico, Indian School. For the 1909 questionnaire she wrote that she had graduated from Drexel Institute in Philadelphia and was currently "staying at home taking care of my baby girl." She lived in a fine adobe house, and had some livestock, but not much land. As for whether she had "done anything for the betterment of [her] people," she wrote,

> I feel I have not done as much as I would like to do. If I have done anything to help them let *them* tell about it. But I will say this

much that I have tried to live so that my father, Gen. Pratt and Carlisle would not be ashamed of me.

Her file contains a brief note from her to the school dated October 18 and either 1910 or 1915—I think 1910 is more likely—in which she writes from Casa Blanca, New Mexico, to announce the birth of her son and an upcoming move to Albuquerque, about fifty-five miles to the east, where her husband is "yardmaster at the Santa Fe RR shop." In 1912 she responded to a questionnaire from Friedman to say that she was once more working as assistant seamstress at the Albuquerque school. That was still her position in 1913, when she wrote to thank Superintendent Friedman for the Carlisle *Arrow* which she was receiving, and to wish him and all at the school a happy new year.

Schanandore had written that he had also seen Yamie Leeds. Leeds, from Laguna Pueblo, was an 1891 Carlisle graduate who had worked as a printer at the school. His information cards list no outing assignments for him, which is unusual, but an undated, unsigned, typed note in his file observes that he is crippled and "unable to walk without a crutch." If that were the case while he was at school, it would explain why he went on no outings, since these usually required farm labor largely beyond the capacity of a young man dependent upon a crutch. His disability would probably also have prevented him from participating in the marching and drilling that were an integral part of the Carlisle experience. There are, however, two school photos of Leeds from 1888 that show him standing without the aid of a crutch. In both he has his arm on a fence, and I cannot say whether that is merely for effect or for support. Leeds may, of course, have been afflicted after leaving school.

He responded to the brief 1907 questionnaire to say that he wasn't married, had been an interpreter for the Indian agent at Santa Fe for a "short time in 1885," and had also been employed as a potter at the Laguna School since 1906. In March 1909 he wrote to Moses Friedman to apologize for not having filled out that year's questionnaire because he had been "at Chicago" when it arrived, and then when he picked it up, he says, "I left the blank at my ranche. And I could not get it for some time." He did later fill it out and send it to the school to say that he was still unmarried and still a potter at Laguna. He owns "Little over fifty head of cattle, sixty head of horses and mules" and has a land claim "of 160 acres, a farm at Seama New Mex," on the western edge of Laguna Pueblo. As for Indian Service employment, he mentions once more his work as interpreter and adds that he had also been "Assistant Post Master for year and half." He had as well been "employed by the Merchantile. Co. at Bernalillo, N.M and then by the St. Fe Railroad Co. for two or three years." So far as working "for the betterment of [his] people," he writes, "Court Interpreter, and often called on to explain the land patents and interpret for the U S Government Lawyers. And help my people out of difficulties when others try to be dishonest with them."

Yamie Leeds's file contains a letter he wrote to Friedman in 1911, thanking Friedman for an invitation to the Carlisle commencement and explaining why he will not be able to attend. There is also some correspondence with the school concerning money owed his younger brother, **Clifford Leeds**, who had attended Carlisle in 1909–11 (his sister, **Alice Leeds**, had been at the school in 1889–91, leaving because of illness). A 1912 form records that Yamie Leeds was "Farming and Stock Raising."

Bennie Thomas, whom Edwin Schanandore had also run into, was another young man from Laguna, in attendance at Carlisle from 1880 to 1884 and, like Leeds, with printing as his trade. His file indicates that he had advanced to the ninth grade—the highest one could go at Carlisle—but he did not graduate. There are no communications from him to the school.

To return to Edwin Schanandore: there is no further communication to the school from him until July 1917, when he writes to John Francis Jr., from the Flandreau Indian School, responding to Francis's request that he recommend some Flandreau students who might go east to Carlisle. Schanandore assures Francis, "I shall certainly do all I can to get certain boys and girls to go to Carlisle," and he names several whom he thinks "ought to go." The Schanandores were Carlisle loyalists; no fewer than sixteen Schanandores attended the school.

Another Wisconsin Oneida and a graduate of the class of 1889 was **Lillie Cornelius**; there is nothing from her after she left the school.

This is the case as well for **Frank Dorian**, an Iowa, also in that first graduating class, and the brother of Mike Burns's friend **Ellwood Dorian**. His information card has the word "Dead" written in the upper righthand corner, with no date given. **Thomas Wistar**, another class of '89 graduate who did not respond to the 1890 questionnaire, also did not correspond further with the school. Wistar died in 1904.

As for **Joel Tyndall**, an 1889 Omaha graduate, he did not receive the 1890 questionnaire because he stayed on at the school until 1891. We know that he had left for a time after his graduation because the *Indian Helper* for July 1889 reported that he had not been able to find work on his return home, something that may have led him to go back east and obtain employment at Carlisle. Responding to Major Mercer's brief 1907 questionnaire to the graduates, Tyndall says he is married to "**Lizzie M. Hill** '97," a Lakota from Pine Ridge who had entered the school in 1889 and left upon her own graduation in 1897. Although he gives his address in 1907 as Macy, Nebraska, site of the Omaha Agency, Tyndall was then employed at the Chamberlain Indian School in Chamberlain, South Dakota, a little over 170 miles northeast of his wife's home in Pine Ridge. Asked about employment in the Indian Service, he writes, "Four years as a teacher. Two years as a Clerk. Four years as a Disciplinarian." In reply to whether he has lived in the east, he says that he spent "Two years in Ohio. attending school. and six months in New York as a clerk."

Lizzie Hill Tyndall responded to the 1909 questionnaire, writing that she and her husband live in Walthill, Nebraska, and that she has attended no other school since graduating from Carlisle. She says she lives in "a frame house three rooms," and owns "Four milk cows, one driving team and chickens," on "Sixteen hundred twenty acres" of land, quite a substantial property. She writes that she has worked in the Indian Service as a "seamstress one year matron four years," and in answer to the question whether she has "done anything for the betterment of [her] people," she responds, "Only thing I can say is that I have kept up my habits and practise my learning while in East. not taking part any of Indian past times. nor encourage its practice." She leaves blank the last question, declining to "tell anything interesting" about her life.

Her husband did not respond to the 1909 questionnaire, but a brief, unidentified newspaper clipping in his file has "1909" handwritten on it, and it reports that "Joel Tyndall, a graduate of Carlisle, spent a day here last week on his way from his home at Omaha Agency, Nebr., to Washington, D.C. He is sent by his tribe to transact some important business." He thus was one of only a few graduates and former students able to visit the school after leaving. The following year Tyndall sent an impassioned letter to Superintendent Friedman in response to the 1910 questionnaire. It is written on Department of the Interior, United States Indian Service letterhead, and he is very much thinking of tribal matters. Here is his letter:

Walthill Neb.
Mr. M. Friedman Supt. Jan. 27th 1910.
Carlisle, Penna.

Sir:—

This is to acknowledge the receipt circular letter Dated Jan. 12th 1910. I have spent fifteen years of best years. in cause of my People neglecting my future warlfare. so Indian problems might be settle and Indians become citizens.

Omahas Indians allowed to be allotted provided after 25 years. under government control they were to receive Patent in Fee Simple for their land. in 1882 we were allotted to meet this requirement. *A Citizen*. Father sent me to Carlisle. I return to my people 1889. Taught school for two terms. finding my education. not equal to my liking, attended Preparatory School. Took up teaching again. but failing in health I took outside work. untill last year. I resigned from Government Service. seeing my people in need of me to meet this 25 years promise of Full fledge citizenship. but only to be denied. so Educated Indian. Carlisle graduate Hampton graduate or any other graduate is not better than old uneducated Indian. Government is wasting millions of good money for nothing [?] non-reservation schools good many good people. waste their time for nothing. If present affairs. keep educated Indian level with uneducated ones. dening them their rights. Having "Boss Farmer" to do business. for them. when will Indian be able to stand alone? "Red Tape" will put me back 25 years. If I let them. but I will not. I shall demand my rights through the courts.

Yours truly,
Joel W. Tyndall[2]

I can illuminate some of the matters Joel Tyndall raises. As early as 1854, an Omaha treaty with the government "allowed for the survey and allotting of the Omahas' northeastern Nebraska reservation" (Swetland 1994, 201); further allotments were carried out in 1871, 1883–84, and in the 1890s after the passage of the Dawes Act. The anthropologist Alice Fletcher not only collected Omaha songs and stories, and collaborated with Francis La Flesche on an ethnography of his Omaha people, but was extremely active in effecting the allotment of the reservation.[3] Mark Swetland reported that when Fletcher returned to the reservation in 1897, she "found that the old ways were gone but the Omahas found the new way unsatisfactory" (227). Joel Tyndall's 1910 letter testifies to the fact that this continued to be the case.

Understanding that it would radically unsettle communal values, many Native people opposed allotment well before the Dawes Act of 1887; most of those who had been to the schools, however, favored it. Zitkala-Ša and her family took allotments; so did Luther Standing Bear and his family, along with many former Carlisle (and Hampton) students. Apart from any material benefits that being a Native landholder might bring—farming in the Dakotas, for example, and in parts of Nebraska looked easy to no one—it also promised the benefit of American citizenship. Upon accepting an allotment—most often, 160 acres per family, 80 acres to an individual, although this could vary—title to the land would be held in custodianship by the government for a period of twenty-five years, after which the allottee would be considered "competent" and receive a "patent in fee simple." This meant that he or she was no longer merely a leaseholder (who could not sell the land) but had full and complete title to the property and any improvements on it (house, barn, outbuildings) in perpetuity. The relevant laws also specified that upon transfer of title to the Native allottee, the new title holder would become a citizen of the United States, something generally desired by those Native people who had been to the schools, and supported by various Native American associations.

The twenty-five-year custodianship was, on the one hand, meant to protect the allottee against fraud and expropriation by rapacious white settlers. On the other hand, it was the purest colonial paternalism, assuming it would take all of twenty-five years for the Native leaseholder to become "competent"—and thus worthy of full title and full citizenship (while also leaving plenty of time for white settlers to advance their aims). But it was also possible for an individual allottee to appeal to a federal Indian agent or to Washington to be declared competent well before twenty-five years had passed.

Although Standing Bear and many other Native people would change their minds in later years about the value of American citizenship, it needs to be recalled that early in the twentieth century, not only white "Friends of the Indian" and eastern boarding school superintendents like Richard Pratt of Carlisle and Samuel Chapman Armstrong of Hampton but almost every Native American activist and writer on record favored full citizenship for Indians. This was something for which Charles Eastman, Luther Standing Bear, the Bonnins, Francis and Rosa La Flesche, Arthur Parker, Carlos Montezuma, Henry Roe Cloud, and a great many other prominent Native people, along with the obscure Joel Tyndall, all worked.

In his letter Tyndall writes of Omaha allotments taken in 1882. This would mean that any 1882 allottee was eligible to receive full title to his or her land along with American citizenship by 1907. Tyndall, writing in 1910, details his own history as a teacher who then pursued further education, obtaining work in the Indian Service, and then, because of ill health, but also because of "seeing my people in need of me," resigning to help "meet this 25 years promise of Full Fledge citizenship." I cannot say why this was denied—to him, and perhaps to other "Carlisle graduate, Hampton graduate, or any other graduate." That educated Native people like himself must have their business attended to by the "Boss Farmer"—usually a white man appointed by the agent or, on occasion, the agent himself—when they could very ably "stand alone," is a painful indignity. But as an educated Indian, Tyndall knows that he can indeed "demand my rights through the courts." Tyndall, as other former students had, addresses his concerns to a Carlisle superintendent, who had no power whatever to intervene in these matters. Tyndall did not go on to become an attorney, as had his fellow 1889 graduate, William Campbell, and I do not know whether he ever instigated or participated in legal action on behalf of Indian title and Indian citizenship.[4]

Finally, we may consider a brief note in Tyndall's Carlisle file that he had written on stationery from a Washington hotel in March 1912, when he was once more there, almost surely on tribal business. But that is not the subject of his communication. Rather, he is responding to an invitation to attend Carlisle's graduation ceremony, addressing his note to "Mrs. N. R. Denny, Carlisle, Pa-," whom he addresses as "Schoolmate:—." This is **Nellie Robertson**, a half-blood Sisseton Sioux, who came to Carlisle in 1880 when she was only nine and graduated in 1890; she and Tyndall would indeed have been "schoolmates." Robertson then attended Metzger College in Carlisle, Pennsylvania, for two years, and went on to the State Normal School in Westchester, Pennsylvania, from which she graduated in 1896. She taught at Carlisle, served briefly as cook for the school's hospital, clerked in different capacities, and was in charge of the outing program during the school's last years.[5]

She married **Wallace Denny**, a Wisconsin Oneida, several years younger. He had come to Carlisle at the age of seventeen in 1896 and graduated in 1906. As a student he served as trainer and occasional substitute for Pop Warner's renowned Carlisle football team and later served the school as the small boys' disciplinarian. The Dennys remained employed by Carlisle until shortly before it closed in 1918. We will see that a great many former students wrote to Nellie Robertson Denny. Her file is very full, and it includes several photos taken of her at the school, along with correspondence with Indian Bureau officials regarding an allotment of 160 acres, which she was granted in 1916–17. Both Nellie and Wallace Denny testified in the government hearing into charges against superintendent Moses Friedman in early 1914, and I return to them briefly in the next chapter.

Tyndall writes his former schoolmate, "Was in hope to attend commcnt for rush [?] of carl from home. I regret very much to be absent to 'roll call.'" He signs, "With best wishes." It is also to "Mrs. Denny" that a brief, typewritten note in Tyndall's file was sent. It reads: "A boy from the Omaha Reservation reported to me that Joel Tyndall died last December. Was in the Service for a number of years and was disciplinarian at Chamberlain for about four years." It is unsigned, except for the typed initials, "EPR," and the date "1914," handwritten on the bottom left. Joel Tyndall's student information card has the notation "Dec 1913," the year someone recorded him as "deceased."

Joel and Lizzie Hill Tyndall had a son named Wallace, born in 1892. From 1901 to 1903 he attended the Chamberlain Indian School in South Dakota, where his parents were employed, going on to the Fort Yuma Indian School in California from about 1903 to 1905, where I suspect the Tyndalls had taken Indian Service jobs. On April 22, 1905, Joel Tyndall applied to have his son accepted at Carlisle. On that application, the line requesting "mother's name" is left blank. Perhaps because no mother's name was given on the application, **Wallace Tyndall**'s enrollment card at Carlisle—he was enrolled in May, less than a month after his father signed the application—lists his mother as "dead." This is incorrect, as I later explain.

Wallace Tyndall's career at Carlisle was brief; he was expelled and sent home to his father in Chamberlain in January 1907. He is not mentioned in any of the Carlisle publications, and I have not found the reason for his expulsion. In 1910, however, he was at the Genoa Indian School in Nebraska, where his mother lived. This is to say that after Joel Tyndall's death in 1913, his widow Lizzie married a Mr. Justice, and the *Carlisle Arrow* for February 9, 1917, noted that Lizzie Hill Justice and her husband were then residing in Cody, Nebraska (1), some three hundred miles west of Walthill, her former home. I don't know what became of Wallace Tyndall. There are, however, presently (2019), a great many people named Tyndall living in Walthill, Nebraska, and some of them are surely descendants of Joel and Lizzie Hill.

Joseph Harris, another member of the class of 1889, became an employee of the school in September 1890, and if he received the June questionnaire, he did not respond. Harris was a mixed-blood Gros Ventre from Montana Territory. His student information card lists his father's name as Michael Harris, with the parenthetical notation that Michael Harris is "Musician 6th Infantry." Harris's Gros Ventre mother's name is not given. He had come to Carlisle in April 1881 at the age of nine or ten, and the Carlisle *School News* for March 1882, under the headline, "A LITTLE NINE YEAR OLD GROS VENTRE WHO HAS BEEN IN SCHOOL LESS THAN A YEAR WRITES TO HIS FATHER," prints the following letter by him:

> DEAR FATHER:—I think you should have a letter from your son. You would be happy if you were here to see me. I will be so happy to go and see you and come back again to school. I can write and spell. I will tell you something about this school. The band boys are going to Philadelphia. This school is learning to speak only English. This is your son writing this letter to you remember your son please. From your little son.
>
> JOSEPH B. HARRIS
> Write soon. (4)

Harris would also become a member of the Carlisle band. As the *Indian Helper* for May 24, 1889, observed, "It doesn't take Joe Harris long to dress when occasion demands, requiring only about two minutes to change his attire and get into his band uniform" (3). The article went on to say that "it is not only in dressing that Joe is quick," but also "in his work, which is carefully and correctly done. There is no more faithful printer than Joe and the Printing office is proud of its graduate" (3). He also played baseball, and although he had graduated in '89, Harris was the center fielder for the 1891 Carlisle Indians baseball team (Powers-Beck 2004, 193). The following year he played for the Union Reserves, another of the school's baseball teams (194).

In 1907 Harris responded to Major Mercer's brief questionnaire to the graduates, writing, "I am not married," and stating that his address was "Langhorne Bucks Co. Pa." He said he was a "Printer by trade, but working on a farm at present." As for work in the Indian Service, Harris writes, "I was employed at Carlisle Indian School as Asst foreman from Sept. 1890 to May 1893. I was employed at the Genoa Indian School, Neb as foreman of the printing office from July 1893 to September 1893." Harris also answered the 1909 questionnaire, stating that he was still unmarried, and still living in Langhorne, Pennsylvania. He says he "attended Middletown Township school for three months during the winter of 1890, after graduating at Carlisle in May 1889." As for his occupation and salary, "I have worked on the farm for at least 14 years. wages vary according to ability. At present I get $15.00 monthly"—about $422 now (2019)—along with, I would guess, room and board. He says that he does not own his own home, and has no property and no money in the bank. As for other positions he has held since leaving the school, he writes, "I have not done any kind of work other than on a farm and its good hard work at that." Asked in the eleventh question, "Have you done anything for the betterment of your people?" and encouraged to "Write fully," Harris responds simply, "I have not returned west since leaving school and living as an individual and don't care about being before the public."

Unmarried, living "as an individual," doing "good hard work," and not caring "about being before the public," Joseph Harris, approaching forty, is a very thoughtful, intellectually aware, and perhaps lonely man. Here is his response to the twelfth question, "Tell me anything else of interest connected with your life":

> I am happy to be among the living. My life out here is about like the general run among persons of my class (working class). The space which my history in your booklet will not consume many pages because I am out here in the country and it keeps me busy to attend to the duties which a farm calls for. I worked for one man six years at present if I live till next March, I will be working here for this man eight years.

Harris's conscious awareness of his class status is in my experience unique among the returned students and suggests that he has used what free time he has to read and perhaps to attend talks or lectures in Philadelphia, some twenty-five miles from Langhorne. But perhaps because he didn't "care about being before the public," he did not engage as an organic intellectual.

Harris did live until the "next March" and responded to an invitation from Friedman to attend that spring's commencement. In a letter dated March 21 he writes:

> Dear Sir—
>
> It gives me great pleasure to think at this season of the year of the Graduating exercises of the Carlisle School. It has been several years since I have graduated from Carlisle, but I still have a warm place for it in my heart. I read the little paper every week and think it is a nice paper. I was a printer at Carlisle when "The Red Man" + "Indian Helper" was published. I am still working on a farm this year makes my tenth. I appreciate the different tokens of rememberances from you from time to time, but I am a poor hand for writing so if I don't write don't mind it. I hope in the future I will get acquainted with you personally. Thanking you for the invitation, but sorry I can not come on this year. I hope the Commencement will excel previous years and make a good impression on the public.
>
> I will close my short letter this time. I will write some more in the future.
>
> I am your friend
> Jos. B. Harris

Upon receipt of Friedman's invitation the following year, Harris wrote in March 1912 that he did indeed wish to come to that year's Carlisle commencement. He asks if it is possible to arrange for reduced rail fare so that he might "be with you and shake hands with you personally for the first time." Unfortunately, as Friedman wrote back to him, although reduced fares had formerly been available to Carlisle students, they were so no longer. I do not know whether Joseph Harris was able to attend the 1912 commencement nonetheless.

Later, in December 1912, Harris filled out a brief questionnaire indicating that he was still a farm laborer in Langhorne, and he provided the same information as he had the year before. His file also contains an unsigned letter to him from the "Superintendent," John Francis Jr., dated January 10, 1918, asking if he would "write . . . a letter giving some interesting facts about your Carlisle outing and naming some special benefits . . . especially those which have helped you in later years." Unless Joseph Harris's circumstances in Langhorne had changed considerably, he might well have found the request ironic. Carlisle closed in 1918, and there is no record of a response from Harris.

Cecilia Londrosh, a Winnebago member of the 1889 graduating class, had entered Carlisle in 1883. She had also been employed by the school after her graduation, serving for two years as an "assistant in sewing room," and so she did not receive the 1890 questionnaire to returned students. She answered Major Mercer's 1907 mailing to the graduates, writing that she had married Mr. Louis Herman, a white man, and that they lived in Homer, Nebraska. Her occupation was "Care of my home and family," although she had "taught at Winnebago for one year" before her marriage, after attending "school at Millersville State Normal, Pa, for two years."

In 1909 she responded that she and her husband were now in Winnebago, Nebraska, where she still kept "house for my family," a five-room house that they do not own but rent. She leaves blank the questions asking about land, stock, and money in the bank, and regarding further schooling and employment in the Indian Service, she repeats what she had said in 1907. As for the question asking whether the former student has "done anything for the betterment of [their] people," Cecilia Herman wrote,

> No. I cannot say that I have been actively engaged in Missionary work of any kind, as I have resided altogether, until recently, among white people. Also I find that my time is entirely taken up in caring for my home and five children.

She leaves blank the twelfth question asking about anything further of interest in her life.

But she did do things "for the betterment of [her] people" once her children grew older. Linda Waggoner, in a note to her biography of Angel De Cora, a Winnebago artist and teacher at Carlisle, writes that Cecilia Londrosh Herman and her sister, Nellie, "served as census takers, government informants, agency teachers, and recruiters for Carlisle and Christian organizations" (Waggoner 2014, 274 n. 20), both sisters acting for "the betterment of their people."

Cecilia's sister, **Nellie Londrosh**, had entered Carlisle with her in 1883 but left in 1887 and did not graduate. The school listed Cecilia as half-blood and Nellie as one quarter Winnebago, but I suspect they had the same mother and father (their Carlisle student information cards do not name their parents). Like Cecilia's husband, Louis M. Herman, Nellie's husband, J. W. Nunn, was a white man.

Nellie had received and responded to Pratt's 1890 questionnaire, and although unlike Cecilia she did not respond to the 1909 questionnaire, she did write toward the end of that year to Nellie Robertson Denny, with whom she too had been at school. She tells Denny that she would like to visit and also asks whether a half-fare ticket could be arranged for her for train travel from Sioux City, Iowa. That fare, as we have seen, was no longer available, and there is nothing on file to indicate whether she made that visit. In April 1910 Nellie Nunn filled out the questionnaire that had been sent to her, giving her husband's name and stating that she lived in Winnebago, Nebraska, where her sister also lived. Her occupation, she writes, is "Mother in our house," but she "also keeps books and help my husband in the store." They live "in a six room cottage," and as for property, she has "Just enough to live and help to educate my children." She does not seem to have gotten any land allotted to her, as she had hoped in 1890.

Nellie Nunn says she had also formerly taught for three years in the Indian Service. The 1910 questionnaire had dropped the question asking whether the recipient had done anything for the "betterment" of Indian people, but it does ask the recipient to "Tell . . . anything of interest connected with your life." Here is Nellie Londrosh Nunn's thoughtful reply:

> Financially, I do not think I would be counted a success. Being of Winnebago blood but not a member of the tribe the only help rec'd from the government was my 3 years and 3 months schooling at Carlisle. For this help I shall always be very thankful for I feel certain that the results are that I have been a better wife, better mother, better woman in every way and more than all, it was through the influence of the Carlisle school and the dear home of Miss Edge at Downington that I became a follower of the Lord Jesus. This year I was elected to my fourth year as President of the Niobrara Presbyterian Society.

Nellie Londrosh had been sent on an outing assignment to the farm of Jacob Edge in Downington, Pennsylvania, in March 1884, where she remained until February 1886. In that she refers to *Miss* Edge, that would be the farmer's sister or his daughter. Sometime later in 1910, Nellie Nunn lost her husband.

Both Cecilia Londrosh Herman and Nellie Londrosh Nunn sent their children to Carlisle. Writing to Pratt in 1890, Nellie had said that she had "a little girl five months old," and two of her daughters, **Mary** and **Alice Nunn**, would enroll at Carlisle in 1910. But Mary was born in 1892, and Alice in 1894, so her first daughter, if she had lived, did not go to Carlisle. Cecilia's son, **Bernard Herman**, born in 1895, also entered the school in 1910, with his two cousins. He had been to the eighth grade in the Winnebago public school, meaning that at Carlisle he could progress only a single year further. Meanwhile, we may note that before entering Carlisle, Mary Nunn had advanced to the eleventh grade in the Winnebago public school, and her sister Alice had reached the tenth: that is, both of them had already gone beyond the grade level offered by Carlisle. It thus seems likely that the main reason for the cousins' attendance at the eastern school was their mothers' desire that they attend, regardless of educational advancement.

Mary and Alice Nunn entered the school on March 10, 1910, and their cousin Bernard Herman arrived some two weeks later. In April the following year he ran away from the school; his file lists him as a "deserter." In the short time he had spent there, he'd taken up "telegraphy" as a trade, and his conduct was recorded as "good," "except smoking." A month after Bernard's departure Mary left to "take a position" somewhere, and it was at this time that Alice "failed to return" to the school because of "Home needs."

Despite their untimely departures, all three cousins responded to Carlisle's 1911 questionnaire. Bernard Herman and Alice Nunn said they were finishing up at the Winnebago high school. But most of Mary's questionnaire has been lost; only the page with the last two questions—other positions held, anything further of interest about your life—has survived. To these, Mary answered no other positions, and she left the final question blank. She did, however, respond to a 1914 request from the school for information, saying she was a clerk at the Ponca Agency in Oklahoma and "always glad to hear from Carlisle."

Other 1889 graduates communicated a good deal less with the school. After graduation **Kish Hawkins**, a Cheyenne, stayed on as assistant disciplinarian until 1891 and thus did not receive the 1890 questionnaire. More than twenty years later he responded to the brief 1913 form, stating that he was "Assistant Indian Farmer" in Darlington, Oklahoma, at the Cheyenne and Arapaho Agency, and offering the news that "Family and myself are in good health, enjoying life the best we can." That is the last record of him in the Carlisle files. Of the remaining members of the class of 1889, **Clara Faber**, a Wyandotte, like Kish Hawkins, had stayed on at the school until 1891 and did not receive the questionnaire, and she did not communicate further with the school. Nor did **Katie Grindrod**, or **Eva Johnson**. I look now at others who had responded to the 1890 questionnaire and continued to maintain contact with Carlisle for years after. I present their communications according to the regional organization of chapter 1.

Susie Young, a Winnebago from Nebraska, had written to Pratt in 1890 to tell him, "A white man is going to marry me" (Part 5), and she did indeed marry a white man, named Louis Cass Kelsey. But as she explains in her response to the school's 1910 questionnaire, the marriage had not lasted. Asked whether she is married and to whom, she writes, "Yes, and Mr. A.R. Mitchell." She gives their address as "Winnebago City, Nebr.," and says she "did not attend no other school after leaving Carlisle." The fourth question asks for her current occupation, and her wonderfully original answer to that is "Good health." As for her "present home," "We are having a good home and Industries." In regard to property, "I have land," she writes. She has "not been in the Indian Service," and she has held "no other position after leaving Carlisle." To the ninth and final question asking her to tell "anything else of interest connected with your life," she responds,

> I am interested in my life, that I got 6 children of one father and having a good behavior, living with my husband 16 yrs. till whisky broke up our home some of my children are attending Government Schools. They are good healthy children. I am now married again to Industries man. I have 160 acre farm and was living on it rented it 2 yrs. and now I will go back to farm again. I make my own living was raising hogs and chickens to sell. also make butter to sell on my farm. I hope I will never sell my land. keep it for my children. Well Mr Friedman I have done my best to answer your questions I am very sorry I wished I had stay longer at Carlisle to get a full education. I must keep my children in schools till they are graduated. This is all
>
> I am very Resptf. yours
> Susie Kelsey Mitchell

That she has 160 acres of land suggests that she had taken an allotment, worked it for a time, rented it, and now will work it once more.

Two years later, in 1912, Susie Mitchell returned the school's brief questionnaire listing her occupation as "Housekeeping," and offering no further information about herself. But two of her six children, **Charles** and **Mary Kelsey**, had already enrolled at Carlisle, and their files contain many letters from their mother. Mary Kelsey, born in 1898, came to the school in March 1911; her older brother Charles, born in 1892, entered six months later, in September. He had by that time reached the eighth grade, having attended public school in Thurston, Nebraska, after which he spent a year at Haskell and three years at the Flandreau Indian School. Unusually (but not uniquely), Charles applied on his own behalf. Mary stayed in the east until 1916, having spent most of her time not at Carlisle but on outing assignments at the home of Mary Deacon in Mount Holly, New Jersey. Several of her outing reports—this, too, is somewhat unusual, although also not unique—are in her file. Also in her file are letters from her mother asking that she be sent home. She was not, however, sent home; mother and daughter did not see each other for a full five years. Mary Kelsey's student information card lists her "character" as "Excellent."

This was not the case for Charles. Moses Friedman wrote to Susie Mitchell in early July, 1913, to inform her that her son had "deserted" in June; in August he wrote once again to say that Charles had been brought back to the school. She responded, asking that her son be sent home, and that some $300 held in his account be turned over to him. This provoked a great many letters between the school, the Winnebago agent, John S. Spear, and Indian School Inspector E. B. Linnen—we will hear more of him in the following chapter—all of which did, in fact, lead to the release of the money to Charles Kelsey. In May 1914 his mother received a letter from the recently appointed superintendent, Oscar Lipps, informing her that Charles was then in the Carlisle guard house; I have not found out his offense. His mother wrote asking for him to be sent home. We know that he was indeed sent home because, at the end of May, Susie Mitchell wrote to tell Lipps that Charles had arrived safely. His student information card says he was "expelled"; his file gives the reason for his discharge as "incorrigible."

Charles Wolfe and **Harriet Stuart**, both Nez Perce people, had responded to the 1890 questionnaire from the Lapwai reservation in Idaho Territory, with Wolfe, as noted, offering the fascinating observation, "Well since leaving dear Carlisle School I have been losing my knowledge, but gained my strength." In differing degrees, both Wolfe and Stuart would continue to communicate with the school. Wolfe filled out the 1910 questionnaire to say that he was married; that he had a good home and some livestock; that he farmed and also worked as a printer, the trade he had learned at Carlisle. Expressing gratitude for his Carlisle education, he noted that he had become a local Sunday School superintendent. In 1912 he returned the brief December questionnaire to say that he was still farming, and continued to be grateful for his schooling. He signed himself "Chas. Wolf Williams," and I cannot account for the change of name.

Harriet Stuart did not return a questionnaire to the school until 1911, and it is one of only a very few to be typed. Then a mature woman of forty-three, she writes as someone pleased with herself and her position in the world. She remains married to James Stuart, about whom she proudly writes that he is "one of my own tribe, a graduate of Chemawa, Oregon and initiated as alumnus of Carlisle, unanimously by the first alumnus under directions of Gen. R. H. Pratt." It is not at all clear what she means by this. Her husband had been a member of the first graduating class at Chemawa in 1886, the graduates having completed sixth grade. But Carlisle did not give out honorary degrees, nor would Pratt have directed the first Carlisle alumni—I think she must be referring to one of them—to "initiate" a Chemawa graduate "as alumnus of Carlisle."

Stuart continues the 1911 questionnaire writing that she has attended no other school than Carlisle, and that her occupation is "staying home mostly, attending to home duties." That home is in Kooskia, Idaho, on "six more tracts of land joining the town" that she and her husband had bought, "and it is one of the most desirable locations." In all, she and her husband "have about 630 acres of land in different places beside's town lots, buildings, etc." As to whether she has ever been in the Indian Service, she writes that she worked "four months nurse in hospital at Ft. Lapwai school under Major E. McConville in the year of 1891." It had been McConville who, as superintendent of that school, had dismissively told her many years earlier that she "ought to work for nothing," as she had written in her 1890 letter to Richard Pratt.[6] Nonetheless, he had apparently seen fit soon after to pay her as a nurse in the school's hospital for four months. As for other positions she has held, Stuart types, "non. only a help mate to my husband in all his work." The ninth and final question of the 1911 form asks for "anything else of interest connected with your life." Here is Harriet Stuart's reply. What to make of it I leave entirely to the reader:

> My husband is a civil engineer connected with the Government service, and he is away from home great deal, so I have to stay home to take care of things, (six little more chicks addit to our stock this mornning,) We have a women missionary society amoung the NezPerce women of which I am the President, and have to take charge the meeting at times. The society will get up a picnic party next week. and no doub't every body will enjoy it. I am trying to make use of what little I learned at Carlisle, and wishing that every girl after leaving Carlisle would try and do her best and show the world that the Indian girls can be some body. During our last meeting I asked the women how they would like to have a nice picnic just amoung ourselves, this was unanimously favored by all. So if you should happen to drop into the beautiful valley of Kamiah next Wednesday June 14, come and join the party and partake some of the refreshment; Although all male visitors strictly forbidding.
>
> I am your friend and former Carlisle student.
> Harriet M. Stuart

Her last correspondence with the school was in response to a very brief form Superintendent Friedman sent in 1913, on which, for "Present Occupation," she wrote, "is not what other returned students would give in account of themselves of something worthy, still I have nothing to complain. Mr. Stuart and myself are living comfortably here at Kooskia. Wishing you a merry Xmas, Harriet." Stuart's file also contains an article published in the *Nez Perce Indian* for April 1, 1915, in which she discusses her garden and Nez Perce homes. From the violent dislocation of her childhood to a comfortable life with her husband at home in the lands of the Niimiipuu, Harriet Stuart's is also a tale structured in the comic mode.

Charles Hood and his wife, **Lucinda Clinton**, both Modocs, had attended Carlisle from the Quapaw Agency in Indian Territory, and after leaving the School both had returned west. Clinton—Mrs. Charles Hood—had not responded to the 1890 questionnaire, nor would she respond to any sent later. Her husband had written Pratt in 1890, and in 1911 he filled out the questionnaire sent by superintendent Friedman in some detail.

Hood says he is married to Lucinda Clinton, "Ex Student Carlisle," and that they live at Fort Klamath, Oregon. He is "Ranching," and living in a rented house. He and his wife have "two boys . . . attending the public school here, ages 9 and 13." As for property, his situation is a bit complicated:

> We have a fine farm of 200 acres and a six roomed cottage in Quapaw Agency Okla. We have due us at Klamath Agency, 8 claims of 160 acres, about 30 head of cattle and 9 head of horses have had some money in the bank on deposit.

The Klamath Agency in Oregon had been allotted in 1895, and when the Modocs who wished to do so returned there from Oklahoma in 1909—as Hood and his wife had done—they were eligible to have lands allotted for them. The *Report of the Sixtieth Congress*, Session II, chapter 253, March 1909, stated that the returned Modocs "be allotted as other Indians on said reservation," provided that the secretary of the interior sell any lands that had been allotted to them in Oklahoma. If "any member of the Modoc tribe of Indians prefers not to have his or her land sold, such allottee may lease his or her land in Oklahoma for a period of not to exceed five years" (*Report of the Sixtieth Congress* 752). I suspect Hood had leased his farm at the Quapaw Agency, and is awaiting action on his claims at the Klamath Agency—the Dawes Act specified 160 acres to each head of household, and I cannot say how it comes about that Hood has eight claims—which would be contingent upon his selling the Oklahoma land within the next three years.[7]

Asked about any Indian Service appointments, Hood writes,

> Have been filling different positions in the Indian Service since coming here from 6 months to over a year. Took a Civil Service Examination in July 21, 1908 for Farmer, successfully passed was appointed at Klamath Training School filled the position nearly two years was transferred and promoted to Ft. Hall Idaho I resigned owing to business necessity and the caring for my stock + etc.

As for other work, he says, "Followed the trade for some time that I learned at Carlisle as a tinner and plumber. have done some carpentering also." For the final question, asking for "anything else of interest connected with [his] life," he writes at length:

> One of the best traits in my life is to do my fellow man some good in the religious way. have fought the evils of liquor at all times. Since coming here have fought the liquor question here in our county as a political issue, being a voter With my assistance and my vote two years ago we voted our County dry again last year we made great effort to keep the sale of intoxicants out of our County but we lost Take considerable interest in all question relating to the laws of our State and right government.
>
> Have endeavored at all times to keep up the good name of Carlisle so that Carlisle will not be ashamed to own me as her *son*. With the best regards and wishes for Carlisle. I am Chas. S. Hood. N.B. Two years ago, I drove sixty miles on the eve of election day to cast my vote against liquor rather than to be absent

As Hood makes clear, the question of whether to keep alcoholic beverages out of Klamath County was contested in his time, and he wishes Carlisle to know which side he was on. Klamath County, however, permits their sale today (2019).

Hood's last communication with the school came in a letter he wrote to Superintendent John Francis on November 16, 1917, less than a year before Carlisle closed. He writes from Yainax, Oregon, just south of the Klamath reservation, and his letter is typed:

My Dear Mr. Francis:

I am in receipt of your, letter of the 26th of October Last. The cordial greeting contained in the said letter, seem to bring back to me the vivid scenes of my best days, when I was a student of the dear old school, *Carlisle*. Since leaving there, I have endeavored to live so, the School would not be ashamed of me. How I wished that I would have been present, there with you, on the 38th anniversary of the School, just a short time ago.

I may be able to pay you a visit, this coming Winter, on my way to the National Capitol, should every thing look favorable and right. I have here lately, got kind of unconcerned and careless about our School, which has been the means of shaping our lives in the way to live upright. This is the first letter, that any Superintendent, has written us, since the founder of the School, Brig. General R.H. Pratt, left there. We thank you, very much for the interest you, Have in us. With the best of wishes, for you and the school.

I am most sure, Mrs. Hood will join with me in this as She is an ex Carlisle student.

I am enclosing you the fifty (50) cents for The Arrow and the Red Man; please send the paper to me, at Klamath Agency, Ore., my future address.

I am yours,
Chas. S. Hood

Hood has probably forgotten the communications he had received from superintendents Mercer, Friedman, and Lipps. But now, thirty-two years since the forty-nine-year-old Charles Hood had seen Carlisle, and on his way to Washington, he hopes to be able to travel to Pennsylvania, along with his wife, Lucinda Clinton Hood. Clearly his goodwill toward the school is ongoing and he sends the postage money that will allow him to receive the *Arrow* and the *Red Man*.

The first two returned students from Indian Territory whose responses to the 1890 questionnaire I have considered, the Reverend Joshua

Given and Cecilia Pickard, did not live many years more, and there are no further communications from them to Carlisle. On November 25, 1892, the Carlisle *Indian Helper* reported that the "Reverend Joshua Given is lying very low with consumption" (2), and the *Helper* for March 31, 1893 reported the sad news of his death. It had come to the school from Given's younger sister, **Julia Given**, then a student at Carlisle, who had been informed of her brother's passing by the Reverend Given's wife. He was only thirty-three years old at the time of his death, and besides his wife he left two young children behind. Cecilia Pickard was even younger, only about twenty-one when she died, something we also learn from the *Indian Helper*. The issue for July 10, 1891, stated that "the news of the death of Celia Pickard some three months since has reached us" (2).

In his 1888 article in the *Indian Helper*, Given had noted the recent death of **Etadleuh Doanmoe** and reported that his wife, Laura, also a Carlisle student, was nonetheless doing well. About 1894 **Laura Doanmoe** married a white man, William Pedrick, although in response to a 1911 questionnaire from Carlisle, Laura Pedrick, in her first communication to the school in more than twenty years, writes, "I am a widow now," having once more lost a husband. She reports that she lives in Anadarko on her own property and lists her occupation as "Housekeeping." She writes that she has "property in town and several farms," and is doing well. As for Indian Service work, she had been "Assistant seamstress, three different times, Laundress two years and field-matron for about five years." She notes that she has also "been an interpreter for my people ever since I left Carlisle." As for anything further of interest, she writes, "I have nothing of interest in my life. I am living in town and taking care of my two children and sent them to town schools. I hope to make them good man and good woman."

Raising her children to be a good man and a good woman was a sufficient task, but about this time Laura Doanmoe Pedrick also took on work for her Kiowa People. A letter in Laura Pedrick's file from Acting Commissioner of Indian Affairs F. H. Abbott dated May 29, 1913, makes clear that when Abbott wrote, the government held no less than $400,000 owed to the Kiowas well over ten million dollars today

(2019). These were moneys long held by the government to be paid out as annuities to the Kiowas for land cessions. Pedrick had discovered that the amount actually paid out in annuities to each individual Kiowa was something like twenty-five dollars a month, hardly sufficient for them to live, and she took on the task of persuading the Indian Office to pay out much more of what legally belonged to the Kiowas.

She did this in part by enlisting superintendent Moses Friedman's help, and from copies of his letters in her file—her letters to him do not seem to have survived—he wrote to the Indian Office several times to praise her and support her claims on behalf of her people. Laura Pedrick was in Washington, at the National Hotel, on March 8, 1912, when she wrote to her old schoolmate, Nellie Robertson Denny:

> Dear Friend:—
>
> I thought I would write you a few lines to let you know that I am still living and well as ever. We have been here for several days in the City on our business and glad to say that we got our business and every things in our favor. I have been thinking of you ever since we came but some how I never have time to write to my friends until today or this afternoon we were in the Indian Office all morning.
>
> Tell Mr. Denny Willie want him to come to Oklahoma again and show him how play ball. I must close, my regard to Mr. Denny, Your friend
>
> L.D. Pedrick

Nellie Robertson's husband, Wallace Denny, had been active in sports at Carlisle, and it would seem he and his wife had visited Anadarko, where he had impressed Willie Pedrick with his athletic skill.

Although Pedrick and her party had "got our business and every things in our favor," there was more to be done. Friedman wrote to Abbott again to press the Kiowas' case further, and as late as May 1913 Abbott acknowledged to Friedman, "Just at present, as you know, the spending of the funds of these Indians is in a somewhat chaotic state," so it would seem that the Kiowas had not yet received what their representatives had requested. Abbott did write in closing, "However, there is nothing to prevent the Superintendent from allowing Indians the use of their individual funds in such amounts as will prevent their suffering," so that despite the government's delay, adequate support for the Kiowas would be forthcoming.

The last item in Laura Doanmoe Pedrick's file is an invitation she had printed inviting its recipients "to attend the Reunion of Carlisle Ex-Students to be held at the residence of Mrs. Laura D. Pedrick, Friday Evening, March 30th, 1917. 8:00 o'clock." This was not the first time she had hosted a Carlisle reunion, for we learn from the Carlisle *Arrow* for December 10, 1915. that she had hosted such a gathering the preceding November, attended by twenty former students (3). I have not found any information regarding the 1917 reunion. Laura Pedrick died in 1942.

Marcus Poko whom the pious Joshua Given had pronounced "no good" in 1888, and who had written to Pratt in 1890 to say that he had "married a camp Indian," did not respond to any of the school's questionnaires until 1910. He then reported that he had some stock, and160 acres of land, and that he was farming. But he also said, "I live as the Indians did in early days, camp around with friends and relatives." He had, it would seem, in his own way, managed to reconcile tradition and modernity, the old and the new.

William Little Elk, a Cheyenne from the Cheyenne and Arapaho Agency at Darlington, returned the 1909 questionnaire to say that he remained married to **Minnie Wolf Face** and was living in a "good three-room frame house." As for land, he wrote that he had his own, his "wife's and two daughters' allotments, beside inherited land," most of which was "under lease," although he did "some farming" himself. As an Indian Service employee, he had been "Policeman, asst Farmer, Laborer and Teamster," and "Was baker at Haskell which is trade I learned" at Carlisle. Regarding work "for the betterment of [his] people," he writes:

> For the past twelve years have been a Christian. Being a deacon in the Baptist church I have tried to walk straight and stand strong and so lead My people into Jesus Road.

> I have attended a good many Christian gatherings, associations, and conventions and have tried to learn all I could so as to teach my people the right way, and also to make the white people more interested in Indians.

As for "anything of interest connected with [his] life," he says,

> I am well and strong. I am living with same wife I married at Carlisle many years ago—about twenty-five—no divorce—no trouble only she is not Christian yet. Four children living. my daughter married.

This must surely have been an interesting household, with Minnie Wolf Face, Little Elk's wife of twenty-five years, "not Christian *yet*" (my emphasis), as he tries to lead his "people into Jesus Road."

Minnie Wolf Face Little Elk also filled out the 1909 form, the only communication from her to the school. She writes that she had worked at Haskell while her husband was baker there many years ago, but she did not attend classes. When she returned home she was employed at the Arapaho school at Darlington. She now lives in a house that is on her father's land, the "good three-room frame house" her husband had mentioned. She leaves several of the questions blank, and in answer to the final one, asking for "anything else of interest with [her] life," she writes, "Im Poor living alt the time I lost 2 my daughters and 2 boys and one girl live yet. all going school Darlington there. I don't How to answer it."

Sadly, she provides a correction of her husband's statement that they had "Four children living." The couple had had five children. On September 24, 1909, before he sent in the questionnaire, William Little Elk had filled out a form listing his children as prospective students for Carlisle. He wrote that his daughter Anna had died four years earlier, and that his oldest daughter, Emma, "she be sick 2 years now." There is no date on the Little Elks' 1909 questionnaires, but they probably would have filled them out toward the end of that year, by which time Emma must have died. Although her father seems to have counted her as among four children still living, her mother acknowledges the unfortunate fact that she had lost "2 my daughters." There is nothing further from her to the school.

Three years later, however, in 1912, William Little Elk wrote to Moses Friedman in response to an invitation to attend the Carlisle commencement that spring:

> Dear friend,
>
> You come on Hand you Letter and I was very glad to hear from you very much. I wishes I go by I had doing on farmer in that time. I and my wif she like to go there but the tak so much money to going there. we got no money to going there. also, I was gethere in 1881 and R. H. P. he sent me 1883 outhere in Lawsece, Kan-Indian School I work there for three years in Bakery, and my wif she be cooking for the children there and I come home in 1885. and I get home here in Darlington I have work in arapaho School both us my woman she do cook again. and never get me work any more in 1892 that time.
>
> that is all.
>
> from you friend
> William Little Elk
> Watonga. Okla.
> R.F.D. 3. Box 74.

Little Elk's written English seems to have liberalized—freed itself a good deal from convention—in the years since he had last written. It was Richard Pratt—"R.H.P."—who had been superintendent in his time, and Little Elk, who had left Carlisle well before Friedman's arrival, wants to tell the new superintendent something of an earlier time at the school. Carlisle records indicate that William and Minnie Wolf Face Little Elk were farming in Oklahoma in 1913.

William Little Elk's younger sister, Florence, had written very briefly to Pratt in 1890 to tell him she was "sorry to say that I am Indian away all the times. I cannot do answered questions, and the other girls all go Back in Indian aways (too)." **Florence Little Elk** had spent just one year at Carlisle, leaving because of illness, and although eighteen years old on her departure, she was recorded as having advanced no further than the first grade. Judging herself unable to do the questions in 1890, Florence Little Elk had nonetheless written to inform the school of that fact. A full twenty years later, she responded to the 1910 questionnaire—although, as becomes clear, she could not then write answers to the questions herself either.

Her 1910 questionnaire came from her home in Cantonment, Oklahoma. Little Elk is married to a man whose name she gives as Red Bird, and she says he has served in the Indian Police but never been to school. For her "occupation," the response is, "Mother of four children. Two have died. Also cares for an orphan nephew." Here it begins to appear as though someone is writing these answers for her. The questionnaire reports that she lives "in a frame square tent. Use the tepee in preference in summer," and the next response to the question about property, stock, and money, does indeed make clear that the writer is not Florence Little Elk Red Bird herself. It says, "In the family there are three farms, all valuable. Red Birds farm has a house of two rooms. She owns horses and wagon, sewing machine, chickens, pigs and three cows. Red Bird, wagon and mules. Oldest boy two horses." The ninth and final question asks about "anything else of interest connected with your life," to which the writer replies, "What she explained under *6*"—the question about property. This is the last record Carlisle has of Florence Little Elk Red Bird, who although she could not "do answered questions," wanted to tell the school something about herself nonetheless.

In 1890 **Leonard Tyler** had written to Pratt, "Since my return I have never made much progress," and offered a detailed plan for a colony of former students. That colony does not seem to have been established, but Tyler did nonetheless make a good deal of "progress" over time. He responded to Moses Friedman's 1910 questionnaire to say that he had married "Nettie Black sister of **Jennie Black** ex student of Carlisle," after the death of his first wife, Jennie Black, in 1904, and that he was a "Stockraiser + farmer." He had been an "Industrial teacher ten years" in the Indian Service, and also an "overseer in road works." He now lived in the town of Calumet, Oklahoma, on an allotment adjoining the town, and had another "ranch place" "five miles from town." In answer to the final question asking about anything of further interest in his life, he wrote "none." He died in 1913, and his daughter, Ruth Tyler, sent the school her father's obituary.

It states that Tyler was born in 1864 at Fort Lawrence, Kansas, and that his "father was Lone Bear, a prominent Cheyenne chief."[8] He and his wife Jennie had five children, but only "Miss Ruth survives him." His home in Calumet was "one of the finest residences in the city, but his health grew so bad that he established his residence on his valuable allotments six miles north of town." About a year and a half before his death "he was baptized into the Reorganized Church of Jesus Christ, Latter Day Saints, and was later made an elder." He was buried "at Darlington on Saturday, April 4th, 1913."

Henry North, an Arapaho who had also responded to the 1890 questionnaire, did so once more to one sent to him in 1910. He writes, "I am married, to Nancy Lee, a fullblood Arapaho, attended Reservation school." After leaving Carlisle, North "attended Haskell Institute, Lawrence, Kansas nearly six month." He says, "I went there in Sept-1890 and returned Mar-1891. never graduated of any school." He is "employed as asst. Farmer for the Government." Of his present home, he writes, "Well, I have a home at Colony, Okla. In Washita County and a home at my wife's allotment. Buildings on each farm. land under cultivation. Some stock and implements." His property consists of "336 acres of land, six head of horses and mares. 2 buildings 1–2 room house on my allotment and 1–3 room house on my wifes allotment only enough money to meet my means." As for employment in the Indian Service, "Yes, I entered the Indian Service in 1894 as asst. Farmer and worked for 1 year and entered the service again in 1900 as additional Farmer held since until 1902. Jan 1 I again entered the service in 1904 as additional Farmer and resigned in April 1 1907 my salary as additional Farmer were $600—a year," or about $16,350 today (2019).

To the ninth and final question, asking for "anything else of interest connected with [his] life," Henry North replied:

> I have done all I could to uphold Carlisle in any breaks made by opposing Indians. and I have done as near as it could by in my knowledge to keep myself busy as I was taught while at Carlisle. my behavior has been better, as would naturally be so the older a person gets to be.
>
> I have eight children, four attending school and, four at home.

North also responded to a brief 1913 inquiry, writing from Geary, Oklahoma, that he was a "Farmer at home," and "Continuing to make use of my learning obtained when at Carlisle school," more than twenty-five years earlier. For all his commitment to "civilization," Henry North continued to be knowledgeable about the Arapaho language and culture, serving as a consultant to the Swiss-born linguist Albert Gatschet, a member of the Bureau of American Ethnology, and to the anthropologist Alfred Kroeber. North died in 1936.

Arnold Woolworth, who had been one of the Arapahos to visit Wovoka in 1891, returned the 1910 questionnaire on January 15, 1911. Woolworth wrote that he was married to an Arapaho woman, Julia Ashley, and they lived in Geary, Oklahoma, where he was farming 240 acres of land. He owns horses, cows, chickens, and hogs, and "$1000 loaned out at 10% interest," a loan worth about $27,000 today (2019). The couple has three boys and a girl; three of the children are in school. Woolworth reports that he has been employed in the Indian Service: "was a Scout six years, assistant farmer five years, ever since am on my own land, farming." He offers nothing further "of interest connected with [your] life." There is no further communication from him to the school.

On November 25, 1910, both **Grant Left Hand**—who had been with Woolworth on the visit to Wovoka—and his wife, **Kate Stalker**, responded separately to the questionnaire sent by Carlisle. They live in Darlington, Oklahoma, and neither has attended any other school. On his form Left Hand writes, "I am clerking in Indian Trader store last 28 years," an extraordinary work record. Those years in the store include his time as an adherent of the Ghost Dance religion, as noted earlier. His wife writes that her "present occupation" is "Bead works"—and that is all she says. Is her bead work for sale in the Indian Trader's store? Does she do it for ceremonial occasions? She says she has a "nice home at Darlington," and that she had been in the Indian Service as a seamstress at the Arapaho school for a year. Left Hand notes that he has "160 acer land house on it wind mill, 3 work horses one good spring." He says of his employment in the Indian Service that he had been a "shoe maker one year at Arapaho school in year 1882. and ever since I work in store."

Although his wife had left blank the final question asking about "anything else of interest connected with [her] life," Left Hand responded to report, "I am one of ahead chief of the arapahoes. I am belong Baptiste church." I believe he meant to say that he is a *son* of a Southern Arapaho head chief, Left Hand, himself formerly an adherent of the Ghost Dance, as I have noted—and also a Baptist. Thus in the year 1910, almost thirty years since he had been at Carlisle, Grant Left Hand, a store clerk for almost all those years and a Baptist, nonetheless wants it recalled that he is the son of Niwot, Left Hand, an Arapaho principal chief.

Kate Stalker Left Hand has in her file a brief letter she wrote to Nellie Robertson. Both had been at the school from 1886 to 1890, and they had probably kept in touch. She gives her return address as "Darlington O.T.," if I am reading her handwriting accurately, although on "Feb. 27, 1912," when she wrote, Oklahoma had been a state for almost five years. Here is Kate Stalker Left Hand's letter:

> My dear Nellie,
>
> I just thought of you this evening so I thought I would drop a few lines to you to let you know that I am still living yet and getting along nicely with my husband and he is still clerk in store yet. Adelia Twiss was down here with us and had a good time why she was down here and I think she saw most of her schoolmates.

The letter ends there, with no close or signature, suggesting that there was at least a second page that has not survived.

Kate Stalker's visitor, **Adelia Lowe Twiss**, had also been a Carlisle student, entering in 1882. Like Nellie Robertson Denny, she was an 1896 graduate and surely would have found a number of former schoolmates near Kate Stalker Left Hand's home in Darlington. Lowe, a Lakota from Pine Ridge, had married **Frank Twiss**, also from Pine Ridge, who had been at Carlisle from 1879 to 1884. If they had not already known each other, they would have met at the school during his last two years there; they married in 1896, the year of her graduation. In answer to a brief 1913 questionnaire, Frank Twiss wrote from Porcupine, South Dakota, to say he was a farmer and stock raiser, and proudly affirmed that he was "One of the first students '1879' one of the first that went on 'Outing System 1880,' one of the first Indian appointees in the Indian Service 1884."

His wife, Adelia, had also replied to the brief 1907 questionnaire to graduates, writing only that she was married, and giving her husband's name. In response to the longer 1909 questionnaire, she wrote that she had attended no other school after Carlisle, and was a housekeeper in her own home of three rooms made of "Sawed logs." She and her husband have many horses and cattle, and "964+ acres" of land, a substantial amount. To the question asking whether she had "done anything for the betterment of [her] people," she writes fully, saying,

> I have attended the Protestant Episcopal Church and the women's societies to help along the uneducated women in their trying to live a christian life. We are pulling along with them slowly but surely. Today they held a meeting in my house and they were greatly pleased that they were allowed to meet in such a cheerful and good ordered home. In their speeches they expressed a desire of having a nice clean house in the future.

In proselytizing "the uneducated women," Adelia Twiss would have addressed them in Lakota, not English. Not to over-read her brief communication, I note nonetheless that, intentionally or not, she seems to equate living a Christian life with "having a nice clean house in the future"—a future more immediately in Porcupine, South Dakota, than in heaven. To the form's last question concerning "anything else of interest connected with [her] life," Adelia Lowe Twiss writes, "I do a great deal of needle work with which I get money." Would she have done her needle work on her visit to her former schoolmate and lifelong friend, Kate Stalker Left Hand—as Left Hand did bead work at her "nice home at Darlington?"

Ernest Left Hand, Grant's younger brother, had written briefly in 1890 to say that he had fallen "back in Indian way." In his case this had happened because no work was available from the agent, a common enough occurrence. Nonetheless, he, too, responded to a questionnaire from the school more than twenty years later, in 1912. Dated July 3, his answer says he is married to "Crooked Star. Daughter of Blackman. (Arapaho)." Himself the son of a chief, Ernest Left Hand is proud of his wife's lineage as well, for Blackman was also an Arapaho leader. Signatory to an important 1865 treaty, he later served as a scout with General Crook after Custer's defeat in 1876 (Trenholm 1986, 212n and 259).[9] Left Hand has attended no other school since leaving Carlisle, and he is a farmer with a family of three children. His property consists of "160 acres land, house, 6 horses, cow and calf, wagon &c." Regarding "anything else of interest connected with [his] life," he writes, "I have been sick a great deal of my life. and my eyes have been very poor for seven years. Thanking you for your interest in me. I remain," and he signs, "Yours sincerely / Ernest Left Hand." Near the end of July 1912, Friedman responded to Left Hand saying he regretted "exceedingly that you have not been in good health and that you have had trouble with your eyes. I hope that your health may improve." He also told him, "I am having your name placed on the complimentary list of THE ARROW." Ernest Left Hand was about fifty-two in 1912, and this is his last communication with the school.

Percy Kable had written Pratt from the Darlington Agency in June 1890 to state grimly that "here we have no means of progress." We hear of him the following year when the *Indian Helper* for March 20, 1891, announced that "Percy has married Susie Vanhorn" (4). Kable did not communicate with the school again until 1910, when he responded to that year's questionnaire from Moses Friedman. Perhaps remembering the procedure from 1890—that was, to be sure, twenty years earlier—Kable sent Friedman both a filled-out form and a letter. On August 31, 1910, he wrote as follows:

> Sir:
>
> I will now trying to answered some questions. very best I know how. I am very business just now working for my family. I make $2.00 a day and I am never forget all what I learne at Carlisle Pa. I am now out from Government or Indian Agent. I am take care of my family. So I get long alright without Agent's care.
>
> That's all,
>
> I remain yours
> Percy E. Kable

He also dated his questionnaire August 31, 1912, and it and his letter come from Okarche, Oklahoma. Okarche was just inside the Cheyenne and Arapaho Agency, but, having been opened to a land run in 1892, it is now "out from Government or Indian Agent." In 1905, two years before Oklahoma statehood, the first post office for Okarche opened, the town's name made up of the first two letters of *Ok*lahoma and *Ar*apaho, and the first three letters of *Che*yenne.

If Kable had married Susie Vanhorn in 1891, he writes in 1910 that he is married to "Emma Bull Bear, Sister of Richard Davis." Emma Bull Bear was not a Carlisle student—there is no record for her—but her brother had been, as Kable knew—and **Richard Davis** is someone who warrants fuller treatment, which I soon offer. As for attendance at other schools, Kable says he had both attended and been employed by the Haskell Institute for a short time in 1888, just after he had left Carlisle. A brief note sent by him from Haskell had appeared in the *Indian Helper* for April 26, 1889, in which he says, "I am now instructor in the tailor shop . . . cutting the boys' suits" and supervising "5 boys and 2 ladies" (4).

As for his occupation in 1910, Kable wrote that he had "some corn and 30 acres. no wheat or oats. I got-Goodbarn." Of his "present home," he says, "I have happy home + Wife she can do most anything. that any woman cando." His property consists of "house 3 rooms I got-2 teams of horses + wagon. + I got some cows + some others thing no money grow [illegible] out." Regarding Indian Service employment, he writes, "I use to in Indian Service + work Tailor for the Cheyenne School about 3 years." He leaves blank the eighth and ninth questions, asking about other positions and anything else of interest.

Kable's last communication with Carlisle came in January 1914, when he responded to superintendent Friedman's brief form. He is still in Okarche, Oklahoma, and he lists his occupation as "Farming." In the space asking for "Remarks," Kable wrote: "I am glad that Carlisle house has not forgot me yet. I will thank that-But I am sorry to say that my wife death 16 of Aug-I am well. at the present."

His deceased wife, Emma Bull Bear, was, as her husband had written Carlisle in 1910, the sister of Richard Davis, and Kable's mention of him once again opens the way to encounters with many interesting Indian people largely unknown to the historical record. Davis himself, for example, was among the earliest students to enter Carlisle, arriving at the age of twelve on October 27, 1879, just three weeks after Luther Standing Bear and the first group of Lakotas from Pine Ridge and Rosebud. He did not graduate, but stayed on to work at the school until 1891, and thus did not receive the 1890 questionnaire. He had come to the school with his older brother, **Oscar Bull Bear**, listed by Carlisle as twenty years old at the time, but probably younger. The two young men, like Emma Bull Bear, Percy Kable's wife, were the children of a prominent Southern Cheyenne chief known as Bull Bear or Old Bull Bear.

Old Bull Bear had been a war chief and a leader among the Dog Soldiers, a group fierce in their resistance to the encroachment of the Americans. He nonetheless was one of the signatories to the 1867 Treaty of Medicine Lodge, establishing a reservation for the Southern Cheyennes and the Arapahos around the town that would come to be called Darlington, after Brinton Darlington, its first agent. In 1872, after Darlington's death, John D. Miles became superintendent of the Cheyenne-Arapaho Agency, serving until 1884. In a letter of 1875 Miles wrote that Bull Bear, "one of the noted old war chiefs," had a son of nine in school at the Agency—the school was the Arapaho Manual Labor and Boarding School, with John Seger as superintendent—"with his hair 'shingled' close and neat, as is required of all and dressed like a white boy." This boy's name had been Crooked Nose, and at the agency school he was called Davis, receiving the name Richard at Carlisle, perhaps from Pratt himself.[10]

Carlisle's *Eadle Keatoh Koh*, or *Morning Star*, for November 1880, prints a letter by Old Bull Bear in which he outlines his thinking about the American schools. Bull Bear did not speak or write English, so the words are those of a Darlington agency Cheyenne interpreter, who would have written them down to be sent to Carlisle by agent Miles, apparently at Bull Bear's request. The letter is dated October 24, 1880, and I present it in full. I have not seen it in print before, and it is an interesting addition to the representations of the speech of nineteenth-century chiefs.

Bull Bear is reported to have said,

> My Dear Capt. Pratt,
>
> A long time ago when you were here with the army I was a big chief among the Cheyennes, when I talked they listened to me and obeyed me. But when I saw that it would be better for me to take up the white man's road, this I did and gave my son to the agent to go to school. His name is Davis, he is a good boy and does not get foolish. I afterwards gave Oscar to the agent to put into school. When you wanted children for your school at Carlisle, I was the first of the Cheyennes to give you my children. Since I have taken up the white man's road I have kept straight on and have not been tired.
>
> The Cheyenne chiefs that visited Carlisle this fall have told me that my boys are doing well, that at work Oscar is a chief—head and shoulders above the other boys. And that Davis is learning

very fast, that he can read and write well, and understand and talk English very well.

Today, as I think about the change that it has made in my children's life by taking up the white man's road and putting them in school, my heart is light—I am very happy.

I would like to have your photograph, also pictures of my two boys Oscar and Davis. I think it will make my wife and the boy's lady friends happy to see their pictures. All the Cheyennes are anxious to see their pictures. All the Cheyennes are anxious to see your picture. When it comes they will all come to my tepe to look at it. When you want more Cheyenne Children I think it would be good to send Oscar for them. He could soon get all you want, for the Cheyennes would hear what he told them. I think it is good for the Cheyennes to send all their children to your school.

Oscar's two sisters are going to the Arapahoe School now.

That is all.

From your friend BULL BEAR

One of those sisters was Emma Bull Bear, who would marry Percy Kable. That Kable had been a Carlisle student would surely have found favor with her father and two brothers, one of whom, as we will see, also married a Carlisle student.

The earliest photo of Pratt in the Carlisle files was taken by John Choate in 1890, and although I am sure Pratt had had many photographs of himself taken before that, I don't know whether he ever sent one to Old Bull Bear. Carlisle has an 1880 photo of Oscar Bull Bear, but in it he is one of a great many Carlisle students and staff working on a roof, and I suspect even his father would be hard pressed to recognize him. There are several photos of Richard Davis, as I describe later, but the earliest of these was taken only in 1885, five years after his father's request for one.

Oscar Bull Bear's student information card says he left Carlisle for home in September 1885, and the *Indian Helper* for November 20 of that year reports: "A letter from Oscar Bull Bear says he cannot find any work at Cheyenne Agency" (3). Three years later, however, the

June 29, 1888, *Helper* noted that Bull Bear, along with the returned students Hubbell Big Horse and Jah Seger—both of whom we have met earlier—were employed at the Seger Colony as assistant farmers. But either Bull Bear was dismissed or perhaps he found his employment unsatisfactory, for the following year's *Helper* for January 1889 reported that he had left his farming duties and was then an army scout at Fort Elliott, Texas.

He did not respond to Pratt's 1890 questionnaire, but in 1893 the August *Helper* observed that he had returned to the position of assistant agency farmer at the Seger Colony. Oscar Bull Bear married a Cheyenne woman named Standing Lightning with whom he had a son in 1906 and a daughter in 1908, two grandchildren Old Bull Bear did not live to see, as he died in 1892. In all this time, however, there is no communication from Oscar Bull Bear to the school in his file.

But then we find a lengthy letter from him to Moses Friedman dated January 3, 1912. He begins by referencing Friedman's cover letter to the 1911 questionnaire and apologizes for not having completed and returned it. That is not, however, the primary reason he writes, nor will he get to that reason before offering a page and a half of the most extravagant praise for Carlisle that I have encountered from one of its students. I quote only some of it. Bull Bear writes,

> You cannot imagine the pleasure it gave me to get a letter like yours coming from My School Boy days and the Carlisle School where I spent many happy hours of my early life in school. There has always has been and as long as life last will be a warm place in my heart for the Carlisle Pa. School and all its Teachers and pupils. These Sweete memorys is deep down in my heart and will never die so long as I live.

There is a good deal more along these lines. Bull Bear writes that he is living on his allotment with his wife and children in Clinton, Oklahoma; that his children are in the public schools; and that he intends to send them "to the Carlisle School Pa. knowing what it has done for me I know it will do the same for my children." He says he is "living a Christian life and Say no bad words drink no whiskey play no cards or use tobacco in any way," all of which, he affirms, are behaviors he learned at Carlisle.

He then comes to his purpose in writing. He recalls having "a good clean record" at school, and he asks superintendent Friedman to send him "a certified copy of my Record in the years I was in School there." He wants that record because he is "asking the government to Remove all my restrictions So I can be and feel free to do as I please with all my private affairs." I don't know when Oscar Bull Bear took his allotment, but it is very likely fewer than twenty-five years earlier than the time he is writing. This is to say that although he does not refer to "patent in fee simple," or for that matter to citizenship, he is surely preparing his case for "competency" in order that he may have full title to his allotment and "feel free to do as [he] pleases with all [his] private affairs." On January 12 Friedman thanked him for his "good letter" and enclosed for him a summation of his Carlisle record, writing, "I trust it may be what you want to help you get your rights."

Born in 1867, Richard Davis, Oscar Bull Bear's younger brother, was enrolled at the school from1879 until 1891. Although he never sent a letter praising the school as effusively as that of his brother and fellow Carlisle student Oscar Bull Bear—indeed, Davis's file contains no communication from him to the school at all—there is no doubt that Carlisle played an important part in his life and that he was important to the school as well. Barbara Landis, the Carlisle Indian School biographer for the Cumberland County Historical Society—one of whose compilations I have already cited, and I cite others later—has gathered "Richard Davis References at Carlisle Indian School." These come to no fewer than twenty pages, and even these do not include every mention of him in a Carlisle publication.

This is to say that during his time at Carlisle, Davis's name appears in the school's publications more times even than did Mike Burns's name, and his writings for them are also abundant. I had noted Davis's comments about one of his early outings in 1882, and there were other such observations that appeared in the Carlisle papers. The *Morning Star* in March 1884, for example, reported that Davis was one of a number of Carlisle students to join the First Presbyterian Church of

Carlisle. The following year Davis's "The Story of my Life" appeared in the *Morning Star* for December, 1885. He was about eighteen at the time, and he had been at the school for six years. Although it has seemed to me that many of the writings by students published in the Carlisle papers were only lightly edited, I think that is not the case with this piece by Davis—or, to be sure, he may have had help with it. It, too, has not to my knowledge been published before, and I include almost all of it.

STORY OF MY LIFE

Soon after General George Custer had slain Black Kettle and his warriors, of the Southern Cheyennes, on the Washita river Indian Territory, some six or seven hundred under my father departed from the Northern Cheyennes of Dakota and joined with those of the south. At the arrival of these Indians, in the spring of 1867, my life began; then the war with the Cheyennes was at hand. In hunting and riding on ponies with my father I early learned that the United States troops could not capture us.

My early life was that of an Indian of the west until 1876 when the Cheyennes marched up with a flag of truce to the military post on the North Fork Canadian river. They were soon disarmed; ponies and prisoners were taken because of their cruelty to the whites in Kansas and other places along their country.

When the last war of 1876 took place, the prisoners were put under the care of Capt. Pratt who brought them away in chains to Florida, and the kindness he had shown towards them was honored by the tribe, and in the summer of 1877 they were willing their children should become educated. A reservation school was opened where I entered and left my blanket and paint. I attended school irregularly.

When 1879 came, a school for all the tribes of Indians was opened at Carlisle Barracks, Pennsylvania. I had the permission from my father to spend three years at that place. When I arrived October 27th, I was put to read from the chart, arithmetic

I began at the first part. I had no knowledge of the English language.

The second year of the school in the summer, I was out at Danboro, Bucks County, Pennsylvania, with a farmer by the name of Henry Kratz; there I learned my first lessons in farm work. . . . I returned to Carlisle and took up my second reader, arithmetic and geography.

The third summer vacation came, and many of my Cheyenne friends who came with me in 1879 bade good-bye to me and they returned to their western homes, but I turned my face towards the east instead of the west, and went to live with another farmer. . . . I found many friends among the white boys, but some of them were not so good, and I soon left them alone. I returned to the school, and entered the school printing office, where I learned how to set type for our monthly paper the MORNING STAR. I worked half a day and went to school the other half. . . . During this year I became a member of the First Presbyterian church. . . .

When our fourth vacation came I again went out to Bucks county to live with a Quaker by the name of Joseph Eyre. . . . From him I learned to do a man's work on the farm. I was called from the west by my father, and on the 18th of [September] some thirty of us started from Carlisle to our homes. On our arrival at the agency very little improvement was made by them and it was greatly discouraging to me, and I begged my father to send me back to Carlisle. By that time I understood and spoke a little of the English language. . . .

The summer of 1884 I was sent to the President of a bank. . . . to be a coachman for him from June to October. When the school opened I returned and began with my studies in Fifth reader, U.S. history, grammar, and went into a higher arithmetic. Last summer I visited Washington where they wanted me to go into a printing office, but Capt. Pratt thought I had better stick to school a while longer and get a higher education and better knowledge of my trade. I can set seven thoussand ems of type in a day and I intend to work until I can set twelve. (5)

Although Davis's language seems to me to have been edited substantially, what he had to say has surely been left just as he offered it, the precise dates differing somewhat from those in the written, historical record. For example, he dates his birth—1867—*after* the Washita massacre of Black Kettle and his southern Cheyenne people. But Custer's murderous attack did not take place until near the end of November 1868. The "last war of 1876" that Davis references is the Red River War, but that ended in 1875, not in 1876. Its conclusion may indeed be marked by the moment, as he says, "when the Cheyennes marched up with a flag of truce to the military post on the North Fork Canadian river," and it was indeed at that time that seventy-two Cheyenne, Kiowa, Comanche, Arapaho, and Caddo people were sent as prisoners to Fort Marion, in Saint Augustine, Florida, where Pratt was in charge.

Davis spent the summer of 1886 at home, taking the time to write to assure the school—his letter was published in the *Morning Star* for September 1886—that he had seen a Cheyenne and Arapaho Sun Dance and that it was not well attended. He noted of his fellow Cheyennes: "It is only their religion and their medicine dances that pull them down. But they will soon see the way," a sentiment sure to be pleasing to Pratt. Once he is back at school, the *Indian Helper* for October 7, 1887, informs its readers that he has been elected president of the Indian Union Debating Club.

It was in 1888 that Richard Davis married **Nettie** (or Nannie) **Aspenall**, a Pawnee woman and a schoolmate at Carlisle. Both were twenty-one years old. Their wedding took place in the Carlisle chapel, the event covered in detail by the *Indian Helper* for March 23, 1888.[11] The wedding ceremony and subsequent festivities over, the *Helper* reported, "the good byes were said—rice thrown after the happy pair—and they were gone—launched on the new life to make for themselves a white man's home in the white man's country" (2). Thus did the *Helper*'s reporter understand what was taken to be the happy ending for an exemplary Carlisle comic narrative. The reality, however, was far more nuanced and complex.

After their marriage Davis and his wife did indeed go to live in West Grove, Pennsylvania, and the *Helper* for September 14, 1888, prints a letter by Davis in which he describes the 1742 house on the farm of William Harvey in which he and his wife live, and which he is painting red and "striping it white" (1). The birth of their first child, a daughter called Richenda—she is named after Richard Pratt's youngest daughter—is announced in January 1889, and the following year the Davises would have another daughter, Mary, who may or may not have been named for Pratt's oldest daughter, Marion. The Davises and both their daughters paid a visit to the school, as reported in the *Helper* for December 5, 1890, and that may have been when John Choate took a photograph of the Davis family. That photo became so popular that the *Helper* for February 27, 1891, reported that the school would now offer it for "20 cents cash, or will be sent free to the person forwarding five subscriptions to the HELPER and a one-cent stamp" (2).

This photograph is the very first item that appears in Richard Davis's digitized file, and it is presented very much as an advertisement for the work of John Choate, the school photographer. The photo has the following announcement below it:

> *RICHARD DAVIS, CHEYENNE.* Born 1867 at Sand Creek, Col., entered Carlisle 1879, learned the Printer's trade. In 1888, married Nannie Aspenall, a Pawnee girl at Carlisle, and worked for a Penna. farmer engaged in raising thoroughbred stock. He has been in charge of the School herd of 65 thoroughbred and graded animals and the Dairying until the summer of 1894 when he was appointed District Farmer of the Cheyenne Agency.

Thus it appears that although the *Indian Helper* had said of Davis and his wife that upon their marriage they were going "to make for themselves a white man's home in the white man's country" (2), before the couple turned thirty they had decided instead to make for themselves an Indian home in Indian country: Davis would not have been "appointed District Farmer of the Cheyenne Agency" unless he had applied for the position.

Neither Richard Davis nor his wife communicated with the school after their return west, although the *Helper* for July 29, 1898, noted that the couple by then had five daughters. Then in 1904 their first daughter, Richenda, wrote to Marianne Burgess to say that "Momma has a new baby boy" (*Red Man and Helper*, March 25, 1904, 3). The last Carlisle references to the couple record that Davis was an interpreter in Kingfisher, Oklahoma, in 1910. He died in August 1913. His widow's file notes that she was still in Kingfisher in 1914 and "Desires matron's position in Indian Service." None of the couple's six children appears to have enrolled at Carlisle.

Of the other students from Indian Territory who wrote to Pratt in 1890, **Hubbell Big Horse** and **Jah Seger** sent no further communications to the school. Big Horse's file records that he died in 1904; Seger's information card has the word "Dead" in the upper righthand corner, with no date given. **Jock Bull Bear**—an Arapaho and no relation to the Cheyenne Bull Bears—responded to the 1910 questionnaire saying that he was married, and that his wife's name was "Noxie [?]." He was then a farmer, who has a "squir house of 32x28 feet + Barn 38x28 feet," with "65 acres caluvation 3 acres archid," and some stock. He has been an Indian policeman, clerked in a store for five years, and served as a government scout and a county deputy sheriff. As for "anything else of interest connected with [his] life," he writes, "I am now as an Indian chief for my tribe to look after their interests." He returned the brief 1913 form to say he was still farming, adding, "am so glad to know that Carlisle still remembers her old student."

Although **Mike Burns** kept in touch with Carlisle from the San Carlos Agency in Arizona Territory, most of his Apache neighbors who had been to the school did not. **Madoc Wind** responded briefly to the 1911 questionnaire, writing from Ray, Arizona Territory, to say that he is married to "Susie," and that his occupation is "Working around the mines." As for his "present home," he writes, "Only temporary as the camp is new." The town of Ray had grown up in the 1880s around the Ray Copper Mine, but the new camp that employs Wind is the one opened there in 1909 by the Arizona Hercules Copper Company. Wind writes that he had formerly been an "Assistant miller 6 or 7 years" in the Indian Service, and also "Foreman at Roosevelt Dam, assistant issue clerk at San Carlos. Was Indian police."[12] The final question asking, "anything else of interest connected with your life" is left blank.

Roland Fish responded briefly to the 1912 questionnaire to say that he was living at San Carlos and married to "Indian Woman Nanohkie [?]" and is a carpenter in the Indian Service. Although he owns ten horses, he has only "about 3 acres" of land, and no money in the bank. To the form's final question asking, "Have you done anything for the betterment of your people," Fish responds, "Not that I know of."

Brian Early Bird had written to Pratt in 1890 as Fish and Wind had not, and more than twenty years later in July 1912, he responded to the questionnaire sent out by superintendent Moses Friedman. Both in printing his name and in signing it, Early Bird spells his first name "Brain," surely an unintentional inversion of the vowels, but one, as we will discover, he could not see to correct. He says he is married "to Indian woman . . . that never went to School," and that he lives in Globe just off the San Carlos reservation in Arizona, which had become a state only five months earlier. He has not gone to any other school and, he writes, "After came back from Carlisle I join the Soldirs for 3 years after that I act as policeman at San Carlos for 6 years." As for his present occupation, he says, "Now I am not doing any thing, I stay one place at home, I am blind now." This misfortune explains what he writes about his home, "My very poor I live in the Indian teepy my children growing up as woman and manhood They are going to school other married. . . . I have not any property at all." To the final question, asking him to tell "anything of interest connected with your life," Early Bird writes, "I will tell you that I can not tell you anything only to say I am blind no way to help my self or help my families I will say that I am poor man [illegible]." He signs, "Your truly / Brain E. Bird."

Less than two weeks later, on July 27, Friedman sent him a short reply—one of his many personal responses to student communications—addressing him as "Mr. Brain Early Bird," respecting the spelling Early Bird himself had used. Friedman sends regrets "that your eye sight is afflicted," and hopes he "may find something to remedy this." He also writes, "I am issuing instructions to have THE ARROW sent to you regularly," something many former students had desired. We may imagine that Brian Early Bird's children, when home from school, would read it to him and hope that it brought some satisfaction to a man whose life story appears as an ironic tale, "no way to help my self or help my families."

Pueblo returned students seem to have been more active in their further communications with Carlisle. **Juan Antonio Chamon**, from Jemez Pueblo, had attended from 1884 to 1889, and had written to Pratt in 1890 to ask his help in obtaining implements for his trade as a blacksmith. In 1909 he responded to the school's questionnaire, writing that he was married to Petra Toya and that they were living at Jemez. He has attended no other school after Carlisle. Of his three children, a daughter, "18 yrs spent 5 years at Santa Fe Ind School, is now housekeeper at the day school here. Oldest boy 12 yrs is at Santa Fe School. The other boy 8 yrs is in the Day School here." Chamon continues to follow the blacksmith's trade, and writes, "I have a shop and do all the work that comes here." He also farms "About fifteen acres of land . . . in corn, wheat + alfalfa." Although he had told Pratt in 1890 that his wife was not "educated," the couple's children are at school, their daughter having attended the Santa Fe Indian School, first opened in 1890, and their oldest son presently in attendance. The younger boy is at the Franciscan Mission's San Diego Day School in Jemez.

Chamon wrote to Friedman on January 12, 1912, in response, he says, to a letter he had received, perhaps an invitation to attend a Carlisle commencement. Now a man about forty-six years old, he addresses the superintendent as "Dear Friend," and writes,

> I received the letter which you wrote to me some time ago. I was very glad and please to hear from you people. But I haven't had no time to answer it soon because I am working hard every day.
>
> I suppose you would like to know how I spend my days now. I am the blacksmith and silversmith I had the shop one side of my house also several other works, but those two I do the work most. But I haven't got all the blacksmith tools that I need but I do the work well.

I repair wagons and make rings, bracelets, earrings things like that. Some one will be round every day that wants his things to be mend or make.

I am married. I have two sons one of them is but round fifteen years of age, the other but nine. The oldest one is at Saint Catherine's Indian School in Santa Fe, the other one go here at the Sisters school.

I guess I will never get to see Carlisle any more because I am so poor. I haven't got no money to go. I am so glad I know some of the blacksmiths work. This help me a great deal in my living and is good business to know blacksmith. Because there will be work all the time no matter when.

I thank you ever so much for the papers you are sending me. I do not know how to read very well but I understand little.

Good bye with best regards to all you people, from all of us.

I am,

Sincerely your friend,
Juan Antonio Chamon

As so many Indian farmers had spoken of the lack of adequate equipment and implements, so too does this modest Indian blacksmith: this is a lack that had not been remedied since 1890. Nonetheless, he manages to do "the work well." One may wonder whether any of his silverwork—a skill he did not learn at Carlisle—has survived to this day. The "papers" the school has been sending are copies of the Carlisle *Arrow*, something many other former students had mentioned receiving. He does not speak, here, of his oldest child, his daughter who had worked as housekeeper at the Santa Fe Indian School. But his boys are still in school, one in Santa Fe at St. Catherine's, run by the Sisters of the Blessed Sacrament, and the other at the Franciscan San Diego Mission at Jemez.[13] Like several former students, he expresses a desire to see Carlisle once more, something his financial situation will not permit.

On December 12, 1912, Chamon returned the brief form he had been sent to say that he was still a "blacksmith and farmer," and the following year, on December 31, 1913, he reported that he was still at work as a blacksmith, adding, "Have just been elected Governor of Jemez Indians. Have two sons attending school. Wish you a Happy New Year."

Lorenzo Martinez responded to Moses Friedman's 1911 questionnaire to say that he had "married Indian girl of this Taos Pueblo," and that he was a farmer. Asked about his present home, he wrote, "I was born in Taos in a beautiful volly big high mt. wheat, corn, oats, potatoes, apples are raised abundantly." As for his property, he has "Cultivated Land Cattles adobe house money I get for value of grain I sell." He has been in the Indian Service as "assistant school teacher 1 year," and he has also been "Interpreter at the Agency." As for anything further about his life, he writes, "Cannot tell much about it have been too good or too bad." To a brief form in 1912 he responded that he was still farming at Taos, "Doing well. also Government Policeman in Indian Liquor Service," the first mention we have had of that federal office. Invited to the 1912 commencement services at the school, he responded warmly, but said that because he would be sowing wheat at the time, he could not consider attending. Responding once more in 1913, Martinez says he is still farming, adding, "I am doing well from what I learned at Carlisle."

The matter of the three young men from Acoma all named Miller does not become any clearer after consulting subsequent communications from them to the school. **F. H. Miller**, the very busy young man who said he was eighteen in 1890 and having good luck with odorless phosphate on his potatoes, does not have a student file containing further word from him. **James Y. Miller**, not yet a returned student in 1890, did fill out one questionnaire, as we will see. And **James H. Miller** has a substantial file. He had written to tell Pratt he was getting along well as a farmer and stock raiser, without mentioning something we learned from a letter Pratt wrote him in December 1890—that he had had difficulties with the conservatives at Acoma Pueblo to the point of being punished by its leaders.

James Y. Miller, living in McCartys, New Mexico, in 1909, said on his questionnaire that he was married to "Andrea Ortize," and had attended no other schools after Carlisle. He is a farmer and sheep raiser, who owns his own adobe house, along with "36 cows, 60 horses +1000 sheep 30 chickens," but he has no money in the bank. His Indian Service employment was only a single year as "Policeman in McCartys Day school." As for doing "anything for the betterment of [his] people," he writes, "I have tried to teach them the best way of cultivating their crops as I learned at Carlisle also any thing that would be of service to them." As for "anything else of interest connected with his life," the forty-three-year-old Jason Y. Miller thoughtfully replies,

> My life has been spent among the Indians and there is nothing new about our mode of life I attend church whenever I can and send my children to school daily I had one boy in the Govmnt School of Albuquerque he finished his term last June. I have very little else to say about myself I never have been in trouble with my people, nor have I ever been in jail
>
> Respectfully, James Y. Miller

There is no further word from him to the school.

As for James H. Miller, he did not communicate with the school until 1911, when he filled out that year's questionnaire in August. In answer to the question whether he is married, Miller wrote, "No. Sir I never was married at all." But this is surprising in that in his 1890 letter to Pratt he had said, "my wife she is very kind we have always live with joyfully she is a good housekeeper just exactly as good as an educated girl" (Part 3). He is writing from Zuni Pueblo, in 1911, a little more than one hundred miles west of Acoma, his home, and what we might have guessed—that it was ongoing conflict with conservatives at Acoma that caused him to move—is confirmed in a letter Miller sent to Friedman later in the year. Can it be that he left his wife behind at Acoma, and now, more than twenty years later, prefers to say that he was never married?

Miller further says that he attended no other school after leaving Carlisle, and that his present occupation is "farming and sheep raiser." He writes that "we had owned afew Cattles and sheep here at Zuni," and that he has "No money at all but we are living better than other here we have a good farmer." Although he said he was not married, his use of "we" implies that he is not alone. He has not been in the Indian Service, but he states that "we have fine crop this year plenty of wheat and corn." The last question, asking about "anything else of interest connected with [his] life," is left blank.

Friedman must have written to him subsequently. Here is Miller's response to the superintendent in full:

> Pueblo zuni
> New Mexico
>
> December 12/31 1911.
>
> Mr M Fraiedman [?],
>
> My dear Sir:
>
> I received your kindest letter and was very glad indeed to hear from you and that my oldest Carlisle father and mothers are still Remembered me. How glad I am and at same time I don't know any what to say or to answer or to please my dear good friends of min and teachers to those who once giving me a good education in the time when I was there and a happy time on that days and it is very ture that I was one off the Carlisle Child and enjoyment with my school brothers and sisters more than, than to be among my own people it have been treaded me my own people very bad for the reason I was been educated and tried to started some living than people get after me or they tried to have me droped in the old costman so is enough to lose my good Education. only the reason why this trouble I did got away from my own home, and here have a good home and enjoy with these family So now I've [?] enclosed this letter with our best regards to all friends and teachers.
>
> I am your friend.
> James H. Miller.

I venture that Miller's reference to being "droped in the old costman" is his version of "draped in the old costume": the preference of some in the Pueblo that he wear traditional rather than "citizen's" clothing. The family he refers to may be his own—wife and children—although it may instead refer to a family with whom he is living. He has left Acoma because his "own people . . . been treaded me my own people very bad for the reason I was been educated," and because he has refused to dress the old way.

Although James H. Miller had seemed to be doing well at Zuni when he wrote to Friedman in late 1911, a letter in his Carlisle file from Robert Bauman, superintendent of the Zuni Indian School, dated March 10, 1914, notes of him: "His occupation for several years has been herding sheep for Mexicans outside any reservation." Does that mean that he had had trouble at Zuni as well and given up farming? James H. Miller was about forty-six in 1914, and I know nothing more of him.

Henry Jiron Kendall from Isleta Pueblo did attend Rutgers University rather than Amherst, as superintendent Pratt had suggested to him in 1890. He would have been in the Rutgers class of 1893, but he left without graduating. Illness had caused him to leave Carlisle in 1890, and he may have been ill at college as well. He died in 1894 with no further communication on file from him to the school.

John Dixon had written to Pratt in 1890 to say that he been pressured to participate in "superstitious" dances at Cochiti Pueblo—although he had also described the governor of Cochiti, the father of his school- and workmate **Cyrus Dixon**, as progressive, at least so far as education and the schools were concerned. There is no word from John Dixon to the school until 1913, when he seems to have returned two short questionnaires, one dated "December 31th, 1913" and one dated "Feb. 27, 1913." It's my guess that Dixon sent the second one out in February *1914*, perhaps having forgotten that he had sent it in earlier. At any rate, both indicate that he is "carpentering and farming," the first of which he may be doing at the Cochiti Day School, which the December form gives as his address. It is on that form under "Remarks" that Dixon writes, "I am always glad + happy to get my yearly letter from the Carlisle Indian School father."

A bit earlier that year Dixon had written to Superintendent Friedman to say he would like his son, "16 to 17 years old," and his nephew, "15 to 16 years" to attend Carlisle. He says both have been at the Santa Fe Indian School, and that the two boys have been reading the Carlisle *Arrow*, which Dixon receives regularly. They wish, he writes, "to be at the Carlisle School. Often they beg me to ask if they could not have the chance to go to Carlisle Indian School." He informs Friedman that "If there is any chance and room for the boys, I might be able to find more boys from my place, Cochiti," many of whom have also been to the Santa Fe School, and who "would like to finish their studies if they can" at Carlisle.

I suspect Friedman wrote back to Dixon—I have several times noted that he was usually good about that—but there is no copy of such a letter in Dixon's file. There is, however, a letter from Friedman addressed to Philip Lonergan, superintendent of Pueblo day schools in Albuquerque, quoting Dixon's letter and informing Lonergan,

> As there is yet room here to accommodate additional students I would be pleased to consider the applications of any whose transfer is recommended by you, and if there is any further assistance I can give from this end I would thank you to let me have suggestions.

I do not know whether Dixon's son and nephew ever did attend Carlisle, and there is no further communication on file from him to the school.

Cyrus Dixon had not written to Pratt in 1890, and his Carlisle file contains no further communication to the school from him. But there is much about this former student's subsequent life that is worth noting. Like his older friend John Dixon, Cyrus Dixon was from Cochiti Pueblo, and his student information card gave his address as "Sarafine Quintana [Ex-Governor]," naming his father and the prominent position he had held and would hold again. Dixon's "Indian name," as I noted, was Santiago Quintana, and in later years he would also be called Santiago Bianco, Santiago Guerro, and Joe Dixon. Like his father, he too would become governor of Cochiti Pueblo, and he would also serve as a consultant to the ethnographers Adolph Bandelier and Elsie Clews Parsons early in the twentieth century and to the photographer

Edward Curtis—who took a portrait of him in 1906. Referred to by people at Cochiti as "mucho sabio" (Babcock 1995, 111), in the mid-1920s he narrated stories that would go into Ruth Benedict's *Tales of the Cochiti Indians* (1931), in which he was identified only as "informant 4." His powers as a storyteller have also been celebrated in the acclaimed "storyteller" pottery figures of his granddaughter, Helen Cordero.

In the 1887 letter from John Dixon cited earlier, published in the *Indian Helper*, he mentioned working at the Albuquerque school not only with Cyrus Dixon but with **John Menaul Chaves** as well. Chaves, from Laguna Pueblo, had not written to Pratt in 1890, but he maintained contact with the school in later years, one of several former students from Laguna to do so. Carlisle records mostly refer to him as Menaul, with an occasional spelling of "Manuel," more commonly found in the Southwest than "Menaul." (Chaves also signed himself "John Manuel Chaves" on a brief 1912 questionnaire he returned to the school.) In any case, John Menaul Chaves was almost surely named for the Reverend John Menaul (1834–1912), who had been born in Ireland, but by 1870 was posted to the American Southwest, where he founded the Presbyterian Mission at Laguna Pueblo, John Menaul Chaves's home.[14] His mission's name notwithstanding, John Menaul Chaves would seem to have been Catholic, not Presbyterian—at least that is the religion listed for his son **John Chaves Jr.** and his daughter, **Martha Chaves**, who went to Carlisle in 1913 and 1914, respectively.

Menaul Chaves responded to the 1909 questionnaire, writing that he was married to an "Indian girl," and although they had lived—and would live again—at Paguate, New Mexico Territory, their current address was "P.O. Bibo, NM."[15] Chaves said he had never attended any other school than Carlisle; that his occupation was farming and stock raising; and that he owned his home, "Three rooms, stone house with flat roof Pueblo style but well lighted and comfortable." He owns cows and horses but only some twelve acres of land. On these, however, are "100 bearing peach + apple trees + 50 younger not bearing yet." He has never been in the Indian Service nor does he have money in the bank, but, he writes, he formerly worked "on the Rail-Road 'Water Service' on this line running through Laguna. Which was then the 'Atlantic & Pacific.'"

In answer to the question asking whether he has "done anything for the betterment of [his] people," he writes, as the instructions had encouraged, "fully," and despite what he calls his "rudimental education," he writes in the wonderfully reflective manner of a Native organic intellectual, offering the telling metaphor of "the manufactured Indian." Chaves says:

> I have always urged my people to send their children to school. I have had held Offices at my Pueblo I was Gov once and I was send to Washington as a delegate for my Pueblo in 1905. That was the time when Pueblos were exempted from paying taxes I am sorry that I could not be much assistance to you but I feel I must answer in some way. As I have got only a rudimental education five years, half day schooling I was one of the first manufactured educated Indians from my Pueblo. When Carlisle was opened for Indian school. If I had studied more I would have—

here he uses the space for the next question—

> assisted you more. What I am trying to say is this, There are some who have had better education and would be of more assistance to you. Anything manufactured at first is not as good as later manufactured and improved. So it is the same with my red brother Each trying to get better education So there are more and better educated Indians now today who would be of good example + of more assistance to you in your good work, wishing you success in convincing the public what good the education did for us Indians. especially those better educated
>
> I am your friend
> John M. Chaves

His answers to the 1910 questionnaire are largely the same as those he had given in 1909, Chaves adding here that his wife's name is Placita Alonzo and that she is an "uneducated Ind." He also writes that he has a "big family, three boys + five girls attending school in Alb. + at

Riverside," probably the Sherman Institute in Riverside, California. In addition, he informs the school that he has been "Govnor of my Pueblo in 1905 had been Interpreter for my Pueblo for several times and as a prin. man"; that is, he had been one of the Principales or members of the tribal council. He writes, "I am John M. Chaves now. When at Carlisle I was John Menaul. I have a son who's name is John Chaves too," and he concludes by quite reasonably noting, "I had send these same ans. once befor."

To the brief 1912 questionnaire, John Chaves responded that he was then back at Paguate, still working as a "Stockraiser + Farmer." In the space for "Remarks" he wrote, "Wishing you a happy New Year and success in your good works + thanking you for the rememberance off me. I'll try to write you a long letter sometime hearafter." The only further letter in his file, however, is to Carlisle's last superintendent, John Francis, sent in November 1917, in which Chaves writes that he is enclosing "fifty cents subscription for the Carlisle Arrow and Red Man." His children, John Chaves Jr. and Martha Chaves, were at Carlisle at the time, and if they were reading the *Arrow and Red Man*, apparently they were not sending it home to their father.

Maria Analla from Laguna Pueblo also kept in touch with the school. On the 1909 questionnaire she wrote that she was still living at Laguna, married to Robert G. Marmon. She had been to no other schools since leaving Carlisle, and her occupation is "Taking care of my home," quite a large one—"7 rooms + kitchen—+cellar"—which she and her husband own. They have "Cows Horses chickens," and, as for land, she writes of an "Interest in Indian Grant and in Calle [?] ranch off the Indian Lands." She has money in the bank, "a few thousand," and "has not been in the Indian Service." In regard to helping toward "the betterment of [her] people," she writes,

> Yes. all I possibly could in way of setting the best example I could + always giving them as good council as I could. Have helped all I possibly could to get my people to take advantage of Education and put their children in school.

Responding to the final question asking for anything else of interest, Maria Marmon wrote,

> I have been married 17 yrs—I have a nice family of children. My youngest is 3 yrs old my children are all in Scholl except the two youngest. I have a nice home + am contented + happy + am proud + pleased with what Carlisle did for me.—

Her file contains nothing further from her.

Laura Reid had written to Pratt from Laguna in 1890 effusively, stating, "I want to come back to Carlisle again"; "I wish I could go back to Dear old school and stay with her there"; "how is Dear old Carlisle getting I like to see it very much"; and "I hope I will see Dear school again." But as noted, despite her attachment to Carlisle there is no student file for her at the dear old school. If she returned any of the subsequent questionnaires the School sent her, they have not been preserved.

Laura's sister, **Mattie Reid**, had been to Carlisle from 1881 to 1885, and in 1890 she had written movingly to Pratt, informing him of her shame at having had a child out of wedlock. There is no record of anything from her to the school until 1910, when she filled out that year's questionnaire. Mattie Reid dates it August 16, 1910, and signs herself "Mrs. Mattie Reid Luther," having married "Mr. Martin Luther, exstudent Albuquerque Gov. School. my own trib. pueblo." They live in Casa Blanca, New Mexico, one of seven Laguna communities, and she responds to the rest of the questions in detail. She writes, "I did not graduate + its in 1885 since I left School from Carlisle and never went to no other School since, but I been making my living among the whitepeople all that time. untill I got married." Her current occupation is "doing my own housework preparing meals for my husband and family, keeping house straight." Of her present home she says, "I am satisfie. What little I have about. I have few things that I am use to have when I was back east to work with." Regarding land, stock, and money, she writes, "We do not own any land yet, but we will. The Gov. is loting out the land now this very year. we have 3 houses but not much money just enough to keep [illegible]." But Pueblo lands were never allotted, and I give a fuller account of Pueblo land and title a bit later.

She writes that she herself has never been in the Indian Service, "but my husband was a policeman once for 3 months and he hauls water for the day School now and last year." As for other positions she has held since leaving Carlisle, "I cannot tell any more this part for myself. I went with my husband. to work on railroad after we were married. until we Sittle down we are having a home he is a blacksmith." As for "anything else of interest connected with [her] life," Mattie Reid Luther responds at some length. She writes thoughtfully,

> Well Mr Friedman, you may try to find out about me. I thought I was to be the only one kept up. Carlisle ways. but I am glad I see others are. I never forgot the dear old Carlisle. I have a son whom was there last year with you James R Luther. Carlisle is like a Christian life to me.
>
> When I was there. they make us be. just what we ought to be. good and honest + earnest in every way. but when some of us get home, did not make use of it. but I try my best. to keep it up. what I had learned and I made use of it and my husband did the same. he only was to Albuquerque School. We have just enough to get along. 3 houses 3 wagons and a blacksmith shop. and a little trading store as big as a nail top of your finger. 13 cows this is the truth. I can tell.
>
> I hope you are Satisfied by this time. I wish Government have enough to pay my fare to see Carlisle once more.
>
> I remain yours truly
> Mrs. Mattie Reid Luther
> Casa Blanca, N.Mex[16]

Friedman read the responses promptly, for only a week later, on August 23, he wrote to tell Mattie Luther that he had been pleased to learn she was doing well, "and would be glad to have you visit Carlisle sometime in the near future." For him to be able to reimburse her fare, however, would require her "to get up a party of pupils," something he encouraged her to do, for "We do not have very many Pueblos now, and we miss them." There is no further communication between the superintendent and the former student on this matter, and I would guess that Mattie Luther did not gather students for Carlisle or visit the school on her own.

She later sent a letter, as several former students had, to Nellie Robertson, with whom she had been at school. The letter, dated December 19, 1910, suggests they may not have been in touch for some twenty-five years. Here is what she wrote:

> My dear friend, Nellie
>
> I no doubt you will be surprise to get this letter from me. I have always had you in mine mind ever since I left the School, and I often talk about you to my husband. I still remember when we were at Germantown + our friend Gertrude Miller. I dont remember all of it and our cook Annie, and please write to me and tell me about the other girls I use to know, at the year 1885. You have seen my boy James. I only have two boys. one is 23 and the other 7. My regards to your husband. I remain your old chum once upon a time. (Mattie Reid)
>
> Mrs. Martin Luther
> Casa Blanca
> N Mex.

There are no Carlisle files for a Gertrude Miller, nor have I found her name in any of the Carlisle publications. I also have not discovered where Nellie Robertson spent her year and a half of outing assignment. But Germantown is in northwest Philadelphia and Mattie Reid had had an outing assignment there in 1882; perhaps Miller and Robertson had visited her there. Her older son, **James Luther**, born in 1887, was indeed a Carlisle student, as we will see further. Robertson's husband, Wallace Denny, had not come to the school until 1896, long after Reid had left, so I don't know whether she had ever met him or had only heard of her schoolmate's marriage.

Mattie Reid Luther filled out superintendent Friedman's postcard questionnaire for 1913 from Riverbank, California, saying that she was

"Housekeeping for my family." In a brief space calling for "Remarks" she writes, "It has been 28 years ago since I was at Carlisle and I have a son, 25 years old. he himself been to the same School." Her remarks were published in the notes on former students, in the Carlisle *Arrow* for February 13, 1914 (2). That is the last communication to the school from Mattie Reid Luther. From what we hear from her in 1890 until her last communication to Carlisle in 1913, she has come through and done well; her story can be read as a narrative in the comic mode.

That same issue of the *Arrow* also printed news of James Luther, who had briefly attended the Paraje Day School in Casa Blanca, and then spent three years at the Albuquerque School, before entering Carlisle and attending from 1906 to 1909. The *Arrow* reports that "James R. Luther writes from Riverbank, Cal., care of A.T. & S.F. round house, that he is at present occupied as boss wiper for Atchison, Topeka & Santa Fe. R. R. Co." (4). The railroad roundhouse was a circular or semi-circular building where locomotives were serviced and stored, and on a Carlisle form James Luther had filled out earlier, in 1907, he said he had "Worked in the round house before entering Carlisle." The wiper's job was to pack engine parts with grease. It was the lowest level railroad job, although if James Luther had become "boss wiper," he might soon hope for a promotion. The *Arrow* had gotten this information in the same way it had received news of his mother: James Luther had sent it in answer to the brief 1913 questionnaire, on which he also noted that he was single, not married.

We know that he had been in California for only a year—that may be true of his mother as well—because he had earlier filled out the brief 1912 questionnaire and listed his address as Casa Blanca, N.M., stating as well that he was a "Bachelor yet. Carpenter." In the brief space for "Remarks" he wrote, "Thanks of your Christmas letter. I am running Black Smith + Carpenter am still keeping up to [illegible] Carlisle's Standard." There is no further record for him or for his mother after 1913.

Frank Paisano had been only fifteen years old when he wrote to Pratt in 1890, after five years at Carlisle. He had written from the Albuquerque Mission School, where he was deeply engaged in religious activities, and strongly affirmed that he "never wear Indian clothes neither do I dance," an issue of concern to many returned students from the Pueblos, as noted. There is no communication from him to the school for twenty years, after which he responded to the 1910 questionnaire.

Asked whether he is married, he says, "Yes I am married to my own Tribe." Despite his time at the Albuquerque school, he writes that he has not attended or graduated from any other school after leaving Carlisle. His present occupation is "Stock raising and farming." He says nothing of his "present home" in the space provided, but in answer to the question concerning what property he has, he writes, "I have a stone building it has four rooms and two rooms I am renting to the Government as a teachers quarters and have cattle and have three thousand dollars in Bank," a substantial sum. He has not been in the Indian Service or held any other positions since leaving Carlisle. The ninth and last question is the one asking for "anything else" about his life he might like to share. He writes, "I have a ranck of my own and been living out there. I have come home on Jan 1st. the Pueblo of Laguna have elect me as a Governor so I have to stay home for a while."

Also in his file is a letter Frank Paisano sent to the school in January 1914. Here it is in full:

> Dear Sir:
>
> Your most welcome letter was received and I am more than glad to know that you take such an interest in the returned students. I, for one, am proud of what learning I received while there and for the Kindness shown me. I am trying to live my life the best I can and am upholding my good character so that the good old school need not be ashamed of me as a return student. I thought Carlisle and its friends had forgotten me. Carlisle has done a lot for me and I can use all that I have learned from the school. I appreciate this very much. I hope to hear more of the dear old school. Please remember me to all my old friends Mr. Siceni Nori is one.
>
> Yours respectfully
> Frank Paisano Ex-student

That is the last communication on file between Frank Paisano and Carlisle.

When he arrived at the Carlisle Indian School in 1884 at the age of ten, Frank Paisano came with another boy from Laguna named **Siceni Nori**, age twelve. Paisano left at the fourth grade level in 1889, but Nori continued, graduating with the class of 1894. He remained at Carlisle, holding various positions at the school until 1914. Siceni Nori played a significant part in Carlisle history, and I describe it further in the following chapter.

In 1926 the governor of New Mexico called a meeting to establish the "United States Pueblo Indian Council," apparently meant to rival the indigenous All Indian Pueblo Council. Many Pueblo leaders refused to attend. It did meet, however, and near its conclusion, those in attendance unanimously elected Frank Paisano president of the new council. The council never again convened, and it disbanded within a year (Sando 1992, 185–88). We may note, though, that in New Mexico's newest county, Cibola County, established in 1981, there is the Frank Paisano Spring.

Frank Paisano's older brother **Willie Paisano** had written to Pratt in 1890, and he also responded to the 1909 questionnaire sent out by Moses Friedman. He writes from Casa Blanca, New Mexico to say that he is still married to **Mary Perry**, also a former student, who as her husband had reported in 1890 had returned to wearing traditional Pueblo clothing. Willie is a "storekeeper" who owns his own home, a "two story adobe building five rooms with iron carogated roofed." He owns some livestock and has "apples peaches other kinds of fruit trees." In answer to the question about "having done anything for the betterment of [his] people," he writes at length, using all the rest of the form. Here is most of what he said:

> I had been appointed the Governor for Pueblo of Laguna in 1908 and served two terms or till 1909 or two years. The Laguna grant have been trying to get the patent years after years by the former Governors but without success. till later part in 1909 was secured by the aid of U.S. Indian Agent, and attorney.

> beside there are two small holding land. These are also secured both patents in 1908 and people mostly are farmers but they have not water enough for iregation purposes. and during 1908 being constructed three dams along the creek build by the Government This was a great help to these people. . . . after I returned from Carlisle in 1886 at once commenced to caltivate the soil for three years. Then I as I say above there was not water enough for the caltivating land this I quited then I began to raise cattle and sheep This I had done well. and kept on for four years. after this I started a store at Laguna in company with my father This kept up till 1899 then I removed from Laguna to this place and sold out my sheep . . . to build me a new home. Indeed I am regret for not getting my education and remain in Carlisle only one year and ten months Capt. Pratt tried hard to let me have full education. but my parents refused. on account of their ignorance. ever since I had in favor in education whenever a chance I found. in 1904 I took a party of 11 to Carlisle another party to Riverside Cal. another party in 1907 to Haskell Institute Lawrence Kans. this I had done without or with receiving any pay from our US Government

From 1598 to 1821 land grants in what is now New Mexico had been made by Spain to individuals and also to communities like the nineteen Pueblos. Upon gaining independence from Spain in 1821 Mexico took over the dispensation of land grants from that year until 1848 and its defeat in the Mexican-American War. The Treaty of Guadalupe Hidalgo at the end of the war provided for Mexico's cession of most of the Southwest to the United States for fifteen million dollars. In1854 the U.S. Office of Surveyor General was established to investigate the Pueblos' claims to lands. A Spanish grant to the Pueblo of Laguna dated from 1689, but a full patent for Laguna land was not issued by the U.S. Government until November 15, 1909. The Pueblo had been to court many times before title was finally granted, but even then there were several disputed land parcels, and these are surely the subject of William Paisano's trip to Washington.[17]

At the end of December 1912 Paisano responded to the survey postcard to say that he was still in Casa Blanca as a "Dealer in General Merchandise," and he also served as postmaster. A month later, he used his personal stationery—with a letterhead indicating both his commercial and his government positions—to request a favor involving Siceni Nori, with whom he too had been at school. He addresses Friedman as "My Dear Friend," and continues:

> I am such in a big hurry in writing to you this I am been elected Governor this year again. and also I have been appointed delegate to Washington D.C. on business Trust Deed proposition. and we have to starte tomorrow on 1st of Feb. and from Santa Fe, N.M. we all have on 2d inst. [?] two delegate each Pueblo. Indians in New Mexico. and if possible for you to do us your help as to allow Siceni Nori to come to Washington. That is when we get there then we can call by phone. that is if he can come at his own expence to do something for the sake his own land, and people. this is only sending ahead so you can have a talk over with him. I will bring two Carlisle man or students as my interpreter Ulysses G. Paisano and Yamie Leeds, all Laguna people in the meeting are expect Mr. Nori him to help less or much That is if he can, and if you can spare him a day or two. either I will be glad. I am your
>
> Sincerely Friend. Wm Paisano.

Edwin Schanandore had spoken of having seen **Yamie Leeds** from Laguna Pueblo in Albuquerque, as noted in chapter 1. Leeds had graduated from Carlisle in 1891, and apparently William Paisano thought that he and **Ulysses G. Paisano**—he was William's brother and had been at the school from 1886 to 1891—spoke and understood English better than he did. Nori was chief clerk at Carlisle at the time, as we will see further. Willie Paisano wishes him to be present in Washington for matters of interest both to him and also to his people.

Paisano wrote to Friedman again from Washington on February 16, 1913, having probably—this is my guess—remained there on tribal business for about six weeks. He addresses Friedman as "Dear Friend" and says:

> I indeed very sorry not able to see you this trip our ticket will not allow us to stop of at Harrisburg as we thought, and this we are intended to do and pay our ticket from Harrisburg to Carlisle but ticket agent told us yesterday that we cannot do that. So my best of regards to you + Mrs. Friedman. Your Friend Wm Paisano

That is the last communication from him in his file.

William Paisano's wife, Mary Perry Paisano, answered the school's 1911 questionnaire to say that she had attended no other schools than Carlisle; had not served in the Indian Service; and considers herself a "housekeeper." To the ninth and final question asking about "anything else of interest connected with [her] life," she wrote:

> Well I am always happy with my nice home and had six children Two are at Haskell School one down Albuquerque school two young ones go to day school and little girl stay at home she only three years old I am so glad that I can write and read when my childrens write to me. I will sent picture of my house. We had little store.

Her file does indeed include a photograph of her house.

On the brief 1912 form she wrote, "Was so glad to get the Arrow, as it is so nice to know what is being done at my old school. I wish I could go and see how Carlisle looks now as I was about the first Laguna girl there." For her "Remarks" on the 1914 postcard, she said simply, "I am so happy with my man and childrens."

Several of the returned Lakotas from Rosebud and Pine Ridge who had responded to the 1890 questionnaire wrote to Pratt, as I have noted, shortly after the massacre at Wounded Knee, their observations appearing in the Carlisle newspapers. But there are very few further communications on file from them to the school.

Luther Standing Bear had written Pratt in 1890 to say he was "working at the Agency school as an assistant," that he attended the Episcopal church, had "married an educated girl," and that the couple had two children. In both his autobiographies, *My People, the Sioux* (1928) and *Land of the Spotted Eagle* (1933), he would write in detail about his experiences during the time of the Ghost Dances and the events at Wounded Knee. In his Carlisle student file the first communication from him to the school after 1890 is his response to the 1910 questionnaire.

In it he wrote that he was now married to May Spicer—the "educated girl" he had first married was Nellie De Cory, and he had also been married for a time to Laura Cloud Shield Levering. He and May lived in Walthill, Nebraska, on the Omaha Reservation, where he clerked in a store. He had 1,120 acres of land on the Pine Ridge Reservation, where he had taken his allotment—a good deal more acreage than typical allotments—and his Indian Service experience amounted to seven years as assistant teacher at the agency school and a year and a half as an agency clerk. To the ninth and final question asking for "anything else of interest connected with [his] life," he writes at length:

> The Schools may not be in favor of the shows but that is where I have seen and learned good deal from too. As the saying goes experience is a good teacher during my travels I have been amongst good and bad. But I never forgot what I was taught at Carlisle not to drink not to smoke not chew tobacco or tell lies. I tell you I have been where temptation was strong especially in the Show-life, but believe me I have lived up to what I was taught.
>
> I went to Carlisle in the year of 1879 October the 6th with the blanket on in fact I was one of the first students. It is easy to be good in school but its hard when you get out into the world.
>
> Respectfully
> Luther Standing Bear

Letters in his file from the following year, 1911, document Standing Bear's efforts to obtain title for his allotted lands and with it American citizenship, which he strongly desired. On February 11, 1911, Standing Bear wrote superintendent Friedman asking for a "copy of certificate that Captain Pratt gave me somewhere between 1884 and 1889," a document he intends to use "for a reference when I apply for my patent in fee." Friedman directed him to Pratt himself for it, sending him Pratt's address in Philadelphia. Whether Standing Bear ever obtained that certificate or not, he was nonetheless successful in his endeavor. On November 8, 1911, he wrote to Friedman from Washington as follows on stationery from the Department of the Interior, United States Indian Service:

> First I do thank you for all the kindness that you have done for me. I would like very much to stop at your school and see the happy faces once more, but owning to my being stay here so long that I have to go right back. But I wish you would tell these few words to your school children for me at last. I step out from back door to front door into citizenship, that what I have been cring for last thirty-two years. Now I can say that I am a man and will enjoy life as citizen.
>
> When the Indians given equal opportunities, is the equal amount of white man in every way. When we compete with equal amount of men with equal chance, we have shown something to show for. In runing, football game, and baseball, we always do our best. Why can we try and do our best in citizenship.
>
> Give my regards to whole school.
>
> Yours very respectfully,
> Luther Standing Bear

Friedman wrote back immediately to congratulate Standing Bear, stating, "I admire you for the splendid way in which you have taken up this matter, and I hope that it will be the beginning of a new era of probabilities for you and yours." He assured Standing Bear: "The students at Carlisle will be pleased to know of the success which attended your efforts in Washington," and he closed, "It always gives me pleasure to hear from our returned students and graduates. . . . Let me hear from you whenever you have time to write." Sadly, Standing Bear was to discover that citizenship for American Indians was not what he and others had hoped it would be. Many years later, President Coolidge having signed the Indian Citizenship Act into law in June 1924, Standing Bear wrote: "The bill signed by President Coolidge . . . was just another hoax" ([1933] 1978, 245).

Standing Bear filled out brief forms from Carlisle in 1912 and 1913 to say that he was once again working in a dry-goods store, this time in Sioux City, Iowa. There is nothing later from him to the school, but there is a newspaper clipping dated August 17, 1917, in his Carlisle student file, reporting that "Chief Standing Bear is at Poli's Theatre appearing in the Race of Man, an act combining six different races of people."[18] Standing Bear had, for a time, returned to "the Show-life." He would marry at least once more; become somewhat active in Indian rights organizations; have a number of small parts in western films; and publish three autobiographies, *My People, the Sioux* (1928), *Indian Boyhood* (1931), and *Land of the Spotted Eagle* (1933). Luther Standing Bear died in 1939 and was buried in the Hollywood Forever Cemetery in Los Angeles, along with his sacred pipe.

There is little further communication to the school from **Plenty Living Bear**, and I reference it shortly, also following up on **Frank Locke**, who had returned home from Rosebud to Pine Ridge.

Dr. Daniel Royer arrived at Pine Ridge as agent in the fall of 1890; he would soon gain the nickname "Young Man Afraid of Indians." Through the fall and into the early winter, active practice of the Ghost Dance at Pine Ridge troubled Royer, who in the last days of December requested that troops be called to the agency. On the 29th of the month, at Wounded Knee Creek, about twenty miles northeast of Pine Ridge, a group of Minneconjous under Big Foot, along with many agency Sioux, were massacred by troops of the 7th Cavalry, George Armstrong Custer's former command. Plenty Living Bear was not there, but he was near enough to hear the big Hotchkiss guns of the soldiers and then, later, to engage in skirmishes with them. On January 8, 1891, he was in the vicinity of a council convened between emissaries of General Nelson Miles and several prominent Lakota leaders to discuss an end to hostilities. One of those present was Army Lieutenant Edward Casey. At some point, Plenty Living Bear, from horseback, fired a single rifle shot and killed the mounted Casey. He was arrested for murder just over a month later, on February 19, 1891.

At trial his lawyers offered in his defense the fact that a state of war had existed between the Sioux and the United States at the time Casey was killed. This meant that Plenty Horses, as I will now refer to him, regardless of the circumstances of his act, could not be prosecuted for killing an enemy combatant. For the government to obtain a guilty verdict against him for murder, it would have to claim that in fact no state of war had existed between the Indians and the United States at the time of the shooting. But if no state of war had then existed, the soldiers who had participated in the killings at Wounded Knee only a week earlier would also have to be tried for murder. The trial ended in a deadlocked jury. A second trial was held, at which testimony by General Miles was entered into the record emphatically insisting that a state of war between the parties had indeed existed at the time his troops had engaged at Wounded Knee, and it had not ceased to exist at the time Casey was killed. On the basis of Miles's testimony, the judge halted the trial and instructed the jury to find for the defendant. Plenty Horses was acquitted.

Dr. Valentine McGillycuddy, former Indian agent at Pine Ridge, was the foreman of the jury that acquitted Plenty Horses. In a biography of her husband, *McGillycuddy, Agent*, his widow Julia reported her husband quoting Plenty Horses as saying,

> Five years I attended Carlisle and was educated in the ways of the white man. When I returned to my people, I was an outcast among them. I was no longer an Indian. I was not a white man. I was lonely. I shot the lieutenant so I might make a place for myself among my people. I am now one of them. I shall be hung, and the Indians will bury me as a warrior. (McGillycuddy 1941, 272)

Plenty Horses was not hanged, and just as he had responded to the school's 1890 questionnaire, so too did he respond to one sent out in

1910, briefly noting that he was then a farmer at Pine Ridge. He died in 1933.

Even before the arrest of Plenty Horses, Carlisle had hastened to deny that one of its students had shot a soldier. The *Indian Helper* for January 30, 1891, on its first page affirmed:

> The despatch which has been sent out over the country, saying that a son of No-Water, "and a graduate of the Carlisle School," was the slayer of Lieut. Casey, is utterly false, so far as it relates to Carlisle. No-Water's son has never been a student of this school, and inquiry among our Sioux students has developed the fact that No-Water has never sent his children to school *anywhere.* (1)

A Lakota named No-Water was a contemporary of Crazy Horse (both born about 1840) who had shot him in the jaw in a dispute over someone known as Black Buffalo Woman. It is probably true that no son of No-Water had ever attended Carlisle, and it is also true that Plenty Living Bear, son of Living Bear, had not graduated.[19] But as the writer for the school newspaper may or may not have known, it was indeed a former Carlisle student who had shot Casey. A lengthy essay by Pratt still denying that Casey's killer had been a Carlisle student later appeared in the *Red Man* for February and March 1891 (1–2).

The January 30 issue of the *Helper* also published some direct reportage concerning the massacre at Wounded Knee by two returned students from whom we have already heard. Here is a letter to Pratt dated January 23, 1891, that the *Helper* printed a week later:

> DEAR SIR—In this letter, I send you a picture of the battle that occurred at Wounded Knee last month. I went to the battlefield, after it was over to pick up the bodies into a wagon to bring to the Agency—that is, the wounded ones. I see in the HELPER that Mack Kutepi, Paul Eagle Star, and some other Carlisle students were killed in the fight. Whoever wrote that letter must have been scared at the time he wrote the letter. Mack Kutepi, Paul Eagle

Star, and the others are here, none of them killed as the HELPER stated.

That is what I want to tell you.

Your friend Moses Culbertson (2)[20]

Mack Kutepi had been at the school from 1882 to 1887, and **Paul Eagle Star**, from Rosebud originally, had attended from 1882 to 1888. Kutepi had briefly responded to Pratt in June 1890; Eagle Star had not, and there is no later communication from them to the school on file. I have a bit more to say about them later.

Following Culbertson's came a letter from **George Means**, a Crow former student. Pratt had written to Means earlier, on December 4, 1890, asking, "Won't you please write me a full letter and tell me all what is going on. . . . Please tell me if any of our Carlisle students are with the Messiah Craze People" (Pratt letters 443). I don't know if Means had written to Pratt before the events at Wounded Knee, but he did soon afterward. He too attested to the fact that those named by Culbertson—and Culbertson himself, whom Means calls "Moses Red Kettle," his Indian name—were not killed; nor, he adds, was **Clayton Brave**, although "Clayton got wounded" (2). The full story of his involvement may be known only by Clayton Brave himself, who had done "slack wire walking" and "got through the hoops too."

It was only in the *Helper* of February 27, 1891, that a frontpage article appeared with the headline, "NOW WE HAVE THE TRUTH." The piece purported to give an account of "WHAT THE PINE RIDGE BOYS AND GIRLS REALLY HAVE BEEN DOING SINCE THEY WENT HOME." The information, the paper said, came from Assistant Commissioner of Indian Affairs A. J. Standing, who had visited the Pine Ridge Agency "three weeks ago" (1), and had just recently brought a group of Lakota students to Carlisle. I strongly suspect that Standing did not see or hear directly from every one of the returned Pine Ridge students he named—not all the information given is accurate—and that some of what he said of several of them comes from the June 1890 letters they had written in response to Pratt's questionnaire, the first two groups of which Standing himself had forwarded to Commissioner Morgan.

The *Helper* names more than sixty former students, and I reference those the *Helper* mentions from Pine Ridge whom we have already encountered and offer what I can about some few others.

"Lucy Day returned June 18, '82: has not always done well," the *Helper* reported, "but is now all right and working in the family of the Rev. Chas. Cook" (1). **Lucy Day** had left Carlisle in 1882 after three years at the school, reentering in January 1889, only to leave three months later because of ill health. Reverend Charles Cook, a half-blood Yankton Episcopal minister, had turned his church into a hospital after the massacre at Wounded Knee, and that was where Dr. Charles Eastman, Elaine Goodale, and others tended the wounded and dying victims of the 7th Cavalry's attack. A notation on Lucy Day's Carlisle file card indicates that she died in January 1898.

"Charles Bird, returned June 22, '86 is a scout and an active worker" (1). **Charles Bird** had also left Carlisle because of poor health. There are no communications from him to the school. His information card says that he died in 1901.

"**Newton Big Road**, returned June 22, '86, is on the police force" (1). There is no further word from him; he died in September 1895.

Of **William Crow** the *Helper* reports only that he is "gone with the Cheyennes" (4), probably to the Tongue River reservation that he did not care for but to which his father, Little Chief, led his people about this time, as we have seen. The *Helper* also reports that "Charles Dakota has gone with the Cheyennes; Arthur Standing Elk and Laura have also gone with the Cheyennes" (4). **Charles Dakota**—despite his name he was Cheyenne—had been a student from 1885 until July 1890, but his file card says "Died 1890"; if that is true, he would probably not in fact have "gone with the Cheyennes." **Arthur Standing Elk** and his younger sister **Laura Standing Elk** had both also left Carlisle in July 1890. There is no further word from either of them to the school, but there is a notation that Laura was living in Lame Deer, Montana, in 1910.

John Rooks had returned from school in 1889 and written to Pratt in 1890 to report that he had seen Clayton Brave wearing Indian clothes. The February *Helper* reported Rooks currently "working in the carpenter and wagon shop; is married" (4). The 1895 *Annual Report of* *the Commissioner of Indian Affairs* lists Rooks as a "private" in George Sword's Indian Police at Pine Ridge in 1894 (558). A notation in his Carlisle file says he "Died 1898."

"**Clayton Brave**, returned June 14, '87, is a government scout; it is said he was with the hostiles, but he himself denies having taken any part; he was trying to get his people to return to the agency and when between fires was wounded in the leg" (1), just as George Means had written to Pratt a month earlier. The report went on to say of him: "He has travelled with a show," as we knew, and also that he had "married **Julia Walking Crane** (Carlisle pupil)" (1). Of her the paper said only that "she wears Indian dress" (4). Walking Crane had entered the school in 1887, leaving in July 1890, a month too late to receive Pratt's June request for information. Her file card has "Dead" written on it with no date given. Neither she nor her husband communicated further with the school.

The February *Helper* reported that "**Emma Hand** returned June 14, '87, married Charles Means," as noted in chapter 1, and that her "husband had left her; she lives with her sister; has done well in so far as she could" (4). There is no communication from her to the school on file.

Of her brother, the *Helper* said, "**Marshall Hand** is a scout" (4). His school file notes that he was a laborer at Pine Ridge in 1910, but there is no further word from him either.

Similarly, we learn, "**Moses Culbertson** is a scout; good report; married an uneducated girl; doing well" (4). His file records that he was a "Stockman" in 1910 in Kyle, South Dakota, and it notes a "Letter dated Feb. 1913 ret'd unclaimed."

"**Wallace Charging Shield**, returned June 14, '87; has done well since his return, and during the latter part of the time has been working at the boarding school and was much valued" (4). This is the Pine Ridge Boarding School, one of the schools at which **Clarence Three Stars** (discussed next) would teach. The paper observes that Charging Shield "returned to Carlisle with the party who arrived this week from Pine Ridge" (4). This is the party the *Helper* said that Commissioner Standing had brought to the school. Charging Shield would stay on at Carlisle until July of that year, when he left because of poor health.

A notation on his student file indicates that he died in May 1895, at the age of about twenty-six.

Of Clarence Three Stars the *Helper* says he "works at the trader's, receives good wages; has a most desirable record since his return; faithful, steady, efficient, an influence for good; everyone speaks highly of him" (1). That same year, 1891, Three Stars would go to Washington with a Sioux delegation that included Young Man Afraid of His Horses and Little Wound (Ricker 2005, 1:350); years later he would serve as Red Cloud's interpreter "when the old chief made his last trip to Washington DC in 1897" (1:344), thus acting on behalf of his people in the manner the elders had hoped the returned students would. He would also become an important teacher at Pine Ridge's schools. Thomas Andrews described Three Stars as "a voracious learner, superb teacher, and tireless advocate for his people whose remarkable teaching career spanned three decades" (2002, 421), beginning in 1895 when he began as a Pine Ridge Day School teacher. Although he also worked at the Pine Ridge Boarding School and had received much of his own education at Carlisle, Three Stars was a strong proponent of local day schools.[21]

Three Stars also served his people through his writings, such as the lengthy letter he would publish in the Carlisle *Red Man and Helper* for December 11, 1903, under the heading, "A Carlisle Ex-Student's Account of the Wyoming Pale-face Uprising," in which he provided a corrective to some of the contemporary news accounts of the events.[22] Like the older George Sword, he also served as consultant to Pine Ridge doctor and amateur ethnographer James. R. Walker. An unidentified and undated clipping in his file speaks of the "new county of Bennett in the Pine Ridge Reservation" having recently been "organized," and of "the Indians voting for the first time." It notes that "several Indians were candidates for county offices," and that "Clarence Three Stars and Edgar Fire Thunder were elected members of the board of county Commissioners." Bennett County was organized in 1909, and I suspect this may have been the first county election in 1910. In 1913 Three Stars's response to Friedman's brief survey reported from Martin, South Dakota, that he was "State's Attorney."

We learn from one of Barbara Landis's compilations that 1910 was also the year when Three Stars married **Jennie Dubray** (https://home.epix.net/~landis/couples.html). She had come to Carlisle from Rosebud in 1883 and remained until 1891 or 1892 (different records give different dates). She did not communicate further with the school. Her husband's response to Moses Friedman's brief questionnaire of 1912 listed his occupation as "Rancher and attorney" and noted, "Just now again a candidate for the office of State's Attorney of Bennett County." Three Stars would seem to have won that election, for the next year, in answer to another brief questionnaire, he reported that he was indeed "State's attorney."

The February 1891 *Indian Helper* said of **Edgar Fire Thunder**, who had returned home in 1884, that he "is now a scout; has been working steadily in the Agency blacksmith shop; a little inclined to be headstrong but is a good worker and a man of character; lost twenty-five head of cattle and some horses by the hostiles" (1). If this comes from Commissioner Standing, I cannot imagine how he could have learned anything about Fire Thunder's temperament and his character. Pine Ridge Agent Daniel Royer had been dismissed on January 8, 1891, a little more than a week after the massacre at Wounded Knee Creek, and his replacement as acting agent, Captain George LeRoy Brown, would hardly have had time to become familiar with the Lakotas at Pine Ridge. Notations in Edgar Fire Thunder's file indicate that he was an assistant farmer in the Indian Service in 1910 and a "well to do ranch man" in 1911. There is also a 1913 letter from Moses Friedman to Edgar Fire Thunder asking whether he would like to enroll his children at Carlisle. There is no response on file from Fire Thunder.

The *Helper* reports on Edgar's brother, **George Fire Thunder**, who had returned home in 1887 but not responded to Pratt's 1890 questionnaire. The paper says he is "working at the agency; has not done altogether as well as he might but well in the main" (4). It is hard to know just what that means. Years later George Fire Thunder himself, responding to Moses Friedman's 1909 questionnaire, writes that he is married to Mary Bissonette and that he is a "Catechist in Episcopal

Church." He owns his own house and has some stock and a fair amount of land, "1920 acres." He had indeed worked at the agency "as Tinner and Painter," and he had also clerked in a store.

As to whether he has done "anything for the betterment of [his] people," Fire Thunder's own sense of the matter is that he has

> always endeavored to make the Indians look at the better side of things in this life to live a better life. And my hope is that eventually they will see the folly of old customs and grow more civilized.

For the final question asking about "anything else of interest with [his] life," he writes no fewer than two pages, offering thoughts that can, I think, be taken as "progressive" and "assimilationist" in a straightforward and uncomplicated manner. He says:

> My most ardent hope is that in the future we will have some educated Indians that will rival in greatness some of our great white brothers. And I see only one path that will make this possible. Have the white people in our midst so that we can get an example from him day by day and assimilate his costums + ways.
>
> The influence of most of the government officers among his People in the past has been, as a whole very bad—because the Indian's welfare was not theirs and their whole ambition was to gain money by any means. . . . Therefore I must insist that the only salvation for the Indian of today lies in the intermingling of the White people among them.

This, of course, is a straightforward restatement of the position of his old superintendent, Richard Pratt. Fire Thunder concludes that

> the returned students should be given an opportunity to fill positions that requires an amount of education which they possess. I think that the educated Indians should be given their rights as a citizen, instead of delaying it for an indefinite length of

time perhaps 25 years. Then the education he has had will be put to a test + be of some practical good.

In 1913 George Fire Thunder became county commissioner for Martin, South Dakota, seat of Bennett County—where, as noted, his fellow Carlisle-educated Indian Clarence Three Stars was state's attorney. I suspect the views of these two men did not exactly align.

The *Helper* reported that **George Means**, "returned Sept. 17, '90; is working as clerk in the office. He is the only Carlisle graduate there" (4). Means, not a Lakota but a Crow from Pine Ridge, had indeed graduated in 1890, with a notation on his file card saying that his "character" was "Very good." But it would appear that neither Means's good character nor his status as a Carlisle graduate worked entirely to his benefit.

For on May 21, 1910, Superintendent Friedman would write to a Mr. William Robertson of Allen, South Dakota, saying, "I enclose herewith a blank requesting information concerning George Means." His enclosure is the 1910 questionnaire to returned students; I believe it had first been sent to Means and had been returned unclaimed. There was an agency office at Allen, and Robertson was probably an Indian Office employee. Friedman asked Robertson "please answer questions 1, 2, and 4" and return the paper "promptly." He would do that, but he also—and likely initially—wrote a paragraph by hand at the bottom of Friedman's typed letter. These are not George Means's own words, but they provide an interesting perspective nonetheless. William Robertson wrote,

George did well for a couple of years or more, got a nice girl for a wife and was all right, and then bad companions, bad habits and finally a divorce the wife's fault I think. George married again with no better success in the way of happiness, he got shiftless and careless, would brace up now and then and get a *job*. but—well, he was on the down grade. Poor boy! lost his hold on "the man higher up," and does not seem to care. He may brace up. I hope so.
Robertson

Robertson also did as Friedman had asked, answering questions 1, 2, and 4 on the 1910 form intended for George Means. Question 1 asks whether the respondent is married, and Robertson answers for Means, "Yes, a daughter of Judge Thunderbear." Thunder Bear, a prominent Teton Sioux, had been a sergeant of the Indian police at Pine Ridge (Ricker 2005, 1:147), and he was elected judge of the Indian court several times. The judge's daughter would be George Means's second wife. Robertson gives "Manderson, S. Dak" in answer to the second question's request for an address. Question four asks for "present occupation," and Robertson writes, "Upon inquiry I learn that he is not doing anything for a living."

But that is not accurate. Upon discovering that Means was living in Manderson, Friedman had written to him there, and George Means responded on July 14, 1910, writing briefly:

> Dear Sir:
>
> Yours of the 7th of July at hand and contents noted.
>
> I have done all kinds of work since I left school and my present occupation is building houses and road overseer.
>
> My present address is Manderson So. Dak.
>
> Very truly yours
> Geo. W. Means.

The last item in George Means's file is a card on which the school had recorded, "No recent data—May, 1914."

The *Helper* reported that "**Dana Long Wolf**, returned June '86, is in the penitentiary" (1). Long Wolf had run away from the school in 1886, and he was indeed incarcerated in the Nebraska State Penitentiary when he wrote to Richard Pratt in June 1890. After his release he came home to Pine Ridge and married a Sioux woman named Maude Apple. We learn this from two 1910 questionnaires Long Wolf returned to Carlisle. He writes on both questionnaires that he has attended no other schools than Carlisle, on one of the forms expansively stating: "I am Educated from Carlisle Indian School [illegible] No other School but only Carlise is good place to get Education In."

As for his present occupation, Long Wolf writes, "Not any" on one form, and "Throngletty Trade an Harness and Black Smith" on the other. The handwriting seems clear for that first word, and I have transcribed what I see, but if I have it correctly, I have no idea what it means. Perhaps something to do with thongs and leather? In answer to the question, "Tell something of your present home," Long Wolf wrote on the first form, "My home is wild place for lonely place," and less poetically on the second, "Well I had 639.68 acres for my own and one log House 4 acres field all Timber spring water." He repeats this in answer to the next question, which asks what property he has, and on the other form offers a slight revision and perhaps an update, writing "639.36 land sale ½ Section $2689.00 down Rosebud my grandfather's property." His responses to whether he had been in the Indian Service are very close to one another on each form. In the longer of the two Long Wolf wrote, "I never had any Indian Service. Since leaving Carlisle No position all in the World I am most working for Chicago + North West Railway Company." As for other positions, "Nothing at all expecting Emply for North Wester Railway Company in most my life Time."

The form's final question asked for "anything else of interest connected with [his] life." To this, Long Wolf replied on one form, "My life is good condition but I hope you will help me to get any position from U.S. Government." On the other form, he put three large x's—XXX—in the space provided for a response, and wrote below, "I would like to have my Discharge paper an [illegible]." In that he had run away from the school, it is not clear what paper he wanted. Still keeping in touch in 1914, Dana Long Wolf sent the news that he was a "Ranchman and Farmer" in Oglala, South Dakota.

In his 1890 letter to Pratt, Dana Long Wolf had asked about his sisters, Lizzie, Hattie, and **Hannah Long Wolf**, the latter two Carlisle students, and about **Emma Bull Bonnet**, also a student there. Lizzie Long Wolf, as noted, was not a Carlisle student, having instead joined the Buffalo Bill Wild West with her parents. I believe she married another of the show's Oglala performers, Charlie Yellowboy, for her name was Lizzie Yellowboy in 1909 when she signed the Carlisle application form for her youngest brother, Nelson Long Wolf—he was born in 1892, the year their father died; Nelson attended until 1912.[23]

The February 27, 1891, issue of the *Indian Helper* I have referenced made no mention of Hannah Long Wolf, **Hattie Long Wolf**, or Emma Bull Bonnet because none of them had yet returned from the school to Pine Ridge. Hannah had entered in 1887 and remained at Carlisle until 1894; the school has no further record of her. Hattie had entered Carlisle with the first group of Lakota students, on October 6, 1879, and remained until 1882, when she returned home. But she reentered in August 1887, when her sister Hannah enrolled, and Hattie went on to graduate in 1892.

In Hattie Long Wolf's student file is her response to Major Mercer's 1907 questionnaire to Carlisle graduates. She writes from "Cheyenne River, S.D." as Hattie Long Wolf Pretty Weasel, the wife, as she states, of Hall Pretty Weasel. For her occupation, she says, "I sew for people + knitting a great deal When I do not fill any places as my hands find plenty to do." She says she has been in the Indian Service "Many times holding different places. first I taught school, Day. school for a year this was at Pine Ridge I was Asst. Laundress + Asst Seamstress here." The final question asks about experiences in the east, and Hattie Pretty Weasel writes, "I went to Madison to attend a normal school to learn how to be a teach + I taught school No. 8 Day school then." She is referring to the Madison State Normal School, in Madison, well over three hundred miles to the east of Pine Ridge, but still in South Dakota.

I believe her daughter, **Lucy Pretty Weasel**, entered Carlisle in 1902. Lucy Pretty Weasel's student file gives her father's name as Harry Pretty Weasel, and I believe Harry is a mistake for *Hall* Pretty Weasel, a less common first name. The file does not give Lucy's mother's name, but it does record that her mother is "Dead." But my guess is that Lucy's mother was indeed Hattie Long Wolf Pretty Weasel, and that she was still very much alive in 1902—and also in 1907, to welcome her daughter home when her school term was up.[24]

Emma Bull Bonnet left Carlisle with her friend Hannah Long Wolf in 1894. In that same year Emma married **Thomas Blackbear**, also from Pine Ridge, who had entered Carlisle in 1886 and graduated with the class of 1894. She returned the brief 1913 and 1914 forms from the school to say that she and her husband lived in Porcupine, South Dakota, and that her occupation was "Housekeeping." Blackbear's forms for those years reported that he was "Stock raising and farming." He had previously responded to Major Mercer's 1907 questionnaire to graduates to report that he, too, had taught at one of the Pine Ridge day schools.

Frank Locke, George Sword's son, had written to Pratt in 1890 about the "confusion" at Rosebud concerning "a lock up man who ran away from the lock up." Of him, the February 1891 *Indian Helper* reported that he "had a most excellent record; is a catechist and blacksmith at the same time; lives at Rosebud" (4). It said as well that "**Hope Blueteeth** is now Mrs. Frank Locke; gone to Rosebud; well spoken of in every particular; a woman of strong character and exerts a splendid influence" (4).

There is nothing to the school from Frank Locke himself before 1912. Although he had indeed been a blacksmith at Rosebud, Locke wrote that he was then living at Porcupine, South Dakota, about nineteen miles northeast of Pine Ridge. He had attended no other school since leaving Carlisle in 1889, and his occupation was "Ranching." Of his present home, he says, "living on mine own land with some improvements a resident, a blacksmith shop, two mills a windmill with a tank, a hay meadow fence [?]." As for property, he writes, "having control of 1920 acres of lands, with a few head of houses and cattle." He has not been in the Indian Service "outside temporary service of assistant farmer with short duration." Regarding other positions held, Locke writes, "none official except at private business, worked mostly at my trade (Blacksmith) Rosebud Agency, S.D. Porcupine S.D. Pine Ridge Agency, S.D. Chadron Nebr. Cranford Nebr. Billing Mont. making living by buying and selling."

In response to an invitation he had received to attend a reunion sponsored by the Carlisle Alumni Association, Locke wrote on February 1, 1912,

> Ladies and Gentlemen,
>
> your letter of Jan 19th has been received without delay and was glad to learn that I am remembered by the Alumni Association. I shall be most gladly to be with you again at your reunion, but

> just now, although I have all kinds of times to be with you, I am unable to figure my way out to come for the one great reason is that the surplus on my part is well emptied.
>
> If you have any further instructions as to the transportations. Please forward to me as soon as you have it ready.
>
> I remained as one your returned students
> F. J. Locke

I suspect the Alumni Association was not able to provide any funds for transportation, and if a 1912 reunion did take place, Locke probably did not attend. In 1915 he returned superintendent Oscar Lipps's brief postcard form, affirming that he remained a "stock raiser and trader" in Porcupine, South Dakota.

Locke's wife, Hope Blueteeth Locke, responded only to the brief form from Friedman in 1913 to say that she was a "House-wife," and "Living on the Ranch." The Lockes' daughter, **Mary Locke**, born in 1896, attended the Oglala boarding school for three years—the couple had gone back to Pine Ridge—after which her parents applied for her admission to Carlisle, which she then attended from 1912 to 1915. Her student file includes a copy of her application to the school signed by her father, and a great many letters between him and the school regarding times when she might be coming home and returning, as well as some "lease money" that the school held for her—and eventually sent on.

The *Helper* briefly mentions a number of others whom we have encountered before. Of the American Horse family—Chief American Horse had been an opponent of the Ghost Dance—the paper reported that **Maggie Stands Looking** was "now Mrs. Belt," as we saw earlier, and observes "her husband kept store on Medicine Root Creek; they lost all by the hostiles" (1). The *Helper* refers to **Guy Bear Don't Scare**, Maggie's brother, as **Guy American Horse**, and says simply that he is "dead" (1). In its notice of her cousin, **Robert American Horse**, the *Helper* is effusive. It says he is

> a catechist for the Episcopal church at an important station at one of the camps; he stands high; is a man of influence among his peo-

> ple; his opinions on matters concerning the interests of the tribe are regarded as that of a leader; he is a strong character in the church and among the young men; his influence is always for good. (1)

Robert American Horse had not communicated with the school for more than twenty years when he responded to the 1911 questionnaire early in 1912. He gives his name as Robert Horse and his address as Kyle, South Dakota. He says that he is married and he gives the date of his marriage but not his wife's name. He is a farmer with eight hundred acres of land, some horses, and some cows. He had been an assistant farmer in the government service and also worked in the government stables at Pine Ridge. As for "anything else of interest," he writes:

> I belong to the Episcopal church. I have been every Sunday in church.
>
> I belong to the Y.M.C.A ever since I was at Carlisle. I have 2 children, 1 boy school who is learning very fast. He is 8 years old and understands English very well.
>
> I am very glad that you remember me at Carlisle. The reason I have not answered sooner is I work every day and am too tired at night to write.
>
> Very Respectfully,
Robert Horse,
Kyle, S. Dak.

Frank Twiss, who would marry **Adelia Lowe** in 1896, as we have seen, is also noticed favorably by the 1891 *Helper*. The paper reports that he "is a valuable hand at the agency; has worked steadily ever since his return and nothing but the most excellent reports were heard of his conduct and true worth" (1). He would indeed go on to become a successful farmer and stock raiser.

We also hear of **Adelia Tyon**, who had been at the school from 1887 to 1889 and would have stayed longer had she not taken ill. The *Helper* says of her only that she "attends school at the agency and so does Lizzie Frog" (4). **Lizzie Frog** had been at Carlisle with Tyon for two years, and she too left in March 1889 because of illness. She would die in 1899, and there was no communication from her to the school before her death. But after some twenty years, a substantial correspondence developed between Adelia Tyon and the school. Among other things, the letters reveal that Tyon was the niece of Adelia Lowe, Frank Twiss's wife, and the cousin of Hattie Long Wolf.

Tyon filled out the 1912 questionnaire in July of that year, informing the school that she was about thirty years old; was not married; that her occupation was "General housework," and that because her "father is a Government employee; do a great deal of his clerical work." She has 320 acres of land and some livestock and has never herself been in the government service. She leaves blank the question asking about "anything else of interest with [her] life." But she had written a lovely letter to Moses Friedman about a year and a half earlier, on January 1, 1911, in response to something he had sent her. It reports much of interest about Adelia Tyon, and I quote it in full.

> Sir—Your letter dated Dec 12–1910 reached me some time ago. Now I will answer you. Though I have been to Carlisle School when I was 6 years old with my aunt Adelia Lowe she is married now did not finish with my Schooling I was sick and stayed at the hospital for a while and after I was doctored I was sent home. I did not remember how long I stayed but I think its a year + half. I stayed at Pine Ridge Oglala Boarding School + after it burned down I went to No 25 Day School thats the last time I went to school though I am not healthy and weak eyes. I love to go to school. I am now 29 years old I am not graduate at any school Will you please sent me the list of the Carlisle pupils and picture of the School my mind is at the Carlisle school yet.
>
> Yours Adelia Tyon

Adelia Lowe was twenty when her six- or seven-year-old niece Adelia Tyon, came to Carlisle in 1887. I can't say why Tyon was put in the hospital; it was probably not for her eye trouble, which was likely trachoma, a contagious bacterial infection of the eyes usually transmitted by poor hygiene. Tyon was at the school—not in the hospital—for about a year and a half, and, although she was "doctored," she writes that her health has not been good and her eyes have been weak ever since. The Oglala Boarding School at Pine Ridge, where Clarence Three Stars and other former Carlisle students had taught and worked, burned down in February 1894, and Tyon then went to day school for a time.[25] She now writes Friedman to ask for a list of pupils—perhaps a current list or maybe a list of those from her time at school—and a photo of the school.

There are also in Tyon's file several letters she wrote to the school about some Lakota girls she hoped would be able to attend Carlisle. The last of these, dated September 29, 1914, was written several months after Friedman had been dismissed, and surely aware of this, Tyon addresses her letter to the school rather than to anyone in particular. Toward the end of the letter she asks after "one of my cousin . . . Hattie Long Wolf." She says, "I been writting to her but never get answer from please let her write to me and also I want a picture of her." She heard back from the school in a letter dated October 10 that Hattie had "died about six years ago," although "the information we have here is evidently not very definite and is not given in detail." The letter was sent by the "Supervisor in Charge"; he had gone to Hattie Long Wolf's file and found the notation, "Deceased: About 1908." That is the last communication to the school from Adelia Tyon.

The 1891 *Helper* reports of **George Little Wound** that he "did not join the hostiles with his father, but remained quietly at the agency; is now a scout" (4). The writer's ambiguous syntax inadvertently points to complications in the positions both of Chief Little Wound of the Oglala Lakota and his son, George. Is it: Little Wound did not join the hostiles as his father had? Or is it: Little Wound along with his father did not join the hostiles?

Although he is less well known outside South Dakota or to specialists than several others, David Bunnell calls the elder Little Wound, born about 1830, "one of the main Oglala chiefs" (2017, 112). Little Wound fought with Crazy Horse and Sitting Bull against Custer and accompanied Red Cloud and Spotted Tail to Washington to meet with President Rutherford B. Hayes. When Sitting Bull, harassed by the soldiers, took his people to Canada in 1877, Little Wound went with him, returning to Pine Ridge only when Sitting Bull returned to the Standing Rock Agency in 1881. Of his several children—Sprague lists his daughters as Won't Give Up Blanket and Jennie Little Wound and his sons as George, Andrew, and James (2004, 47)—only George went to Carlisle. He did not go east until 1885, when he was seventeen years old. He returned home in 1889 because of illness, and as we will see from what he would write to the school in 1911, he had not fully recovered even many years later.

Enochs quotes Little Wound on his 1877 visit to Washington as having said he wanted farm implements and animals for his people "so I can learn and bring my children up in the same way the whites do theirs" (in Enochs 1996, 22). Had the government been more liberal in its provision of these things, perhaps he might have become a farmer committed to bringing his "children up in the same way the whites do theirs."[26] But matters transpired very differently. Thus years later, in the spring of 1889, Little Wound joined Red Cloud and Young Man Afraid of His Horses in rejecting the offer of General Crook's second Sioux Land Commission for the government to purchase reservation land—something that American Horse, after some hesitation, approved (Greene 1970, 53–54). At Rosebud the elder Standing Bear, Luther's father, had been among the first to speak in favor of the sale (51).

Little Wound, Red Cloud, and Young Man Afraid also had an opinion different from that of American Horse regarding the education of Lakota young people, and some of Little Wound's thoughts are recorded in the Minutes of the Land Commission. Thomas Andrews writes that while American Horse told the commission "that children learned more in four years of boarding school than in eight years of day school" (quoted in Andrews 2002, 417), Little Wound "pleaded," to the contrary, "We can't send them here to this boarding-school" (417). Perhaps he meant the Pine Ridge boarding school, on the reservation, but I suspect he may have been thinking of the boarding schools in the East. "Oglalas such as Little Wound," Andrews observes, "felt that day schools provided an antidote to the heart-breaking separation of parents and children that boarding school entailed," and, moreover, that they might offer "immunity from the contagious diseases that brought many Oglala children home from distant institutions in caskets" (417).[27] What Andrews does not say is that the objection to the boarding schools' dangers to the children's health that Little Wound expressed in the spring of 1889 did not arise from general observation alone but from personal experience. Little Wound was speaking to the Land Commission in June 1889. Earlier, at the end of March of that year, his son George had come home from Carlisle not in a casket, fortunately, but very ill.

When Pratt's 1890 questionnaire arrived at Pine Ridge in June, Little Wound's son was not doing well and nor were his people. Here is some of what Chief Little Wound said to Agent Hugh Gallagher at a meeting held at Pine Ridge on July 23, 1890:

> Look at these people around you, see their sunken cheeks and emaciated bodies. Many of these you will notice have drooping heads and an expression of unconcern in their faces that shows plainly the ravages of hunger has reduced them to the verge of idiocy. This has been a hard winter upon us. Many of our children have died from hunger. (Quoted in Andersson 2019, 149)

Dire as the situation was, nonetheless, "In August 1890, the annual appropriations for all Lakotas was reduced" (Andersson 2019, 150 n. 11), and "Later in the summer and early fall, the Ghost Dances started in earnest and Little Wound joined the dancers"(149). By the time troops arrived at Pine Ridge in late November, "Little Wound had been singled out as one of the main instigators of trouble" (50). Nonetheless, when asked by General John Brooke in December if he was a Ghost Dancer, Little Wound's response was, "No my friend, over sixty winters have passed over me and I am too old for dancing" (quoted in Andersson 2019, 152).[28] By December 1890 he, Big Road, and Hump had indeed given up the Ghost Dance (Andersson 2019, 392). Whether George Little Wound had formerly danced with "the hostiles" as his father had, it is likely that at least since December he, like his father, had "remained quietly at the agency."

George Little Wound did not respond to Pratt's 1890 questionnaire, nor did he respond to any others he may have received until he decided to answer the one sent to him in 1910 by Moses Friedman. He says he is married to Bell Yellow-Wolf and lives in Kyle, South Dakota. Asked about his occupation, he writes, "not capable to work. I come home from Carlisle sick as"—and here I believe he names his illness. He writes two words, the first of which is almost surely "scarfler," and I suspect refers either to scrofula or to scarlet fever. "Scarfler" is followed by a second word that I cannot make out, although it, too, almost surely begins with an "s," not an "f." Scrofula is an infection of the lymph nodes by tuberculosis bacteria, and it most usually affected children under ten. Little Wound had not gone to Carlisle until he was seventeen—but the disease was spread by unpasteurized milk from infected cows, and he certainly could have picked it up at Carlisle even in his late teens. Children from five to fifteen were most susceptible to scarlet fever; it too is highly contagious and, untreated, can cause later kidney and heart trouble. Whatever he caught at the Carlisle School, it continued to afflict George Little Wound.

He writes to say that he has "320 acres" and a log house; he has gone to no other schools, nor has he had any position in the Indian Service. It is in answer to the final question, asking about "anything else of interest connected with [his] life," that he expresses himself with strong feeling. Little Wound writes,

> I went to school to get a good education to go out this world and to do something but I greatly mistaking when I went to school I come home with sickness and do not know any thing I generally obey the law of the U.S. and believe it I never get well the sickness which I brought from the school. you have sent me this question a half dozen time but I am in mizer place and bad condition which I can not answer the question which you sent me. Dear friend I am very sorry to sent this to you. I am a shame to sent this to you. all return student hold us down let the white people fil all the positions. We try make our self supporting but Indians hold down too.
>
> Yours truly
> George Little Wound

A number of photographs of George Little Wound as a mature man can easily be found online. All of them show him in some form of traditional regalia; if as a returned Carlisle student he wore "citizen's clothing," he did not allow himself to be photographed in it. Like his father, he was an advocate for local day schools. On a copious (and sometimes inaccurate) website, I have found the information that George Little Wound died at Pine Ridge on August 15, 1936.[29]

The 1891 *Helper* makes mention of **Edward Jannies** and **Frank Jannies**, who were cousins. Edward had entered the school at the age of seventeen in 1886 and remained for a year. The *Helper* said of him only "works on home ranch" (1). He did not communicate with the school. At the end of his student file is a notation reporting that he was a stock raiser in Kyle, South Dakota, in 1910, but this is mistaken. Early in 1912, Jannies's wife wrote to Friedman to say that the reason he had not answered the questionnaires sent by the school was that he had died in April 1907.

Frank Jannies, about three years older than his cousin, attended Carlisle from 1883 until 1889. The *Helper* writes that he "had a good record; gone to Rosebud" (4), his home agency. Opening his student file is a photograph of Jannies in army uniform. To his right is someone identified as Samuel Little Hawk and, to his left, **William C. Bull**. They too are in uniform, and the caption to the photo, reproduced here, says Jannies enlisted in 1891, while the other two, also said to be Carlisle students, enlisted in 1892. (Jannies would later write that in fact he too had enlisted in 1892.) William C. Bull is William Crazy Bull, who would be known later in his life as William Girton, sometimes William C. Girton. Both he and Frank Jannies—sometimes Janis or Janniss—kept in touch with the school. But there is no Carlisle record at all for Samuel Little Hawk. He has neither a student information card nor a student file; he is not mentioned in any of the Carlisle publications or in the school's documents; and the only photo Carlisle has of him is the one with Jannies and Crazy Bull.

Frank Jannies responded in some detail to the 1909 questionnaire. He said he was married to Josephine Young, who does not seem to have been a Carlisle student, and he has attended no other school. He farms and owns a good-sized house along with some horses and cattle on 1,120 acres. He has money in the bank, and, except for assisting the agency carpenter "for one year in, 1891," he has not been employed in the Indian Service. He writes, "In 1892 I inlisted in the Army and service two years." As for doing "anything for the betterment of [his] people," he says,

> Yes. I have tried to help my people who never had the chance as I have to learn the way of living and getting along like the whites. I have tried to show good example to all in every thing that I can.

As for anything else of interest, Frank Jannies, now a man in his early forties, reflects thoughtfully on the benefits but also the deep frustrations he has experienced as a result of the government's Indian education policies:

> My wish and hope was to learn to know how to make my living when I entered Carlisle I was a grown boy when I first went there so I have to work hard to learn what I know now. I was always willing to work when I had the chance after I came home depending on the promise made to the Carlisle students for government position I have applied several times but it seems that the students of these reservations have been forgotten or neglected either for their own faults or what I do not know. but never being able to get a solid position from the government I have with the aid of what I learned at Carlisle made my way through this life with a wife + two children to support which I never could if I did not hold on to what Carlisle school has taught me. It seems I can't thank the school enough + I will hope for employment from the government as carpenter which was my trade.

This is not the first time we have seen one of the returned students disappointed to discover that a government position he had thought secure upon his home-coming was not to be had after all. As noted, Carlisle could not promise its students work at their respective agencies on their return, but it is more than possible that some of its recruiters and staff nonetheless made or implied such a promise. In 1909 Frank Jannies continued to hope for a position as one of the agency's carpenters, but it was not to be. Nonetheless, some connection to the school remained important to him.

In 1910 superintendent Friedman wrote to Jannies, as he had written to many other returned students, asking for a photograph of his home to be published with those of other students' homes, and Jannies responded that he would send one. In 1912 Jannies wrote to the school twice on the same day, February 6. He sent a brief note to the Alumni Association at Carlisle to say that he hoped to attend its meeting that year. And there is a warm letter to Friedman. Frank Jannies wrote,

> Dear Friend—
>
> I take the greatest pleasure to answer the Christmas letter you wrote me. If I ever received a letter that was full of cheer and encouragement it was the Christmas letter I received from you. The letter was worth more to me than other gift. I am always very grateful and glad to hear of the good wishes and kind remembrance from the dear old school and friend, to the returned students.
>
> Sincerely your friend
> Frank Jannies

Jannies had also received an invitation from Friedman to attend that year's Carlisle commencement exercises, and he wrote in March to say that although he had hoped to do so, his wife's slow recovery from an illness made that no longer possible.

He returned the brief postcard form sent by Friedman in 1914, listing his occupation not as "carpenter" but as "Farm and stock raising." He also squeezed a substantial commentary into the brief space given for "Remarks," writing,

> Upon the reservation there is not enough work for all the returned students and they must not expect it. The only way I can

> see out is to take a hold and farm or stock raise. A student may want a position but he either have to remain in the east and get it, or unless the Gov. secure a position him or her their own.

There are many more communications between Jannies and Carlisle, all of these involving anticipated transportation costs for the enrollment of his daughter, Ruth, and two of her friends at the school, the last of these a letter Jannies sent on August 24, 1916. But there is no student information card or file for a Ruth Jannies at Carlisle; for whatever reason, it appears that she did not attend.

Frank Jannies's fellow enlistee in the army in 1892, William C. Bull, as he was then known, responded to the 1909 questionnaire as William Girton. He lives in Kyle, South Dakota, within the Pine Ridge reservation, and is married to Fannie Yellow Bear. He owns a small log house, and unlike his older Carlisle schoolmate, Frank Jannies, he has a position as assistant farmer at the agency. In fact, since leaving the army he has been regularly employed in the Indian Service, having been on the Indian police force for three years, and several times serving as assistant farmer. During his three-year enlistment in the army, he was stationed in Salt Lake City, Utah, where, as sergeant, he served as company clerk. Asked whether he has done anything "for the betterment of [his] people," he writes,

> Yes I have been more less every day been with my people and I have endeavored in all my efforts to enlighten them in either in religion, agriculture or other branches of work so far as my intergerity would permit.

To the final question about "anything else of interest," he writes briefly but suggestively, "There is nothing of any interest connected with my life but if I were to tell you the haps and misshaps concerning my people it would have to have several sheets like this." William Girton did not provide that account of the "haps and misshaps concerning [his] people" to superintendent Friedman in 1909, but surely it would have been a powerful narrative.

The following year, in March, he wrote wondering why he hadn't heard back from Friedman. He says, "I have been looking for you answer me as I answered carefully your questions which you sent me I mail it 4 or 5 months ago and I have not heard from you." He seems to be referring to the 1909 questionnaire, which he had indeed mailed several months earlier. He also tells Friedman that he had not been able to obtain a photograph of his daughter to send, and that instead of having a photo taken of his home—Girton would have been one of the many returned students who were asked for a photo of their home—he is sending one of himself and his wife, with which his file opens. As I have said, Friedman was generally good about responding to mail from former students, but there is no copy of a response from him to Girton in Girton's file. The file contains only one further communication from Girton. It is in answer to the brief 1914 form, on which he writes that he is now a "Forest Guard" in government service, and "Have my Fee Simple patent and support myself."[30] That is, he had taken his allotment and managed to prove "competency," giving him full title to his land, along with an American citizenship he may or may not have wanted.

A final letter worth attention in William C. Girton's file is from someone we have already encountered, Girton's neighbor in the Medicine Root district of Kyle, South Dakota, and his former schoolmate at Carlisle, George Little Wound. Little Wound's letter is addressed to "Horace Lipps, supt.," and it is dated "Jan. 1st 1914." The superintendent's name was Oscar Lipps, and Little Wound's first sentence makes clear that he meant the date to be 1915. Here is Little Wound's moving letter about his friend:

> sir
>
> In regard to Mr. William C. Girton death on Dec 25 1914 on Chiristmas night 10 'o clock living one girl and a boy. when he was a boy he went to first day built by the government at Pine Ridge Agency after that when Oglala boarding was built at the Agency he went school there from there he went to Carlisle Indian school. from there he joined U.S. infantry at Salt Lake City he was sergent at that time since he returned to Pine Ridge

> he hold important position as Indian Police, night watch, at Ogalala Boarding school after ward he was special police at Kyle S.D. after wards he was asst Farmer of Kyle S D. Later he was appointed as Forest Guard he hold this work when he dead it show that he was perseverance what ever he under take in his life he is good Christian an beliving God therefore he leaves many good friends sorry for him behind He was not afraid to die on account of beliving O. Might God I respectfully and earnestly request of you to put the history of W*m* C. Girton to the Arrow to know all friend of his returned student what he has when he was living
>
> Yours friend
> George Little Wound
> returned student

William C. Girton was about forty-five at the time of his death, and George Little Wound, with complicated feelings about Carlisle, nonetheless wanted his old friend and fellow student remembered by all who had known him at school.

4

“One of the most trusted members of the faculty”

Siceni Nori, Some “Successful” Carlisle Indians, and the 1914 Congressional Hearings

Siceni Nori, from Laguna Pueblo, entered Carlisle in 1884 and graduated with the class of 1894. He remained at Carlisle after his graduation, holding various positions at the school until 1914. He did not like to write nearly as much as Mike Burns did—Burns had left the school the year Nori arrived—but he does have an autobiographical piece in the *Indian Helper* for March 30, 1888. Here it is in full:

> I have a home where I used to live. I used to take care of cows every day. In the evening I would put the cows in the yard and in the morning my mother would take her pail and I would help her. Sometimes we would get two pails or four pails full of milk and she would give me my lunch and I would go out to take the cows out of the cow yard and I would take them where there are lots of grass and sometimes I would catch rabbits and I would play with them. I did not know who made me. Some people worship idols but I never went to church.
>
> We play every day, we did not know about Sunday. The people used to paint their faces and they would not go to church. We used to swim every day when it was sunshine. We have houses like blocks and flat roofs and a chimney or two are on the top of the houses.
>
> We don't sleep on beds as we do here but we sleep on floors with some little beds under and mice would run over us in the night time. The cats would get after them sometimes we would

hear them scream when the cat catch them. When I got up I would go down to the water and then I would eat my breakfast and I would play with bows and arrows.

SICENI NORI (4)

Nori was about twelve when he went to Carlisle in 1884, and his record indicates that his mother had died by that time. These seem the recollections of a boy younger than sixteen—and he does not mention his father.

The "home where I used to live" is Laguna Pueblo in New Mexico Territory. Nori recalls milking the cows with his mother in the morning, and then taking them out to pasture, but he does not say who—he, his mother, or someone else—brought them back in the evening. He then shifts abruptly to the matter of not knowing who made him, a sentence that might well have begun a new paragraph, followed as it is by the observations "Some people worship idols but I never went to church," and—pluralizing the first person to observe of his Laguna people, or at least the children—"We play every day," and "we did not know about Sunday."

One may wonder about this. The young boy's entertaining himself with rabbits notwithstanding, the routine he describes of caring for the cows is not play. Meanwhile, the Saint Joseph or San Jose Church at Laguna, originally built just before the end of the seventeenth century, was still in use when Nori was growing up. Even if he and his family did not attend, he would have known the church and that many in the community worshiped in it—on Sunday. The Presbyterian minister John Menaul—whom we met in chapter 3—was active at Laguna from 1876 to 1890 (Banker 1982, 30–31), and he might have considered both Catholic rites and traditional Laguna ceremonial practices to be worshipping idols. Were these views that the young Siceni Nori had picked up? As for his people's sleeping arrangements, Nori's point for the most part seems to be that they were less satisfactory than what he had become accustomed to at Carlisle.

I have been able to learn almost nothing about his experience at the school as a student. The *Helper* for July 29, 1887, referred to him as

Superintendent Pratt's "orderly" (3); his trade at the school was printing, and there is an 1894 photograph of him with twenty-three other Carlisle student printers. He also pitched successfully on several of the school's baseball teams, and he had farm outings in 1890, 1892, and 1893—and then again in 1895 and '96, after his 1894 graduation. It is unclear whether he went home in all that time, but in any case his file, while substantial, as I explain later, includes only letters from him after he had left the school in 1914, and they say nothing about his time as a student.

After graduating from Carlisle Nori attended nearby Dickinson College for two years, and he attended but may or may not have graduated from Scranton Business College. He married **Ida Griffin**, a half-blood Okanagan from the state of Washington, who had come to Carlisle in 1896 at the age of fourteen with her younger brother **Thomas**. Both brother and sister graduated in 1903, the year in which Ida married Siceni Nori. The Noris would have two daughters at Carlisle, Verna and Hazel, and they would later divorce. Ida Griffin Nori seems to have taught for a time at the school, as her husband did as well. But his chief employment was as clerk. According to his own testimony—this is from the congressional hearing of 1914, from which I quote later—he had been appointed chief clerk by Richard Pratt in September 1900 (*Hearings Before the Joint Commission of the U.S. Sixty-third Congress*, 1914, 1293), retaining that position during Major Mercer's time as superintendent (1292), and continuing under Moses Friedman's superintendency, which began in April 1908. A newspaper clipping in Nori's file from 1910 or 1911 confirms that

> Siceni Nori, a Pueblo, of the class of 1894, who was an expert pitcher in his day, and after graduation took up further training in business, is now chief clerk at the Carlisle School, and is one of the most trusted members of the faculty.

He held that position until 1914, when he and Friedman were both dismissed.

In the summer of 1909 a dispute of such proportion had arisen between Siceni Nori and a Carlisle matron named Jennie Gaither as to require the intervention of the commissioner of Indian Affairs. Superintendent Friedman wrote to the commissioner on August 13, 1909, explaining: "When Mrs. Nori was sick in bed, with a newly born child, Miss Gaither refused to assign a girl to the Nori household." Jennie Gaither was the matron in charge of the girls' building, and Nori's request for one of the girls to assist his wife, as Friedman affirmed, was not, as Gaither may have alleged, for "any special privileges that could not consistently be given to any other member of the faculty." The superintendent also noted that "in the assignment of girls," Miss Gaither had previously "had difficulty with other employees besides Mr. Nori."

The dispute had apparently led Nori to use abusive language to Gaither, which she reported to Friedman and very likely to the Office of Indian Affairs as well. Here I note only in passing what I point to again later: the difficult position of the Carlisle superintendent, who could not take any substantive actions regarding faculty and staff at the school without the approval of the Indian Office. In the end Friedman "gave instructions" to Miss Gaither that Nori "be furnished with a girl the same as any other married employee" (August 13, 1909), on the condition that Nori first apologize to Miss Gaither in writing. This he had done in a letter to Friedman dated August 11, 1909. He wrote, in part,

> while I do not for a moment question the integrity and veracity of Miss Gaither, nor do I have any recollection of calling her a name such as she accuses me to have said, but if I did use undignified and discourteous language to her in a moment of anger, I do most truly and sincerely apologize to Miss Gaither, and hereafter endeavor or to so conduct myself amicable and with proper courtesy, and to cooperate with Miss Gaither in the proper discharge of our respective duties for the best interest of the school.

Friedman's letter of August 13 to the commissioner concluded, in summary, that

> Mr. Nori is one of the best employees at Carlisle; he is quiet, faithful, efficient and unassuming, and from his past record,

> and native excellence as a man, would not, I believe, ask for, nor expect, anything which was not his due.

By 1914 Friedman would think very differently.

In 1911 the Carlisle *School News* observed that Nori was "now acting as treasurer of the school fund, handling every year upwards of $150,000" (2), equivalent to well over four million dollars today (2019). It would be his handling of those funds that would be investigated by Congress in 1914. Other news clippings in his file indicate that this was a busy time for Siceni Nori. One records, for example, that he had been made a "thirty second degree mason . . . the first Indian in the East to receive this distinction."[1] Another reports that in October he had addressed the twenty-ninth annual conference of the Friends of the Indian at Lake Mohonk, New York, speaking on behalf of "the exceptional position of the Pueblo Indians of New Mexico." It was around this time as well that Nori became active with another group of white friends of the Indian, the Indian Rights Association and, in particular, with a prominent figure in its Philadelphia office, Matthew Sniffen.

In the spring of 1911 Nori was invited to address the Carlisle graduating class. His talk—it can be found in his file—was called "Some Successful Indians." Here it is in its entirety:

> Has it ever been your privilege to listen to the inspiring music by the famous Indian band which toured the country under the leadership of Dennison Wheelock, a graduate of this school, and was for a number of years band leader of our own school organization, but who is now a prosperous business man in Wisconsin? If it shall be the pleasure of anyone here to take a trip to Cuba and it becomes necessary to have the assistance of a dentist, just look up Dr. James E. Johnson, who is enjoying an annual income of $4,000, and his wife, also a graduate, employed by the government at a salary of $1,200 per annum; or if you do not desire to take the water trip, take the Pennsylvania Limited and go to Tiffin, Ohio, where you will find Dr. Caleb Sickles, another graduate and a prominent den-

tist who is equally successful; then, if you have time, go to Oneida, Wisconsin, where you will find Dr. Powless, a prominent physician who has the largest practice at his home at De Pere, Wis., and is a real leader and missionary among his people. Then proceed to Minnesota state and find Carlisle graduates practicing law and other professions in the persons of Thomas Mani, Edward Rogers, and Dr. Oscar Davis. Or, if you took the southern way you would find along the Santa Fe route, Carlisle graduates and ex-students working in the various railroad shops and taking care of sections of that great railroad system, preferred above all other kinds of skilled labor, for they have shown their worth as good workmen. Or, you might meet Chas. A. Dagenett, a graduate who is National Supervisor of Indian Employment, who has by experience gained here at this school under the Outing System, been able, by untiring effort, to systematize and build up what is really the Carlisle Outing System for the entire Indian Service, and for 300,000 Indians. It is not often possible to find a man who can be equally successful in everything that he attempts, but we have in a Carlisle graduate, Chas. A. Bender, the world-famous pitcher of the Philadelphia Athletics, a crack marksman and a jeweler by trade, and a pastmaster in all. So I might cite hundreds of others, but time forbids, hence I shall only repeat that the Carlisle graduate has shown that Indian Education has not been a failure, but has paid.

As commencement talks go, this one is rather narrowly focused. Addressed as much to a broad American audience as to the graduates, their friends, and families, Nori's speech names as exemplary Carlisle graduates Native people who have been successful in the professions, government, and athletics. (He does not give the names of those who work in the railroad shops, like James Luther.) This represents a shift of emphasis from Carlisle's longtime goal of training Indian (male) students for agriculture and the trades (as Nori himself had been trained as a printer), while Carlisle women—he mentions only Dr. Johnson's wife, and does not give her name—were instructed in the "domestic sciences."

Before continuing with the further history of Siceni Nori at Carlisle, it is worth looking more closely at the "successful" Indians he names. Their student files are once more a rich source of hitherto unknown boarding school voices, opening a window once more, on

> an interesting and as-yet-unexplored cast of historical characters . . . an incredibly complex Indian world . . . people who stayed engaged with Indian politics, education, law, and culture; and people who melted into reservation communities, small towns, and big cities as dentists, clerks, farmers, and mechanics. (Deloria 2013, 39)

Most of the former students Siceni Nori names as having achieved success were athletes at Carlisle before they became dentists, lawyers, government officials, or jewelers. This is surely no accident. Nori was well aware of superintendent Friedman's concern to show that the school's emphasis on athletics was no hindrance to its educational program, an important matter that would come up during the congressional hearing in 1914.[2]

We have earlier met **Dennison Wheelock, Julia Powless Wheelock**'s brother-in-law. A schoolmate of Siceni Nori, he had entered Carlisle at the age of fourteen in 1885, graduated in 1890, and as a virtuoso cornetist had become the Carlisle bandmaster two years later. In 1900 he led the Carlisle Band on a tour of the Northeast that was meant to culminate in a trip to the Paris International Exposition, although in the end a lack of funds prevented the band from traveling abroad. Compared in his day to John Phillip Sousa, Wheelock had written an acclaimed "Carlisle Indian School March"; he was also interested in classical music and composed "a symphony in three parts" titled "Aboriginal Suite" that was to have debuted in Paris during the Carlisle band's visit (Hauptman 2006, 127). Although that did not come about, the symphony did have its premier at New York's Carnegie Hall near the end of March 1900.

Wheelock responded to the 1909 questionnaire to say that he was married to **Louise La Chapelle**, a Chippewa from White Earth who had come to the school in 1892. They lived with their two children—one of them born at Carlisle—in West De Pere, Wisconsin, where Wheelock then earned a living selling real estate. He wrote that he had a large, nine-room house with "electric light etc.," and several land holdings, along with "Various amounts" of money in the bank. In addition to his eight years of employment as the Carlisle bandmaster he had worked as a disciplinarian at the Flandreau Indian School and also served for a year as the Haskell Institute's band leader. Asked whether he had "done anything for the betterment of [his] people," Wheelock wrote,

> I have never attempted to do very great things for my people or even to do anything in particular other than to point out their opportunities. I try to set a good business example for them and although they all fall into the ditch with me once in a while yet we manage to get along fairly well.
>
> There is not another reservation in the country which is as prosperous as the Oneida reservation today.

In a letter he wrote to **Nellie Robertson Denny** dated December 4, 1909—their time at the school had overlapped—he offers some thoughts on Oneida tribal divisions of the period. Wheelock wrote:

> In every Tribe, of course, you know there are all kinds of leaders of the Injun factions, and then others who are the leaders of the Progressives. It is the same way with the Oneida Indian.
>
> Of the Indian faction, are Indians who desire to remain as Indians forever. . . .
>
> Of the Progressive element, there are several prominent young men who may be set to lead their people.

Wheelock named two men of the "Injun faction," and three—one of them, Dr. **Josiah Powless**, a Carlisle graduate of whom we will hear further—of "the Progressive element," whose views he clearly shared.[3]

In 1911, having received his law degree, Wheelock passed the bar to become the first Native American lawyer in Wisconsin, and in the same year he was active as one of the founders of the Society of American Indians. Siceni Nori chose to emphasize Wheelock's prosperity above all else, something Dennison Wheelock, a complex man of many talents, might well have approved. Nori would do the same in regard to the next "successful" Indians he brings to his audience's attention.

James Edward Johnson was a Stockbridge Indian, also from Wisconsin. He had entered Carlisle in 1897, and although he was a member of the 1901 graduating class, he stayed on to continue playing football under Carlisle coach Glenn "Pop" Warner. In 1903 Johnson was quarterback and captain of a Carlisle football team that included **Jim Thorpe.**[4] Johnson made all-American that year, as he had also done in 1901.[5] Like Thorpe, he also played baseball. Nori himself had pitched and played both second and third base in 1895, and went on to play center field in 1901 and outfield on the same 1902 team as Johnson (Powers-Beck 2004, 200). In track Johnson ran the 400-yard relay on a 1902 team that included his fellow Oneida, Nellie Robertson's husband **Wallace Denny** (Powers-Beck 2004, 184), and he was also "Carlisle's star hurdler" (Benjey 2010, 178). Not least, Johnson was also a member of the Carlisle band and occasionally "allowed to leave the baseball team for band trips" (Powers-Beck 2004, 43): here is another young man of extraordinarily varied abilities.

Johnson attended the Dickinson College Preparatory School and then Dickinson College proper, going on to Northwestern University, where he continued to play football while attending the Northwestern Dental School, from which he graduated in 1907. Had any members of Nori's audience in 1911 sought out Dr. Johnson in Cuba as directed, however, they would have been sorely disappointed, because the doctor actually practiced dentistry in San Juan, Puerto Rico, from 1909 to 1916, at which time he returned to the United States to enter medical school in order to specialize further in his dental practice.[6] Dr. Johnson was indeed doing well financially; the $4,000 salary Nori reports would be worth about $108,500 today (2019).

Nori does not name Johnson's wife: she was Florence Welch, a Wisconsin Oneida and a Brothertown Indian.[7] She was indeed a U.S. government clerk, as Nori says—although in San Juan, with her husband, not in Cuba—and her "$1,200 per annum" salary would be worth about $32,400 today (2019). Dr. Johnson fell ill in 1941 and returned to the United States, where he died in January 1942 (Benjey 2010, 188).

Dr. **Caleb Sickles**, a dentist "equally successful" to Dr. Johnson, was also a Wisconsin Oneida, from the Green Bay Agency. He was a member of a large and interesting family whose successes might be measured in ways other than financial. Like Dr. Johnson, Dr. Sickles had played football, baseball (Powers-Beck 2004, 197–98), and basketball (Benjey 2010, 222). In answer to the 1909 questionnaire sent out by superintendent Friedman, Sickles wrote that after his graduation in 1898, he too had spent a year at Dickinson Prep School, where he also ran track and participated in other sports. He "Entered Ohio Medical Univ. at Columbus O. Sept. 1900—Graduated in dentistry in class of 1904. Took one year in Pharmacy there." He helped pay for his studies by coaching baseball and football at Heidelberg University in Tiffin, Ohio, where Sickles would settle and establish his dental practice. In answer to the 1909 form's last question, inviting the former student to tell "anything else of interest connected with [his] life," Dr. Sickles, who seems to have been a voluble man, wrote in detail, and I quote him at length:

> From my own experience I think the pupil who has attended Carlisle should never go back to the reservation to live. If he has holdings I would advise him to sell them, put the money in bank and seek employment or attend a school and obtain a professional or technical education. I started to attend the Ohio Medical Univ. with 53.00 in my pocket. Of course my football ability helped me as schools then were seeking men who could play football. I was given employment at the school and in this way was enabled to help myself. I played professional baseball during the summer and earned enough money to pay my expenses during the school year. When I graduated I had nothing, but determined to make a success of my life. I came to Tiffin, O. to coach the football team—when the season ended I opened up an office, that was in 1904—have applied myself to business with successful results. Belong to two secret orders here, the Improved order of Redmen and Elks. Am proud to state that I am looked upon as one of the leading businessmen of the city.

To the question about doing "anything for the betterment of [his] people," Dr. Sickles responded somewhat off-handedly: "I am not prepared to state whether or not I have benefited or bettered my people any. I have never lived among the Indians to any extent." Nor would he ever choose to do so.

His membership in the Improved Order of Red Men, it should be noted, had nothing to do with Indians. The Improved Order of Red Men was formed in Baltimore in 1834 and traced its origins to the Sons of Liberty, the secret patriotic group whose members, dressed as Indians, had dumped the tea into Boston Harbor in 1773. The order had no relation whatever to Native American people, and still has none, although it continues to exist; until 1974 it was a "whites only" organization, the aims of which were patriotic and ethical.

This is to say that if Dr. Sickles's fellow "Red Men" had known he was a real "red man," he would not have been permitted to remain in the fraternity. The Improved Order of Red Men—along with its women's division, the Degree of Pocahontas—had a membership of probably a couple of hundred thousand when he wrote in 1909. Then U.S. president Theodore Roosevelt was a member of the Improved Order of Red Men, as his distant cousin Franklin D. Roosevelt would be as well. The Benevolent and Protective Order of Elks, in which Dr. Sickles also held a membership, was founded by minstrel show performers and actors in New York, in 1868, as a private club, thereby allowing members to drink together on Sundays without paying additional taxes. But until 1973 the Elks too were a white-men-only fraternity, so that once more, had Dr. Sickles been known to be an Indian, he would have lost his membership.

Former Carlisle student Dr. Caleb Sickles, an Oneida from the Green Bay Agency, was "passing"—to use the term for light-skinned Blacks living as whites in this period—as a response to American race prejudice. In fact, in a January 1909 letter to Moses Friedman referencing the questionnaire he had sent in, Dr. Sickles stated clearly, "It is very hard for the Indian to succeed among the white people on account of race prejudice." He added, "I find it no handicap because very few know I have the strain of Indian blood in my veins, but I heard on all sides about this being a white man's country." We may compare Dr. Caleb Sickles's sense of the matter here to Dr. Charles Eastman's remark a couple of years later at the Society of American Indians' first meeting in 1911. Contrary to what Dr. Sickles had found, Eastman said to those who thought "a great deal of injustice" had been "done to our tribes," that "really no prejudice has existed so far as the American Indian is concerned" (quoted in Warrior 1999, 6), especially in the professions. Some four years later, as we will see, Dr. Caleb Sickles, beset "on all sides" by the fact that America was indeed "a white man's country," would voice his renunciation of an Indian identity.

Although Dr. Sickles preferred that his neighbors not know he was an Indian, he continued to have warm feelings for Carlisle, the Indian school he had attended and from which he had graduated. In 1907 he had written to tell Superintendent Mercer that he and his wife would like to visit the school, and in 1910, when superintendent Friedman wrote to ask for photos of himself, his home, and his office, he responded very positively. The photos he sent are in his file, so that we may see the prosperous Dr. Sickles himself and also view the dentist at work. He described to Friedman the thoroughly modern equipment with which his office was outfitted and noted that he was successful enough to "keep a servant all the time."

Sickles's wife, Mabel Teachnor, was white. When she died in April 1911, after a long illness, Dr. Sickles wrote to "Mr. and Mrs. Denny"—Nellie Robertson and her husband, Wallace Denny—to inform them of her passing; as noted earlier, both were Carlisle graduates, employed at the school while Sickles had been a student, and they were employees there in 1911. Writing lovingly of his wife and her painful death, he also asked: "Tell Mr. and Mrs. Nori and give them my regards." In 1912 he sent his regrets to an invitation to come to that year's commencement exercises, and went on to express in some detail his views that Indians ought to pursue a college education and enter the professions. The next year he filled out the brief 1913 questionnaire, and in 1916 he proposed to come to the school to give lectures on the proper care of the mouth and the teeth. Dr. Sickles promised not to use technical terms the students would not understand.

In August 1915 Sickles married "Miss Nina M. Hankey, of Tiffin," and on the couple's "extensive trip through the East," they stopped off "at Carlisle for a few days visit" (Carlisle *Arrow*, December 10, 1915, 4). Clearly the second Mrs. Sickles, like the first, knew that the doctor was an Indian. That issue of the *Arrow* published a "Biographical Sketch of Caleb M. Sickles," reporting that he "has been very successful in his profession," and that he owns "among other things, a fine farm and an automobile." The sketch continues, "He is an Oneida Indian, or as he said with a smile. 'I used to be, but am now a true American'" (4). Contrary to Dr. Eastman, Dr. Sickles seems to have found American race prejudice, even in the professions, sufficient to provoke an abandonment of his identity as an Oneida Indian. It is interesting that he did so at Carlisle, and he is the only former Carlisle student I know of to have done so. I imagine the doctor's smile perhaps to have been tinged with some sadness.

The Sickles family was large; I have counted seven siblings, all but one of whom attended Carlisle. (Raymond, probably the youngest, was living with Dr. Sickles in Tiffin, Ohio, in 1910 and going to school locally.) While their experiences at school, and their lives after leaving, were various, four of the seven Sickles who had been to Carlisle—including one who had run away—kept in touch with the school. Taken together, their Carlisle files allow a look into the lives of a progressive Oneida family in the early part of the twentieth century. I quote the Sickles siblings liberally and also reference a first cousin of theirs who attended Carlisle and appears in what I find a fascinating photograph. I'll then continue with the other "successful" Indians mentioned by Siceni Nori in his 1911 commencement address before returning to his story.

The doctor's sister, **Elizabeth Sickles**, was the oldest of the children and attended Carlisle only from 1891 to 1893 when, her file reads, she was "needed at home" and she left the school. She returned to Wisconsin, where she married **Thomas Metoxen**, a member of a prominent Oneida family, an 1892 Carlisle graduate, and also a baseball player for the school (Powers-Beck 2004, 193). The couple lived in West De Pere, Wisconsin, where Dennison Wheelock had established himself, and where other Sickles siblings would live.

Thomas Metoxen completed the lengthy 1909 questionnaire and also sent the school a lovely formal photo of himself, his wife, and his four children. Near the end of the questionnaire, in answer to whether he had "done anything for the betterment of [his] people," he functions very much as an organic intellectual, offering a much more deeply thoughtful response to the question than that offered the same year by his brother-in-law Dr. Caleb Sickles. I quote it in full:

> I have not undertaken any special line of work for these people as those of my own age all know their own business, and those of the older generation are doing fairly well, and as all elderly people have their set ways, so have these. Therefore if I have been of any special benefit to the Oneida tribe it has been by setting the example "to do your best in your own line of duty and be as good a citizen as possible."
>
> A large number of our tribe have become citizens. We have been voters for some years. The Govt. does not do very much for us financially considering what it does for other tribes. Therefore what we own we work for and we work against odds too. Our annuity this year amounted to only 44 cts a piece. We are to have a Rural Route this coming season which will speak of the progressiveness of the Oneidas. I have not a picture of my home but here is one of the family. My wife is a Carlisle student and she is well posted for her people to help, and well advanced as I am.

He completes his thoughts in the space after the question asking about "anything else of interest," writing, "I am always glad to help Dear old Carlisle and am pleased I can do this much in helping to uphold Carlisle standard."[8]

Thomas Metoxen's wife, Elizabeth Sickles Metoxen, did not respond to the 1909 questionnaire, but she wrote at length in 1911 and 1912. By 1911 she and her husband had had a fifth child, and she says despite poor health her work is caring for her family. She writes, "We see our old school mates quite often. There are quite a number of them living around here and the most of them are doing quite well." She closes by inviting Superintendent Friedman to come and visit "whenever you pass this way."

In answer to the following year's questionnaire, she gave much the same information as she had earlier, and then wrote very fully in response to the last question inquiring about anything further of interest in her life. Her manner differs from her husband's, but it is equally thoughtful, and some of what she says is personal, to the point that she clearly informs Friedman that it is "not for publication." She is thus indicating her awareness that the school often published letters or parts of letters received from former students in the *Indian Helper*, the *Red Man*, or the Carlisle *Arrow*, as we have seen, and she makes clear that she does not want her words made public in that way. As for the broader sense of "not for publication," perhaps now, more than a hundred years later, she would not object to her descendants and other sympathetic persons reading what she so movingly wrote. In the hope that this is true, and in the interest of recovering voices from the boarding schools, I quote her at length. Here is what Elizabeth Sickles Metoxen wrote to Moses Friedman on the 1912 questionnaire:

> Dear Friend (If so I may call you)
>
> Altho I do not personally know you, I feel a deep interest in you and your noble work and often think of the dear old place where I have spent so many happy and profitable hours. I have wished to go back + visit the scenes of my girlhood days, and to be present at the graduation exercises but have never been able to do so.
>
> My health has been such that it has been hard for me to get along with my ordinary housework and to care for the little family I have intrusted to my care. I have neglected my correspondence on account of always being pushed by my work against a weak body, and also felt that I had nothing worthwhile writing of.
>
> But I do know, and God knows, I have always did my best, or the best I could do under all circumstances and always spoke a good word for Carlisle. I thank you *now*, for the kind and cheerful letter I received from you at Christmas time. I

appreciated it very much in my lonely hours. Cheer is what I often need. (This is not for publication.)

Yours most respectfully, E. Sickles Metoxen

She continues on a separate sheet of paper:

P.S. I will thank you very much for the catalogue of the school and as we have received the arrow for some time and several of the Reports and Craftsman, I want to thank you for them and as we have both been getting the arrow, (but Thos.'s I think has been sent to Kaukauna no. 10, it is always a day or two later). . . . Thanking you for your kind interest in us, oldest of old children of Carlisle, I am with respects

E. Sickles Metoxen

She adds a second postscript, now addressing a practical matter:

P.S. again.

If my husband would wish to get a Gov't position could you help him in any way? in recommendation or such? He has been talking of trying to get a position as this clearing the land business and heavy farming is getting to be too hard for him. he is nearing the 50 mark + has always worked hard. He is a harness maker by trade but he does not like indoor work its too confining. he would rather a job of bossing [?] out of doors.[9]

Yours respt
E.S.M.

Although he usually responded to former students, and copies of his letters are often in their files, there is no copy of a response from Friedman to Elizabeth Metoxen in her file. The Metoxens were still in West De Pere in 1913, the last record of them in the Carlisle files.

Martha Sickles, born in 1877, was two years younger than Elizabeth and two years older than Caleb. She entered Carlisle in 1891 and graduated in 1898, marrying **James Cornelius**—also from a prominent

Oneida family—who had been at the school from 1885 until 1890, leaving just after Pratt had sent out his questionnaire. Martha Cornelius responded to the 1909 questionnaire to say that she and her husband also lived in West De Pere, Wisconsin, where they farmed. Most of her responses are brief, but she is more expansive in regard to the last question asking for anything else of interest about her life. She writes,

> I was married in the fall of '98 and have always lived in our own home just doing the work that usuly falls to a farmers wife and little children. I have four girls the oldest one is five years. The next almost three and on the 5th of June we had twin girls: I've never done anything very exciting but nothing can be said against my character to hurt Carlisle or the Oneida.

On December 22, 1910, she wrote to Friedman from a hospital in Green Bay, Wisconsin. Like her sister Elizabeth, she too thanked him for his Christmas letter and offered some local news. She wrote,

> Supt. Friedman,
>
> Dear Friend you never can know how much pleasure your Christmas rememberance gave me. It came soon after my operation and I could just lie here and look from one building to another and think of my old friends and wonder what each one were doing now. and if any were sick if they had such good care as I have from these good Sisters. I'll be able to be taken home for Christmas. They are all doing fine at Oneida.
>
> My classmate and now my sister-in-law Cora Cornelius Adams lives next door to us. she has three children and is kept quite busy but they are doing well. they built a nice big house this fall. They had been living in Buffalo, N.Y. since they were married.
>
> John Powlas, who has been teaching the day school at Oneida was married a few weeks ago. I got a letter from Mary Mitchel an old student of Carlisle, she is now married but I don't remember the name. They live in Michigan and have about fourty borders to cook for.

Well I must close by wishing you all a Merry Christmas and Happy new year. I'll be Happy to get back to my dear little twins again.

Mrs. Martha Sickles Cornelius '98

Cora Cornelius had indeed been Martha Sickles's classmate at Carlisle, and she too had graduated with the class of 1898. **John Powlas** was a member of the 1901 graduating class, and as Martha Cornelius notes, he had recently been married, to **Meg Hill**, a Seneca and also formerly a Carlisle student. After teaching school at Oneida, Powlas would go west to teach at Pine Ridge, and Manderson, South Dakota. **Mary Mitchell**, an Ottawa woman from Michigan, had also been a classmate of Martha Cornelius, attending Carlisle from 1889 to 1895. She had married Ben Ettawageshik, also a Michigan Ottawa—with a name Mrs. Cornelius did not recall. There is no record of him at Carlisle, although at least two other students named Ettawageshik did attend. It is clear that Martha Cornelius, like so many other Carlisle students, kept up with former classmates.

She filled out the brief 1912 form thanking Friedman "for kind letter and card," and adding, "we are getting along fine. My husband who learned the carpenter trade at Carlisle has built us a nice home." What I believe to be a photo of that home accompanies a note—undated, but probably 1912—that Martha Cornelius addressed to Nellie Robertson Denny. Sending regrets at not being able to attend the Carlisle commencement to which she had been invited, she adds, "I suppose you will recognize our house. The Town Board meets here tomorrow. James is serving his second term as supervisor of the town of Oneida." Nellie Denny was from Sisseton, South Dakota, and she might have visited her old schoolmate on a trip home—or this may simply mean that James Cornelius had earlier sent the school a photo that Denny had seen.

James Cornelius had been elected to his first term as town supervisor in 1910, as we learn from his response to one of the questions on the 1910 Carlisle questionnaire:

> The new town of Oneida which was opened last April elected me as one of the three supervisors which is quite an honor since

> better educated men tried so hard for the position. it is rather hard studying up the laws of the county opening new roads and building new bridges and still please everybody. There are almost as many white people as Indians live in this town. We had an election on the liquor question and only 18 voted for the saloon so I guess it will be a long time before we have a saloon here at that rate which is a very good thing.

Caleb Sickles was next after Martha, born in 1879, and after him came Arthur, who entered Carlisle in 1891 and remained—probably leaving and reentering—to graduate in 1902. His student information card says he trained as a printer and that his "character" was "very good." But that is all the Carlisle records say of **Arthur Sickles.** If he had received the brief 1907 questionnaire to graduates and the lengthier 1909 form, for example, he does not seem to have returned them. This was also true of the 1910 questionnaire, prompting superintendent Friedman to write to Dr. Sickles to ask after his brother. Here is the Ohio dentist's reply, dated May 24, 1910:

> Dear Sir,
>
> Our folks have not heard from Arthur Sickles for nearly three years. The address given in the list is the last one we received from him. He has been away from home for 9 years. If he is anything, he is independent—which is one good mark in his make up—he is not depending on the father and mother to support him. He is among strangers making his own way.

Arthur Sickles had come home in 1901 and returned to Carlisle to graduate in 1902. In August of that year, a letter Martha Sickles Cornelius had sent was published in Carlisle's *Red Man and Helper* in which she reported, "My sister and brother, Arthur and Florence, are both working in Green Bay, Arthur in a printing office and Florence in a private family" (vol. 8, no. 7 [August 29, 1902]: 1). Arthur may well have remained in Green Bay for some five more years, but he then appears to have gone off "among strangers making his own way." There is a photograph of Arthur with his older sister, Elizabeth, at the school about 1892, a year after he had arrived, and he is surely in a photograph of the class of 1902—although the individual students are not identified. Superintendent Friedman continued trying to reach him, for his student information card has the notation, "Letter dated Feb. 1913 unclaimed." Whether a "good mark in his make-up" or not, he was indeed "independent": there is no further mention of him on record by his siblings or the school.

Curiously, **Florence Sickles**'s file contains exactly the same item, "Letter dated Feb. 1913 ret'nd unclaimed," although she was not off "among strangers," like her brother Arthur. Born in 1886, Florence Sickles had enrolled at Carlisle in 1898, graduating with the class of 1902. She left Carlisle in June that year but returned in September, and perhaps employed by the school, she seems to have lived there while attending Normal School in West Chester, Pennsylvania. She left Carlisle in September 1905. The Carlisle *Arrow* for December 12, 1909, noted that Florence S. Rickman—she had married Earl G. Rickman—"has a happy home in Seattle where her husband is a carpenter and contractor. . . . Before her marriage she taught in the [Indian] service, being stationed at Fort Shaw, Montana." There is also in her file the information that she was living in West De Pere in 1914, near her family, so that unlike Arthur's, her whereabouts were known to them. There is no word of her after 1914.

When she returned to Carlisle in September 1904, Florence Sickles brought with her a young man named **Fred Sickles,** whom I believe to have been her first cousin.[10] The school listed his age at the time as eighteen, and if that was correct, he would have been the same age as Florence. The first item in his student file is a striking photograph. It is undated and seems to have been sent as a postcard. (Fred was a printer, and he could have made it himself.)

He left the school in June 1909, only to reapply for admission in the fall. He applied on his own behalf, and the birthdate he put on his application was November 22, 1889, which would make him three years younger than what had been recorded when he first entered. He trained to be a printer, although his "Trade Record" for 1910–11 stated that while his conduct was "splendid," and he was a "Good worker," the printer's trade was "a poor match for him." He had several outing assignments and returned to Carlisle to graduate in 1913. One of his outings had been in Allentown, New Jersey, from where he wrote to the school on October 5, 1913, about getting $87.30 in his account released to him. Superintendent Friedman sent him a check for that amount just a week later. There are no further communications between Fred Sickles and the school in his file, although the Carlisle *Arrow* for September 10, 1915, noted that he was still employed "at Allentown, N.J.," and that "He wishes to be remembered to all old friends" (3).

Herbert Sickles, the last of the Sickles family I mention at Carlisle, was born in 1888 and entered Carlisle in 1903. In April 1906, he went on a farm outing assignment, and a month later the Carlisle *Arrow* for May 25 reported, "We are pleased to know that Herbert Sickles is enjoying his work at farming in Robinsville, New Jersey, and wishes to be remembered to his friends" (3). He continued to work on the farm through that summer and the fall. Then, either because he was no longer "enjoying his work at farming," or because he was scheduled to return to the school and did not wish to do so, he "ran" on December 2 and was listed as a "Deserter" by the school. Either returned to the school against his will or coming back of his own volition, he remained for the spring semester, finally leaving Carlisle at the beginning of July 1907.

"Deserter" though he had been, Herbert Sickles sent Carlisle a long and fascinating letter dated May 28, 1909. It describes a truly historical experience, and I quote it in full:

> U.S.S. Kiarsarge
> League Island Navy Yard
> Philadelphia, Pa.
>
> May 28th 1909
>
> Dear Friend,
>
> You have no doubt given up hopes of hearing from me. It has been so long since I left Carlisle that I will not ask you to excuse

me. Since the time I broke away from the rules of Old Carlisle I have had many and varied experiences.

But I am now in the U.S. Navy. The navy suits me. I will remain in the service 3 years and 11 months longer. I already have 1 year and 1 month in.

I have been all the way around the earth. I enlisted in Minneapolis, Minn. and was sent to Newport, R.I. to the U.S. Naval Training Station. There my previous military training received at Carlisle gave me the rate of petty officer. I had charge of my company. I was sent aboard the training ship Cumberland. That is a fine large sailing vessel, a steel ship too. She has the highest mast in the navy.

On the afternoon of June 12th, 1908 about 700 [?] of us who were the best trained were transferred. We went aboard the U.S. gunboat Prairie and the next morning at 10 o'clock got under way. We sailed down the beautiful bay and out to sea. We were going to join the "Big Sixteen" which would be in San Fran-cisco Bay by the time we would get there.

Our first stop was to Colon, Panama. It is a distance of 2200 knots. It took just 7 days and 5 hours. But it would not have taken so long but for about 2 ½ days of rough weather while crossing the Caribbean Sea. We had all kinds of funny experiences on that run and as it was our first it of course impressed us very much.

Besides we were most all green hands and the spectacle of the high running seas was very aweinspiring to the more timid ones. A good many as I ought to say nearly all of us were seasick. But I can truthfully say that I have never been seasick. And I have only been slightly frightened once and then for only a moment when I kicked myself for being so foolish. This was in a terrible typhoon in the China Sea. I was the only one on the hurricane deck or super-structure deck at the time when the storm was at the hight of its furry. The navigator had lost the course and the storm was getting worse it seemed. the maintop mast was carried away with the wireless apparatus leaving us out of communication with the rest of the ship.

The lifeboats were being carried away one after another and other pieces of tackle on the forecastle and quarter deck were torn loose and carried away. Joints that had stood other storms easily were now leaking badly. Water was three feet deep in the 6 forward coal bunkers and two forward holds. All the overboard discharge pumps were working full capacity, but the water gained in by inch as the long hours wore on. Even the hand pumps were manned constantly for one day and one night to keep back the water. That storm lasted three days and three nights. The sea ran 60 feet high according to the estimates of the navigator. The ship rolled 38 degrees 45 being the limit.

We couldn't get the food cooked the way it was in calm weather and we couldn't use the tables to eat from on account of the rolling and the pitching of the ship.

My ship is now in League Island. We are likly to be tied up here a couple of years. I am detailed to remain aboard until this Sept. perhaps I will be detailed for even longer. I hope you will not be displeased with me and I also hope you will answer this letter soon. I beg to remain your friend and ex-scholar

Herbert A. Sickles

Leaving Carlisle, Pennsylvania, in July 1907, Herbert Sickles, an Oneida man of about twenty-one, seems to have headed west; he may have stopped to visit his brother, Caleb, at his practice in Tiffin, Ohio. Perhaps he then continued to visit others of his family in West De Pere, Wisconsin. In April 1908, as he told superintendent Friedman, he enlisted in the United States Navy. Having engaged in a good deal of marching and drilling at Carlisle, Sickles says he entered the navy not as a simple seaman, but as a petty officer. He is first assigned to the training ship *Cumberland*, a steel-hulled sailing ship. He then transfers to the gunboat *Prairie*, which had seen action in Cuban waters during the Spanish-American War before being recommissioned as a training vessel. From its berth in Newport, Rhode Island, the *Prairie* heads out to sea, to the Atlantic Ocean. It is destined for the Pacific, and San Francisco Bay, to join the "Big Sixteen" or the "Great White Fleet."[11]

Sailing south 2,200 knots—2,640 miles—the *Prairie* stops in Panama—but not to use the Panama Canal as a route from the Atlantic to the Pacific Ocean, as American ships would later do: the canal, then under construction, would not open until 1914. This means that to get to San Francisco Bay, Petty Officer Sickles's ship would continue down the coast of South America in order to pass through the Straits of Magellan in Chile, the only natural passage from the Atlantic to the Pacific. It would then head north to San Francisco Bay.

But we next hear of the powerful typhoon in the South China Sea. This means that Sickles's ship, the gunboat *Prairie*, upon entering the Pacific, had not turned and headed north to San Francisco, its stated destination, but instead had continued south. Now, in May 1909, Sickles is writing from on board the USS *Kearsarge*, but of course that was not the vessel on which he had been sailing. Rather, he seems to have been detailed to the *Kearsarge* while his severely damaged ship, the gunboat *Prairie*, undergoes repairs. Curiously, for all his far-flung travels, he is now at League Island, a navy repair yard in the Delaware River, part of Philadelphia, not far from Carlisle.

Sickles's description of riding out a typhoon in the South China Sea is powerful; one may well read it in the context of literary evocations of similar experiences. Although Petty Officer Sickles had requested a response, there is no copy of a letter from superintendent Friedman to him in his file.

Siceni Nori's next example of a "successful" Indian in the professions is "Dr. Powless, a prominent physician"—not in West De Pere, but in nearby Oneida, Wisconsin, where he was in charge of the agency hospital. First educated at the Oneida Mission School, Josiah Powless had gone to Carlisle in 1885 at the age of fourteen and graduated in 1892. He attended Dickinson Preparatory School but did not immediately go on to further studies. He returned home and took "a teaching position at the newly established government school" (Hauptman and McLester 2015, 28), and in 1897 married **Electa Skenandore**, also an Oneida and a Carlisle alumna. In 1900 Powless entered the Milwaukee

Medical College and graduated in 1904, "the first Oneida Indian to graduate from a medical school in the United States" (Hauptman and McLester 2015, 26). In 1911 he would join Dennison Wheelock, and **Charles Dagenett**, whom Nori mentions later, and a number of other prominent Native people in launching the Society of American Indians.

Dr. Powless seems to have been a modest man of few words. In response to the 1907 questionnaire to graduates, for example, he simply gave his wife's name and noted that he had been a schoolteacher and physician at the Oneida school. He was equally reticent on the lengthier 1909 form. Unlike other "successful" Indians Nori had named, he chose not to describe his home and listed only "a span of ponies" for the stock he owned. As for whether he had "done anything for the betterment of [his] people," the doctor wrote, "Trying to get a system of town government," and he left blank the question about anything further of interest about his life.

As Nori could not know, the quiet Oneida doctor would die a hero in World War I. The Oneidas had fought on the American side during the Revolutionary War; Powless's grandfather, Peter Powless, had "served in Company K of the 17th Wisconsin during the Civil War"; and his "oldest brother Emmanuel served . . . during the Spanish American War" (Hauptman and McLester 2015, 28). Following in their footsteps, a month after America's entry into World War I in April 1917, Dr. Josiah Powless joined the army at the age of forty-five. He soon found himself in combat on the Western front in France as a first lieutenant in the Army Medical Corps. On October 14, 1918, he attempted to rescue Captain James McKibben, another Medical Corps doctor, who had been badly wounded. Under heavy German fire, Dr. Powless was himself hit, his wounds leading to his death a month later, "just five days before the armistice" ending the war (Hauptman and McLester 2015, 30). Josiah Powless was awarded the Distinguished Service Cross, the nation's second highest military decoration "for extraordinary heroism in action." He was buried in Oneida.

Of the three next mentioned by Nori, **Thomas Mani** and **Edward Rogers** were prominent attorneys and elected officials in South Dakota and Minnesota, respectively; Rogers had been a Carlisle football star as well. Their files provide a fair amount of information about them. But there is no student file for Dr. **Oscar DeForest Davis**, a White Earth Chippewa. His information card records that he entered Carlisle in 1896 at the age of eleven and graduated with the class of 1903, with printing as his trade. In the 1911 *Report, U.S. Indian School, Carlisle, Pa.*, Friedman says Davis "worked his way through the University of Minnesota and graduated near the head of his class" (10). A written notation on his student information card indicates that he was "Band leader at Tomah Indian School 1904," and Friedman specified that Davis had become a dental surgeon. But there is nothing more.

Thomas Mani, a Sisseton Sioux, was a 1902 graduate with several letters in his file between himself and Nellie Robertson—whom he addressed as "cousin"—mostly about the possibility of land sales. His 1909 questionnaire indicates that he had married Ada Louise Woodman and attended Dickinson College Preparatory School before being admitted to the University of Minnesota Law School, from which he graduated in 1906. He writes that his past year's income was $4,000, thus matching the impressive sum Nori had cited as Dr. James Johnson's income. He says he has a fine home, some land, and money in the bank. Asked whether he has "done anything for the betterment of [his] people," Mani writes,

> I have been trying to set an example for others to follow and have made an independent living. I have always abstained from drinking intoxicants which fact I consider a great deal for the betterment of the race as well as for the white people who are my neighbors.

As for "anything else of interest connected with [his] life," Thomas Mani movingly wrote, "I have now a son named Delphin Delmas Mani, born Dec. 22, 1907. He has been an inspiration to me for nobler things and has made the home more cheerful than before." In 1912 Mani ran successfully for state's attorney on the Republican ticket.

Edward Rogers, a White Earth Chippewa, graduated from Carlisle in 1897, then went to Dickinson College and to the Dickinson Law School before he too entered the University of Minnesota Law School, graduating in 1904. At Carlisle he was a nationally recognized end on the football team and captain of the team in 1896. Like Thorpe and several others, he also ran track, specializing in the hurdles and the pole vault. In addition, he excelled as a baseball player. According to the rules of the period, he was eligible to play football for the University of Minnesota as a law student, and he was captain of its 1903 team. Upon his graduation from law school Rogers, at the age of twenty-seven, was still eligible to play for another year, but chose instead to return to Carlisle to coach the football team, after the departure of Glenn "Pop" Warner in 1904.

As he details in several responses to the school's surveys, Rogers first practiced law in Mahnomen, Minnesota, where he was appointed judge of the Probate Court. He then moved his practice east to Walker, Minnesota, where, as he informed the school in 1912, he was "elected county attorney of Cass C. Minn. at the last election. Only about 75 Indian votes in the county so was elected by white votes. Doing well." Earlier, on his 1909 questionnaire, in response to the question about doing anything for the "betterment of [his] people," he had scrawled a large "No." But a letter to Friedman dated "Jan. 18th 1909"—it may have accompanied the questionnaire, which is not dated—suggests that he had indeed given the matter some thought.

Rogers wrote,

> I herewith take pleasure in submitting to you the report of my career since graduating from your school in 1897. You will note that I have been most fortunate in my endeavor to better myself and have had a comparatively easy road to travel.
>
> What little degree of success I have attained I attribute entirely to my early training at Carlisle.
>
> I might add although the subject is not mentioned nor no opinion is requested that to abolish non-reservation schools is

a mistake and would be a serious detriment to the progress and welfare of future young Indians.

In 1913 Rogers was elected "Chief"—I'm not sure just what the office entailed—of ten Ojibwe tribes, with much newspaper coverage of his election.

The other materials in Edward Rogers's capacious file are mostly laudatory news clippings about him, with nothing further from him in his own voice. But there is a single clipping from the Saint Paul, Minnesota *Dispatch*, dated February 14, 1917, that sounds a different note. It begins, "Ed L. Rogers, county attorney of Cass county, was charged with misfeasance or non-feasance in office in a complaint filed with Governor Burnquist by Thomas Pederson, a Cass County citizen, asking that the attorney be removed." The complaint's allegations range from Rogers being "absent from his office for weeks at a time," to failing to investigate charges against county employees and "violation of the corrupt practices act in transporting Indian voters to the polls." It is, of course, difficult to see how simply "*transporting* Indian voters to the polls" could be a "violation of the corrupt practices act"—unless they were not allowed to vote in Minnesota at the time, something I have not been able to determine. But the other charges are abundantly detailed.

Rogers was acquitted, or in any case was not removed from office, if an article by Curt Brown in the *Minneapolis Star Tribune* for June 29, 2019, is correct. (The piece does have some errors.) Brown writes that Rogers served as Cass County Attorney for forty-six years, with apparently no break in that service. He died in 1971 at the age of ninety-five; in 1997 a bronze bust of Edward Rogers was installed on the lawn of the Cass County Courthouse in Walker, Minnesota.

Of the remaining "successful" Indians named by Siceni Nori, we have already learned something about Charles Dagenett from his own words and from the copies of letters from and to him concerning the subject of his Indian Office duties as supervisor of Indian employment. As we will see, it would not be long before Dagenett would be called upon to find employment for Siceni Nori.

Charles Albert Bender, known as "Chief"—all early twentieth-century Native American professional baseball players were called "Chief," sometimes affectionately, but more usually with disparaging racial intent—was born in either 1883 or (more probably) 1884 and grew up on the White Earth Reservation. He spent several years at the Educational Home in Philadelphia and entered Carlisle in 1896, graduating in 1902, by which time he had already come to attention as a promising baseball pitcher. After a year at Dickinson Preparatory School he signed with the professional Philadelphia Athletics in 1903. He had by that time also worked as a watchmaker and would become, as Nori reported, "a crack marksman." Bender had an extraordinary professional career, including a no-hitter and winning the World Series in 1910; the following year he became the only player in history to pitch three complete games in a World Series. Bender was elected to the Baseball Hall of Fame in 1953 and died the following year, just before his induction into the hall.

A great deal has been written about him, but because Charles Bender, like so many other former Carlisle students, returned the 1909 questionnaire to Superintendent Friedman, we can hear an account of his early life in his own words. He says that he is married, but instead of giving his wife's name—she was Marie Clement and they were married in 1904—he writes "German-American." He lists his occupation as "Professional baseball player," and he describes his home and considerable property, including an allotment, "160 acres of land on the White Earth Reservation."

Bender crossed out the question about having "done anything for the betterment of [his] people," and wrote above it, "Just an outline of my life." Here is that outline:

> Born in Brainerd Minn. Parents: Father German American, one of the early settlers in Minnesota. Mother Chippewa. Parents moved to White Earth Res when I was quite young.
>
> At the age of eight—1891, I was sent to the Educational Home 49th + Greenway Ave Phila, where I received my early training. 1896 was allowed to go home. At the end of two months, decided

> to run away from home and go to Carlisle Indian Training School. Arrived the 1st week in Sept. My record while there can be easily found. The best training that I received was from the good Quaker folks of Bucks County. The outing system is O.K. in my estimation.
>
> Graduated in Feb 1902 with one of the largest classes ever turned out.

He crosses out the next question, "anything else of interest," to continue:

> Played ball for Carlisle during 1901 + 02. Joined the Harrisburg Athletic Club 1902 summer. made good but saved little money. Had to scratch to make both ends meet during winter. Started in to learn watchmaking and jewelry business. spent four or five winters at it.
>
> In 1903 signed a contract as pitcher with the Phila. "Athletics" of the American League; and the coming season will be my 7th one with the same club. Wouldn't advise any of the students at Carlisle to become a professional ball player. It's a hard road to travel. Many temptations along the wayside.

Except for a brief note thanking Superintendent Friedman for sending him two tickets to a Carlisle v. Penn football game, there is nothing more in Charles Bender's Carlisle file from him to the school. These are the "successful" Indians Siceni J. Nori called to the attention of the Carlisle graduating class of 1911, and I return now to his further history at the school.

On February 6, 7, and 8, and March 25, 1914, E. B. Linnen, an inspector of Indian schools for the Department of the Interior under Franklin K. Lane, led the *Hearings Before the Joint Commission of the U.S. Sixty-third Congress, Second Session*, an inquiry into conditions at the Carlisle Indian Industrial School. Charges against the school had been made by Matthew Sniffen of the Indian Rights Association, and letters and petitions from students and faculty of the school complaining of a variety of conditions had been sent to the Office of Indian Affairs. Superintendent Friedman believed that the charges had been instigated by Richard Pratt because he wished to return as head of the school, although Pratt vigorously denied this. It was not, in fact, true but arose from a rumor originating in a misleading article in a local newspaper. There was also speculation that the attack on Carlisle was intended to move it to the west, or perhaps close it entirely, and the latter speculation may well have had some truth to it.

Of particular concern was the leadership of superintendent Friedman. Also questioned were the place of athletics at Carlisle; the handling of funds for the athletic programs; the quality and quantity of food provided to students; the thoroughness of industrial and agricultural instruction; use of corporal punishment and of mandated detentions for students, both in the school jail and in the town jail; drunkenness on campus; "immorality" among the students; dissension among the teachers and staff; and general disrespect for the superintendent.[12]

Friedman had been superintendent since the spring of 1908. What had happened, almost six years into his tenure as head of the school, to lead to these charges? A thorough history of the affair does not exist—one would, to my mind, be valuable—but I will outline the matter as best I can.[13]

Moses Friedman took over as head of the school from Major William Mercer, who had replaced Colonel Richard Pratt upon his dismissal in 1904. Friedman had worked for two years at the Phoenix Indian School, and had served as assistant superintendent at Haskell, so he had had solid experience in federal Indian education. But he was only thirty-four years old; he was not a military man like Carlisle's first two superintendents; and he bore an obviously Jewish name at a time when anti-semitism was common. Let me note again here that while Friedman's parents were Jewish immigrants from Germany, he had married the daughter of a Presbyterian minister and converted to Christianity. Many notices in the Carlisle newspapers over the years described him as giving sermons and leading church services at the school, and several of those who gave testimony to the congressional committee in 1914 spoke of him attending the Episcopal church; he and his wife had also been active among the Presbyterians. In other words, everyone at the school would have known that despite his name, Moses Friedman was a practicing Christian.

Like the military officers who had preceded him as Carlisle's superintendent, Friedman was in an odd position for a chief executive, for as noted, the Carlisle superintendent could not hire, fire, suspend, or transfer an employee of the school—with one important exception—without the approval of the Office of Indian Affairs. In much the same way, decisions about which students to accept or reject, or, after their admission, to send home for unsatisfactory behavior, tended to become entangled not only with officials in Washington but likewise with the government-appointed agents in charge of the various reservations.

It is also the case that Friedman was on record as opposed to corporal punishment in an era that resorted to it frequently, although his position on this matter was inconsistent. Disciplinarians, faculty members, or staff at the school had sometimes insisted that there were occasions on which "nothing could be done" with a student without the use of physical force, and Friedman had apparently acceded to the occasional use of it, provided his consent was first obtained. Carlisle graduate and former athlete Wallace Denny, in charge of the small boys, for example, had several times been reprimanded by Friedman for excessive use of force, and Denny—along with his wife, Nellie Robertson Denny—testified against Friedman in 1914.[14] Indeed, a 1913 instance of corporal punishment involving a student named **Julia Hardin** took up much space in the congressional hearings. I describe it briefly here.

Julia Hardin was listed in the Carlisle records as a quarter-blood Potawatomi woman of seventeen or eighteen years old. She had refused to go on two outing assignments—assignments she herself was said to have requested—because she claimed not to have a proper trunk in which to pack her clothes. On both those occasions, she was not required to go, on the assumption that she would obtain the necessary trunk and go at some later date. In June 1913, when she refused once more to go on the outing, the matron, a Miss Ridenhour, sent her to Friedman in order that he might solve the problem. But Friedman sent her back to the matron for the two to work things out on their own. At that point Mr. Claude Stauffer, a music teacher and bandmaster, became involved, and Stauffer slapped the girl in the face, threw her down, and beat her with—testimony varied—a three-inch wide wooden slat or something more substantial. Stauffer claimed that he had Friedman's permission to do this, Friedman presumably having told him on some occasion that he might do as he thought necessary with this young woman or with students generally.

Enter, now, John Whitwell, a principal teacher, or assistant superintendent, who strongly disliked Friedman. He comforted the girl. In regard to what had been done to her, the commissioners seemed most troubled by the fact that Hardin was three-quarters white, and they demonstrated a certain erotic uneasiness about the rough handling of not a little girl but a young woman in her late teens.

Politics and changing educational philosophies were also involved in the decision to subject Carlisle to congressional investigation. Friedman was a Republican, and after Woodrow Wilson's 1912 Democratic victory for the presidency, Cato Sells, the commissioner of Indian Affairs, and Franklin K. Lane, secretary of the interior, both Democrats, may have had some interest in installing a Democratic superintendent at the Carlisle Indian School. Or, for that matter, they may have favored closing the school entirely: around the first decade of the twentieth century a number of Indian reformers had come to believe that local public schools might better acculturate—they would perhaps have said "assimilate"—Native students than the off-reservation boarding schools, a move that would also save the federal government money. And there was the complex matter of Carlisle athletics.

Glenn "Pop" Warner had first come to Carlisle as athletic director under Pratt in 1899, and he left the school when Pratt was dismissed in 1904, later to return under Mercer in 1907. Warner, who had coached baseball and track, was actively in the process of building up the football program—and side-lining the baseball program—when Friedman arrived. But Warner was not a government employee; he had been hired by the athletic association at Carlisle. The composition of that association, its fund-raising, and disbursements remained unclear, even by the end of the Linnen investigation. That Warner received a salary of

$4,000 in 1914—over $100,000 today (2019)—however, is undisputed, as is the fact that at least during his early years at Carlisle, his methods with the football players led several of them to refuse to play until he changed his ways; as was common at the time and sometimes since, those ways involved cursing at and belittling them. He did change his ways—at least in sufficient measure to field a powerful team.

Its star was Jim Thorpe. Thorpe had briefly been to the Haskell Institute before coming to Carlisle in 1904, and it was reported that in 1907, visiting Carlisle, he casually beat the best high jumpers on the track team while still in his street clothes.[15] Upon joining that team, he, like Dr. Johnson, participated in several events, and Warner also put him on the football team. By 1911 both Thorpe and Carlisle football were nationally recognized and regularly covered by the *New York Times*. Thorpe would go on to win medals at the 1912 Olympics in Stockholm, Sweden, and as is fairly well known, he would subsequently be stripped of his medals for having played baseball professionally one summer, thus violating the required "amateur" status for Olympic athletes.

One of the charges against superintendent Friedman was that he was ineffective in stamping out drunkenness at the school—apparently a problem of long standing—and this was particularly marked when it came to the athletes, who were known to imbibe a good deal of beer on campus. Thorpe and other football players had been found drunk on many occasions, something that was attributed to inattention—if not actual encouragement—on Coach Warner's part. This was a problem Friedman had not managed to solve. It was also the case that the athletes ate at special tables in the dining room and got an abundance of excellent food, while—it was alleged—rations, in particular bread, were both scarce and unpalatable for the rest of the students. It was charged as well that student mattresses were of insufficient quality, and that "immorality" between the boys and girls was common. In this regard, two teachers also reported that Mrs. Friedman, the minister's daughter, sometimes wore make-up, and had on occasion danced so heartily at band functions as to have her knees show.

A number of students and faculty members also testified that superintendent Friedman was lacking in his concern for the well-being of his students, and that he was generally not respected, this disrespect marked in particular by some calling him "Mose" and "Old Jew." Regarding the matter of Friedman's concern for the students, I repeat that his record in responding to former students is excellent, a judgment I base on the many copies of letters he wrote them that repose in the Carlisle files, several of which we have noted. There is no question that antagonism toward the superintendent was largely organized by John Whitwell and some other teachers and staff for reasons not entirely disinterested.[16] But it is nonetheless clear that Friedman had lost control of the situation, to the point where some government-sponsored remedies were in order.

On February 25, 1914, among the last witnesses called to testify before the congressional committee was Siceni Nori. As chief clerk, Nori was in charge of ledger books, account books, vouchers, and "mileage books"—these were used to document official travel by Friedman and other school staff. Nori admitted to having altered some of these records and destroyed others by burning them at home in his stove. He did this, he said, on Friedman's orders (*Hearings Before the Joint Commission of the U.S. Sixty-third Congress,* 1914, 1293–94), Friedman "intimating," he testified, that he was to "fix" the accounts (1255). Nori's testimony was sometimes confusing, but the gist of it was that Friedman had misused funds and directed his chief clerk to try to hide that fact.

Linnen's final "Report" concluded that "Superintendent Friedman and Bandmaster Stauffer be suspended and tried" (1390), and that Glenn Warner be dismissed. Inspector Linnen recommended that Nori "be suspended at once and undoubtedly dismissed from the Government service" (1387). While Linnen believed that Nori "is likely to be dishonest" (1379), and reported that "rumors were afloat connecting him to certain women in the town of Carlisle" (1378), he nonetheless did not recommend criminal charges against Nori. This would seem to be for reasoning of a racist nature, Linnen stating that Nori was an Indian who had been at Carlisle for a long time and thus believed he had no choice but to obey Friedman's direction (1387).

But when Friedman learned of Nori's charges against him, he had a warrant sworn out for Nori's arrest on the charge of embezzlement.

The *Harrisburg Telegraph* for April 25, 1914, reported that at the subsequent trial, a Miss Beatrice Herman, who had been assistant to Nori, testified "that she knew Nori had diverted student moneys to his personal account" (10). It was observed as well that having separated from his wife and been ordered by a court to pay support for her and their two children, he was in need of money. Before a verdict was reached, Nori's attorneys had the case transferred to federal court—where the charges now included destruction of government property.

Friedman resigned from Carlisle in May 1914, and refused government offers of immunity on some of the charges, insisting that he be allowed to defend himself at trial. Just over a year later, on June 18, 1915, the *New York Times* reported that Friedman had been acquitted of all charges, and as William Cook has written, he insisted "that he had been harassed out of his position by . . . a Democratic administration in Washington that wanted Republicans out so they could make appointments of their own" (Cook 2011, 111). The *Adams County News* of Gettysburg, Pennsylvania, reported on October 23, 1915, that

> Dr. Friedman was acquitted and completely vindicated of the charges brought against him by a prompt decision of the jury at the June session of the Federal Court at Williamsport. Chief clerk Nori, who testified against him at the trial was sent to the penitentiary.[17]

Although the article noted that Friedman had gone on to be "appointed to a most responsible position," with a large salary, in fact his subsequent employment as school superintendent was at places far less prestigious than Carlisle.

At this point we may pick up the story by returning to Nori's Carlisle student files. Sentenced to prison in October 1915, Nori did not serve long. As we learn from a letter by Charles Dagenett, Carlisle graduate and supervisor of Indian employment, to Matthew Sniffen of the IRA, dated December 17, 1915, Nori had already been paroled by that time, although not yet released. In his letter Dagenett asks Sniffen to provide what is called a "statement of first friend," a letter in support of Nori required by the parole board before he could actually be set free.

Sniffen provided that "statement," and he would subsequently make a number of efforts to find employment for Nori. Nellie Denny, still at the school, also offered Nori help.

Meanwhile, on February 2, 1916, Nori wrote to ask that three employees of the school be allowed release time to testify on his behalf in his suit against his wife for divorce on the grounds of desertion. Wherever his daughters had been during his time in prison and for a year after his release, they were now, as he wrote on February 6, 1917, "temporarily in care of friends in Carlisle." Nori explained that having obtained work with the Pennsylvania and Reading Railway Company "at the Loco shops in Reading, PA,"—basic locomotive repairs and maintenance—he goes "up to see them Saturday afternoon and evenings," a trip of about eighty miles. It was Dagenett's opinion that it would be best for Nori's daughters to attend public school in Pennsylvania, although (for reasons I have not discovered) their father preferred that they go to the Mount Pleasant Indian School in Michigan. With Nellie Denny's help, the girls were examined by the Carlisle physician in 1917, a requirement for their admission to the Mount Pleasant School, which they subsequently attended. Whether Nori found work near them or remained in Pennsylvania cannot be known from his Carlisle files.

Immediately after Moses Friedman's dismissal, Oscar H. Lipps, of the government Indian Service, was appointed Carlisle superintendent. Lipps's career had included work at the Nez Perce agency and service as superintendent of the Chemawa School in Oregon. He was in charge at Carlisle from the spring of 1914 until relieved of his duties in February 1917, when he was replaced by John Francis Jr., who would be Carlisle's last superintendent.

Francis's personnel file, a full 137 pages, can be read at the Carlisle Indian School Digital Resource Center website. One of the more interesting items in it is a letter by none other than Dennison Wheelock to Indian Commissioner Cato Sells, dated March 3, 1917, favoring Francis's appointment. I don't know who solicited Wheelock's opinion, but he wrote that while he had approved of Lipps and valued him as an educator, he believed Francis's military training—he had attended

St. John's Military Academy, in Manlius, New York—would suit him well in putting things in proper order at Carlisle.

In April 1917, just a month after Wheelock's letter and Francis's appointment, the United States entered World War I. Francis served as wartime superintendent at Carlisle until July 1918, when at age thirty-eight he resigned to enter active duty in the army reserves. Two months later, on September 1, 1918, the American flag was lowered for the last time at the Carlisle Indian School, less than a year short of graduating its thirtieth class. Perhaps the band played Dennison Wheelock's "Carlisle Indian School March" for the occasion. The war ended on the eleventh hour of the eleventh day of the eleventh month, 1918. I know no more of Siceni Nori, and there would be no more Carlisle boarding school voices.

Appendix

Carlisle Students Named in this Book

The married names of several of the women are given in parentheses but all are alphabetized by the names by which they were known as Carlisle students. Tribal affiliations are those recorded at the time (e.g., Winnebago, not Ho-Chunk; Chippewa, not Anishinaabe).

Alice American Horse	Sioux
Ben American Horse	Sioux
Joseph American Horse	Sioux
Lucy American Horse	Sioux
Robert American Horse	Sioux
Sophia American Horse	Sioux
Maria Analla	Laguna Pueblo
Nettie Aspenall (Davis)	Pawnee
Boisie Bassford	Paiute
Charles Bear	Nez Perce
Guy Bear Don't Scare/American Horse	Sioux
Charles Albert Bender	Chippewa
Hubbell Big Horse	Cheyenne
Newton Big Road	Sioux
Charles Bird	Sioux
Thomas Blackbear	Sioux

Jennie Black Kettle (Tyler)	Cheyenne
Hope Blueteeth (Locke)	Sioux
Martha Bordeaux	Sioux
Clayton Brave	Sioux
Constant Bread	Apache
Lewis Brown	Sioux
Jock Bull Bear	Arapaho
Oscar Bull Bear	Cheyenne
Emma Bull Bonnet (Blackbear)	Sioux
Mike Burns	Apache/Yavapai
William F. Campbell	Chippewa
Juan Antonio Chamon	Jemez Pueblo
Wallace Charging Shield	Sioux
John Menaul Chaves	Laguna Pueblo
John Chaves Jr.	Laguna Pueblo
Martha Chaves	Laguna Pueblo
Charles Chickenny	Menominee
Ramona Chihuahua	Apache
Lucinda Clinton (Hood)	Modoc
Cora Cornelius	Oneida
James Cornelius	Oneida
Lillie Cornelius	Oneida
William Crazy Bull/Girton	Sioux
William Crow	Cheyenne
Moses Culbertson	Sioux
Frank Cushing	Zuni Pueblo
Charles Dagenett	Peoria
Asa Daklugie	Apache

Charles Dakota	Cheyenne
Oscar DeForest Davis	Chippewa
Richard Davis	Cheyenne
Lucy Day	Sioux
Rendell Delchey	Apache
Wallace Denny	Oneida
Eva Dezey	Apache
Charles Dickens	Yavapai
Cyrus Dixon	Cochiti Pueblo
John Dixon	Cochiti Pueblo
Etadleuh Doanmoe	Kiowa
Laura Doanmoe (Pedrick)	Kiowa
Dora Her Pipe	Sioux
Ellwood Dorian	Iowa
Frank Dorian	Iowa
Charlie Driscal	Shoshoni
Jennie Dubray (Three Stars)	Sioux
Paul Eagle Star	Sioux
Brian Early Bird	Apache
Casper Edson	Arapaho
Harriet Elder (Stuart)	Nez Perce
Charles Elk	Cheyenne
Amelia Elseday	Apache
Clara Faber	Wyandotte
Edgar Fire Thunder	Sioux
George Fire Thunder	Sioux
Roland Fish	Apache
James Fox	Sioux

Lizzie Frog	Sioux
Joshua Given	Kiowa
Julia Given	Kiowa
Dolly Gould	Nez Perce
Christopher Goggles	Arapaho
Ida Griffin (Nori)	Okanagan
Thomas Griffin	Okanagan
Katie Grindrod	Wyandotte
Emma Hand (Means)	Sioux
Marshall Hand	Sioux
Julia Hardin	Potawatomi
Joseph Harris	Gros Ventre
Kish Hawkins	Cheyenne
Bernard Herman	Winnebago
Meg Hill	Seneca
Lizzie M. Hill	Sioux
Charles Hood	Modoc
Edward Jannies	Sioux
Frank Jannies	Sioux
Samuel Johns	Nez Perce
Arthur Johnson	Wyandotte
Eva Johnson	Wyandotte
James Edward (Jimmy) Johnson	Stockbridge
Percy Kable	Cheyenne
Mabel Kelcusaway	Apache
Charles Kelsey	Winnebago

Mary Kelsey	Winnebago
Henry J. Kendall	Isleta Pueblo
Stiya Kowacura	Laguna Pueblo
Annie Kowuni (Abner)	Laguna Pueblo
Mack Kutepi	Sioux
Louise La Chapelle (Wheelock)	Chippewa
Alice Leeds	Laguna Pueblo
Clifford Leeds	Laguna Pueblo
Yamie Leeds	Laguna Pueblo
Ernest Left Hand	Arapaho
Grant Left Hand	Arapaho
William Little Elk	Cheyenne
Florence Little Elk	Cheyenne
Rebecca Little Wolf	Nez Perce
George Little Wound	Sioux
Plenty Living Bear	Sioux
Frank Locke	Sioux
Mary Locke	Sioux
Cecelia Londrosh (Herman)	Winnebago
Nellie Londrosh (Nunn)	Winnebago
Amos Long Wolf	Sioux
Dana Long Wolf	Sioux
Hannah Long Wolf	Sioux
Hattie Long Wolf/Porcupine (Pretty Weasel)	Sioux
Nelson Long Wolf	Sioux
Adelia Lowe (Twiss)	Sioux
James Luther	Laguna Pueblo

Thomas Mani	Sioux
Lorenzo Martinez	Taos Pueblo
Jimmie McAdams	Shoshoni
George Means	Crow
Thomas Metoxen	Oneida
Esther Miller (Dagenett)	Miami
F. H. Miller	Acoma Pueblo
James H. Miller	Acoma Pueblo
James Y. Miller	Acoma Pueblo
Mary Mitchell	Ottawa
Edward Myers	Pawnee
Jose Nadilgodey	Apache
Siceni Nori	Laguna Pueblo
Henry North	Arapaho
Alice Nunn	Winnebago
Mary Nunn	Winnebago
George Nyrnah	Yuma
Maggie Old Eagle	Sioux
Frank Paisano	Laguna Pueblo
Mary Paisano	Laguna Pueblo
Minnie Paisano	Laguna Pueblo
Ulysses G. Paisano	Laguna Pueblo
William (Willie) Paisano	Laguna Pueblo
Jesse Paul	Nez Perce
Emily Peatone	Kiowa
Mary Perry (Paisano)	Laguna Pueblo

Luke Phillips	Nez Perce
Cecilia Pickard	Wichita
Eva Pickard	Wichita
Helen Pickard	Wichita
Rose Pickard	Wichita
Marcus Poco	Comanche
John Powlas	Oneida
Josiah Powless	Oneida
Julia Powless (Wheelock)	Oneida
Lucy Pretty Weasel	Sioux
Sophia Rachel	Nez Perce
Obed Rabbit	Apache
Laura M. S. Reid	Laguna Pueblo
Mattie Reid (Luther)	Laguna Pueblo
Nellie Robertson (Denny)	Sioux
Edward Rogers	Chippewa
John Rooks	Sioux
Conrad Roubideaux	Sioux
Edwin Schanandore	Oneida
Jah Seger	Arapaho
Neathah Seger	Arapaho
Nancy Seneca	Seneca
William Shakespeare	Arapaho
Christine Showtemutsey	Laguna Pueblo
Arthur Sickles	Oneida
Caleb Sickles	Oneida
Elizabeth Sickles (Metoxen)	Oneida
Florence Sickles (Rickman)	Oneida

Fred Sickles	Oneida
Martha Sickles (Cornelius)	Oneida
Ruben Sioux	Sioux
Electa Skenandore (Powless)	Oneida
Simon Smith	Winnebago
Kate Stalker (Left Hand)	Cheyenne
Luther Standing Bear	Sioux
Arthur Standing Elk	Cheyenne
Laura Standing Elk	Cheyenne
Maggie Stands Looking (Guy Belt)	Sioux
Hortie Stevens	Wichita
Raymond Stewart	Sioux
Carl Sweezy	Arapaho
John Tatum	Wichita
Joe Taylor	Sioux
Bennie Thomas	Laguna Pueblo
Jim Thorpe	Sac and Fox
Clarence Three Stars	Sioux
Lucy Tsisnah	Apache
Frank Twiss	Sioux
Leonard Tyler	Cheyenne
Joel Tyndall	Omaha
Wallace Tyndall	Omaha
Adelia Tyon	Sioux
Julia Walking Crane (Brave)	Sioux
Thomas Wistar	Ottawa
Josiah Wolf	Ottawa
Cleaver Warden	Arapaho

Charles Wheelock	Oneida
Dennison Wheelock	Oneida
James Reilly Wheelock	Oneida
Ida Whiteface	Apache
Reuben Whiteman	Apache
Madoc Wind	Apache
Thomas Wistar	Ottawa
Charles Wolf	Nez Perce
Minnie Wolf Face (Little Elk)	Cheyenne
Arnold Woolworth	Arapaho
Silas Yellowboy	Sioux
Susie Young (Kelsey Mitchell)	Winnebago
William Young	Nez Perce

Notes

Introduction

1. In the introduction and in the chapters to follow, the name of each Carlisle student referenced is **in bold** on first mention. An appendix to the book lists all of their names.
2. Genevieve Bell's (1998) dissertation is the fullest source for facts, figures, and statistics about Carlisle. For further information about the school, see also Fear-Segal (2004, 2007); Fear-Segal and Rose (2016); Witmer (2000), and Carlisle Indian Industrial School (2017, 2019a, 2019b, n.d., being items compiled by Barbara Landis at https://carlisleindianschool.org/). Articles in the *Eadle Keatah Toh* or *Morning Star* as well as in other Carlisle newspapers can all be referenced at the Carlisle Indian School Digital Resource Center under "Publications."
3. I know of two significant exceptions to the generalization just made. In 1884 Apaches at the San Carlos reservation in Arizona Territory were ordered to send some of their children to Carlisle. There was a measure of negotiation possible, but parents could not, for the most part, withhold their permission. Then in 1887 Pratt himself went to Fort Marion, Florida, to select young people to attend Carlisle from among the Apaches held there as prisoners of war. Once more, there was some latitude; for example, **Ramona Chihuahua** went north to Pennsylvania, while her brother, **Eugene Chihuahua**, who did not wish to go, was allowed to stay behind. Then Pratt "went down the line choosing forty-nine boys and girls to return with him to Carlisle," as **Jason Betzinez** described this occasion many years later, when, despite the fact that he was "twenty-seven, too old to be a school boy," he was chosen to go as well (149).
4. On plot structures generally see Hayden White and, before him, Northrop Frye.

5. See in particular White's *Metahistory* and Clifford and George Marcus's edited volume, *Writing Culture*.
6. For a fuller account of these structures in Indian autobiography, see my discussion in *Changed Forever*, volume 2, of the life stories of Carl Sweezy and "Jim Whitewolf" as, respectively, comic and ironic narratives. I do not discuss tragedy and romance here because the materials under consideration do not take those structures or imply their meanings. It is at least imaginable that the stories of some of the students who did not write to the school, if we knew them, might on occasion approximate tragedy.
7. See my *"That the People Might Live"* for an account of how Jefferson learned of a possible speech by Logan, and of the appropriation of presumptively noble orations by Chief Sealth and Chief Joseph. Robert Berkhofer's classic study *The White Man's Indian* provides a general account of these matters.
8. I date the modern critical conversation about the boarding schools from 1928 and what has become known as the Meriam Report, which studied the government Indian schools as part of its examination of federal "Indian Administration" generally. Brewton Berry (1968) provided an overview, as did Margaret Szasz in [1974] 1999. Significant subsequent studies are those by Michael Coleman (1993), David Adams (1995), and Jon Reyhner and Jeanne Elder (2004). The following list covers only book-length studies, and by no means all that are available; there are many more studies in the relevant journals. Works focused on particular schools and topics include:

   Bloomfield Academy: Amanda Cobb (2000)
   Carlisle: Bell, Fear-Segal, Fear-Segal and Rose, Landis, and Witmer (see earlier note 2)
   Cherokee Female Seminary: Devon Mihesuah (1993)
   Chilocco Indian School: Lomawaima (1994); Brumley (2010)
   Flandreau school: Brenda Child (1998, 2014)
   Hampton Institute: Jon Brudvig (1996); Donal Lindsey (1993)
   Haskell school: Brenda Child (1998, 2014); Myriam Vuckovic (2008); Zuzanna Buchowska (2016)
   New Mexico Indian schools: John Gram (2015)
   Oklahoma Indian schools: Sally McBeth (1983)
   Phoenix school: Robert Trennert (1988)
   Rainy Mountain school: Clyde Ellis (1996)
   Rapid City Indian School: Scott Riney (1999)

Santa Fe Indian School: Sally Hyer (1990)
Sherman Institute (Riverside, California): Diana Bahr (2014); Trafzer, Gilbert, and Sisquoc (2012)
Sherman's Hopi students: Gilbert (2010)
St. Joseph's Indian School: Sarah Shillinger (2008)
"Boarding-school experience and American Indian literature": Katanski (2006); Krupat (2018, 2020)
"Boarding-school poems": Robert Dale Parker (2011)
"Native American writings in the boarding school press": Jacqueline Emery (2017).

1. "I talk white nicely"

1. The class photo does not provide the graduates' tribal affiliations, and I have given them as they appear on a 1915 list of Carlisle graduates up to that time. The list reports that half of the original graduating class had died by 1915. Articles in the *Eadle Keatah Toh* or *Morning Star* and other Carlisle newspapers can all be referenced at the Carlisle Indian School Digital Resource Center under "Publications."
2. Standing's letter may be found at the Carlisle Indian School Digital Resource Center, carlisleindian.dickinson.edu, "Correspondence Regarding Student Surveys, 1890."
3. For the 103 digitized responses, see http://carlisleindian.dickinson.edu/documents/former-student-survey-responses-1890. They represent a very small percentage of the total number of students who had returned home from Carlisle from its opening in November 1879 to June 1890, when Pratt sent out his questionnaire. I cannot say exactly what percentage that might be because I haven't been able to calculate the total number of returned students. Carlisle had opened in 1879 with just under 150 students, and in his *Annual Report of the Commissioner of Indian Affairs* for 1890, Thomas Morgan's table 1 put Carlisle's capacity at 500 students, while his table 2 recorded its "average attendance" at 789 students (*Annual Report* 1890, ix). Morgan's attendance numbers are larger than Carlisle's actual capacity because they include enrolled students who were not physically present at the school, but on outing assignments, usually on nearby farms. On September 22, 1890, Pratt wrote to **Hortie Stevens**, a returned student (see also Stevens's letter later in this chapter), to say that the year's enrollment was 700, with 230 out on farms and attending public schools (Pratt letters binder 242). A bit later, on November 5, 1890, he said in a letter to **Susie Young**, also a former student (see also her letter later in this chapter), that Carlisle then had 759

students enrolled (Pratt letters binder 368). The reference numbers are to pages in the binder in which Pratt's letters for June 1890 to January 1891 have been collected. It may be found in the Richard Henry Pratt Papers at Yale's Beinecke Rare Book and Manuscript Library, WA MSS S-1174, box 10–17. I give page numbers to this binder when referencing others in this group of letters.

4. Rarely noted is the fact that after the United States acquired Puerto Rico as a territory from Spain at the end of the Spanish-American War in 1898, a number of Puerto Rican students attended Carlisle.
5. Few Paiutes attended Carlisle, and I have found only one from before 1900. This is **Boisie Bassford**, who arrived in 1886 at age twenty-one and died at the school in 1892.
6. Alvin Wilcox's *A Pioneer History of Becker County, Minnesota* (1907) describes William Campbell as having been born in 1865, which would make him twenty-three when he entered Carlisle. His father, Frank Campbell, was a white man who had married a Native woman and moved with his family to White Earth in 1868, the year the reservation was established. I am grateful to Gerald Vizenor for this information (personal communication, September 3, 2018).
7. I provide an endnote number only at the end of letters quoted so as not to interrupt the speaker, as it were. The 1890 responses, as noted, were divided into five parts, and I give the part number in which each can be found. Jay-Eye-See was a harness racehorse that broke the trotting record for the mile on August 1, 1884. With a new gait, the horse would break the pacing record in 1892, and by the time of its death in 1909 it had become sufficiently famous to warrant an obituary in the *New York Times*. Maud S—named after Maud Stone, daughter of its owner, George Stone—was an even more famous trotting racer, which broke Jay-Eye-See's mile record on August 2, 1884, the day after it was set, and then lowered that record seven times in six years. The Lake Mohonk Conference was an annual meeting of wealthy white men who called themselves "The Friends of the Indian." Their program sought to break up the reservations, obtain citizenship for Indians, and promote education. From 1883 to 1916 they met annually at the Mohonk Lodge in New York. Campbell's reference is to the journalist and novelist Edward Bellamy (1850–98), whose novel *Looking Backward: 2000–1887*, published in 1888 but set in the year 2000, was enormously popular. It was generally socialistic, and as Campbell correctly notes, it did not think well of competition.
8. Some of Pratt's letters are addressed to Campbell at the Minneapolis School of Law and offer financial advice and encouragement.

9. His younger brothers, Dennison and **James Reilly Wheelock**, were also Carlisle students and were associated with the world-renowned Carlisle Band. James was a clarinetist, and Charles was a cornetist, as was Dennison, who was also a composer. In 1892 Dennison Wheelock became the Carlisle bandmaster. A great many students named Powlas (sometimes spelled Powless) and Wheelock attended Carlisle.
10. For a full account of this matter, as well as of Menominee allotment, see Beck (2005), chapter four, in particular pp. 46–59.
11. Although there is no copy of an immediate answer from Pratt to Susie Young, he did write to her on November 5, 1890, to offer congratulations on her marriage.
12. For more on the exile specifically see Pearson and Hilden (2008) and also Trafzer (1985).
13. Of many references, see Greene (1970).
14. Other Nez Perce students who went from the Ponca Agency to Carlisle in October 1879 were two teenaged boys from Chief Joseph's band, **Charles Bear** and **William Young**. The following year Pratt himself went to the Ponca Agency and recruited Elder and Paul along with **Samuel John** and **Sophia Rachel**. In 1883 **Luke Phillips, Dolly Gould**, and **Rebecca Little Wolf**, along with Charlie Wolfe, went from Indian Territory to Carlisle.
15. She is best known for an ethnography of the Omaha people done with Francis La Flesche (it was not published until 1911, although the two had begun work in the 1880s). During her time in Idaho Territory Fletcher continued to gather ethnographic materials, along with her partner, the photographer E. Jane Gay. Fletcher's "Ethnologic Gleanings Among the Nez Perces" appeared belatedly, in 1995. See also Caroline Carley's (2001) compilation of Fletcher's "Letters from the Field."
16. Donald Berthrong (1956) writes that although they had signed the treaty establishing the reservations, the Cheyennes and Arapahos "refused to occupy" them (138), and it was not until 1875 that their military resistance ceased. Berthrong's account is detailed and useful, although—it is a product of the 1950s—it refers unself-consciously to "the Messiah *Craze*" and "the Peyote *Cult*" (my emphases).
17. Lee had already had an interesting history. As an army lieutenant, he had been agent at the Spotted Tail (later Rosebud) Agency and was detailed by General George Crook to escort Crazy Horse as a prisoner to Fort Robinson in 1877. There Crazy Horse, most likely while trying to escape—the actual sequence of events remains in dispute—was bayo-

neted by a guard. Dr. Valentine McGillycuddy, post physician, of whom we will hear more, attempted unsuccessfully to save Crazy Horse's life. A brief speech purported to be Crazy Horse's last words before he died was published and attributed to Lieutenant Lee. I believe the speech to have been entirely fabricated, and Lee himself never referenced any speech. For the "farewell speeches" of noble Natives, see my *"That the People Might Live"* (2012).

18. See Earenfight (2007). A drawing by Doanmoe, captioned "Where Capt. Pratt lived on the north side of the Fort," is number 30 of the sketches.
19. *Plymouth Church* is underlined in the handwritten original. The school Given had attended was as the Ashmun Institute, founded in 1854. Following the assassination of President Abraham Lincoln, the school changed its name in 1866 to Lincoln University. It continues to operate today and is considered an historically Black college, although it was always open to all. At Lincoln Given would have had an experience similar to that of the Native students at Hampton Institute, who also studied and worked with Blacks. Henry Ward Beecher (1813–87) was a Congregationalist minister and a prominent abolitionist, the father of Harriet Beecher Stowe. His Plymouth Church was in Brooklyn, New York. The cost of Given's "frame cottage" today (2019) would be about $22,000.
20. Richenda and Nana were superintendent Richard Pratt's daughters.
21. It was in 1868 that George Armstrong Custer attacked the camp of the southern Cheyenne leader, Black Kettle, on the Washita, giving rise to what had been called the Battle of the Washita, and is generally—but not by all historians—called the Washita Massacre today.
22. See Cutler (1971).
23. Buffalo Good gave a lengthy speech in Boston, in 1871, protesting President Grant's assignment of Wichita lands to the Cheyennes and Arapahos. It has been preserved in the *Documents of the Senate of the United States* for 1892, 17–18.
24. Tatum was in his late twenties at the time, so that Mooney's calling him a "schoolboy" does not reference his age but rather the fact that he, like his wife Eva, his sister-in-law Cecilia, and his brother John, had attended school—not Carlisle, but perhaps the Riverside Indian School in Anadarko.
25. There were two Southern Arapaho chiefs named Left Hand. The older was a man born in the 1820s who died in 1864 at the Sand Creek Massacre carried out by Colorado Volunteers under Colonel John Chivington. Later, a follower of the deceased Left Hand "received the name in

a council held sometime after Sand Creek and before 1867" (Coel 1981, 117). This Left Hand also became an important Arapaho chief. He was the father of Grant and Ernest Left Hand, listed as "Living" on both boys' student files (1879 and 1883).

26. The identification of Chief Left Hand as a Cheyenne is an error and one that should have been avoided: the student information cards of both his sons record them as Arapahos and Left Hand as their father.
27. Referring to Wovoka, Virginia Trenholm (1986) wrote that "while the Ghost Dance leader was at the height of his career, Chief Left Hand sought his advice" (286), so that Grant Left Hand was following his father in his commitment to the movement. Belief in the Ghost Dance was largely over among the Arapahos by late fall 1893 (291).
28. He missed Zitkala-Ša at White's by a year, her attendance at the school being 1884–87.
29. The name I have put in quotation marks is an error on the part of the letter's transcriber. The correct name is in boldface later.
30. The "dog soldiers" were a military society among the Cheyennes and Kiowas, sufficiently numerous and powerful to constitute almost a separate division within the tribes. They were adamantly opposed to any accommodation with the whites, refusing to sign treaties, and pressuring families to keep their children out of the schools.
31. Mike Burns, whose life and work I consider in the following chapter, references the Modoc War of 1872–73 and I describe it briefly there.
32. In his *Report to the Commissioner of Indian Affairs* in August 1890, Major T. J. Moore—whom Hood mentions—wrote: "Too much cannot be said in praise of the Modoc day school. It has always a good attendance, and I am told that every child over eight years can read and write" (85). Charles Hood was about seventeen when he went east to Carlisle.
33. Upon surrendering, 153 Modoc people were put on a train east in the fall of 1873. In his 1890 *Report*, Agent Moore recorded only 84 Modocs at the agency at the time (83). Most of the Modocs in Oklahoma remained there and today constitute the federally recognized Modoc Tribe of Oklahoma. Others, like Hood, went to Oregon and joined the federally recognized Klamath Tribes.
34. I have no information about Summers, although Crawford is worth a few words. He had commanded a cavalry company for the Union Army in the Battle of Bull Run and then resigned his commission to enlist in the Confederate Army. He rose to the rank of general and he is the only Confederate general to have fought on both sides in the Civil War. After

serving as Indian inspector he became assistant commissioner of Indian Affairs from 1893 to 1895.

35. The Carlisle *Indian Helper* for January 10, 1890, reported: "On the 6th of December [1889] there were six men hung [*sic*] for committing crimes" (2) at San Carlos. This may or may not have prompted Bread's comment to Pratt later in June.
36. Not long afterward, on September 3, Pratt wrote to Delchey to say he was glad to hear Delchey was doing well, but that it was best for him to stay at San Carlos (Pratt letters 208). I infer from this that Delchey had written to Pratt and asked to return to the school. But Bullis may have denied Delchey permission to leave, thus prompting Pratt's response.
37. More than twenty years later, in 1913 when he was convicted of grand larceny for rustling, Obed Rabbitt's prison record at the State Prison at Florence, Arizona—(both his Carlisle student file and the prison record spell his name with two "t's")—gave "No" as the answer to the questions "Can read?" and "Can write?" The question "Where educated?" is left blank (in Herman 2012, 239). His Carlisle student file, however, states that Rabbitt was enrolled at the school for no fewer than ten years, 1884–94.
38. Mike Burns, whom Carlisle listed as Apache, also wrote from San Carlos in answer to the 1890 questionnaire, but as I explain in the next chapter, he had gone to the school from Fort Laramie, Wyoming Territory, not from the San Carlos Agency.
39. These numbers are also approximate because not all records were preserved and digitized, and because there are occasional errors, duplications, or other uncertainties in them.
40. He would have been named for the anthropologist Frank Hamilton Cushing, who worked at Zuni from 1879 to 1884, and would almost surely have been involved with the boy's going east to school. The young man was buried in the Carlisle cemetery. As had been the case with many Apaches at Carlisle, a number of Pueblo students also were sent home ill or died at the school.
41. Dorchester (1827–1907) was an ordained Methodist Episcopal minister, much of whose later career was dedicated to the temperance movement. His 1892 *Report* contains shrewd insights based on careful observation, along with blind religious bigotry. He found the religious ceremonies of the Pueblos dark and pagan, but like Elaine Goodale—who was superintendent for Indian education for the Dakotas—he favored reservation schools, very much in opposition to Richard Pratt.
42. Kendall was named after the Reverend Henry Kendall, secretary of the Presbyterian Board of Home Missions, who had been involved in estab-

lishing reservation boarding schools at Isleta, Jemez, Laguna, San Juan, Santa Clara, and Zuni Pueblos.

43. "Hattie Porcupine" is also listed as **Hattie Long Wolf**, from Pine Ridge. She had entered Carlisle at the age of fourteen in 1882 and would graduate with the class of 1892. Soon to follow is a lengthy letter from her older brother Dana, where we learn more about the Long Wolfs.
44. As Kendall summarizes it, Dr. Spinning had urged the Carlisle students not to follow bad friends, and to adhere to the good, and always to value careful work and resist any temptation to work hastily. Kendall initially reports of Dr. Spinning's talk that "he said when he was a boy he used to be an Indian," and went on buffalo hunts (8). This is Dr. George L. Spinning, a Presbyterian minister, who was pastor of a church on Madison Avenue in New York and went west to work on behalf of Pimas, Papagos, and homeless Indians in California. I have found no information about Reverend Spinning other than these few facts.
45. Ostensibly based on a true story, the novel represents the determination of Stiya, the Carlisle girl who had gone home, to resist the insistence of the governors of her pueblo that she engage in the communal ceremonial dances that she, like John Dixon, now believes to be "superstitious." The author of the novel was "Embe," a transcription of "M. B.," Mariana Burgess, a teacher in charge of printing, and also editor of the *Indian Helper* and other Carlisle publications. The novel's title borrows the name of **Stiya Kowacura** or Koykuri, a Laguna Pueblo student at Carlisle who entered in 1886 and was discharged because of ill health in 1892. (Her death was mourned in the *Indian Helper* for February 23, 1900.) Jacqueline Fear-Segal (2004) and Amelia Katanski (2006) offer useful discussions of *Stiya*.
46. Marmon's first wife was Maria Analla's sister, whose name I have not discovered. After his wife's death he married Maria. Maria Analla Marmon was the great-grandmother of Leslie Marmon Silko, who spells her name Anaya, and in several places refers to her as Grandmother A'mooh.
47. This young woman appears in the school records as **Christine Showtemutsey**. She had been at Carlisle in 1884–89 with Maria Analla and would have been about nineteen when she died.
48. The Albuquerque Indian School, or Pueblo Industrial Boarding School, opened in 1881 as a Presbyterian "contract" school—run by the Presbyterian Home Mission Society and partially subsidized by the government—until 1886, when it was completely taken over by the federal government (Banker 1982, 35–36). Reverend Robert Coltman was superintendent in 1888–91, and as Paisano's letter makes clear, the school continued to provide a full range of religious activities.

49. Policing one's own people was not an alien notion to the Lakota, who had long had tribal members act as *akicitas*, or communally appointed enforcers. See in particular Mark Ellis (1999), who gives a good account of Sword's police service, and Julian Rice (1985) for *akicitas* in Black Elk's great vision. Also generally useful is Hagan (1980).
50. See, for example, Walker's *Lakota Belief and Ritual*. An interesting interview with Captain Sword is in Ricker (2005, 1:326–30), and a recent study of Sword's oral narrative style is Delphine Red Shirt's *George Sword's Warrior Narratives*, from which I have quoted.
51. James Mooney would call his monumental study *The Ghost-Dance Religion and the* ***Sioux Outbreak*** *of 1890* (my emphasis)—although he did quote Valentine McGillycuddy's observation that "up to date there has been *neither a Sioux outbreak nor war*. No citizen in Nebraska or Dakota has been killed, molested, or can show the scratch of a pin, and no property has been destroyed off the reservation" (quoted in Mooney 1973, 78, my emphasis).
52. The identity of the Man-on-the-Bandstand was addressed in a verse published in the *Indian Helper* for November 29, 1889: "Who can this Man-on-the-Bandstand be?" / "You ask if it's Captain or even Miss B / With special good spectacles on? / . . . / I'll tell you the secret you want to find out / About this strange man on the stand: / Just any one truly, who happens to see / A thing that is worthy of note, / And gossips a little about helpful things, / Gets bits of the "news" that's afloat." This amiably suggests or less amiably warns that surveillance was total and anonymous. For more see Fear-Segal (2004 and 2007).
53. Elaine Goodale, who would become superintendent of Indian education for the Dakotas at Pine Ridge just a year later, although she greatly admired Pratt, nonetheless favored reservation schools for Native children. It was her sense that although the students' regular contact with their families might slow their progress somewhat, that was more than compensated for by minimizing their loneliness and, in effect, culture shock. (It is worth noting, though, that students ran away from on-reservation boarding schools just as they did from Carlisle.)
54. The school does, however, have a record for a **George Means**, a Crow Indian, who had arrived at Carlisle in 1886 and graduated with the class of 1890. He remained at the school until September 1890, and so did not receive Pratt's questionnaire. Means wrote to Pratt from Pine Ridge in January 1891, to provide an account of what he knew of the fate of Carlisle students there after the Wounded Knee massacre at the end of December 1890, as I explain in chapter 3.

55. In his *Annual Report of the Commissioner of Indian Affairs* for 1890, Gallagher had written of the "Indian Police" that "the best men that can be induced to enter the force are always sought after, but the compensation is not adequate for the work required and many of the best Indians will not serve" (45). Culbertson would seem to have been an exception. I suspect he does not complain of his wage because he is a young man just back from school, although as he further notes, earning a living on the reservation is not easy.
56. The Pine Ridge Agency had been established by congressional action on March 2, 1889, reducing the Great Sioux Reservation established by treaty in 1868. Further complicating matters was the fact that the Dawes General Allotment Act had been passed in 1887—while Culbertson and many of the respondents were at Carlisle—although actual allotment of the Pine Ridge reservation did not begin until 1904.
57. The Genoa Indian Industrial School was the fourth federal off-reservation boarding school and one of the largest. It opened in 1884 and operated until 1934.
58. Neither did **Josiah Wolf**, an Ottawa, who writes from the Quapaw Agency in Indian Territory, describing his particular sort of performance: "I don't wear no Indian clothes, only when I was working for Dr. J.E. Fraser Specialist in Indian Remedies. I put on the leggin, Buckskin shirt feathers & painted my face. I worked for him two months then I wanted to quit. I used to prepare the medicine, boiled it, bottled it, labeled it, and corked it, and sold it on the streets in ~~Which~~ Wichita Kansas but I dress citizen clothes all the time" (Part 1). Wolf had run away from the school in 1883, but the questionnaire clearly found him, and he chose to reply.
59. In his autobiography Pratt quoted from an article in one of the Carlisle newspapers about some of the returned Lakotas at home: "Baldwin cut hay four weeks and Guy worked two months" (281). That is almost surely Guy Bear Don't Scare, but of course it does not tell us much. The *Indian Helper* for February 27, 1891, refers to him as Guy American Horse, as I note further in chapter 3, and says of him only that he is "dead."
60. Either Pratt was mistaken about Guy Belt's role or Belt was demoted, for the *Annual Report of the Commissioner of Indian Affairs* for 1895 lists him as a "private" in the Indian police at Pine Ridge in 1894 (558).
61. This seems to have been a matter of conscious determination on Long Wolf's part, as I suspect Burgess did not know. There are anecdotal reports of occasions when, given "citizen's" dress, he folded it neatly and returned it.

62. Although Carlisle's policy was English-only, there are many instances on record of Pratt giving students permission to talk to visiting relatives in their own language, one of which Luther Standing Bear described when his father visited him at the school. See *My People, the Sioux*, 149–50.
63. See buffalobill.org/pdfs/buffalo_bill_visits.pdf. A much younger son, **Amos Long Wolf**, born about 1880, was with his parents when they first traveled abroad with the Wild West. He too would enter Carlisle, enrolling in 1891, after Dana wrote to Pratt.
64. In 1997 his direct descendants were able to bring his body home to be buried in South Dakota. The re-interment was covered by the *Washington Post*, September 26, 1997 (washingtonpost.com/archive/politics/1997/09/26/chief-long-wolfs-last-journey) and an account is given in Gallop (2001, 260–61).
65. In a summary of how the returned students are doing, the *Helper* of February 27, 1891, mentions Dana Long Wolf and describes him as "In penitentiary, *on doubtful charge*" (my emphasis), further complicating the picture.

2. "I have always liked to write"

1. All of Burns's publications in the Carlisle newspapers can be found at the Carlisle Indian School Digital Resource Center under "Publications." Standing Bear's column can be accessed there as well, and it has also been reprinted by Jacqueline Emery (2017, 43). Emery prints none of Burns's writings.
2. **Ruben Sioux** is almost surely Reuben Kills the Enemy, also known as Reuben Quick Bear, from the Rosebud Agency, who entered with Carlisle's first Lakota students on October 6, 1879. **Joe Taylor**, also from Rosebud, was likewise part of that first group.
3. The only **Lewis Brown** I have found at Carlisle entered much later, in 1911. **Edward Myers** entered in October 1879 and left because of ill health in 1883. I suspect that "Raymond, Sioux" is **Raymond Stewart**, also called Raymond White Bear, another Rosebud Lakota who entered with the first Carlisle students.
4. In July 1881 Charles J. Guiteau shot President James Garfield, who died in September. Guiteau's family had earlier tried, unsuccessfully, to have him judged insane and institutionalized, and at trial Guiteau pleaded innocence on the grounds of insanity. He was nonetheless convicted and hanged at the end of June 1882. Guiteau's sentence was announced just after the January 1882 issue of the *School News* came out.

5. Curiously, on Saturday, December 21, 1872—exactly one day before Hoomothya was captured by American troops—Carlos Montezuma "was on stage for the first time" playing "the young Apache captive, Azteca" in a performance of the Buffalo Bill Wild West in Chicago (Marino 1998, 45). Montezuma had been captured by Pima Indians the year before, and, as we shall see, had been taken to Chicago by his benefactor, Carlo Gentile.
6. For captivity narratives, see Axtell (1975) and Strong (1999). I am calling Burns's story—and I later call Carlos Montezuma's story—an "inverted captivity narrative" because most captivity narratives studied have been the stories of whites captured by Indians, not the other way around, like that of Burns and, ultimately, of Montezuma, as I will explain further.
7. For the Modocs and the Modoc War see McNally (2017).
8. Burns's autobiographical writings have had a complicated history. Working from his manuscripts at the Sharlot Hall Museum in Prescott, Arizona, Susan Rockwell published an edition of his autobiography, with critical commentary, as her 2001 doctoral dissertation. The following year she published a facsimile edition of the autobiographical manuscripts themselves. What will probably remain the definitive scholarly edition of the autobiography appeared in 2010, edited mostly by Dr. John Langellier, and published by the Sharlot Hall Museum. A somewhat rewritten and abbreviated version was published by Gregory McNamee in a 2012 paperback. Timothy Braatz's introduction to his *Surviving Conquest* (2003) begins with a section called "Hoomothya and Wassaja," referring to Mike Burns and Carlos Montezuma, and references the Sharlot Hall manuscripts. Victoria Smith's *Captive Arizona* (2009) links the two men as well, as it also references Burns's manuscripts. Louise Aflen's 2011 masters dissertation on the Fort McDowell Yavapai Casino summarizes the autobiography, and Daniel Herman mentions it in his 2012 book. Burns's letters have not been collected and published, although Rockwell in her 2001 dissertation transcribes and prints seventeen of them. Franklin Barnett's brief biography, *Viola Jimulla: The Indian Chieftess* (1968) does not mention Burns, who was about fourteen years younger than Chieftess Jimulla, and from the same tribal background.
9. I quote from the 2010 edition of Burns's autobiography called *All of My People Were Killed: The Memoir of Mike Burns (Hoomothya), a Captive Indian*. Ellipses and bracketed words are those of the principal editor, Dr. John Langellier, and I quote the text exactly as published. Langellier noted: "Despite Burns's contention that more than two hundred men, women, and children were slaughtered at Salt River Cave, the best

current estimate of Yavapai casualties, drawn from forensic evidence, is seventy-six dead" (325 n. 15). Daniel Herman writes that "in all some ninety Kwevkepayas lost their lives" (2012, 78), although he gives no source for that number. Langellier, however, also points to a letter from Burns to Montezuma dated October 27, 1912, in which Burns wrote, "About that 'Salt River Cave Massacre.' I could not truthfully say: 'just exact number Indians were killed, but I only got the number from the soldiers. Because I could not count anything at that time: nor did I went to see to every one was killed that I think unreasonable for any one to state the exact numbers were seen dead in that Cave: because; good many were on top the others: and were mashed so it could not tell whether awhole or pieces'" (Sharlot Hall Museum, Series 1, folder 12).

10. Apaches spoke a southern Athapascan language, completely different from the Yavapais' Yuman language. In the 1870s and '80s, however, "one thousand Yavapais shared the [San Carlos] reservation with four to five thousand Western and Chiricahua Apaches" (Braatz 2003, 14), and there were many inter-tribal marriages. Braatz used different spellings for Burns's Yavapai band in 2003 and 2010, as I have quoted him.

11. A matter of concern since Burns's time has been whether or the degree to which the boy, Hoomothya, helped the soldiers find the well-hidden cave. Captain John Bourke, who was there and who noted Burns's presence at the time, wrote that "'Nantaje,' one of our Apache scouts, who had been brought up in the cave in the canon of the Salt River, . . . had expressed a desire to lead us there, provided we made up our minds to make the journey before day-dawn" (188). Timothy Braatz stated that "Apache scouts and Kwevkepaya captives provided directions" (2003, 138). One of those captives was the boy Hoomothya, although my sense is that Braatz did not mean to say that he contributed to these directions. Later, in his 2010 foreword to the autobiography, Braatz wrote that "soldiers . . . took him [Burns] along as they searched for a remote Kwevkepaya cave encampment in Salt River Canyon" (vi). John Langellier, the principal editor of the autobiography, concluded that upon Burns's return home, some held him responsible for having led army troops to the Salt River Cave, a plausible scenario given that the cavalry located the band in this remote and hidden cave only four days after Burns's capture. He conjectures that this may be the reason "that the officers subsequently kept Burns under their care rather than finding a home for him among his people" (Langellier 2010, Afterword 274–75). There are, however, other reasons why they may have kept him with them. For more about American troops "adopting" Indian children, see

Sherry Smith (1990), in particular pp. 72–74 ff, and also Victoria Smith (2009). More recently, Daniel Herman's (2012) account of the remote cave in which the Yavapais were discovered states simply that "Apache scouts found them" (78). Burns himself told Carlos Montezuma in 1911 that it was an Apache woman captured by Apache scouts who led the troops to the cave, stating, "Even I was there once; I could never found the real camp because they had moved down over close to the River" (quoted in Langellier 2010, Afterword 438).

12. Captain John G. Bourke (2014), aide to General Crook, had written in detail about the massacre—he did not call it that—in 1891, his account noting the presence of "a small but very bright and active boy, whom the men had promptly adopted, and upon whom had been bestowed the name 'Mike'" (188). In that Bourke had died in 1896, Burns is probably correct in stating that at the time he wrote, he was "the only one *living* to tell what happened to [his] people" (my emphasis). Certainly Burns was the first to tell of what happened from a perspective other than that of the soldiers.
13. It was, however, First Lieutenant Earl Thomas of the 5th Cavalry who suggested making him "an Irish Indian by naming him Mike Burns" (Burns 2010, n. 5, 319). Lieutenant Thomas had also seen action at the cave. Bourke had made it clear that Captain Burns was especially resourceful in killing Hoomothya's People at Salt River Cave. He wrote that Burns "had two of his men harnessed with the suspenders of their comrades, and made them lean well over the precipice" to get clearer shots at their targets, and then "ordered his men to get together and roll several of the huge boulders, which covered the surface of the mountain, and drop them over on the unsuspecting foe" (197), inflicting further casualties. It is impossible to say the degree to which the captive child knew of the actions of the officer with whom he would live.
14. Fort Brown was established in 1846 as the first military post in Texas, a year after Texas became a state. That Burns had been there would explain how it is that he had been "as far south as to Texas"; he would later visit another Texas fort. Fort D. A. Russell was in Wyoming Territory, established in 1867 to protect workers on the Union Pacific Railroad. Fort Laramie was also in Wyoming Territory, about 110 miles north of Fort D. A. Russell, just south of the Montana border, so that in his time there, Burns would indeed have got as "far north as to Montana."
15. Contrary to widely held belief, Abner Doubleday did not "invent" the game of baseball in 1839, in Cooperstown, New York, where the Baseball Hall of Fame is located today. Doubleday, who would become a Civil War general, was a cadet at West Point in 1839, had not been to Coo-

perstown, and never himself spoke of inventing baseball. Burns's editor points out that "the game's roots date to colonial times, although its popularity grew considerably during the mid-nineteenth century." He observes that soldiers played the game as "early as 1866" (n. 10, 422), so that Burns could well have learned it from them. Jeffrey Powers-Beck (2004) writes that Daklugie, Geronimo's nephew, and other Apache prisoners at Fort Marion in Florida brought the game to Carlisle (6) when they arrived at the school in December 1886, very likely having learned it from the soldiers guarding them. He also says that **Conrad Roubideaux**, a Lakota from Rosebud Agency, formed an intramural team at the school in May 1886, before Pratt had uniforms made for the official Carlisle nine in June of that year (38).

16. This is **Ellwood Dorian**, a few years older than Burns, who had also been enrolled at Carlisle in 1880–84.
17. Timothy Braatz quotes from Burns's manuscript the statement that "I spent there at this school"—Haskell—"about a week" (2010, ix), something that did not get into the published autobiography. Victoria Smith found records showing that Burns was, in fact, an enrolled Haskell student (2009, n.3, 203).
18. There is no digitized Carlisle file for Tom Roberts, so he and Burns may have been schoolmates elsewhere.
19. Nor is there a Carlisle record for James Roberts. It is on this same page that Burns writes, "On that afternoon an old captain I used to know [came there]. His name was Captain J. G. Bourke. . . . He was still an aide to General Crook. He also was as much surprised to see me as the Indians were" (247). Bourke had noted of Burns, "we have met at the San Carlos Agency, and talked over old times" (188). One may wonder whether that talk included mention of what had happened at Salt River Cave some thirteen years earlier.
20. February 27, 1875, is known to the Yavapai People as "Exodus Day" and it commemorates the time when, after the closure of the Rio Verde Reservation, the government force-marched—this has been called "The March of Tears"—Yavapai and Tonto Apache Peoples two hundred miles southeast to the much-inferior San Carlos Agency. Exodus Day is observed each year, the most recent commemoration I know of organized by the Yavapai-Apache Nation on March 23, 2019.
21. **George Nyrnah** or Nyruah is listed in the Carlisle files as a Yuma who entered the school at the age of fifteen in 1884 and left in 1889. The *Indian Helper* for August 2, 1889, had reported, "George Nyrnah at San

Carlos Agency says his people did not recognize him" (2). Mike Burns did, finally, recognize him—and, I'm sure, in time others did as well.

22. The Afterword I am citing is to *All of My People Were Killed*, and it is unattributed, as are the very copious notes to the book. It is, however, the work of Dr. John Langellier, former director of the Sharlot Hall Museum, who also compiled the notes with the museum's anthropologist, Dr. Sandra Lynch (Langellier, personal communication, May 16, 2019).
23. Langellier reports that Burns's wife's name had other spellings, like Chahadya or Che Haled, and that in English she was also called Mary. He found that the San Carlos census for 1888 listed her "as fifteen and Burns as twenty-two," and it also recorded that they had a son named Ga-me-ja or Jim Burns. "The 1893 San Carlos census," however, "states her age as twenty-two" (Burns 2010, 318, n. 13), and the couple as then having two children. They would have several more.
24. Indian raiding for captives to sell to Americans, Mexicans, or on occasion other Indians was one of several activities that led to what Victoria Smith (2009) studies as "captivity in Arizona." Although she does not discuss either Burns or Montezuma—she explains why she does not—her book outlines the little-known inverted captivity story of Bessie Brooks, also a Yavapai girl, who was taken by whites when she was three. For Gentile, see Marino (1998).
25. The letter is to be found in the Carlos Montezuma Papers at the Newberry Library, Chicago, box 1, folder 26. Burns is referring to Anne Eli, Mariana Burgess's older partner, who ran the outing program and also taught at Carlisle. Transcription is mine, and while the handwriting is for the most part easily read, I am less sure when Burns gives Yavapai names.
26. Montezuma Papers, box 1, folder 26. In view of the reason Burns states his people would go to that "large mountain north of Florence," Arizona, I will guess it to be Cholla Mountain, about seven and a half miles more nearly to the west of Florence.
27. Date Creek or Fort Date Creek was an important settlement for Yavapai people about sixty miles south of Prescott, the capital of Arizona Territory in 1864–67. A great deal of information about Howard, Date Creek, and other names and places in Burns's account is given in the copious notes to his autobiography.
28. Pattern numbers are numbers that appear frequently in folk tales, such as three and seven in traditional Western stories. Four is the most common pattern number in Native American cultures, as it might be here with Burns from the Southwest. Five is also common in the Northwest; Burns

will later use four and five; six, said to reference the four directions plus above and below, is also found.

29. Donald Worcester (1979) notes in passing that the Indians who made this trip to Washington were housed at Howard University (137), of which, of course, General Howard was president. Had any of these Native people remained to study at the school, Howard would have preceded Hampton University by six years in educating freedmen and Native people together. (Hampton's Indian program was begun in 1878 by Captain Richard Pratt at the request of another Civil War general, General Samuel Chapman Armstrong, in charge at Hampton.)
30. Neither Pakota, later known as Jose Coffee, nor Takodawa, who acquired the name Washington Charley (Braatz 2003, 127), was a tribal leader. The Yavapai headmen, apparently distrustful of the whites' intentions, refused to make the trip, and the two who did go were simply volunteers who had no authority to negotiate tribal business.
31. Braatz gives the date of this letter as January 7, 1914 (2010, vii); Langellier gives it as January 7, 1913 (2010, Afterword 277). One of them is mistaken, but I have not been able to see the letter to determine the correct date.
32. It is the sense of the autobiography's editors that Burns actively worked on it from about 1913 to 1929.
33. Friedman's communication is in Mike Burns's student file, to be found at the Carlisle Indian Industrial School Digital Resource Center under "Student Records."
34. I quote at length from the responses of former students to this and other Carlisle questionnaires in the next chapter, but because the questions overlap considerably from year to year, I will not later cite them for each year. Burns's responses appeared in print as Appendix G to *All of My People Were Killed*. My own transcription differs only slightly from that of Burns's editors.
35. The handwritten original appears to me to have colons where one might expect periods, and I have transcribed it that way. The letter is available in Burns's Carlisle file.
36. The letter assumed to be from Lipps is in Mike Burns's student file at the Carlisle Indian Industrial School Digital Resource Center under "Student Records."
37. I find Crandall's implication that there is a single "Yavapai perspective" for which he speaks—"we Yavapai"—unfortunate. While the perspective he offers may be that of the tribal council, or even of a majority of the enrolled members of his Yavapai-Apache Nation, it is simply not

credible that all Yavapais share a single "Yavapai perspective." Crandall is correct, however, in pointing to the high regard in which Montezuma is held by Yavapai people. This is demonstrated, among other things, by the elaborateness of his gravesite, and by the fact that the Yavapais' traditional point of emergence into the present world has been named Montezuma's Well. No such attention has been paid Michael Burns.

38. For a fuller account of Du Bois and Eastman, see my *Changed Forever*, volume 2.

3. "I am interested in my life"

1. As noted in chapter 4, toward the end of his tenure as superintendent Friedman was occasionally referred to derisively by some of the students as "Mose" with overtly anti-semitic intent. They would have known that Friedman, although born of Jewish immigrant parents, had converted to Christianity at the time of his marriage and was active in church activities at Carlisle.
2. Once again, periods in my transcription are not where one would expect them—and, of course, they may be blemishes, or defective scanning. But I have placed them where the scan of Tyndall's letter seems to show them.
3. I comment later on Fletcher's work allotting the Nez Perce reservation, work that brought her into contact with another former Carlisle student.
4. The Supreme Court's verdict in *Elk v. Wilkins* (112 U.S. 94) in 1884 is relevant to these considerations, and although Tyndall does not refer to it, it may have played a part in his thinking. John Elk, a Winnebago man, attempted to register to vote in Omaha, Nebraska, in 1880. Charles Wilkins, the registrar, denied Elk's registration on the grounds that he was a member of the Winnebago tribe and thus not a citizen of the United States. Elk claimed he had renounced membership in his tribe, and that the first sentence of the Fourteenth Amendment adopted in 1868, the "citizenship clause," granted him United States citizenship. That sentence reads: "All persons born or naturalized in the United States, and subject to the jurisdiction thereof, are citizens of the United States and of the states wherein they reside." This reversed Justice Roger Taney's ruling in the Dred Scott case (1857) that the U.S. Constitution did not grant citizenship to blacks, whether enslaved or free, and Elk claimed that since he had been born in the United States, he too was a citizen and entitled to vote. But in a ruling supportive of tribal sovereignty, but not of John Elk's right to vote, the Court ruled that he had been born a citizen of the Winnebago Nation, and since he had not been naturalized, he was not an American citizen and thus was not eligible to

vote. Nonetheless, because the right to vote is governed by the states, in some states Native Americans were not guaranteed the vote until 1957.

5. A substantial description of her achievements was given by Moses Friedman in his *Annual Report, U.S. Indian School, Carlisle, Pa.* for the year ending June 1911, 22–23.
6. On James Stuart at Chemawa, see chemawa.bie.edu/history.html. Edward McConville, like Pratt, Samuel Armstrong, and others, was a Civil War veteran who went on to become superintendent of a government Indian school. After the war, he had served with the troops pursuing Chief Joseph and his Nez Perce followers in 1877, and upon leaving the army, he had helped found the Chemawa School in Oregon before being transferred to Lapwai. His treatment of Harriet Stuart in 1890 seems somewhat out of character, but I am not aware of the circumstances. Alice Fletcher had called McConville "an excellent man . . . known, loved & trusted by the people" (quoted in Toncovitch 2012, 85), and sought unsuccessfully to have him replace the imperious and arbitrary C. E. Monteith as agent at Lapwai. McConville would be promoted to the rank of general and lead Idaho troops in the Spanish-American War, dying in battle in 1899.
7. McNally (2017) writes: "The Klamath Reservation to which some of the exiled Modocs returned . . . no longer exists. The reservation's 880,000 acres . . . were removed from Indian ownership by the 1954 Klamath Termination Act despite the clear opposition of the reservation's Native residents. . . . A decades-long struggle to restore federal recognition succeeded in the 1986 Klamath Indian Tribe Restoration Act. This law returned no reservation lands to the Klamath Tribes" (354).
8. Lone Bear, also known as Ochinee or One-Eye, had been committed to peaceful relations with the whites, and he had been given a written certificate attesting to this by none other than Colonel John Chivington. Nonetheless, Lone Bear was killed in 1864 by Chivington and his men at Sand Creek.
9. He was also an imposing figure. He appears standing, in full regalia, in a photograph by Frank Albert Rinehart taken at the Omaha Indian Congress in Nebraska in 1898. E. A. Burbank did a vivid painting of him in 1899, and Edward Curtis photographed him as a much older man, mounted on horseback, in 1927.
10. There is a brief note from him in the *School News* for September 1882 about his outing assignment, which he signs "Davis," and the *News* for the following month reports, "We have a new boy in the printing office. His name is Davis. He is a very good boy." A year later, however, when

Eadle Keatah Toh or the *Morning Star* lists him among its Indian printers, his name is given as Richard Davis (https://home.epix.net/~landis/richarddavis.html, 1and 3). On being dressed "like a white boy" see https://home.epix.net/~landis/bullbear.html.

11. See https://home.epix.net/~landis/richarddavis.html. The *Helper* lists among the "bridesmaids and groomsmen" (2) Joel Tyndall, whom we have already met, and John D. Miles. Miles, of course, was the agent at Darlington who had sent Old Bull Bear's words to Carlisle many years earlier, and who had known Davis since he was a boy.
12. This is the Theodore Roosevelt Dam on the Salt River, northeast of Phoenix. It was constructed during the years 1905–11, with a construction crew of Apaches, Mexicans, African Americans, and European immigrants. It had been dedicated by Roosevelt five months before Wind filled out the Carlisle questionnaire.
13. Mother Katharine Drexel, an heiress to a banking fortune and a Catholic convert, founded the order of the Sisters of the Blessed Sacrament in 1891 for the purpose of addressing social inequities and spreading the Gospel to "Indians and Colored People." The Sisters of the Blessed Sacrament established Saint Katherine's Indian School in 1897. A 1908 issue of the Carlisle *Arrow* notes that she had contributed a gold medal as first prize for a competition among Carlisle's Catholic students, and years later it reported a visit she paid to the school in 1911. Mother Katharine Drexel was canonized in 2000.
14. More about him and about this period in the Southwest may be found at the Menaul Historical Library, opened in 1974 on Menaul Boulevard Northeast in Albuquerque, New Mexico.
15. Bibo, New Mexico, is about thirteen miles north of Laguna. It is named for Solomon Bibo, who, however, was mostly associated with Acoma Pueblo. Bibo (1853–1934), a Jew born in what was then the Kingdom of Prussia, immigrated to the United States and, with his brothers, was a trader at Acoma in the 1870s. In 1885 he married Juana Valle, daughter of the governor of Acoma Pueblo, Martin Valle. He thus became a member of her tribe—and she converted to Judaism. When Martin Valle died that year, Bibo was elected governor, the first and only non-Indian governor of the Pueblo. He was elected three more times and was a strong supporter of the American schools and a strong opponent of traditional Acoma religious practices.
16. I have once more put periods where I see dots in the text of Mattie Reid's letter. And once more it is possible that she did not intentionally insert those marks as punctuation.

17. Worth consulting on this matter is the *U.S. General Accounting Office Report to Congressional Requesters, Treaty of Guadalupe Hidalgo: Definition and List of Community Land Grants in New Mexico*. Its Appendix 1 offers "Data on 295 Spanish and Mexican Land Grants in New Mexico."
18. I do not know which paper ran the article or at which Poli's Theatre Standing Bear was performing. Sylvester Z. Poli was an Italian immigrant who had opened his first establishment in New Haven, Connecticut, in 1892 and by 1916 controlled some thirty theaters throughout the Northeast.
19. A note in Frank Twiss's file—he had been among the first Lakota students at Carlisle—says that he was a "Grandson of Chief No Water."
20. The editor noted: "The photographs sent by Moses were views of Wounded Knee Battlefield, taken shortly after the fight, the bodies of those killed still on the field" (1). Jim Gerencser of the Carlisle Digital Resource Center said they are not among the Carlisle materials catalogued (personal communication, February 15, 2019), and Richard Tritt of the Cumberland County Historical Society has not found any trace of them there (personal communication, March 9, 2019). It would, of course, be very interesting to see them if they have somehow survived.
21. Andrews provides a useful brief discussion of Three Stars's teaching methods (2002, 421–23). Three Stars himself described them in an essay called "Teaching Beginners to Talk English," in the *Oglala Light*, April 1907. A biography of Clarence Three Stars would be good to have. On his later marriage to Jennie Dubray see home.epix.net/~landis/couples.html.
22. For an excellent brief account of this event, see Deloria (2004, 15–21).
23. Carlisle has records for a **Silas Yellowboy** who entered the school in 1905. But his parents are Alfred and Mabel Yellowboy, so he was not Lizzie Yellowboy's son. There were and presently are many people named Yellowboy at Pine Ridge.
24. Handwritten on the upper right of Hattie Pretty Weasel's file is the word "Dead"; in addition, her student information card, next to "Deceased," has the notation "about 1908."
25. The boarding school was rebuilt in 1898 (*Indian Leader*, May 25, 1917, 8). There were twenty-nine day schools at the Pine Ridge Agency around that time, many just one-room schoolhouses (Andrews 2002, 408). Adelia Tyon attended #25, and Clarence Three Stars would teach at #27 (Andrews 2002, 422).
26. His comments at the time also include a request for a Catholic priest, although Little Wound became an Episcopalian.

27. The Little Wound School, named in Little Wound's honor, opened in Kyle, South Dakota, in 1934. It was destroyed by fire in 1938, but soon rebuilt, eventually to operate as a K–12 institution.
28. His speech continues with an account of "what I know and have heard about the Messiah and the Ghost Dance" (Andersson 2019, 152). Andersson prints—sometimes in new translations—all of Little Wound's comments on the Ghost Dance (2019, 149–55).
29. See www.Ameri-Tribes.com and amertribes.proboards.com/thread/1955/george-little-wound.
30. The file also contains what appears to be a letter "To Carlisle Arrows" from someone who identifies himself as Judson Shook, "Additional Farmer" at Kyle, South Dakota. The letter lists William C. Girton's activities since leaving Carlisle, and it offers the information that he had two children named May and Daniel, and "he has allotted 1000 acres of land." Girton almost surely asked Shook to prepare and send this, and he may have done so—this is entirely speculation on my part—as part of his case for "competency." If the *Arrow* ever published Shook's communication, I have not been able to find it.

4. "One of the most trusted"

1. The Freemasons are a fraternal order dedicated to good works and high moral purpose. A thirty-second degree Mason of the Scottish Rite—there is also a York Rite—has attained essentially the highest rank.
2. See *Annual Report, U.S. Indian School, Carlisle, Pa.* for the year ending June 30, 1911, which gives Friedman's detailed accounting of former Carlisle students who have succeeded in a variety of endeavors, mentioning those whom Nori had named.
3. His wife was like-minded. In her Carlisle file is an extraordinary letter dated March 3, 1916, to the Carlisle paper, the *Red Man*. In it Louise La Chapelle Wheelock objects to an article announcing a program to teach the female students to "cook over a cook stove, take care of kerosene lamps, and to prepare three meals a day" in a "model home cottage" that the school had built. This, she asserted, was either superfluous or shamefully retrograde. Rather than envisioning Carlisle's women returning to what she calls "reservation imbecility," the school should instead encourage them to "aspire to have good homes with electric lights, gas stoves, bath rooms, just as the white girls do"—and as Mrs. Wheelock herself did.
4. Nori does not mention Thorpe because, having left Carlisle in January 1911 and continuing to excel athletically, he had not achieved vocational or professional excellence, the focus of Nori's address.

5. Johnson would have been twenty-four in 1901 and twenty-six in 1903, and so older than most of the players on the college teams Carlisle played, as was Jim Thorpe; eligibility rules were different then. Johnson was inducted into the College Football Hall of Fame in 1969.
6. Only a year earlier the Johnsons had visited Carlisle and "Mr. and Mrs. Siceni Nori hosted a surprise party for [them] the evening before they left for their return trip to Puerto Rico" (Benjey 2010, 186). Apparently Nori had forgotten to which Spanish-speaking island the Johnsons were returning.
7. Brothertown or Brotherton Indians, originally from southern New England and Long Island, were Christian Indians who, along with the Stockbridge, Munsee, and some Oneidas, moved to Wisconsin in the 1830s. In 1839, to avoid further removal, the Brothertown Indians accepted U.S. citizenship and the allotment of their lands. They are currently the only Native American nation in Wisconsin not to have federal recognition.
8. Annuity payments were for Native American land sales to the federal government. Whatever the purchase price agreed upon, in some cases that sum was to be paid for by annuity, which meant that over a number of years, the government would pay each tribal member a sum of money, an annuity. Some of these land sales had been concluded at grossly unfair prices, and as Metoxen indicates, the amount received by individuals could be absurdly low. A rural route is a mail delivery route in a rural area. Once there is a rural route in West De Pere, it will no longer be necessary to pick up mail at the post office because the mail carrier will deliver to each individual mailbox along the route. It is possible that the Oneidas Metoxen speaks of had gained citizenship as a result of having their lands allotted. But qualifications for voting are determined by the individual states, and I cannot say exactly when Wisconsin Oneidas got the vote.
9. Her reference is to the Carlisle *Arrow*, to any number of reports sent by the school to former students, and to the *Indian Craftsman*, published 1909–10 for one dollar a year. Her husband's copies come a bit late, she says, because they are probably still being sent to Kaukana, Wisconsin, where they had formerly lived.
10. His father's name is Isaiah Sickles; Florence and her siblings' father was Martin Sickles. Fred's student information card states, "Brought here by Florence Sickles."
11. The "Great White Fleet" was made up of sixteen warships painted white instead of standard navy gray by order of President Theodore Roosevelt. They were to sail around the world making courtesy stops in many ports and also—an example of speaking softly and carrying a big ship—to

flaunt American (white) naval might. The fleet left Hampton Roads, Virginia, early in December 1907 and arrived in San Francisco Bay in May 1908. It would remain anchored in the bay until July 7, before sailing around the world, completing that voyage by February 1909. The *Kearsarge*, named for Mount Kearsarge in New Hampshire, was the only one of the ships not to be named for a state.

12. My information comes mostly from the *Hearings*, which have been digitized—and which I cite—and from a brief compilation of materials by Cumberland County historian Barbara Landis, at https://home.epix.net/~landis/investigation.html.
13. A 2012 undergraduate honors thesis in history by Afrora Muca includes a brief section on the "Hearings" (15–22) and contains some inaccuracies. Benjey provides a very brief account (2010, 25–28) that also is deficient in accuracy. The Carlisle files contain a "Brief of Charges, Answers, and Evidence in Case of Moses Friedman, Superintendent, Carlisle School, PA, Based on Original Report of Inspector Linnen," that is marked as having been "Received" by the Office of Indian Affairs on July 29, 1915. It summarizes the charges and gives Superintendent Friedman's responses to them. It also contains copies of letters from Cato Sells, commissioner of Indian Affairs, and others, and is a further source for my account.
14. A 1914 report in his file included the observation that Denny was "successful as a disciplinarian by reason of force rather than gentleness and moral suasion," and that he had been informed of charges of "harshness" against him. A number of such charges are on record.
15. He was as well a champion hurdler, long jumper, and hammer thrower. Thorpe was officially enrolled at Carlisle from 1904, when he was seventeen, until 1911. His file, the largest of any Carlisle student, contains 97 pages almost entirely made up of newspaper clippings and some correspondence asking for information about him. It does not contain a single word from Jim Thorpe himself.
16. The particular point of friction between Whitwell and Friedman seems to have been this: before Friedman's arrival, there had been an evening study hour for students monitored by faculty; Whitwell had abolished this. Friedman reinstated the study hour, which he believed was advantageous to the students. But this meant that many teachers once again lost part of their free evenings, which some resented—and which resentment Whitwell seems to have mobilized against Friedman. Oscar Lipps, who succeeded Friedman as superintendent, continued the evening study hour.
17. See https://home.epix.net/~/landis/investigation.html.

Bibliography

Carlisle Indian School and U.S. Government Publications

Adams County News, October 23, 1915.

Annual Report of the Commissioner of Indian Affairs. Washington DC: Government Printing Office, 1890, 1892, 1895.

Annual Report of the Department of the Interior for 1890. Washington DC: Government Printing Office, 1892.

Annual Report, U.S. Indian School, Carlisle, Pa. for the year ending June 30, 1911. Carlisle PA: Carlisle Indian Press.

"Appendix 1: Data on 295 Spanish and Mexican Land Grants in New Mexico." *U.S. General Accounting Office Report to Congressional Requesters, Treaty of Guadalupe Hidalgo: Definition and List of Community Land Grants in New Mexico*. Washington DC: Government Accounting Office, 2001, 22–29.

"Brief of Charges, Answers, and Evidence in Case of Moses Friedman, Superintendent, Carlisle School PA, Based on Original Report of Inspector Linnen." Carlisle Indian School Digital Resource Center. carlisleindian.dickinson.edu.

Mike Burns (Hoomothya) Collection, Sharlot Hall Museum Library and Archives, Prescott AZ. Series 2 and 3.

Carlisle Indian School Digital Resource Center. carlisleindian.dickinson.edu.

Carlos Montezuma Papers, Newberry Library, Chicago.

Census of Wichita and Caddo Indians on the Wichita and Caddo Reservation, Kiowa Indian Agency, Anadarko, Oklahoma, 1915. Extracted from NA film M-595, roll 214, frames 272–300.

Documents of the Senate of the United States. Washington DC: Government Printing Office, 1892.

Eleventh Census of the United States. Washington DC: Government Printing Office, 1890.

Hearings Before the Joint Commission of the U.S. Sixty-third Congress, Second Session. Washington DC: Government Printing Office, 1914.

Report of the Sixtieth Congress, Session II, March 1909. Washington DC: Government Printing Office, 1909.

Richard Henry Pratt Papers. Letters, June 1890–January 1891, WA MSS S-1174, box 10–17. Beinecke Rare Book and Manuscript Library, Yale University, New Haven CT.

Twelfth Census of the United States. Washington DC: Government Printing Office, 1900.

Other Published Sources

Adams, David Wallace. 1995. *Education for Extinction: American Indians and the Boarding School Experience, 1875–1928*. Lawrence: University of Kansas Press.

Aflen, Louise. 2011. "Yavapai Indians Circle Their Wagons: Indians to Arizona: 'It's a Good Day to Declare War.'" Master's thesis, Arizona State University.

American-Tribes. 2018. "George Little Wound." Updated November 7, 2018. amertribes.proboards.com/thread/1955/george-little-wound.

Andersson, Rani-Henrik. 2008. *The Lakota Ghost Dance of 1890*. Lincoln: University of Nebraska Press.

———. 2019. *A Whirlwind Passed through Our Country: Lakota Voices of the Ghost Dance*. Norman: University of Oklahoma Press.

Andrews, Thomas. 2002. "Turning the Tables on Assimilation: Oglala Lakotas and the Pine Ridge Day Schools, 1889–1920s." *Western Historical Quarterly* 33, no. 4 (Winter): 407–30.

Axtell, James. 1975. "The White Indians of Colonial America." *William and Mary Quarterly* 32, no. 1 (January): 55–88.

Babcock, Barbara. 1995. "Not in the Absolute Singular." In *Women Writing Culture,* edited by Ruth Behar and Deborah Gordon, 89–121. Berkeley: University of California Press.

Bahr, Diana Meyers. 2014. *The Students of Sherman Indian School*. Norman: University of Oklahoma Press.

Ball, Eve, with Nora Henn and Lynda Sanchez. 1988. *Indeh: An Apache Odyssey*. Norman: University of Oklahoma Press.

Bandelier, Adolph. [1890] 1971. *The Delight Makers*. New York: Harcourt.

Banker, Mark. 1982. "Presbyterians and Pueblos: A Protestant Response to the Indian Question, 1872–1892." *Journal of Presbyterian History* 60 (Spring): 23–40.

Barnett, Franklin. 1968. *Viola Jimulla: The Indian Chieftess*. Prescott AZ: Classic Prescott.

Beck, David R. M. 2005. *The Struggle for Self-Determination: History of the Menominee Indians since 1854*. Lincoln: University of Nebraska Press.

Bell, Genevieve. 1998. "Telling Stories out of School: Remembering the Carlisle Indian Industrial School, 1879–1918." PhD diss., Department of Anthropology, Stanford University.

Benedict, Ruth. 1931. *Tales of the Cochiti Indians.* Washington DC: Smithsonian Institution Press.

Benjey, Tom. 2010. *Wisconsin's Carlisle Indian School Immortals*. Carlisle PA: Tuxedo.

Berkhofer, Robert. 1979. *The White Man's Indian: Images of the Indian from Columbus to the Present.* New York: Vintage Books.

Berry, Brewton. 1968. *The Education of the American Indian: A Survey of the Literature*. Washington DC: U.S. Department of Health, Education, and Welfare Bureau of Research.

Berthrong, Donald. 1956. "Federal Indian Policy and the Southern Cheyennes and Arapahos, 1887–1907." *Ethnohistory* 3, no. 2 (Spring): 138–53.

Betzinez, Jason, with Wilbur S. Nye. [1959] 1987. *I Fought with Geronimo.* Lincoln: University of Nebraska Press.

Bourke, John. [1891] 2014. *On the Border with Crook*. New York: Skyhorse.

Braatz, Timothy. 2003. *Surviving Conquest: A History of the Yavapai Peoples.* Lincoln: University of Nebraska Press.

———. 2010. "Foreword" to Mike Burns, *All of My People Were Killed: The Memoir of Mike Burns (Hoomothya), a Captive Indian*, iii–xii. Prescott AZ: Sharlot Hall Museum.

Brown, Estelle. 1952. *Stubborn Fool: A Narrative*. Caldwell ID: Caxton.

Brudvig, Jon. 1996. "Bridging the Cultural Divide: American Indians at Hampton Institute, 1878–1923." PhD diss., College of William and Mary.

Brumley, Kim. 2010. *Chilocco: Memories of a Native American Boarding School.* Fairfax OK: Guardian.

Buchowska, Zuzanna. 2016. *Negotiating Native American Identities: The role of Tradition, Narrative, and Language at Haskell Indian Nations University*. Poznan, Poland: UAM.

Buffalo Bill Museum and Grave. Comp. 2010. "Did Buffalo Bill Visit Your Town? A Comprehensive Country/State Listing of William 'Buffalo Bill' Cody's Tour Destinations." Revised 2010. buffalobill.org/pdfs/buffalo_bill_visits.pdf.

Bunnell, David. 2017. *Good Friday on the Rez: A Pine Ridge Odyssey*. New York: St. Martin's.

Burns, Mike. 2010. *All of My People Were Killed: The Memoir of Mike Burns (Hoomothya), a Captive Indian*. Prescott AZ: Sharlot Hall Museum.

Carley, Caroline. 2001. "Letters from the Field: Alice Cunningham Fletcher in Nez Perce Country, 1889–1892." *Northwest Anthropological Research Notes* 35, no. 1 (2001): 55–133.

Carlisle Indian Industrial School. 2019a. "C&A Letterbook, Vol. 1, pg. 7" (and other items). Accessed September 4, 2019. https://home.epix.net/~landis/bullbear.html.

Carlisle Indian Industrial School. 2019b. "Richard Davis References." Accessed September 4, 2019. https://home.epix.net/~landis/richarddavis.html.

Carlisle Indian Industrial School. N.d. "Some of the Names." https://home.epix.net/~landis/couples.html.

Chemawa Indian School. 2017. "Chemawa History." Updated August 8, 2017. chemawa.bie.edu/history.html.

Child, Brenda. 1998. *Boarding School Seasons: American Indian Families, 1900–1940*. Lincoln: University of Nebraska Press.

———. 2014. "The Boarding School as Metaphor." In *Hemispheric Perspectives on the History of Indigenous Education*, edited by Brenda Child and Brian Klopotek, 267–84. Santa Fe NM: School for Advanced Research Press.

Clark, J. Stanley. 1945. "The Nez Perce in Exile." *Pacific Northwest Quarterly* 36: 213–32.

Clifford, James and George Marcus, eds. 1986. *Writing Culture: The Poetics and Politics of Ethnography.* Berkeley: University of California Press.

Cobb, Amanda. 2000. *Listening to Our Grandmothers' Stories: The Bloomfield Academy for Chickasaw Females, 1852–1949*. Lincoln: University of Nebraska Press.

Coel, Margaret. 1981. *Chief Left Hand, Southern Arapaho*. Norman: University of Oklahoma Press.

Coleman, Michael. 1993. *American Indian Children at School, 1850–1930*. Jackson: University Press of Mississippi.

Cook, William A. 2011. *Jim Thorpe: A Biography*. Jefferson NC: McFarland.

Crandall, Maurice. 2014 . "Wassaja Comes Home: A Yavapai Perspective on Carlos Montezuma's Search for Identity." *Journal of Arizona History* 55, no. 1 (Spring): 1–26.

Cutler, Lee. 1971. "Laurie Tatum and the Kiowa Agency." *Arizona and the West* 13 (Autumn): 221–44.

Deloria, Philip. 2004. *Indians in Unexpected Places*. Lawrence: University Press of Kansas.

———. 2013. "Four Thousand Invitations." *Studies in American Indian Literatures* 25, and *American Indian Quarterly* 37, no. 3 (Summer): 23–43.

Du Bois, W. E. B. [1903] 1989. *The Souls of Black Folks*. New York: Bantam.

Earenfight, Phillip, ed. 2007. *A Kiowa's Odyssey: A Sketchbook from Fort Marion*. Seattle: University of Washington Press.

Eastman, Charles. [1916] 1977. *From the Deep Woods to Civilization: Chapters in the Autobiography of an Indian*. Lincoln: University of Nebraska Press,.

Ellis, Clyde. 1996. *To Change Them Forever: Indian Education at the Rainy Mountain Boarding School, 1893–1926*. Norman: University of Oklahoma Press.

Ellis, Mark. 1999. "Reservation *Akicitas*: The Pine Ridge Indian Police, 1879–1885." *South Dakota History* 29: 185–210.

Ellis, Richard N. 1985. "'I would raise him to be Indian.'" In *Essays on Nineteenth and Twentieth Century Native American Lives*, edited by L. G. Moses and Raymond Wilson, 139–58. Albuquerque: University of New Mexico Press.

Emery, Jacqueline. 2017. *Recovering Native American Writing in the Boarding School Press*. Lincoln: University of Nebraska Press.

Enochs, Ross. 1996. *Jesuit Mission to the Lakota: Pastoral Theology and Ministry, 1886–1945*. Kansas City MO: Sheed and Ward.

Fear-Segal, Jacqueline. 2004. "Eyes in the Text: Mariana Burgess and *The Indian Helper*." In *Blue Pencils and Hidden Hands: Women Editing Periodicals, 1830–1910*, edited by Sharon Harris with Ellen Garvey, 123–43. Boston: Northwestern University Press.

———. 2007. *White Man's Club: Schools, Race, and the Struggle of Indian Acculturation*. Lincoln: University of Nebraska Press.

Fear-Segal, Jacqueline, and Barbara Rose, eds. 2016. *Carlisle Indian Industrial School: Indigenous Histories, Memories, and Reclamations*. Lincoln: University of Nebraska Press.

Fletcher, Alice, and Francis La Flesche. [1911] 1992. *The Omaha Tribe*. Lincoln: University of Nebraska Press.

Fowler, Loretta. 1978. "Oral Historian or Ethnologist? The Career of Bill Shakespeare, Northern Arapaho, 1901–1975." In *American Indian Intellectuals*, edited by Margot Liberty, 227–40. New York: West.

Frye, Northrop. 1957. *Anatomy of Criticism: Four Essays*. Princeton NJ: Princeton University Press.

Gallop, Alan. 2001. *Buffalo Bill's British Wild West*. Thrupp, UK: Sutton.

Geronimo. [1906] 1973. *Geronimo's Story of His Life*. Edited by S. M. Barrett. Williamstown MA: Cornerhouse.

Gram, John. 2015. *Education at the Edge of Empire: Negotiating Pueblo Identity in New Mexico's Indian Boarding Schools.* Seattle: University of Washington Press.

Greene, Jerome. 1970. "The Sioux Land Commission of 1889: Prelude to Wounded Knee." *South Dakota History* 1 (Winter): 41–72.

Griffis, Joseph (Chief Tahan). 1915. *Tahan, out of Savagery into Civilization: An Autobiography.* New York: Hugh H. Doran.

Haes, Brenda. 1997. "The Incarceration of the Chiricahua Apaches, 1886–1914: A Portrait of Survival." Master's thesis, Texas Tech University.

Hagan, William. 1980. *Indian Police and Judges.* Lincoln: University of Nebraska Press.

Hauptman, Laurence. 2006. "From Carlisle to Carnegie Hall: The Musical Career of Dennison Wheelock." In *The Oneida Indians in the Age of Allotment, 1860–1920,* edited by Laurence Hauptman and L. Gordon McLester III, 112–38. Norman: University of Oklahoma Press.

Hauptman, Laurence, and L. Gordon McLester III. 2015. "Death in the Ardennes: Dr. Josiah A. Powless, Oneida Hero of World War I." *Magazine of the Smithsonian's National Museum of the American Indian* 16 (Spring): 26–30.

Herman, Daniel. 2012. *Rim Country Exodus: A Story of Conquest, Renewal, and Race in the Making.* Tucson: University of Arizona Press.

Hittman, Michael. 1997. *Wovoka and the Ghost Dance.* Edited by Don Lynch, expanded edition. Lincoln: University of Nebraska Press.

Hoare, Quinton, and Geoffrey Nowell Smith. 1971. "Introduction" to Antonio Gramsci, *Selections from the Prison Notebooks,* ed. and trans. by Hoare and Smith, xvii–xcvi. New York: International.

Howard, Oliver O. [1907] 2019. *Autobiography of Oliver Otis Howard, Major-General, United States Army.* N.p.: Forgotten Books.

Hyer, Sally. 1990. *One House, One Voice, One Heart: American Education at the Santa Fe Indian School.* Santa Fe: Museum of New Mexico Press.

Iverson, Peter. 1982. *Carlos Montezuma and the Changing World of American Indians.* Albuquerque: University of New Mexico Press.

Johnston, Terry. 1991. *The Modoc War, 1872–3.* New York: St. Martin's.

Jordan, Julia. 1967. "Interview with Jess Rowlodge, Arapahoe." University of Oklahoma, Doris Duke Western History Collection, volume 5, T-170, December 5, 1967.

Katanski, Amelia. 2006. *Learning to Write "Indian": The Boarding School Experience and American Indian Literature.* Norman: University of Oklahoma Press.

Krupat, Arnold. 2002. "America's Histories." In *Red Matters: Native American Studies*, 48–75. Philadelphia: University of Pennsylvania Press,.

———. 2018. *Changed Forever: American Indian Boarding-School Literature*, vol. 1. Albany: State University of New York Press.

———. 2020. *Changed Forever: American Indian Boarding-School Literature*, vol. 2. Albany: State University of New York Press.

———. 2012. *"That the People Might Live": Loss and Renewal in Native American Elegy*. Ithaca NY: Cornell University Press.

LaBarre, Weston. [1938] 1989. *The Peyote Cult*. New York: Schocken.

Langellier, John. 2010. "Afterword" to Mike Burns, *All of My People Were Killed*, 273–83. Prescott AZ: Sharlot Hall Museum.

———. 2010. "Preface" to Mike Burns, *All of My People Were Killed*, xiii–xviii. Prescott AZ: Sharlot Hall Museum.

———. Personal communication, May 16, 2019.

Leap, William L. 1993. *American Indian English*. Salt Lake City: University of Utah Press.

Lesser, Alexander. 1933. *The Pawnee Ghost Dance Hand Game: A study of Cultural Change*. Columbia University Contributions to Anthropology, vol. xvi. New York: Columbia University Press.

Lindsey, Donal. 1995. *Indians at Hampton Institute, 1877–1923*. Urbana: University of Illinois Press.

Littlefield, Daniel, and James Parins, eds. 1984–86. *American Indian and Alaska Native Newspapers and Periodicals*, 3 vols.. Westport CT: Greenwood.

Lomawaima, K. Tsianina. 1994. *They Called It Prairie Light: The Story of Chilocco Indian School*. Lincoln: University of Nebraska Press.

Long Soldier, Layli. 2017. *Whereas*. Minneapolis MN: Graywolf.

Marino, Cesare. 1998. *The Remarkable Carlo Gentile: Pioneer Italian Photographer of the American Frontier*. Nevada City CA: Carl Mautz.

Mattina, Anthony, ed. 1985. *The Golden Woman: The Colville Narrative of Peter J. Seymour*. Tucson: University of Arizona Press.

McBeth, Sally. 1983. *Ethnic Identity and the Boarding School Experience of West-Central Oklahoma American Indians*. Lanham MD: University Press of America.

McGillycuddy, Julia B. 1941. *McGillycuddy, Agent: A Biography of Dr. Valentine T. McGillycuddy*. Redwood City CA: Stanford University Press.

McNally, Robert. 2017. *The Modoc War: A Story of Genocide at the Dawn of America's Gilded Age*. Lincoln: University of Nebraska Press.

McNamee, Gregory, ed. 2012. *The Only One Living to Tell: The Autobiography of a Yavapai Indian*. Tucson: University of Arizona Press.

Meriam, Lewis, et al. 1928. *The Problem of Indian Administration: Report of a Survey Made at the Request of the Honorable Hubert Work, Secretary of the Interior and Submitted to Him, February 21, 1928*. Baltimore: Johns Hopkins University Press.

Mihesuah, Devon. 1993. *Cultivating the Rosebuds: The Education of Women at the Cherokee Female Seminary*. Urbana: University of Illinois Press.

Mooney, James. [1896] 1973. *The Ghost-Dance Religion and the Sioux Outbreak of 1890*. New York: Dover.

Muca, Afrora. 2012. "From Classroom to Battlefield: The Role of Students in the Closing of the Carlisle Indian Industrial School, 1918." Honors thesis, Temple University.

"Newspaper Items on House Committee of Indian Affairs Investigation of Moses Friedman and Carlisle Indian School Staff (January 31, 1914 to October 23, 1915)." 1914–15. https://home.epix.net/~landis/investigation.html.

Parker, Robert Dale, ed. 2011. *Changing is Not Vanishing: A Collection of American Indian Poetry to 1930*. Philadelphia: University of Pennsylvania Press.

Pearson, J. Diane, and Patricia Hilden. 2008. *The Nez Perces in Indian Territory: Nimiipuu Survival*. Norman: University of Oklahoma Press.

Pico, Tommy. 2018. *Junk*. Portland OR: Tin House.

Powers-Beck, Jeffrey. 2004. *The American Indian Integration of Baseball*. Lincoln: University of Nebraska Press.

Pratt, Richard Henry. 1964. *Battlefield and Classroom: Four Decades with the American Indian, 1867–1904*, edited and with an Introduction by Robert Utley. New Haven CT: Yale University Press.

Red Shirt, Delphine. 2016. *George Sword's Warrior Narratives: Compositional Processes in Lakota Oral Tradition*. Lincoln: University of Nebraska Press.

Reyhner, Jon, and Jeanne Elder. 2004. *American Indian Education: A History*. Norman: University of Oklahoma Press.

Riney, Scott. 1999. *The Rapid City Indian School: 1898–1933*. Norman: University of Oklahoma Press.

Rice, Julian. 1985. "*Akicita* of the Thunder: Horses in Black Elk's Vision." MELUS 12, no. 1: 5–23.

Ricker, Eli S. 2005. *Voices of the American West: The Indian Interviews of Eli S. Ricker, 1903–1919*, edited and with an introduction by Richard Jensen, vols. 1 and 2. Lincoln: University of Nebraska Press.

Rockwell, Susan. 2001. "The Autobiography of Mike Burns, Yavapai Apache." PhD diss., Arizona State University.

———. 2002. *The Journey of a Yavapai Indian: A 19th-Century Odyssey*. Princeton NJ: Philip Leif.

Sando, Joe. 1992. *Pueblo Nations: Eight Centuries of Pueblo Indian History.* Santa Fe NM: Clear Light.

Sappington, Robert Lee, and Caroline D. Carley. 1995. "Alice Cunningham Fletcher's 'Ethnologic Gleanings Among the New Perces.'" *Northwest Anthropological Research Notes* 29, no. 1 (1995): 1–43.

Shillinger, Sarah. 2008. *A Case Study of the American Indian Boarding School Movement: An Oral History of St. Joseph's Indian Industrial School.* Lewiston NY: Edwin Mellen.

Shklovsky, Viktor. [1917] 1965. "Art as Technique." In *Russian Formalist Criticism: Four Essays*, edited by Lee T. Lemon and Marion J. Reiss, 3–24. Lincoln: University of Nebraska Press.

Smith, Sherry L. 1990. *The View from Officers' Row: Army Perceptions of Western Indians.* Tucson: University of Arizona Press.

Smith, Victoria. 2009. *Captive Arizona, 1851–1900.* Lincoln: University of Nebraska Press.

Speroff, Leon. 2004–5. *Carlos Montezuma, M.D.: A Yavapai American Hero.* Portland OR: Arnica.

Sprague, Donovin Arleigh. 2004. *Pine Ridge Reservation.* Charleston SC: Arcadia.

Standing Bear, Luther. [1928] 1975. *My People, the Sioux.* Lincoln: University of Nebraska Press.

———. [1933] 1978. *Land of the Spotted Eagle.* Lincoln: University of Nebraska Press.

———. [1931] 1988. *My Indian Boyhood.* Lincoln: University of Nebraska Press.

Strong, Pauline Turner. 1999. *Captive Selves, Captivating Others: The Politics and Poetics of Colonial American Captivity Narratives.* Boulder CO: Westview.

Sullivan, Robert. 2010. "Introduction" to Mike Burns, *All of My people Were killed*, xxi–xxiii. Prescott AZ: Sharlot Hall Museum.

Swetland, Mark. 1994. "'Make-Believe White-Men' and the Omaha Land Allotments of 1871–1900." *Great Plains Research* 4, no. 2 (August): 201–36.

Szasz, Margaret. [1974] 1999. *Education and the American Indian: The Road to Self-Determination since 1928.* 3rd ed. Albuquerque: University of New Mexico Press.

Toncovich, Nicole. 2012. *The Allotment Plot: Alice C. Fletcher, E. Jane Gay, and Nez Perce Survivance.* Lincoln: University of Nebraska Press.

Trafzer, Clifford. 1985. "The Palouse in Eekish Pah." *American Indian Quarterly* 9, no. 2 (Spring): 169–82.

Trafzer, Clifford, Jean Keller, and Lorene Sisquoc, eds. 2006. *Boarding School Blues: Revisiting American Indian Educational Experiences*. Lincoln: University of Nebraska Press.

Trafzer, Clifford, Matthew Sakiestewa Gilbert, and Lorene Sisquoc, eds. 2012. *The Indian School on Magnolia Avenue*. Corvallis: Oregon State University Press.

Trenholm, Virginia. [1970] 1986. *The Arapahoes, Our People*. Norman: University of Oklahoma Press.

Trennert, Robert, Jr. 1988. *The Phoenix Indian School: Forced Assimilation in Arizona, 1891–1935*. Norman: University of Oklahoma Press.

Tritt, Richard. 2019. Personal communication, March 4, 2019.

Vizenor, Gerald. 2018. Personal communication, September 3, 2018.

Vuckovic, Myriam. 2008. *Voices from Haskell: Indian Students between Two Worlds, 1884–1928*. Lawrence: University Press of Kansas.

Waggoner, Linda. 2014. *Fire Light: The Life of Angel DeCora*. Norman: University of Oklahoma Press.

Walker, James R. 1980. *Lakota Belief and Ritual.*, Edited by Raymond DeMallie and Elaine Jahner. Lincoln: University of Nebraska Press.

Warrior, Robert. 1999. *Tribal Secrets: Recovering American Indian Intellectual Traditions*. Minneapolis: University of Minnesota Press.

Webster, Anthony. 2017. "'I don't write Navajo poetry, I just speak the poetry in Navajo': Ethical listeners, poetic communion, and the imagined future publics of Navajo poetry." In *Engaging Native American Publics: Linguistic Anthropology in a Collaborative Key*, edited by Paul Kroskrity and Barbra Meek, 149–68. London: Routledge.

White, Hayden. 1973. *Metahistory: The Historical Imagination in Nineteenth-Century Europe*. Baltimore: Johns Hopkins University Press.

Wilcox, Alvin. 1907. *A Pioneer History of Becker County, Minnesota*. St. Paul MN: Pioneer.

Witmer, Linda. 2000. *The Indian Industrial School, Carlisle, Pennsylvania, 1879–1918*. Carlisle PA: Cumberland County Historical Society.

Worcester, Donald. 1979. *The Apaches: Eagles of the Southwest*. Norman: University of Oklahoma Press.

Index

Women are indexed by the names they used at school.

www.ingramcontent.com/pod-product-compliance
Lightning Source LLC
Chambersburg PA
CBHW060816310726
48980CB00002B/311

9781496228017